Emily Post's

WEDDING ETIQUETTE

SIXTH EDITION

Essential Manners for Men, 2nd Edition

Emily Post's Etiquette, 18th Edition

Emily Post's Great Get-Togethers

Emily Post's Manners in a Digital World

Emily Post's Wedding Parties

Do I Have to Wear White?

How Do You Work This Life Thing?

"Excuse Me, But I Was Next . . ."

Emily Post's Wedding Planner, 4th Edition

Emily Post's Wedding Planner for Moms

Emily Post's the Etiquette Advantage in Business, 2nd Edition

Essential Manners for Couples

A Wedding Like No Other

Playing Through: A Guide to the Unwritten Rules of Golf

Mr. Manners: Lessons from Obama on Civility

Emily Post's the Gift of Good Manners

Emily Post's Teen Manners

Emily Post's Prom and Party Etiquette

Emily Post's Table Manners for Kids

Emily Post's the Guide to Good Manners for Kids

Emily's Everyday Manners

Emily's Christmas Gifts

Emily's New Friend

Emily's Magic Words

Emily's Sharing and Caring Book

Emily's Out and About Book

WEDDING ETIQUETTE

SIXTH EDITION

Anna Post
and Lizzie Post

WITH ILLUSTRATIONS BY HAPPY MENOCAL

WILLIAM MORROW
An Imprint of HarperCollinsPublishers

EMILY POST'S® WEDDING ETIQUETTE, SIXTH EDITION. Copyright © 2014 by The Emily Post Institute, Inc. All rights reserved. Printed in the United States of America. No part of this book may be used or reproduced in any manner whatsoever without written permission except in the case of brief quotations embodied in critical articles and reviews. For information address HarperCollins Publishers, 195 Broadway, New York, NY 10007.

HarperCollins books may be purchased for educational, business, or sales promotional use. For information please e-mail the Special Markets Department at SPsales@harpercollins.com.

Designed by Kris Tobiassen / Matchbook Digital
Illustrations by Happy Menocal

Library of Congress Cataloging-in-Publication Data has been applied for.

ISBN 978-0-06-232610-2

16 17 18 OV/QG 10 9 8 7 6 5 4

To all of the couples who say "I do"—
We wish you every happiness!

CONTENTS

ACKNOWLEDGMENTS

Many thanks go to all the couples, their parents, and attendants who shared their insights and wedding questions with The Emily Post Institute, either through our website, Facebook page, or columns in the *New York Times*.

We can't say thank you enough to Tricia Post, who has helped shepherd this book from start to finish. It's been a pleasure and a singular honor to be able to work so closely with our mom.

For their unwavering support and for always willing to be the voice of reason, we thank the team at The Emily Post Institute, particularly Elizabeth Howell; Matt Goodman; Peter Post; Daniel Post Senning; Virginia Keyser; Dawn Stanyon; Emma Crockett, our intern; and our agent, Katherine Cowles.

A special thanks to Emily Krump, our intrepid, cheerful, and unflappable editor, who saw the book through editing and production, and to the team at William Morrow: Liate Stehlik, Lynn Grady, Jennifer Hart, Kathryn Gordon, Joseph Papa, Joyce Wong, Leah Carlson-Stanisic, and Karen Lumley. They were joined by the creative talents of designer Kris Tobiassen and illustrator Happy Menocal, whose work gave shape and life to the stories and advice within.

We have been fortunate to be able to call on our network of professionals who work within the wedding industry. They have been generous with their advice and defining the gold standard in their fields: Matt Bushlow, Kris Engstrom and Britta Johnson of In Full Bloom, Scott Flynn, Sabin Gratz and Melissa Mercer of Sabin Gratz Photography, Mike Hakim, Deborah Jarecki, Adrea Kofman, Dale Loeffler of Catering by Dale, Scott MacMillan (DJ SMac), Katherine Meyers, Elizabeth Singleton of Events by Elizabeth Palmer, and Terrell Titus. Special thanks also go to friends who have shared their wedding experiences and wisdom: Nicole and Michael Atherton, Suzanne Flynn, Michelle Lambert, and Leigh and Peter Phillips.

Thank you to all of the wedding magazine editors for whom we have written, especially Marilyn Oliveira, previously of *Inside Weddings*.

We owe a debt of gratitude to Emily Post, our great great grandmother who started it all, and to our grandmother, Elizabeth Post, and our aunt, Peggy Post, who took on Emily's mantle and have led thousands of couples to the altar with grace and courtesy. We are proud to continue the tradition.

FOREWORD

It is my great pleasure to tell you about Anna Post and Lizzie Post—my nieces and key spokespersons for The Emily Post Institute—and their most recent accomplishment, *Emily Post's Wedding Etiquette*, 6th edition. This updated book is the ultimate go-to guide for brides, grooms, and their families as they plan their weddings.

Most recently, Anna, Lizzie, and I had the opportunity to collaborate on the extensive revision of *Emily Post's Etiquette*, 18th edition, so I can tell you with confidence that they bring a fresh perspective to the complexities of wedding planning and the etiquette dilemmas that often arise. Anna is the author of two previous wedding etiquette books, *Emily Post's Wedding Parties* and *Do I Have to Wear White?: Emily Post Answers America's Top Wedding Questions*. She also writes for *Inside Weddings* magazine and for regional bridal magazines such as *St. Louis Bride*, *Orlando Weddings*, *Charlotte Weddings*, *Vermont Vows*, and *Well Wed*. Lizzie is the author of *How Do You Work This Life Thing?*, a comprehensive guide for young adults heading to college, their first apartments, and jobs. Together Lizzie and Anna co-authored *Emily Post's Great Get-Togethers,* a modern guide for home entertaining, inspired by their own passion for hosting par-

ties. Both Anna and Lizzie have answered literally hundreds of wedding etiquette questions posed by couples on The Emily Post Institute website, when they meet with brides and grooms at wedding events, and when they have been interviewed by the media about the latest questions in the world of weddings.

The entire process of planning a wedding is thoroughly covered in the 6th edition, but what makes this book unique is the warm and level-headed way Anna and Lizzie address the decisions that involve the *relationships* of weddings—much the same way that a good friend would help solve a problem. They are passionate about helping brides and grooms tailor their weddings in innovative ways that weave in their personalities and focus on their guests, and by merging traditions with the many new options available to today's brides and grooms. Anna's and Lizzie's insights focus on positive planning and individual needs—not on the "musts"—allowing each bride and groom to decide what works best for their particular wedding. They have a way of putting people at ease, whether it's a stressed-out bride, a nervous groom, or a demanding mom.

There have been many changes in the world—and in the world of weddings—since the previous edition of *Emily Post's Wedding Etiquette* was published in

2006. This 6th edition of the book covers the latest wedding trends and realities, from the best way to keep a wedding green to the impact of technology. For example, does "going green" mean that it's okay to send wedding invitations via email or as a text? Mobile devices have become essential wedding communication and planning tools, and Anna and Lizzie look at how to use them effectively and considerately. Social media, also, plays a big role in most of our lives and it's not surprising that it has an impact on your weddings, too. Wedding websites are now standard, but couples still need solid advice on keeping them gracious and guest friendly. Anna and Lizzie tackle what works and what doesn't in our ever-changing world in a way that helps couples build confidence as they make decisions about their weddings.

This 6th edition of *Emily Post's Wedding Etiquette* is the gold standard for brides and grooms. It is with my best wishes that I encourage you to enjoy reading these pages and planning your wedding.

The best is yet to come! May you have a joyous wedding and a lifetime of happiness.

PEGGY POST

January 2014

THE HEART OF YOUR WEDDING

You're engaged! As the couple of the moment, it's likely that you're in a whirlwind of rejoicing with your parents and friends and picturing a life of married bliss. With all the excitement comes another vision—that of a perfect wedding. But what does "perfect" mean? For one thing, it no longer describes only the storybook formal event with six bridesmaids and yards of white tulle. In truth, the ideal wedding is one that is a reflection of who you are as a couple; is considerate, inclusive, and patient with your closest family; and takes your guests' comfort into account at all times. Today's idea of "perfection" is about planning your wedding and any related celebrations with the following ideas in mind:

* Let consideration be your guide. Make decisions based on maintaining and caring for the important relationships in your lives.

* Rely on diplomacy: Employ tact and sensitivity when involving others—including stepparents and extended family members.

* Give thought to the kind of occasion that you, your family, and friends will feel comfortable with and enjoy.

* Try to include traditions that mean a great deal to someone important to you. Forgo a tradition if it doesn't make sense for you or if it could cause more problems than it would solve.

* Be considerate of your guests with special needs, such as elders, parents with very young children, or guests with disabilities. Find ways to give children special roles if they're included.

* Anticipate and take steps to avoid potential problems that may lead to friction. Give people time to adjust to decisions that might not be their first choice.

The same attention and respect you give your family and guests applies to your relationship with suppliers and contractors. No matter the size or budget of your wedding, your goal is to form positive, collaborative relationships with everyone providing you with wedding services.

Keeping Joy in the Process

Planning a wedding is a time of joy and community that can bring people together in the most wonderful of ways. At the same time, this closeness can breed friction, and the land mines involved in making deeply emotional (and expensive) decisions can detonate unexpectedly. Take care that your family and close friends feel included in the planning. Most important, you'll want to find ways to take good care of yourself and your fiancé(e) so that you can enjoy the planning. There are also *Emily Post's Wedding Planner*, the companion to this book, and www.emilypost.com to help keep you organized along the way. Here is some tried-and-true advice to help smooth your wedding preparations:

You're a team. The two of you need to be a united front and, most important, each other's support amid a barrage of sometimes conflicting wedding advice or unexpected pressure as you make the big decisions. Although such advice is well meant, it can also be overwhelming to sort through. Help each other stay grounded and focused.

Remember the three C's. Always keep your focus on the three C's of good relationships:

- Consideration

- Communication

- Compromise

How you handle the decisions involved in your wedding plans can set the tone for how you'll handle the other major decisions in your life together. This is the time to develop a way of reaching consensus—or good compromises.

Delegate duties. Others will want to help, and what bride and groom couldn't use some assistance? You may discover how fortunate you are to have friends and family willing to help out. Your wedding day may be the most important time to delegate tasks so that you can focus on your ceremony and enjoy the reception afterward.

Once you have relinquished a responsibility, don't dwell on it, second-guess yourself or others, or micromanage. When you've put someone in charge, let others know. For example, tell the florist your sister is in charge of flowers and to contact her, not you, or have your fiancé(e) contact the tent supplier and arrange all of the details.

Stay organized. It doesn't take long for chaos to reign if you don't have some sort of system of organization. Whether you use the *Emily Post Wedding Planner*, an online site, or an app; set up computer files; or devote a binder or filing drawer just to wedding-related papers, you'll find everything is easier to manage when you can locate it quickly. Here are a few tips from the most efficient brides and grooms:

- Create a master to-do list, preferably in time sequence.

- Keep fabric swatches, photos of gowns, photos of locations, and table measurements with you—either physically or on your phone or tablet—in case you get a phone call while you're out.

- Design a contact list with the names of everyone you're working with, including email and business addresses, web address, phone and even fax numbers.

- Carry a paper or digital calendar with all your appointments highlighted, and set alerts for them on your smartphone.

- Create a paper or electronic folder for all contracts. Staple copies of contracts to the appropriate pages in your organizer or scan completed contracts and file them electronically. Don't leave home without them—either in your binder or on your phone or tablet—in case you have to check details from one supplier when working with another.

- Keep copies of important papers you will need (birth certificates, any divorce papers, driver's licenses) in one envelope or folder. Again, it's a good idea to scan and save these documents electronically.

- Check off completed to-dos as you accomplish them. Seeing the number of check marks grow will feel great!

Stay calm. Even if you've lived together or are an older couple with grown children, don't let the details bog you down or send you into an emotional tailspin; when things get tough, keep reminding yourself that it's the marriage, not the wedding, that's important. Try to step back and imagine the view from 30,000 feet. Here are three ways to keep things on an even keel:

1. **Include, don't exclude.** Even if you're doing everything yourselves, keep others—your mothers, children, or friends—in the loop. Don't let them feel left out. You may see yourself as adding to your family with this wedding, but your family may feel they are losing you. Give them extra attention. Ask their advice periodically—but not about things you've already decided on, or you'll have to either reject their advice or change your plans and give up something you really want to do.

2. **Be forgiving.** When things get touchy between you and your family (or your fiancé(e)!), make an effort to get things back on the right foot, which might mean being the first to apologize.

3. **Stop reacting.** If someone is being difficult, take a deep breath and think about what might be motivating them. Is your brother feeling left out of your life? Is your mom worried about what your relationship will be with her once you're married? If you can't figure it out, have a calm chat with them and ask what is upsetting them. (Don't go into a conversation like this with a bone of your own to pick—the goal is to be understanding and helpful.)

Take care of your relationship with your fiancé(e). Throughout your engagement, remember to make time to enjoy each other. Take time out with scheduled date nights that are "wedding free."

Take care of yourselves. To keep yourselves from burning out:

- Eat right—you need the energy.

- Exercise—you need the release (and you'll look great, too!)

- Get enough sleep—you can think much better when you're rested.

- Look for the bright side when things don't go your way—and when you can't . . .

- Find humor.

Family Matters

As much as your commitment to marry is between you as a couple, you each bring your own families along with you. We can't stress enough how important it is to commit to getting to know each other's families. This means accepting them for who they are and giving them the benefit of the doubt when something hits a nerve. Keep your communications open and clear, but if there is a misunderstanding or disagreement, remember to support each other first and foremost. At the end of the day, your goal is to build good relationships with people who mean a tremendous amount to your future partner.

If your family or families are complicated by divorce, remarriage, step relationships, or family feuding, give serious thought to these issues as early in the planning process as possible. Your marriage is highly unlikely to heal rifts among family members, but with forethought and tact, you can prepare yourself to head off serious difficulties.

Unfortunately, divorced parents aren't always on friendly terms. Although most adults will lay their differences aside for a wedding, you should avoid putting divorced parents in awkward and uncomfortable situations. For example, seating divorced parents together at the ceremony or reception isn't necessary. If you plan to have your stepdad walk you down the aisle, let your biological dad know well in advance so he has time to accept the idea. Most parents will do everything in their power to make your wedding special, but you have responsibilities to them as well, which may mean adjusting what you want to what others need.

The traditional wedding vows include the words *for better and for worse*. Couples would be wise to apply these words to their families. Will your plans make difficult family relationships better or at least keep them on an even keel? When you look back on your wedding in ten or fifteen years, you'll want to be proud of everything you did and remember a day that was happy for everyone.

The 21st-Century Wedding

Emily Post knew that the magic of a wedding lay less in the details than in the tender quality of the occasion and the radiance of the couple. "The radiance of a truly happy bride is so beautifying that even a plain girl is made pretty, and a pretty one, divine," she wrote in *Etiquette* in 1922. "She and the groom both look as though there is sunlight behind their eyes, as though their mouths irresistibly turned to smiles."

While that sentiment has stayed the same, weddings themselves haven't. Changes in society, from a more culturally diverse population to the redefinition of the family, have revolutionized weddings today, giving rise to more informal ceremonies and the inclusion of customs and traditions reflecting the couple's heritage. Weddings have become more adventurous and imaginative, with destination and theme weddings part of the evolution. They feature more guest-focused receptions and a more active role for the groom's family. Here are some of the hallmarks of weddings today:

Personalized weddings. This is one "trend" that seems here to stay. Many couples make a concerted effort to differentiate their wedding by planning intimate and individualized ceremonies and receptions that express their personalities and interests.

Financing the wedding. The economic downturn has given wedding budgets a reality check. Today, wedding expenses are no longer the exclusive responsibility of the bride's parents but are frequently shared by the couple, the bride's and groom's parents, or any combination of the three. More and more couples pay most or all of the expenses. With the average cost of a wedding clocking in around $27,000, it's no wonder that "How will we pay for it?" is one of the first conversations that engaged couples have.

The wedding weekend. With so much to plan and many guests coming from afar, the wedding day has expanded to the wedding weekend. Many couples schedule events that bracket the wedding day for the wedding party and their guests to take advantage of the fact that their closest friends are already gathered together.

Good-bye, Bridezilla. We have happily waved good-bye to the imperious, self-absorbed bride; instead couples are once again as focused on providing a meaningful, memorable experience for their guests as they are for themselves.

Encore and family weddings. Nearly 40 percent of today's weddings are "encore" events, meaning that the bride, the groom, or both have been married before. More remarrying couples with children are hosting "family weddings" that actively involve their children in the ceremony and often have them join them during their vows, or as part of a statement of support.

Social media. Social media, such as Facebook and Twitter, are deeply woven into the fabric of our everyday lives and extend naturally to sharing wedding news. Image sharing sites like Pinterest that help organize your inspirations are still emerging. These can make planning your wedding day easier and more fun. It's also important to put on the brakes sometimes to avoid oversharing and to make your offline communication with friends and family your top priority, especially when first sharing news and plans about your wedding.

More wedding attire choices. Modern brides are continuing to express their individual taste and style in their attire. Wedding dresses and accessories increasingly include color, and many incorporate designs and fabrics that reflect the bride's culture or ethnic heritage. Bridesmaids' dresses allow for individuality, and are often chosen with complementary cuts or colors instead of all being identical. Black is no longer "out" for bridesmaids or female guests (or even very adventurous brides!), and though most guests still shy away from it, white can be acceptable for guests as well.

Colorful weddings. Traditional white still reigns in many aspects of weddings, but color is also blooming in more than just the flowers, including attire, invitations and announcements, reception decorations and table linens, wedding cakes, and gift wrappings.

Destination weddings. More couples continue to invite guests to join them in exotic and distant locations for their big day, with many guests turning the trip into an opportunity for a longer vacation. Even when it's not an exotic locale, there's a good chance that your wedding will involve travel plans for many of your guests.

20/20 HINDSIGHT

As we were writing this book, we reached out on The Emily Post Institute's Facebook page to recently married brides and asked for their best piece of wedding advice. Here's a sampling of what they were kind enough to share, along with good advice from past brides:

THE BIG PICTURE

"Remember that ultimately, it isn't about the wedding—it's about the marriage." —TANA

"Don't put too much pressure on yourself for everything to be absolutely perfect. At the end of the day, if you're married to the one you love, then that's all that matters!" —ERIN

BALANCE

"Take advice graciously, but ultimately make your own decisions. You will be inundated with advice (both solicited and unsolicited!), which can become confusing." —JENNIFER

"Know your audience! It will help you have a balance of everything from music to food. Grandma does not want to dance to LMFAO! And your construction worker uncle wants an adequate amount of food so he does not have to go to fast food after dinner." —KRISTIN

DELEGATE

"Hand over your cell phone to your maid of honor / best man / wedding planner—just make someone else your 'point person' that weekend and endow them with the power to make decisions on your behalf. Notify all your vendors and family of this. This was the best thing I did—then I could just enjoy the day and focus on getting married!" —NICOLE

"Don't be afraid to ask for help and let others contribute in different ways to your special day. Involving close friends and family in different wedding-day elements can save you time and stress, plus it can bring loved ones joy to have had a hand in bringing your dream to life." —ALLISON

"Have someone designated to run the rehearsal. The bride and groom should be relaxed and just let that person stage-manage. Also, build in time for delays (traffic, logistics) for getting to the ceremony, photos, getting to reception, etc." —TAMMY

GUEST LIST

"I would invite everyone. I was so scared of going over numbers, I didn't invite everyone I wanted, and in the end, I missed having some great friends there." —LISA

"Really narrow down your guest list to the people *you* want to invite, not who your *parents* want to invite. My husband and I were married three and a half years ago, and I have no idea why I invited some of the people that I invited." —TIFFANY

APPRECIATION

"One thing that I think is still so important yet often overlooked is the thank-you note! After an occasion where you are on the receiving end of so much generosity and well-wishing, it is the least you can do, and I think it says a lot about you whether you do or don't!" —SALLY

MONEY

"As you plan, think how no day should cost more than a car. You will need several cars, a mortgage, college funds, savings, healthcare, and emergencies all your days together. Always, always say thank you for whatever gesture is made." —COLEEN

"Save up, and don't use credit to pay for your wedding." —HERRY

"We are going with a grocery store cake, it will look great and taste just fine and we can spend money elsewhere. No one other than us will know the difference." —MELISSA

DETAILS

"Come the wedding day, I couldn't have cared less about chair covers—and I have a feeling that not a single guest noticed. In retrospect, chair covers would have looked silly—but this topic definitely caused a major meltdown during wedding planning." —SOPHIE

"Figure out what's important to you, for example food, flowers, dress, and alcohol. Number them in the order of priority and stick to it! If it didn't make the list then forget about it. It's one less thing to spend money on or make a decision about." —ALYSON

"Have fun with the planning! Don't get too caught up in all the little details or obsess about decisions to be made. Remind yourself that the whole purpose of the day is to celebrate your love and the beginning of your lives together." —ANNE MARIE

"There will inevitably be something that will go wrong or not be exactly as you wanted it, but your guests will never notice, and (hopefully!) you'll be too blissfully happy on the big day to care." —MORGAN

TAKE CARE OF YOURSELF

"When bride and attendants are getting ready before ceremony, make sure to provide food and water so nobody goes to ceremony hungry or dehydrated. The bride and groom should make sure to eat at the reception." —CAROLINE

"Don't forget to eat!" —ANDREA

The More Things Change . . .

Sometimes these changes can be confusing and stressful to sort through, especially when different generations have different traditions and expectations. Your wedding may be quite different from that of your parents or grandparents. While you all said (or will say), "I do," the manners and traditions surrounding the wedding experience have changed over time.

You may run into resistance or skepticism from upper-generation guests or family who expect that for a wedding to be "proper" it must conform to the manners of their day. Having families finance and host the wedding together may be a concept foreign and somewhat suspect to your grandmother, whose parents alone paid for and hosted her wedding. (And it's still perfectly fine today if the bride's family continues to do so.)

These differences of opinion and generational custom are not insurmountable. The best way to bend or break with a tradition is first to understand it. Why is it important, and did it serve a greater purpose that might make it worth holding on to, or at least still achieving another way? For example, you might not choose to send formal wedding invitations or announcements or have a receiving line, but we encourage you to read about them to give context to wedding traditions that have endured for generations. Knowing that you are aware of and have considered all your options will also go a long way to gaining support for more contemporary wedding ideas.

The wedding questions we answer on a regular basis come from all quarters—brides, grooms, parents, attendants, guests, wedding professionals—and whether the asker wants to hold on to tradition or push forward, the questions all reflect a relaxing of "rules" and an increase in alternatives. Tradition for its own sake alone is hollow; it must have meaning and value to make it special. So long as the answer to a dilemma reflects thoughtfulness to the feelings and comfort of all who will be affected by it, practicality may indeed trump tradition—and may in turn create a new tradition of lasting significance.

Best Wishes

Whatever questions and challenges come your way, we hope this book will give you the guidance you need. Most important, we hope you'll have fun, whether your wedding is small and informal or grand and traditional. Really, all that's needed for the "perfect" wedding is the love the bride and groom feel for each other, the confidence to make decisions, and the consideration to make sure that everyone involved is treated with courtesy. A sense of humor comes in handy, too, to help you negotiate any unexpected bumps along the way.

As the two of you approach one of the most important days of your lives, just remember to keep the details in perspective and your happiness and joy in the forefront. May it all turn out beautifully—the perfect wedding for you.

ANNA POST
LIZZIE POST
January 2014

PART ONE

GETTING ORGANIZED

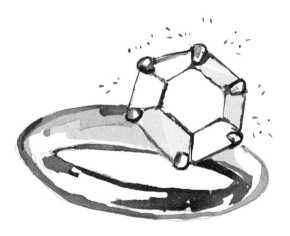

CHAPTER 1

RULES OF ENGAGEMENT

An engagement may encompass only a few days or weeks, or extend over a number of years. For most couples, the engagement period lasts as long as it takes to plan the wedding, and the average period is almost sixteen months. However long, it is always a busy, exciting time for the couple and their families.

If you want to marry at a specific time of the year, on a certain date, or have your heart set on a special location, you may need to reserve wedding and reception sites as much as a year to eighteen months in advance. Religious requirements can be a factor in the equation; and sometimes an engagement is affected by events beyond a couple's control, such as military service or education or work commitments.

For most couples, an engagement is a happy time. It seems as if everyone wants to share in your happiness and celebrate it with parties and presents, indulging almost your every wish. This exhilarating time also includes being attentive to the feelings and needs of other important people in your life. And that starts with how you share the news.

MAKING IT OFFICIAL

The term *officially engaged* is really a misnomer. There is no official validation for an engagement—no tests to take, papers to sign, or fees to pay. What is generally considered an "official" engagement is one that includes both a direct proposal (and often but not necessarily) and an engagement ring, and that has been announced to family and friends and perhaps in a public forum such as the newspaper or Facebook.

If you were previously married, wait until you are divorced before announcing an engagement. Even if an annulment or divorce is imminent, an engagement shouldn't be announced until it is final.

Sharing the Good News

Who you tell and how you tell is at the heart of sharing well. You may be bursting to tell everyone you see and your fingers may be itching to tap out a post on your social network, but before informing the world of your engagement, consider the people closest to you. Usually people know when romance is in the air and marriage is a possibility, but family and good friends deserve your special attention. It's important to tell parents and children in person or, if that's not possible, then by phone. They'll want to be with you when they hear the news or at least be able to hear your voice. Email is just too casual and impersonal a way to share the news with close family.

Children. If one or both of you have children, tell them first before anyone else. This is critically important for young children and teens—and even for adult children—whose lives will be dramatically changed by the addition of a stepparent and perhaps stepsiblings. Your children may be thrilled, but it's also possible they may be doubtful, reluctant, and even frightened and resentful. It takes love, honesty, and patience to transform individuals into a family, so respect every child's need to question your decision and seek your reassurance.

You should also tell an ex-spouse if you share children from that marriage. It may help to smooth the way for your children's involvement during your engage-

ment and at your wedding. Even if you didn't have children but are on speaking terms, it's kind to inform your ex before the news becomes public knowledge. (See also Chapter 18, page 242.)

Parents. After children, parents deserve priority. Tradition holds that the couple tells the bride's parents first. In the past, the suitor spoke first with the father of the young woman to declare his intentions and get her father's consent before proposing. Although this tradition is obsolete, it's still a sign of respect for a prospective groom to meet with his future in-laws and discuss his career and life plans. This conversation might take place before the engagement, when the couple tells their parents of their engagement, or soon thereafter—whenever seems most appropriate. When parents are separated or divorced, convey the news to each. Even if a parent and child are somewhat estranged, a parent should hear the news directly from their child instead of others.

You can each inform your own parents or speak as a couple with both sets of parents. If your parents don't know your fiancé(e), it's your responsibility to introduce them. If your parents live at a distance, you can make introductions by phone, but also plan to visit as soon as you can. Nothing is better than getting together in person.

In the event that the announcement will be a total surprise, each member of the couple should talk privately with their own parents first. This allows parents to ask questions and express perfectly normal worries—such as how long you've known each other—without their future son- or daughter-in-law present. Some parents may need a day or two to get used to the idea and patience at this stage is worth the investment.

Relatives and close friends. Depending on your family structure, there are probably some relatives—siblings; grandparents; close aunts, uncles, and cousins—and good friends who you'll want to inform soon after you tell your parents. Always include them as special people in the know before the rest of the world finds out. When and how you spread the word is up to you as long as you're sensitive to people's feelings and thoughtful of what is going on in their lives.

Your social network. Of course you and your fiancé(e) are excited and want to share the news with everyone you know, but make sure you have told those closest to you first before you post or tweet the news, the "we're engaged" or ring photo, or change your relationship status on your social network page. Think how hurt you might feel to find out about your best friend or sister's engagement in such an impersonal way. Because social networks can spread news very

---

AVOID THE RUSH TO GUSH

Don't make promises before you have planned the wedding. For example, some couples find themselves with a much larger wedding party than they wanted because in the euphoria of becoming engaged, they asked too many people to be bridesmaids and groomsmen. Others risk hurting the feelings of people they care about by having to rescind such invitations. The same can occur if you initially invite more people to your wedding than can fit on your guest list. Stop and think before inviting anyone. If asked, you can always say, "It's so early in our planning, we haven't even decided on a venue yet."

FACEBOOK FAUX PAS

Q: My daughter posted on her Facebook page, "Who wants to come to a wedding!" A large proportion of her 500-plus friends responded, "Yes!" and asked for directions. The wedding is to be at our house. We are prepared for 40 guests, total. I immediately posted on her Facebook page: "Jenny is so enthusiastic about her wedding! Of course, she's not actually inviting everyone she knows on Facebook. It's a very small, private wedding. If you are on our list, you will receive an invitation in the mail." Then I emailed Jenny, who emailed me back, saying she hadn't thought anyone would take her seriously. Fortunately, she has never met most of these "friends," and they don't know where we live. Still, should I hire someone as a security guard and have him check invitations?

A: Many an overexcited couple wishes they had curbed their enthusiasm when spreading the news—and invitations—about their wedding. Hard enough when it's a blanket announcement to coworkers. But a blast to 500-plus Facebook friends, in jest or not, definitely requires some damage control. You've done the sensible thing with your reply post and your chat with your daughter. However, given the scope of the circumstances, it might be wise to be prepared for some uninvited "invited" guests.

As you mention, the simplest way to be sure that only the invited 40 get past your front gate is to check invitations, either the invitation itself or names against a list. So the onus doesn't fall on you, the father of the bride, or a guest, consider hiring a gatekeeper for an hour or two around the wedding start time.

quickly, ask those early birds in the know to let you share your own news on social media first.

Colleagues and coworkers. Before telling your office mates, you may want to inform a boss or supervisor first as a matter of courtesy. The easiest way to spread the news among your colleagues is to tell people as you see them and let them know it's okay to tell others. At some point, meet with the person in charge of employee compensation and make necessary alterations in benefit, insurance, and retirement plans effective following your wedding. (See also Chapter 3, page 41 and page 42.)

During sad times. If you become engaged during a time of difficulty—when a family member or close friend is seriously ill or there has been a death—share your good news, but keep it low key and don't expect everyone to react as they would under happier circumstances. Depending on the situation, a couple may delay an engagement celebration.

If Parents or Children Disapprove

When parents or children disapprove of an engagement, it's natural to feel hurt, sad, or disappointed. Whether they express their concerns or not, some parents may feel somewhat anxious when their children become engaged. As the bride or groom, don't be too overly surprised if your parent's reaction isn't quite what you expected. That anxiety usually disappears once wedding plans are under way and they get to know their son or daughter's fiancé(e). But if the tension increases or a parent clearly voices objections, then it's best to address the problem openly.

- First and foremost, *stay calm* and approach any discussion as one adult to another.

- Be willing to listen to parental concerns and to take them seriously. Address those concerns as best you can.

AS A COUPLE

Besides planning your wedding, your engagement is a time for contemplation and mutual consideration of the commitment you're preparing to make. During this time, you will begin to sort out what it means to act in tandem as you plan and prepare not just for your big day, but also for your future together. There will be parties and presents and friends and family focused on celebrating the two of you. But there will be times when the barrage of planning details or tricky relationship management moments will cause stress.

- Don't give in to pressures to stage a celebration that is more about show and less about you.

- Stay focused on your vision.

- Delegate tasks to others who have offered to help.

- Stick to the day-to-day routine activities of your life.

And, whether the time between your engagement and your wedding is twelve weeks or twelve months, remember to take time off from organizing every now and then to enjoy each other, and to immerse yourself in the fun and happiness your engagement brings.

- ❖ Try to remember how important your happiness is to your parents and don't let minor disagreements get out of hand.

When parents are on board, most other family members will follow. Yet it may be impossible to overcome parental objections, and you will have to proceed on your own. But don't sever family ties. Be sure that your parents—or any other family members who disapprove—know when and where the wedding will be and how much it would mean to you to have them there.

When children disapprove the dilemma is even greater, and family relationships can become quite strained. If time and communication cannot bridge the gap, then pro-fessional counseling may be a good option to help the entire family understand one another's feelings.

Getting Families Together

A wedding isn't just the joining of two people; it's also the joining of two families—and sometimes more in the case of remarriages. The purpose of much wedding etiquette is to provide a framework for the two families to interact and get to know each other without causing offense—a tall order! For generations, formal etiquette assigned hosting duties of the first parent meeting to the groom's family and hosting duties for practically everything else to the bride's family. It was presumed that the marrying couple were too young to have much experience of the social obligations of the adult world, so to be safe, the parents ran the show.

Today, engaged couples are likely to be socially independent and perfectly capable of arranging and facilitating a meeting between their respective parents if they don't already know each other.

Parents meeting parents. While traditional etiquette calls for the groom's parents to contact the bride's parents soon after they've all learned of the engagement, today it really doesn't matter who makes the first move. If you're the parents of the bride, give the groom's parents a few days to honor the tradition. The key here is that the parents get in touch with each other in the spirit of friendship, so this isn't the time to stand on ceremony.

Whichever set takes the initiative, a phone call or an email is a good way to introduce yourselves and set up a date to meet with the "kids" to celebrate the good news. Even if it's not possible for the parents to get together at this point, aim to establish a line of communication so that when planning questions arise you feel comfortable calling each other.

If the "who should call whom" scenario seems too awkward, the engaged couple can smooth the way and help parents get the ball rolling by arranging and hosting the first parental get-together themselves.

Who hosts? As with all invitations, the person doing the inviting does the paying. So if the groom's parents invite the bride's parents to Sunday brunch, the groom's parents pick up the tab, and vice versa. If the couple arranges, hosts, and pays for the event at home or at a restaurant, it removes any "who pays" awkwardness from that first meeting.

The bride and groom are in the best position to know what kind of gathering is most likely to put everyone at ease. A casual event, such as a barbecue or weeknight supper, is often most comfortable. But if one set of parents has a more formal lifestyle than the other, a good compromise might be a dinner or weekend brunch at a nice midrange restaurant.

When parents are divorced. Think carefully about family structures and have realistic expectations. Arrange separate meetings with each set of parents so that everyone involved has a chance to meet. Don't force divorced parents into social situations that have the potential to make them—and others—feel uncomfortable. As much as you may want to have your parents put aside grievances in honor of your wedding, it may be too much to hope for.

WHAT TO CALL THE FUTURE IN-LAWS?

Q: I'm unsure what to call my future in-laws. Up until our engagement, I've been addressing them as Mr. and Mrs. Jenkins.

A: Continue to call them exactly what you have been calling them until they suggest otherwise. Sometime during the engagement period, parents usually ask their future son- or daughter-in-law to call them by their first names, just as other adult friends and family do.

By the time you are married, if your in-laws still haven't suggested a less formal option, ask them directly what they would like you to call them.

If they want you to call them "Mom" and "Dad," it's okay—if you feel comfortable doing so. However, if you don't, you'll have to say, "I'm honored, but I have to be honest and tell you that I'm only comfortable using "Mom" and "Dad" with my own parents. Would it be all right with you if I call you Roger and Ann?"

PRINTED ANNOUNCEMENTS

Printed social announcements are often sent to mark life's milestones, such as the birth of a child or a wedding. Since an engagement is a temporary state, printed announcements aren't sent to friends and family. The news is shared in person, by note, phone call, via email or social media, or with a newspaper notice.

Newspaper Engagement Announcements

As it is a long-held tradition, lots of couples still want to spread the happy news beyond immediate friends and family with an announcement in the bride and groom's local, regional, or hometown newspaper.

Most newspapers provide forms for couples or their parents to complete and submit online, and many allow for photo submissions as well. Before contacting a paper, look at its engagement section. This will tell you what kind of details the paper normally reports and whether they use photographs of the couple.

Even if you haven't set a date for the wedding, it's a good idea to submit your announcement soon after you are engaged. Newspapers vary as to when they print the announcements, so submit early to avoid a delay.

Engagement announcements are usually brief and follow a format similar to the one below. But some papers use an informal style, include more information, and ask couples about details of their courtship and engagement.

A public engagement announcement should never be made if either member is still legally married to someone else. Nor is a public announcement usually appropriate when there has recently been a death in either family or when a member of the immediate family is critically ill. And don't forget to tell your closest friends and family before making any public announcement! (See also page 3.)

Basic Wording

Traditionally, the parents of the bride make the announcement. The basic wording of a formal announcement includes full names with courtesy or professional titles; city and state of residence if not the same as the hometown of the newspaper; highest level of education of the couple; and their current employment.

> *Mr. and Mrs. Allen Perry of Fairview, Maryland, announce the engagement of their daughter, Jane Ellen Perry, to William Paul Kruger, Jr., son of Dr. and Mrs. William Paul Kruger of Newcastle, Missouri. A September wedding is planned.*
>
> *Ms. Perry, a graduate of Richmond Nursing College, is a physical therapist with Bonaventure Hospital in Baltimore, Maryland. Mr. Kruger was graduated from Monroe University and is employed as a loan manager with First Bank of Baltimore.*

Engagement and wedding announcements are a public service of the newspapers—though many papers now charge fees—and you can't dictate or edit the contents. Using or dropping courtesy titles, for example, is determined by a publication's overall style, not the preference of people whose names appear in the paper. Larger newspapers tend to have a more concise announcement style than suburban and rural publications, and virtually all publications give some precedence to prominent community members.

The following samples indicate how a number of different situations may be treated in print:

When the couple make the announcement. In today's less formal world, many couples make their own announcement. The wording is simple:

> *(Ms.) Gayle Ann Parker and (Mr.) James Newsom are pleased to announce their engagement. [This may be followed by information about their parents or simply about the couple and their planned wedding date.]*

When parents are divorced. Divorced parents are listed as individuals, by their current legal names and places of residence, and never as a couple. If the bride's parents are divorced, her mother usually makes the announcement.

> *Ms. Martine Cousins of Hartsville, Colorado, announces the engagement of her daughter, Sarah Louise Baker, to . . . Ms. Baker is also the daughter of Mr. Albert Baker of Boulder.*

When the groom's parents are divorced, the announcement follows this pattern:

> *Mr. and Mrs. Lamar Hughes announce the engagement of their daughter, Caroline Hughes, to Justin Marc DuBois, son of Mrs. Thomas Shelton of Centerville, Ohio, and Mr. Jean Marc DuBois of Brighton, Michigan.*

When the parents of both the bride and the groom are divorced, the usual form is:

> *Mrs. Walter Murray announces the engagement of her daughter, Elizabeth Leigh Considine, to John*

Carter Lowndes, son of Mrs. Harriett Lowndes of
Seattle and   Mr. Houston Lowndes of Palmetto,
California. Ms. Considine is also the daughter of Mr.
Horace Considine of Melbourne, Australia.

A stepparent usually isn't included in a formal announcement unless he or she is an adoptive parent or the biological parent is not a part of the bride or groom's life,
but stepparents might be mentioned in a lengthier or
more informal announcement.

**When divorced parents make a joint announce-
ment.** Divorced parents of the bride-to-be may want
to make the announcement together. Both are listed
by their current legal names (whether or not they have
married again) and places of residence:

> Mrs. Walter Murray of Gladstone, Washington,
> and Mr. Horace Considine of Melbourne, Australia,
> announce the engagement of their daughter,
> Elizabeth Leigh Considine, to . . .

When a parent is deceased. When one of the bride's
parents is deceased, the surviving parent makes the
announcement:

> Mr. Gerald Mackenzie Brown announces the
> engagement of his daughter, Leslie Brown, to . . .
> Ms. Brown is also the daughter of the late Marie
> Compton Brown.

When a parent of the groom is deceased, this form is
generally followed:

> Mr. and Mrs. Gerald MacKenzie Brown announce
> the engagement of their daughter, Leslie Brown, to
> Peter Carelli, son of Mrs. Benjamin Carelli and the

late Mr. Carelli [or when the mother is deceased: Mr.
Benjamin Carelli and the late Mrs. Carelli or the late
Katherine Boyd Carelli].

If both the bride's parents are deceased, a close family member (or members) may make the announcement:

> *Mr. and Mrs. Seth Sheridan announce the engagement of their granddaughter, Cynthia Sheridan, to . . . Ms. Sheridan is the daughter of the late Mr. and Mrs. Frederick Sheridan [or the late Margaret and Frederick Sheridan].*

Announcements for same-sex couples. The *New York Times* and a number of large city newspapers print engagement, marriage, and commitment ceremony announcements for same-sex couples, as do gay and lesbian publications, but be aware that not all newspapers do. Many gay and lesbian couples choose to issue the announcement themselves. But whether the couple or one or both of their parents make the announcement, the wording follows the same form as for heterosexual couples. The only decision to make is whose name comes first. There's no etiquette to this, it's up to you—though going alphabetically or flipping a coin might settle any debate.

> *(Mr.) George Barnes and (Mr.) Claudio Manelli are pleased to announce their engagement . . .*
>
> *Mr. and Mrs. Henry Barnes of Garden City, Long Island, are pleased to announce the engagement of their son, George, to Mr. Claudio Manelli. . . .*

The Engagement Ring

A new sparkler on a woman's left hand can be the only clue needed for people to realize a wedding is in her future. An engagement ring, however, isn't essential for you to be "officially" engaged, and many cou-ples choose to put the money toward other purposes. Some couples even postpone purchasing an engagement ring until later in their marriage, when they can afford it. (This can be a romantic way to celebrate a special wedding anniversary.)

Engagement rings can be new or antique, bought from the showcase or custom designed. Rings may be passed down in a family, and heirloom stones might be reset in a more contemporary style. Traditionally, the man selects and purchases the ring, and that's often still the case today. According to a joint survey released by *Men's Health* magazine and The Knot, 44 percent of men chose the ring on their own, while only 16 percent chose it with their fiancée. And they must be doing a good job because only 3 percent of the women surveyed exchanged the ring for another. The women also said that "size didn't matter" (96 percent), but 32 percent said that not having a ring was the biggest proposal mistake a man could make.

Diamonds: The Five C's

The traditional gemstones for engagement rings, diamonds are the emblems of love and engagement. Knowing the five C's of diamonds allows you to converse comfortably with jewelers when you are shopping for a diamond engagement ring. (For choosing wedding bands, see Chapter 2, page 23.)

CARAT

Carat is the weight of a diamond. One carat is one-fifth of a gram (200 milligrams). There are 142 carats to an ounce. One carat also has 100 points. This system of measuring diamond weight began in India and was based on the weight of the seeds of the carob tree, which were used to balance scales.

CLARITY

Diamonds are rated on the basis of blemishes that occur naturally, such as inner cracks, bubbles, and specks that are hard to detect with the naked eye. The size and placement of the blemishes determine a diamond's clarity rating, which ranges from flawless to varying degrees of small inclusions to the least-desirable rating: imperfect. When a diamond is rated flawless (FL), it is given the highest clarity rating; a flawless diamond is rare.

CUT

The way a diamond is cut determines its brilliance. In fact, cut is generally considered the most important of the four C's of diamonds. When cut, a diamond is faceted in a series of flat, angled surfaces that reflect light off one another. This is what causes the stone to sparkle.

SAYING "I DON'T" TO THE FAMILY HEIRLOOM

If a bride feels uncomfortable accepting the family heirloom, she may decline graciously.

Turning down the ring can be especially awkward if it's the groom's family making the offer. While a groom's parents may be focused on honoring a family tradition when they pass along an engagement ring, they may put the bride-to-be in an awkward position if she has her heart set on having her own ring or simply doesn't like the ring being offered. If she refuses, she may seem ungrateful; if she accepts, she may feel resentful. It's best if parents make the offer to their son *before* rings are chosen. They should also let him know that they understand completely if the couple chooses a different ring or creates a new setting.

Princess   Marquise   Cushion   Round

Asscher   Oval   Emerald   Pear

COLOR

Another criteria for determining the value of diamonds is color. If a diamond is clear and colorless, it is rated D, the highest color ranking. The lowest rating is Z, yellow. This indicates a stone that contains traces of earthy color. Some diamonds that naturally have some tint of color are placed in a special category called fancies.

CERTIFICATION

A fifth C for diamonds is certification. This is the written proof of a diamond's weight, grade, and identifying characteristics from the International Gemological Institute and should come with your ring. Keep this certification in a safe place; it will be important for insurance purposes.

Gemstones

Instead of a diamond, many couples prefer a gemstone—a perfectly acceptable choice—for the engagement ring. Gemstones are classified as "precious" and "semiprecious," with "precious" stones being emeralds, rubies, and sapphires. Long prized as symbols of mystical powers, gemstones were also graced with symbolic meaning during Victorian times, when they became especially popular in engagement rings. Some couples select gemstones for engagement rings based on the birthstone of the bride or the groom or both.

The Engagement Party

An engagement is definitely something to celebrate, and a party may be the perfect way for family and friends to toast the future bride and groom. Modern engagement parties may be as formal or informal as you like and are by no means mandatory.

The hosts. Although the bride's parents usually host the engagement party, another family member or friend may do so. When the couple's families live in different parts of the country, the parents of the bride and groom might each host parties in their hometowns— an alternative to the more traditional post-honeymoon party given by the groom's family to honor their new daughter-in-law.

What kind of party? Cocktail and dinner parties are popular, but there is no standard party format. Everything from a casual brunch to a formal reception is appropriate. Sometimes the purpose of the party isn't stated on the invitation and the engagement is announced as a surprise. Whatever suits the hosts, the couple, and the guests is just fine.

The guests. Generally the guest list is limited to the couple's relatives and good friends. It can be as small or as large as you want and can comfortably accommodate. Under most circumstances, engagement party guests are wedding guests, so plan with the long view in mind.

SURRISE!

Whether you let a cat out of the bag with your names written on a ribbon around its neck, or you distribute bouquets and boutonnieres tagged with both names, or whether guests receive the glad tidings in telegrams used as place cards, there is not a rule in the world to hamper the complete freedom of your own imagination. You can literally give any variety of party you choose, invite whom you choose, and serve whatever you choose.

—EMILY POST, *ETIQUETTE*, 1945

GIFTS FOR ENGAGEMENT PARTIES

Q: I've attended a number of engagement parties, and I still can't figure out the etiquette of gifts. Some people bring presents; others don't. Should I expect gifts at my engagement party?

A: It depends. In the past, engagement gifts weren't obligatory or expected, and this is usually still the case. However, in many parts of the country, bringing a gift to an engagement party has become a "must." Close friends and family members usually do give a gift, but ultimately, the decision whether to give an engagement gift depends on local custom, your guest's relationship to you, and their budget. Gift instructions shouldn't be included on invitations, but a guest might call the host and ask. If you're worried about taxing your friends' budgets, you can tell your hosts that you prefer "no gifts."

An engagement gift is really a good-hearted gesture of affection, and it doesn't need to be expensive or elaborate. Something simple such as a cookbook or a good bottle of wine—intended to help a couple establish a collection—are typical engagement gifts.

Invitations. Written or printed invitations are the norm, but for a small gathering, phoned or emailed invitations are also acceptable. Send three weeks ahead.

The announcement. Whether the news will be a surprise or the guests already know, it's traditional for the host (often the bride's father) to make the official announcement and lead a toast to the couple. At a large party with guests who already know about the engagement, the couple and their parents might form an informal receiving line to welcome guests and make introductions.

WHAT IS A TROUSSEAU?

A trousseau traditionally included the personal possessions—clothing and household goods—that a bride brought to her marriage. The word *trousseau* is derived from a French term meaning "bundle." The trousseau was originally part of a dowry (the financial arrangement between the families of a betrothed couple) and is associated with a time when marriages were arranged and the bride ceded all her possessions to her husband.

Beyond her wedding dress, party clothes, and honeymoon outfits, today's bride-to-be is unlikely to acquire a vast new wardrobe before her wedding. Items including linens, tableware, silver, and basic kitchen equipment, which made up the household trousseau, are now purchased by the couple, acquired as wedding gifts, or assembled when the couple merges their households.

One tradition that has survived is the hope chest—a good-sized wooden (often cedar) chest for storing linens and blankets. Although few mothers begin sewing and embroidering linens when their daughters are born, as they once did in anticipation of a distant wedding day, hope chests remain a popular gift from parents to their engaged daughters and, like handmade wedding quilts, are often passed from one generation to the next.

Gifts and thanks. Since guests aren't expected to bring engagement gifts, save any you receive to open later, after the party. You might receive a few unexpected gifts after your announcement appears in the newspaper or on your Facebook page, too. Follow up promptly with a note of thanks and appreciation, even if you said thanks in person. (See Chapter 14, page 177.)

When the Engagement Doesn't Work Out

One of the underlying purposes of an engagement is to give a couple time to test their commitment, and not every engagement ends in marriage. When an engagement is broken, it can be a time of great sadness, and confusion, which, all too often, can lead to animosity. But whatever the feelings of the people involved, they shouldn't be embarrassed about taking a difficult step that prevents future and even greater unhappiness.

There are important dos and don'ts associated with a breakup—some are grounded in respect and consideration for all involved, whereas others concern practical matters.

Do tell close family as soon and as tactfully as possible. As with announcing an engagement, your children and your parents should be the first to know. When children are involved, particularly if they have developed a good relationship with the person you were engaged to, they often feel an intense loss. Explain the breakup as best you can without demeaning the other person.

Don't expect family and friends to choose sides. A broken engagement should not be a declaration of war by either party. Some people will instantly rally around you, but many who know you both won't want to be drawn into your very personal decision, no matter how much sympathy they express.

Do inform everyone involved in the wedding as soon as you can. A family member, friend, or members of the wedding party may be able to help you out by getting in touch with people who have been contracted for services (caterers and the like), but you should personally speak with the officiant, attendants, and others who agreed to participate in the planned wedding. Remember to contact anyone who has planned a social event in your honor.

Do inform invited guests. If there is enough time, when an engagement is broken after invitations have been mailed you can send a printed card like the following:

> *Mr. and Mrs. Nathan Morris announce that the marriage of their daughter Ashley to Mr. Josh Sandburg will not take place.*

If there isn't time to print and deliver notices, call the people on the guest list. While it's preferable to speak personally with guests, you can leave a message. Send an email if that's the most efficient way to reach someone, but do request a response so you know the message was received. The bride can enlist the help of her maid of honor or other bridesmaids with this task. (See also Chapter 8, page 104.)

Do return all engagement, wedding, and shower gifts, including monetary gifts. This is generally the bride's responsibility, since gifts are traditionally sent to her. But there's no reason why the man can't return gifts given to him and his former fiancée as a couple by his friends. Accompany returned gifts to the giver with a brief note such as the following:

Dear Claudia,

   I am sorry to have to tell you that Josh and I have ended our engagement. I'm returning the beautiful crystal bowl that you were so thoughtful to send.

Love,

Ashley

If One of a Couple Dies

When one of an engaged couple dies, the survivor is unlikely to be able to handle the details of canceling any wedding plans. It's good for relatives and friends to take over certain painful but necessary tasks, including notifying members of the wedding party, the officiant, the wedding location, anyone hired for services, and the people on the guest list if wedding invitations have been sent.

   A bereaved fiancée can certainly keep her engagement ring if she wishes. Returning wedding and engagement gifts is a personal decision. If the survivor chooses to return some or all gifts, there is really no time limit. Only the most insensitive people would complain if gifts are not sent back or are returned after weeks or months. A brief note should be included with a returned gift, and family members can handle this task as well.

SHOULD I RETURN THE RING?

Q: My fiancé and I have just broken off our engagement. Our decision was mutual, so I hope we can be friends again someday. But what should I do with my engagement ring? He hasn't asked for it, and my friends say I should keep it.

A: Most states consider an engagement ring to be like any gift—the property of the person who receives it—so you have no legal obligation to return it. But ethics trump law in this situation. Do you really want to keep a ring that was given to symbolize a pledge that you have both agreed not to honor? Since your decision was mutual, what is more important to you now, the ring or keeping some kind of positive relationship with your ex-fiancé? The decision is yours, and your conscience is a much better guide than the opinions of friends.

   The unique circumstances of a broken engagement often determine what is done. When the man purchases the ring, he traditionally relinquishes it if he ends the engagement, though the woman may choose to return it to him. If the woman cancels the engagement, it is correct for her to give back the ring—especially when it's an heirloom of the man's family—along with any other jewelry she received as an engagement gift from her ex-fiancé. But when a couple shared the cost, then the one who keeps the ring ought to refund the other person's money, regardless of who precipitated the breakup. Or they might sell the ring and either split the proceeds or divide the return based on the proportion each person originally contributed.

CHAPTER 2

THE BIG DECISIONS

The engagement is on! You and your loved ones are thrilled; the future is bright with hope and possibility. A beautiful bride, a beaming groom, an elegant wedding party, and a happy complement of family and friends. To make the dream come true requires time, planning, and huge doses of the "three C's"—consideration, communication, and compromise.

This chapter focuses on the major decisions and initial steps of planning. While there will be many more decisions to come, start by making these "top ten." Many of your future to-dos and choices will be based on these determinations:

1. Guest list

2. Budget

3. Season, date, and time of day of the wedding

4. Ceremony and reception location

5. Ceremony officiant

6. Style and formality

7. Wedding consultant

8. Wedding party

9. The rings

10. Honeymoon location and date

Turning Wedding Dreams into Reality

This stage of planning is the opportunity for both of you to explore your wedding dreams. Many brides have imagined their weddings since they were young and they have definite ideas about what they want. However, you may be surprised to learn that you're not the only one who has visions of this day. Your parents, grandparents, and even siblings and good friends may harbor ideas and thoughts about how they picture your wedding. Grooms are more closely involved in wedding planning than in past generations, and your fiancé may have his own ideas about your wedding.

If you've always longed to float up the aisle in a long white gown and your groom-to-be thinks a casual ceremony on the beach would suffice, don't worry. This is the time to consider all kinds of different options. Blending your ideas is bound to be interesting, and there are many ways to personalize your wedding and to bring in elements that you both think are important. Couples who consider the feelings of their partners, communicate honestly about matters large and small, and who are willing to make compromises usually find that their wedding planning goes smoothly.

This is the time to look for inspiration and gather ideas that visualize your dreams. Before you start debating the merits of large versus small or formal versus informal, enjoy some creative time. Build a Pinterest board with different categories for attire, flowers, and reception ideas; even creating an old-fashioned scrapbook is a fun and worthwhile exercise. Write a list of the qualities you have admired about weddings you've attended or you see as important to your own wedding. What kind of celebration do these images and words describe? A small gathering in your parents' backyard? An evening gala in a ballroom, with everyone decked out in formal dress? Let the qualities you consider most important guide your decisions.

The Primary Decisions

Whether you have a long or a short time to plan your wedding, start by separating your primary decisions from those that can wait. Think of the primary decisions as the foundation for all the other choices you make. Once you've made the big decisions, secondary decisions often fall into place.

Let's take a look at the top ten big decisions and how to start making them.

The Guest List

Any decisions about the type of wedding you will have hinges on the size of the guest list. While your available budget is the fundamental determining factor, the size of your guest list governs how that money is spent. For example, if neither of you can imagine celebrating without your mutually large families and numerous friends in attendance but your budget is modest, you may have to forgo a formal sit-down dinner reception.

If the sit-down dinner reception is your top priority, the easiest way to cut costs is to shorten your guest list. In the long run, it's easier to modify spending than to leave out people who really matter to you. Also, by starting with a preliminary guest list, you'll be better able to pare it down if you have to make cuts. (See also Chapter 7, page 87.)

The Budget

The days when the bride's parents were automatically expected to bear all the expenses of the wedding and reception are over. It's now more common for engaged couples, especially established wage earners, to pay all, most, or at least to share some of the expense with their parents. Although not expected, the groom's family may also contribute to the wedding funds.

As soon as possible, everyone—you, your parents, as applicable—needs to discuss finances and determine how much each would like to contribute. In the early days of planning, people have a tendency to overestimate their financial capabilities (and underestimate actual costs), so the first rule of budgeting is to be realistic. The second is to be considerate. A parent may be willing to take a second mortgage or deplete retirement savings in order to finance an elaborate wedding, but is this the kind of sacrifice you want? If you're paying for the wedding, you may have to borrow some funds. How much debt are you both comfortable taking on?

If your parents have given you a figure that is the most they can spend, it is up to you to be appreciative and to work with that amount, combining your resources with theirs. Review the projected costs for all of the wedding expenses (see chart, Chapter 3, pages 33–35), and compare it against your resources.

Since the reception will account for the bulk of your wedding expenses, get general estimates from a few of the reception sites that are at the top of your wish list. That way you can determine if you are dreaming within your financial abilities. At this point, don't worry about cutting costs or quality. There are many smart ways of cutting corners without sacrificing quality. For now, you are just trying to get a sense of the cost so that you can determine how many guests and what type of reception you can plan.

If you are paying for your own wedding, take an honest look at your finances. If your budget is limited, decide what takes priority: a glamorous wedding and elaborate meal with a smaller guest list, or a larger guest list and a casual reception? Make compromises jointly. Ideas include shortening the guest list; marrying at a time of year or time of day when costs are less; and choosing a more affordable reception site.

Season, Date, and Time of Day

TIME OF YEAR

The time of year for your wedding is a key consideration for several reasons. The most popular months for weddings (starting with the busiest) are June, September, August, May, October, and July. However, this can vary regionally. In New York City, October is the second most popular month in which to marry. Accordingly, the most popular wedding locations will be at a premium during those months, in terms of both availability and cost. It's worth asking about rate changes throughout the year. In general, reception venues offer better rates in January, February, and March. Of course, if you plan a destination wedding or a honeymoon in February at a popular wintertime retreat like Florida, Hawaii, or the Caribbean, expect to pay peak prices.

Some religions have restrictions on weddings that take place during holy days, such as those of Lent or Easter, Passover or Ramadan. If you're hoping for an early-spring wedding, check the calendar—and then check with your priest, minister, imam, or rabbi.

Finally, consider the impact the timing will have on guests. Thanksgiving, Christmas, and the Fourth of July are prime family vacation times, when people have longtime traditions and obligations they may find hard to forgo. When school is in session, it may be difficult for families to carve out a three-day wedding weekend. Consider as well any difficulties guests will have in making their travel plans.

On the other hand, having your wedding on a secondary holiday weekend, such as Memorial Day or Labor Day, may be a smart choice: Guests who have to travel will have an automatic three-day weekend and won't have to take an extra day off from work, but remember, travel tends to be more expensive.

DAY OF THE WEEK

Most weddings are held on weekends, and for obvious reason: Weekend days are the customary days off from work. Within the weekend, Christians don't usually wed on a Sunday and Jews don't usually wed on a Saturday, because these are their respective Sabbath days of prayer and rest. A weekday wedding can reap the benefits of lower prices and almost certain availability of popular ceremony and reception sites. A weekday wedding, particularly in the late afternoon or evening on a Thursday, is also a logical consideration for a destination wedding. It provides an entire weekend for guests to fit in a mini vacation along with the festivities.

TIME OF DAY

The time of day your wedding takes place can make a big difference to your budget, especially reception costs. A late-afternoon or early-evening wedding is generally more expensive than a morning or early- to mid-afternoon wedding. The most popular time blocks to get married (no surprises here) include Saturday afternoon, Saturday morning, Friday evening, and Sunday afternoon.

Guests expect to be fed a meal or its equivalent at a reception in the middle of the day or anytime from 4 to 8 P.M. If you're looking for a way to rein in your expenses, consider holding your celebrations during a less frequently booked time of day, that will give you more options—heavy hors d'oeuvres or brunch rather than a plated dinner.

Traditionally, the later the wedding, the more formal it is likely to be. But that's not always the case. A morning wedding doesn't have to be any less elegant than one held at night. And an evening wedding reception could be a casual clam bake or barbecue.

The Locations

CEREMONY LOCATION

If you want to be married in a house of worship, make inquiries as soon as you have an approximate wedding date. It may be possible to make a tentative reservation and then confirm the day and time when you have reserved your reception site.

When selecting both your ceremony and reception sites, be certain there's adequate space for your guests, including parking. Aside from a house of worship, your choices for the ceremony and/or reception might include your or a relative's home, a hotel, a wedding hall, a restaurant, a club, city hall, a historic or cultural facility, park, and even a beach. (See also Chapter 15, page 185.)

RECEPTION LOCATION

Once you have drawn up your guest list and determined a date and time for your wedding, you can focus on the kind of reception you want and your location preferences. Begin checking out possible sites immediately, in terms of approximate cost and availability. In some parts of the country, reception sites are booked at least a year in advance. (See also Chapter 16, page 207.)

THE CHICKEN AND THE EGG

Which comes first, the date or the place? There's no science here, but at some point the date, the venue, or the choice of officiant will guide your planning decisions, and suddenly, everything magically falls into place.

The Availability of Your Officiant

If you place great importance on who performs your ceremony and wouldn't consider getting married without having him or her officiate, check on that individual's availability before making any other decisions about the date of your wedding. (See also Chapter 15, page 185.)

Style and Formality

When determining the style of your wedding, you're really deciding on how formal or informal you want it to be. The formality is related to the location of the ceremony and reception, and the time of day. Evening weddings and those held in a place of worship tend to be more formal. Afternoon, at-home, or beach weddings are generally less formal. Any combination is possible, though, so choose what suits your circumstances. The style of your wedding will also impact the small touches and how you personalize the space and experience. A wedding held in the fall may reflect the season in everything from the color of the bridesmaid's attire to the frosting on the beautifully wrapped cupcakes each guest receives as a wedding favor.

THE FORMAL WEDDING

What makes a wedding formal? The clothing for one thing. From the guests to the groom, everyone at a formal wedding is decked out in their finest. The bride and her attendants wear long gowns, sometimes even long white gloves. The groom and his groomsmen may be in tuxes. In addition to clothing, the setting, the time of day, a formal invitation and an adherence to tradition are also the hallmarks of a formal wedding. (See Chapter 19, page 251; Chapter 8, page 95; and Chapter 9, page 107.)

THE INFORMAL WEDDING

Afternoon, at-home, or beach weddings are generally informal. The ceremony may take place in a place of worship, or in a home or garden presided over by a justice of the peace. At an informal wedding, the bride and her attendants wear more simple floor-length gowns or ballerina, tea-length, or knee-length dresses. The groom and his attendants might wear suits or sport jackets and slacks. Guests' attire ranges from cocktail dresses to sundresses for ladies and from suits to jackets and slacks for men. The reception can take place in a restaurant or at a home with a caterer and/or friends providing refreshments. A breakfast, brunch, or lunch follows a morning or early-afternoon wedding, and an informal buffet or simple hors d'oeuvres and wedding cake for an afternoon reception.

Wedding Consultants

For busy people with hectic schedules, hiring a professional wedding consultant is a smart alternative to trying to do it all. Wedding consultants can be a great help to a busy couple: They can scout sites and oversee the budget, the caterer, the band, the florist, and any number of service providers. Often they can obtain discounts from vendors. In short, they can lift the load from your shoulders simply because they have encountered and solved the same problems you may be facing in hundreds of unique ways. Their purpose isn't to take over your wedding but to help make your dreams come true and your plans a reality. Plus: Wedding consultants can save you money in the long run.

Think about what kind of help you need before making a decision. There are many different levels of service and types of consultants. A full-fledged wedding consultant can do anything and everything for you. A wedding day coordinator springs into action on the day of the wedding, making sure everything goes according to schedule. Many hotels and resorts employ full-time wedding coordinators who are available to you when you book their venue to plan both your ceremony and reception at no additional charge. The ceremony site may provide a wedding day director to supervise all the details of the ceremony and make sure that the rules of the house of worship are followed. There are consultants and coordinators who handle varying responsibilities in between. Here is a general guide on the services of a wedding consultant:

What, exactly, does a wedding consultant do? In general, a wedding consultant will:

- Listen carefully from the very beginning to understand your wedding vision, and then be your advocate for realizing it in the best way possible.

- Help you set up a budget, and commit to sticking to it.

- Help you locate and reserve ceremony and reception sites.

- Help you select and hire reputable suppliers and vendors, such as the florist, the caterer, musicians, the photographer, and the videographer; advise you on vendor contracts and handle any negotiations.

- Advise you on selection and wording of invitations, as needed.

- Coordinate communication among vendors, suppliers, and sites, so that, for example, the florist knows when and how to obtain access to the ceremony site to decorate.

- Draw up a timeline to keep everyone on schedule, both before the wedding and on the wedding day.

- Serve as a referee, friend, budget adviser and watcher, etiquette expert, shopper, detail manager, and organizer.

- Coordinate your rehearsal with the officiant.

- Supervise all the last-minute details of your wedding day.

What are the qualities of a good wedding consultant? Wedding consultants are known for saving time, money, and stress for their clients. When interviewing candidates, look for these qualities:

- **Experience.** A good track record is usually the best guide, so check references and talk frankly with some of the consultant's previous clients.

- **Professionalism.** The consultant should understand the business of weddings. Certification and/or membership in a consultants' association may be indicative of professional commitment.

- **Congeniality.** A congenial consultant works with you; he or she isn't dictatorial and won't pressure you into decisions you aren't comfortable making.

- **Good chemistry—with you.** It's important that you feel comfortable with the consultant that you'll work with. Is this someone you'll want to spend time with? Confide in? Many couples refer to their consultant as "their new best friend."

- **Excellent listening skills.** Your consultant is going to plan your wedding. Is he or she a good listener?

◆ **Courtesy.** A consultant's manners may indicate how well he or she will work with you and others. This person will be your wedding etiquette expert and will also serve as your intermediary with officiants, site managers, suppliers, vendors, and even members of the wedding party. You want to be represented positively.

How much does it cost to work with a wedding consultant? You don't have to be among the wealthy to hire a wedding consultant, planner, or coordinator. Costs for a consultant's services depend on what the person does for you. In general, a consultant who provides full service will charge either a flat hourly rate or a flat fee. Allocate 10–15 percent of your overall budget for the services of a wedding consultant who does everything for you. The many couples who have used the services of these professionals will tell you that the money was well worth it.

On the other hand, you might need only planning advice and referrals. If so, you'll find that planners usually charge an hourly rate for consultations. Or you might hire a consultant at a daily rate to help with specific events. For many couples, hiring a consultant for the day of the wedding means they (and their parents and wedding party) aren't burdened with overseeing schedules, deliveries, and last-minute details. All options are worth investigating.

Once you have an initial budget in mind, calculate what the cost of a consultant will be and weigh that against the value of your time. Keep in mind that a successful consultant may be able to pass along enough savings to defray much of his or her cost—and that time can be just as important a commodity to you as money.

To avoid unscrupulous consultants who attempt to increase their fees by adding extras or who have under-the-table agreements with suppliers and vendors, it's best to look for someone who provides wedding packages at fixed rates, or charges a flat fee based on the services you request.

Choosing the Wedding Party

Selecting bridesmaids and groomsmen is an opportunity to blend family and friends into a harmonious, helpful unit as well as a way to honor the people that are most important to you. Pick your attendants early enough in the process so they can assist with decision making but not so soon after your engagement that in the glow of excitement you make choices you may later regret. This will be the group of people you spend the most time with during the celebrations surrounding your wedding. (For more information, see Chapter 6, page 71.)

Wedding Rings

Wedding rings may be selected at the same time as the engagement ring, but more often they are selected and ordered during the engagement period, when the bride and groom can take the time to find what will be a meaningful purchase. Even when the groom has selected the engagement ring as a surprise, you both should participate in the selection of your wedding ring or rings. The groom may or may not choose to wear a wedding ring. If he does, decide whether you want matching rings. (Generally his wedding ring will be a little wider and heavier than the bride's.) In the United States, men and women wear their wedding ring on the fourth finger of the left hand.

Types of wedding bands. Wedding bands are designed in platinum or yellow or white gold and come in a variety of finishes. For men, titanium is a popular modern choice. (If nothing else, it will match his golf clubs!) If the bride is going to wear her engagement ring with her wedding band, two rings of the same metal work best together. Some brides choose to have their engagement ring and wedding ring soldered into one unit after the wedding.

Narrow or wide? As with engagement rings, bands should be chosen with an eye to the shape of the bride's hand. If her hands are small, a narrow band looks best. Larger hands with longer fingers can wear wider and more elaborate rings. Still, for both the bride and the groom, comfort is of the utmost importance. A ring that's too wide or heavy or that gets in the way isn't the right ring.

Engravings. Wedding bands may be plain or engraved with designs on the outside. The inside can be engraved with words, initials, or simply the date or the engraved words may be a message that is a sentiment known only to the bride and groom. Before finalizing your purchase, ask the jeweler how many letters can be engraved on the inside of your wedding bands so that you can write out an inscription that will fit.

Planning the Honeymoon

Many couples consider making honeymoon plans a top-priority decision, particularly if they plan to marry and vacation during a peak season or travel to a popular honeymoon site. In some instances, couples will make their other top-level decisions around their honeymoon plans. At the very least, make some preliminary choices regarding the honeymoon date, location, transportation, accommodations, and length of stay.

Today, a couple's honeymoon may not follow immediately after the wedding, and some couples forgo one altogether. But if a honeymoon is in your future, it needs to be planned in advance not just to ensure a place to stay and transportation reservations but for budget considerations as well. In the frenzy of planning the wedding and reception, couples often forget to include the cost of a honeymoon. The expenses of a honeymoon trip are greater than just those of transportation and lodging—the honeymoon budget should also allow for meals; transfers; souvenirs; sightseeing; outing and activity-related costs; tips; taxes; and the little luxuries, like a massage or poolside charges for lounge chairs and towels. (See also Chapter 27, page 356.)

The Second-Level Decisions

Once you have settled the who, when, and where of your wedding, take a deep breath. You've knocked some of the major to-dos off the planning list! Next, it's time to start shopping, interviewing, and booking vendors, suppliers, and services. Because each of these next steps generally requires a good amount of lead time, there is no time like the present to:

- Shop for and make decisions about clothing and accessories—for the bride, groom, and attendants. (See also Chapter 19, page 251.)

- Order invitations, enclosures, announcements, and other printed material. (See also Chapter 8, page 95; Chapter 9, page 107; Chapter 10, page 121; and Chapter 11, page 131.)

- Visit stores and build your bridal registry. (See also Chapter 13, page 161.)

- Begin reviewing reception menus. (See also Chapter 16, page 207, and Chapter 23, page 313.)

- Interview and talk to florists. (See also Chapter 20, page 267.)

- Decide what type of music your reception will feature, then interview and listen to bands or DJs. (See also Chapter 21, page 287.)

- Interview photographers and videographers and look at their portfolios. (See also Chapter 22, page 297.)

The Third-Level Decisions

Once all your outside resources are in order, you can turn your attention to the details that will make your wedding day personal and unique. That to-do list may include the following:

- Listen to and choose music for your ceremony.

- Select readings for your ceremony.

- Make lists of music choices for your reception.

- Plan the special elements you'd like to include, such as your first dance at the reception, a bouquet toss, and any special decorations, photo displays, or favors.

- Incorporate family and cultural traditions into your ceremony and/or reception.

- Decide if you will host any additional wedding events such as a party for your attendants or a morning-after brunch.

- Select gifts for your attendants, perhaps for your parents, and for each other.

- As acceptances come in, begin to chart seating arrangements for your ceremony and reception.

THEME WEDDINGS

Theme weddings are becoming more and more popular: sixties, eighties, Hawaiian luau, Southern barbecue, Western square dance, even Halloween, complete with costumes. The theme may be carried into every aspect of the celebration, from the invitations to the attire, food, and decorations.

Same-Sex Commitment Ceremonies and Weddings

There are various resources available to help you plan your same-sex ceremony. Many of the traditional wedding etiquette guidelines are applicable and adaptable—from how to word the invitation to what questions to ask a potential photographer or florist. Other elements of your celebration should cater to your personalities and tastes.

Vendors and suppliers. The wedding industry is ready to help same-sex couples celebrate, and suppliers offer products such as invitations, rings, and cake toppers that are customized for gay and lesbian couples. Particularly in larger cities, you will find wedding consultants with considerable experience in staging commitment ceremonies or same-sex weddings and receptions. Even in less cosmopolitan areas, there are likely to be consultants or event planners who will happily help you plan your event.

Gay-friendly vendors and suppliers—those that cater to providing a wide array of options to gay customers—may identify themselves as such or be recommended via word of mouth. If as a couple you want to use gay-owned businesses, contact local gay and lesbian organizations and also consult online directories of retailers and service providers.

Whether or how extensively you explain your relationship depends on what you are seeking. Use common sense: The company that rents tents or folding chairs probably doesn't care what kind of party you're having. But wedding consultants, caterers, photographers, and travel planners need to know if they are to fulfill your dreams for the perfect ceremony, reception, honeymoon trip, and wedding album.

Locations. Even though couples may not have a house of worship in their area that permits same-sex ceremonies, location options are many and varied. Your own home or that of a family member or friend; a hotel, club, or restaurant; a civic or historic site; a park or beach setting; a fabulous resort destination—the choice comes down to what you want and fits your budget. If a clergyperson will officiate, you'll need to coordinate with him or her. (See also Chapter 15, pages 188 and 190.)

Destination Weddings

Exchanging vows as the sun sets over the ocean. Marrying against the backdrop of a majestic mountain lodge or an ancient European castle. Destination weddings are increasingly popular, currently comprising up to 24 percent of all weddings. Choosing a dream location to marry, celebrate, and even spend your honeymoon is ideal for the couple who wants to get away with a few close friends and family for a combined celebration and vacation. It's also a smart solution for the couple who envisions both a wonderful honeymoon and a grand wedding but has to choose one over the other.

Guests

Unless you have the wherewithal to charter a plane for a slew of guests and rent rooms for all of them (customarily, these expenses are the guests' responsibility), you can't expect all of your invited guests to be able to afford such an expense. Begin with an assessment of your guests' ability to finance what is usually a three- or four-day vacation—especially if you won't be helping out by covering accommodations (which is something you need to communicate up front). Understand that because of the costs, scheduling, and travel involved some people you'd really like to be at your wedding probably won't be able to attend. Some couples schedule a second reception back home so that important friends and family who couldn't attend the destination wedding have a chance to celebrate their wedding as well. (See also Chapter 7, page 88.)

Calling on Experts

Unless you can commute back and forth to the location during the planning process, you'll need someone on-site to manage the preparations. You might work with a wedding consultant in your area who can coordinate with a planner in the wedding location. Hotels in popular travel locations may have a wedding planner on staff, and resorts or cruise lines that specialize in destination weddings have full-time wedding coordinators at your service. There are also travel agents who specialize in destination weddings and can advise on the best times to travel and advise on discount rates for fares and lodging. With expert help, couples can sometimes achieve savings over a traditional at-home wedding—for themselves and their guests.

Communication

It's very important to inform guests of your plans as far in advance as possible—well before the traditional mailing of wedding invitations. Therefore, consider sending out save-the-date notices to your guests as soon as you have nailed down the date and venue. (See also Chapter 11, page 132.) Also, have a Plan B up your sleeve in case anything happens to prevent that planned wedding. If the site is struck by a hurricane or snowed in, for example, do you want to reschedule at another time or go ahead with your wedding in another location?

Legalities

If your destination is outside the country, you and your guests will probably need passports and perhaps visas, so make sure there is enough time to apply for and receive them. It can take up to six weeks, although expedited service is available for additional processing and delivery fees. (See http://travel.state.gov/passport.) There may be recommended medical precautions and inoculations. Consult with both the U.S. State Department and the embassy of the country, and provide all necessary information to your guests. Also check on any legal requirements, such as a period of residency or a published announcement of intent to marry.

Remember, too, that the perfect destination may be closer than you think. There may be locations in your own state or region that meet all your requirements for romance, adventure, and convenience.

CHAPTER 3

BUDGETS, EXPENSES, AND OTHER PRACTICALITIES

Whatever the size or style of your wedding, the end result will depend not on how much money you spend but on how well you spend it. A wedding is an important milestone and should be a time of special indulgences. But that doesn't mean bankrupting yourself or your family to make it happen. Thankfully, there are many ways to save without scrimping.

A large, elaborate wedding can cost tens of thousands of dollars. In fact, the average wedding in the United States in 2012 costs $27,000—although there are major regional variations. Excess does not necessarily equal a more meaningful wedding. A less elaborate wedding can be equally elegant and memorable. Remember: Your relationship is what is important, not the extravagance of your celebration.

The lists on pages 30–31 outline the traditional wedding expenses as well as how these expenses would be traditionally divided. Its intention is to give you a structure for planning. Today, nearly all weddings include some form of combined financial contribution from the couple, the bride's parents, and possibly the groom's parents.

There is also an extensive budget chart on pages 33–35. None of the budget items listed are "mandatory." Any of them may be omitted entirely without making your wedding any less beautiful or meaningful. Use the chart as a guide—you can begin to fill in estimates and make your own adjustments, giving you a sense of how your budget will be allocated.

Who Pays?

Tradition called for the bride's family to assume the burden of most wedding costs, a custom most likely translated from the ancient practice of providing a large dowry to attract a good husband. In Victorian times, the custom had evolved into the provision of a settlement from the bride's family to the groom's family, along with a substantial trousseau, usually a year's worth of clothing and household items. Today, however, only about 30 percent of weddings are paid for solely by the bride's parents.

Modern Alternatives

These days, it's quite common for both the bride's and the groom's families to share the costs of the celebration or for the bride and the groom to pay for all or part of the expenses themselves. In fact, up to 70 percent of weddings are currently financed this way. Modern couples are older and generally employed and independent by the time they get married, enabling them to plan and pay for their own weddings.

Traditions evolve, but etiquette still leads the way. It is still not correct for the bride's family to ask the groom's family to pay any of the wedding costs. If, however, his family offers to pay a share, it is quite appropriate for the bride's parents to accept.

When families are willing to share the costs, the bride and groom should agree on their wedding priorities and how they would allocate the funds ahead of time before sitting down with their parents to discuss the budget. If they accept financial help, they should be willing to compromise on some of their wishes for the wedding. Any conversation about money should be dignified, respectful, and candid.

Traditional Division of Costs

The following are lists of traditional expenses and responsibilities. It's a good checklist of the expenses involved, but feel free to assign the responsibilities to fit your circumstances.

Traditional Expenses of the Bride and Her Family

- Services of a bridal consultant
- Invitations, enclosures, and announcements
- Bride's wedding gown and accessories
- Floral decorations for ceremony and reception, bridesmaids' flowers
- Bride's bouquet (unless in a region where it's customary for the groom to pay for it)
- Tent, awning, aisle runner
- Musicians for church and reception
- Transportation of bridal party to ceremony and to reception
- A traffic officer or security if necessary
- All reception expenses

- Photographer, wedding photographs, wedding albums
- Videographer and finished DVD
- Transportation and lodging expenses for officiant if from another town and if invited to officiate by bride's family
- Accommodations for bride's attendants
- Bridesmaids' luncheon if hosted by bride
- Bride's gifts to her attendants
- Bride's gift to groom
- Groom's wedding ring

Traditional Expenses of the Groom and His Family

- Bride's engagement and wedding rings
- Groom's attire
- Ties and gloves for groomsmen if worn and not part of their clothing rental package
- Accommodations for groom's attendants
- Accommodations for groom's parents and siblings
- Bachelor dinner if groom wishes to give one
- All costs of rehearsal dinner
- Officiant's fee or donation
- Transportation and lodging expenses for officiant if from another town and if invited to officiate by the groom's family
- Marriage license
- Transportation for groom and best man to ceremony
- Bride's bouquet (only in those regions where it is local custom for the groom to pay for it)

- Bride's going-away corsage if wearing one
- Boutonnieres for groom's attendants
- Corsages for immediate members of both families (unless bride has included them in her florist's order)
- Groom's gift to his bride
- Gifts for groom's attendants
- Expenses of honeymoon

Bridesmaids'/Maid of Honor's Expenses

- Purchase of apparel and accessories
- Transportation to and from the wedding location
- A contribution to a gift from bridesmaids to bride
- An individual or group gift to the couple (if being in the wedding is not the gift)
- A shower, luncheon, or bachelorette party for bride (optional)

Groomsmen/Best Man's Expenses

- Rental or purchase of wedding attire
- Transportation to and from the wedding location
- A bachelor dinner if given by groom's attendants
- A contribution to a gift from groomsmen to groom
- An individual or group gift to the couple (if being in the wedding is not the gift)

Out-of-Town Guests' Expenses

- Transportation to and from wedding
- Lodging expenses
- Wedding gift

Determining a Budget

A carefully prepared budget can spare you the nightmare of falling prey to impractical plans or running up unnecessary debts. Whether you plan an elaborate wedding with 300 guests or a simple ceremony with thirty friends in your own home, a realistic budget will help make your preparations less stressful. If money becomes a source of tension, remember that the quickest way to decrease expenses is either to cut the guest list or plan a less elaborate reception, such as cake and punch or afternoon tea.

Simply put: Base your budget strictly on what those contributing to the wedding can afford. A budget for a large wedding will likely include allotments for each of the expenses listed on page 33–35. The budget for a simple wedding can include the items that you can't provide yourself and intend to purchase, as well as the things you plan to do on your own or with the help of friends and family.

With imagination and good planning, a beautiful wedding can be held within any limits. Whatever you plan, stick to your budget, or the worry and insecurity will carry over to your relationship and you'll start your marriage in a sea of bills and a state of anxiety and stress.

Start with a figure. Before you sign a single contract or make a firm commitment with any vendor, establish a dollar amount of what you believe you can spend on your wedding. If you have $25,000 to spend on your wedding, and the reception site you are hoping for will cost $15,000, you are probably not leaving enough money to cover other costs—flowers, fees, food, a band or DJ, wedding attire, and so on—unless some of those items will be paid for by someone else or given as wedding gifts. If you will be paying all the expenses, adjust your sights and find a reception location that isn't as costly. Choose a public garden or a friend's beautiful backyard. Have a morning wedding followed by a brunch, or have an afternoon cocktail reception instead of a seated dinner. The variations are endless.

Economy versus value. Value is really knowing precisely what you want and what you are willing to pay for so that you can satisfy your expectations for quality and service. If you pay for extras you don't want, you're not getting good value. For example, a band that charges for a master of ceremonies when you don't want a master of ceremonies is of no value to you, just as a reception package that includes printed cocktail napkins or dining chair covers has less value if you don't care about these incidentals. You can achieve economy if you plan well and give yourself the time to shop around and compare costs.

Tips on budgeting. Almost every component of your wedding will have a wide range of choices and costs. Decide which components you consider important enough to splurge on; then find ways to economize with style in the other areas.

The fastest way to economize on big-ticket items? Cut your guest list, find a smaller but no less elegant reception site, and choose a time of the year, a day of the week, and time of the day when prices are not at a premium. For fairly formal weddings, 50–60 percent of the costs generally go toward the per-person reception fees. Some caterers suggest making a budget for the reception and then cutting it back by 25 percent to cover any possible overruns or unforeseen expenses. So if your budget is $20,000, plan as though you have $15,000 available, leaving you $5,000 worth of wiggle room.

Budget Categories

The following chart includes traditional costs associated with a wedding. Some are mandatory, such as marriage license fees, and some are optional, such as limousines and a videographer. Whether an optional category is mandatory to you is your decision. For example, if it is really important to you to arrive at the ceremony in a white stretch limousine, then this will become a fixed cost in your budget. A fixed cost, yes, but adjustable—if you must have a stretch limo, call around and compare prices.

Don't forget the little costs that add up quickly. Things like stockings and lingerie are considered "bride's accessories," not just shoes and jewelry. Be as thorough as you can to get the most realistic picture.

ITEM	BUDGET	ACTUAL COST
Attendants		
Accommodations		
Bridesmaids' luncheon (if hosting)		
Ceremony Fees		
Officiant's fee		
Site fee		
Organist's fee		
Cantor / vocalist / instrumentalist fee(s)		
Flowers		
Ceremony		
Reception		
Bridal bouquet		
Bridal attendants' flowers		# x $ =
Corsages		# x $ =
Boutonnieres		# x $ =
Gifts		
Engagement ring		
Bride's gifts for attendants		# x $ =
Groom's gifts for attendants		# x $ =
Bride's gift for groom		
Groom's gift for bride		
For people who host parties or do special favors for you		

ITEM	BUDGET	ACTUAL COST
Honeymoon		
Transportation		
Accommodations		
Meals		
Incidentals		
Invitations / Announcements / Stationery		
Save the date		# x $ =
Invitations / enclosures (per set)		# x $ =
Announcements (per set)		# x $ =
Extra envelopes		# x $ =
Calligraphy		# x $ =
Postage		# x $ =
Thank-you notes		
Ceremony program		# x $ =
Place cards / pew cards		# x $ =
Legalities		
Marriage license		
Health / physical / blood test fees		
Music for Reception		
Musicians / DJ / MC / MP3		
Equipment rental		
Photography		
Engagement photographs		
Wedding photographer		
Wedding videographer		
Prints/albums/discs		

ITEM	BUDGET	ACTUAL COST
Reception		
Location fee		
Food / beverage (per-person cost)		# x $ =
Reception favors (per-person cost)		# x $ =
Wedding cake		
Rehearsal Dinner		
Location fee		
Food / beverage (per-person cost)		# x $ =
Transportation		
Limousines / cars for bridal party		
Traffic officials at ceremony, reception		
Valet parking		
Travel costs for officiant, if necessary		
Guest transportation to postreception lodging		
Wedding Attire		
Bridal gown		
Bridal accessories		
Groom's outfit		
Bride's ring		
Groom's ring		
Beauty costs (hair, nails, makeup)		
Wedding Consultant Fees		
Miscellaneous		
Telephone bills related to planning		
Trips home during planning if you live away		
Wardrobe costs for wedding-related events		
Tips (if not included in above costs)		
Taxes (if not included in above costs)		
Insurance		

ALL ABOUT TIPPING

Tipping can be tricky, and whether to tip or not depends on the vendor and your contract. Tipping amounts can also vary by region and are often on the higher end in major metropolitan areas, so ask around about the norms.

Ceremony services. Ask about the fees or suggested donations for the use of the house of worship when you meet with your officiant or the person who organizes weddings. Usually, you don't tip the officiant, the organist, or other members of the church or synagogue's staff. If your officiant isn't affiliated with a house of worship, or is traveling to be at your wedding, you should cover all his or her travel and lodging costs. Additionally, your officiant (and his or her spouse or significant other) is a guest at both the rehearsal dinner and the reception. A letter of thanks to your officiant, perhaps accompanied by a personal gift, is a good way to show your appreciation to someone who played a major role in your wedding.

If a tip isn't included in the contract for any outside musicians that you hire for the ceremony, add 15 percent or tip a flat fee of $15–$20 per musician.

Deliver all fees (or the balance on fees) and tips right after the ceremony. Prepare labeled envelopes several days ahead, and include a short note of thanks. (See page 38.) It's the best man's duty to deliver them; if that's not possible, then the father of the bride (or groom in some cases) should put this on their to-do list.

Reception services. Today, it's likely that your contract with a reception venue will include tips as a percentage of the entire *pretax* package. Do ask which members of staff are tipped and how tips are handled. Since tips are the host's responsibility, make it clear that no tip jars or coin plates will be displayed.

Typically, restroom and coatroom attendants, waitstaff, bartenders, the maître d', catering manager, and sometimes the chef are all tipped. If these tips aren't included in your contract, count on:

- $1–$2 per guest for restroom and coat attendants. Make an estimate from your final guest count and round up a little.
- Tip the bartenders as a group, 10 percent of the total liquor bill.
- The maître d' or headwaiter is tipped 1–3 percent of the contracted food and beverage price, and waiters each receive about $20 or more.
- Tip the chef $100 or more.

As with ceremony fees and tips, prepare labeled payment envelopes and have the best man or father of the bride deliver them to the reception manager or maître d' for distribution.

Musicians or a DJ are tipped at the end of their gig and any final payments are also delivered at the same time.

- Tip a DJ 15 percent of the fee.
- Tip musicians $25–$50 per musician if tips aren't included in the contract.

Transportation services. Tipping drivers and valet parking staff is also the host's responsibility. If not included in the contract, let service providers know that you, not your guests, will be taking care of it.

- Limo, taxi, bus, and shuttle drivers are tipped 15 percent if the tip is not included in the contract.

- Parking attendants $1–$2 per car.

- Tip more for valet parking; if the valet parking is contracted, then 15 percent is the norm.

Professional services. Your wedding planner, florist, photographer, videographer, and reception manager fall into this category. These are the people with whom you will develop a close relationship and work with the most. In general, you don't tip professionals, but a note of appreciation is always welcome. If you're very satisfied, you can offer to be a reference, always a valued "thanks." When given, most couples consider any extra remuneration more as a gift than a tip, whether it is in the form of cash, a gift certificate, or an actual gift. However you decide to style your thank-you, send it personally from you as a couple along with a heartfelt note expressing your appreciation soon after your wedding day.

All About Contracts

You should expect to sign a contract with every supplier, from the stationer to the florist to the limousine service to the wedding consultant. The contract should cover every single detail in writing, including taxes, gratuities, dates, delivery schedules, payment plans, cancellation fees, and refund policies. Take the time to read everything thoroughly; if you don't understand something, ask questions until you do. Never sign a contract under pressure. If you're still unclear about some aspect of the contract, take a copy of it to a friend who has experience in contractual agreements. Be sure you are clear on how and when payments are to be made. And check to see that there are clauses in the contract that guarantee proper restitution in the event of a snafu that is clearly the vendor's responsibility.

Check for Hidden Costs

Even deciphering the fine print on a contract can leave you with unanswered questions. You're entitled to know exactly what is included—and what is not—before agreeing to the service. If the service provider or contractor is unwilling to give you a detailed listing or breakdown of costs, consider looking elsewhere. For example, confirm that alterations to your gown (both service and price) are included in the contract with a bridal salon. If they're not, ask for a range of what these costs generally run. Does the salon charge extra to press your gown after alterations? Would it be less expensive for you to take the gown to a reputable and experienced dry cleaner for pressing?

Don't forget taxes and gratuities, which can add a significant amount to the total bill—especially in states

Fees for the officiant, the organist, the soloist, and use of a church or other house of worship aren't tips but should be delivered as you would tips, in sealed envelopes, addressed to each person, with the couple's "thanks" included. It's the groom's responsibility to cover these fees. Some grooms prefer to make the payments directly themselves, but most rely on the best man to distribute the envelopes, just after the ceremony.

that have a high sales tax. Make sure that taxes and tips are included in the estimates you receive so there are no surprises later. And inquire about such hidden costs as a "slicing fee." (See Chapter 23, page 313.)

Marriage Legalities

Along with the romance, fun, and excitement of a wedding come the absolutes—the legally required paperwork and to-dos without which a marriage cannot take place. In the eyes of the law, a couple must live up to the letter of the law in order to be married—and the law can vary not just from country to country but from state to state and even city to city. It's your responsibility to check, in advance, what is required—whether you are getting married in your hometown or on an exotic island on another continent.

Where do you start? Check the website of the state and town where you plan to marry. It will likely list the legal requirements for acquiring a marriage license. Some states require that you register in the same state and even county where the ceremony will be performed, and some ask that you do so in person. The most important point is to start your research well in advance of the ceremony so that come your wedding day, all will be legal and aboveboard.

Particular Legal Factors

Age. In most states, the age one may be married is much younger than the age one may legally drive, drink, vote, or apply for a credit card. Age restrictions vary widely from state to state, so be sure to determine the requirements for your state. Be prepared to submit documentary proof of age, such as a birth certificate.

Familial restrictions. In the United States, a marriage may not take place between those of the following relationships, regardless of whether they are legitimate or illegitimate offspring:

- Ancestor and descendant (parent, grandparent, great-grandparent, child, grandchild, great-grandchild)
- Brother and sister (full- or half-blood)
- Uncle and niece, aunt and nephew

In most but not all states, marriage between family members closer than second cousins is prohibited. If this is an issue, it is important to check with the town or city clerk or the marriage license bureau in the town where the marriage will take place.

Capacity to consent. It is the law that marriage requires two consenting people. If either person cannot or does not understand what it means to be married because of mental disability or illness, drugs, alcohol, or other factors affecting judgment, then that person does not have the capacity to consent and the marriage is not valid. If fraud or coercion is involved, the marriage may also be invalidated.

Gender. In most states couples must be of the opposite sex to form a valid marriage. The majority of Americans support gay marriage, but laws are slow to change and it's legal in just over a quarter of our states. State laws can also limit who can perform your union. For example, civil servants like judges, clerks, and justices of the peace who work in states that do not recognize same-sex marriage would not have the authority to perform a marriage in spite of their positions. In states that do recognize same-sex marriage, either civil or religious officials may seal the union.

Remarriage. Applicants for a marriage license who were married before must provide information regarding previous marriages, either a copy of the Decree of Divorce, a Certificate of Dissolution of Marriage, or a death certificate. Clerks and marriage licensing officials say the biggest problem that occurs for those who have been married before is that they neglect to bring the original document or a certified copy. The information the applicant needs to provide includes but may not be restricted to:

❖ The month, day, and year of the final divorce decree

❖ The county and state where the divorce was granted

❖ The grounds for divorce

❖ Whether the former spouse or spouses are living

Similar documentation may be required for an annulment, and of a widow or widower. Check and double-check the requirements. Even one missing document can delay the wedding—a disaster if that means postponement.

The Marriage License

A marriage **license** authorizes you to get married; a marriage **certificate** is the document that proves that you are married and is issued by the county office where you were married, usually within a few weeks after the ceremony. Your officiant (and perhaps witnesses) signs your marriage license, validating it, and then has a prescribed time period to send the license to the county office for recording.

In general, a marriage license may be used only in the place it is obtained, and then within a certain period of time, usually between twenty-four hours and sixty-five days, depending on the state; otherwise the license expires. Some states require a several-day waiting period from the time applicants apply for a license to the time the license is issued. Those states with the strictest requirements strongly advise the bride and groom to obtain their marriage license two to three weeks before their wedding day. (See www.usmarriagelaws.com for state-by-state information on marriage laws and license requirements.)

Health Certificates

The purpose of premarital health requirements and examinations is not to keep a person with an illness from marrying but to ensure that the future spouse knows of the condition. Most states no longer have requirements for premarital blood tests in order to obtain a marriage license, but make sure you check the requirements if you're marrying abroad. Even in states where no blood test or physical exam is required, failing to tell your prospective spouse that you have a venereal disease, are HIV positive, or have a physical impairment (such as impotence or infertility) before you marry may make the marriage invalid. Find out the requirements in your state by visiting the state's website or www.usmarriagelaws.com.

Religious Factors

Mastering government legalities is just one step toward ensuring the legality of your marriage. Some religions also have rules and regulations that must be adhered to—points that are best checked, up front, with the priest, rabbi, minister, or imam who will officiate.

In some religions, if one or both members of the couple have been divorced, the divorce is not recognized and they may not be married in the church. Then there is the matter of membership. For a wedding to take place at a Quaker meetinghouse, for example, at least one of the couple should be a Quaker. Otherwise, written support for the marriage must be obtained from two adult members of the Society of Friends.

The bottom line: Even if you are a lifelong Roman Catholic, Lutheran, Presbyterian, Jew, or a convert who has seriously studied the tenets of the religion, inquire in advance whether the institution has any special requirements. If it is important to you to be married by a priest, rabbi, or minister or in a church, temple, or synagogue, you will need to know the requirements to make that happen. (See also Chapter 15, page 185.)

Odds and Ends

Marriage by an American to a foreign national requires its own set of documents and qualifications, including certified English translation of any required documentation. You can get information on obtaining a visa for a foreign spouse from any office of the U.S. Citizenship and Immigration Services; U.S. embassies and consulates abroad; or the U.S. Department of State Visa Office.

If you are using an officiant from out of state, know that some states require that he or she have a Certificate of Authorization from the state in which the wedding will take place.

Some states require witnesses—in addition to an authorized member of the clergy or a public official—to be present during the wedding ceremony. In some of these states, there is no minimum age for a witness, but it is suggested that he or she be considered competent enough to testify in a court proceeding regarding what was witnessed. In other states, no witness is required other than the officiant.

Premarital Counseling

Premarital counseling, whether mandated by certain religions or merely recommended, is a short-term way to identify and work through important issues to avoid potential long-term conflict in the marriage. The purpose is to raise issues regarding marriage and your relationship that you might not have considered, to discuss potential sensitive areas, and to give words to some of the things a couple may be thinking but may not know how to express. The couple who treats one another with respect and consideration has a much greater chance of making their marriage a success, and this counseling can help establish patterns of positive communication that will stand them in good stead for a lifetime.

When premarital counseling is completed, it's thoughtful of the bride and groom to write a thank-you note or a letter to their clergyperson or counselor to express their appreciation for the guidance they received.

The Legalities of Marrying in Another Country

Many brides and grooms dream of being married outside the United States in a romantic spot like Tahiti or Paris or St. Thomas. But before you call that little French patisserie for the perfect wedding cake or put down a deposit on a Caribbean island resort, check the wedding legalities of the country you wish to be married in. Each country has a different set of requirements. Some have residency requirements of a certain duration. Others require a specific number of witnesses. And if you're marrying in another country,

don't forget to look into your legal and religious requirements at home as well. Check your passport, medical requirements, and the documentation you need to bring back home to ensure your marriage's validity in the United States.

There are plenty of resources available to help you. One surefire way to get answers is to visit the country's consulate or tourist website. In some countries, such as Mexico, the requirements vary slightly from town to town, so once you've gotten the basic information, you will need to call the registrar's office in the town where you are getting married.

Wedding consultants who specialize in destination weddings and travel agents who do wedding planning can also provide information on the documentation required and any restrictions.

Name Changes

In the 1800s and into the 1900s, married women took their husband's last name because under the common law doctrine of couverture, a woman was not allowed to own property or enter into a contract and had no rights to her name. Hence, the husband was the legal entity in the marriage. Today, there is no law, rule, religious dictate, or mandate that says a bride must take her groom's last name. Many established businesswomen keep their maiden names, and other women choose to hyphenate both their and their husband's surnames. In spite of the range of acceptable choices, approximately 88 percent of today's U.S. brides make the traditional choice of adopting their husband's names.

A bride who takes her husband's last name either keeps her given middle name or uses her own surname as a middle name. The only law governing the name chosen by the bride is that it be used consistently and without intent to defraud.

The name change occurs simply by entering the new name in the appropriate space provided on the marriage license. Once the license is signed by the officiant (and in some localities by two witnesses, usually the maid of honor and best man), your name change can take place. Your officiant will send the license to the county office who registers the marriage and issues a marriage certificate in the name you have chosen. It's a good idea to request (and pay for) at least three copies: one for the DMV, one for the Social Security Administration, and one to file in a safe-deposit box.

Why Change Your Name?

The matter of changing names is traditionally more of a consideration for the bride than it is for the groom; it's still rare for a man to change his name upon marriage. If a woman is being married for a second time, she probably has already changed her name once. She may have kept her ex-husband's surname, or she may have reverted to her maiden name. Another marriage can bring about more change. If the bride has kept her married name from her first marriage, it is likely that she will take her new husband's surname—if for no other reason than to avoid confusion for all concerned but also out of consideration and love for her new husband. Widows often use their first husband's surname as a middle name.

Professional considerations. One way to deal with a name change professionally is for the bride to continue to use the name she has been using in work or professional situations and to use her new name in social situations. Therefore, she is Ms. Jane Johnson at work; socially, she is Mrs. Franklin Pierce (or Jane Johnson Pierce if she retains her maiden name as her middle name).

Children and names. When the bride has children from a previous marriage, their last name will very likely be that of their father, whereas their mother may be using her maiden name or taking the name of her new husband. How this is sorted out is up to each couple, but it is important to let relevant persons and organizations know who is who and how each person is to be addressed. You may want to send an email with your proper name, phone numbers, and addresses to your child's school, to your pediatrician and dentist, and to any extracurricular groups to which your child belongs.

Official Notifications

When a bride changes her name, she must notify a vast number of people, companies, agencies, and organizations, starting with the DMV and the Social Security Administration. It's a good idea to meet with the HR department at work several months before the wedding to complete any forms and make beneficiary changes. Other important agencies to notify are the IRS; your state tax department; voter registration authority and the post office; and your bank, investment companies, and credit card companies. Otherwise, deal with them as they come up—when paying bills, renewing magazine subscriptions, gym, library and professional association memberships, or making appointments at the salon or dentist. Some organizations require proof of the name change and will ask for a copy of the marriage certificate, which is issued *after* the marriage, so be sure to order extra copies. When an address change is occurring as well, it is a good idea to make both changes at the same time.

Advising Others

It can be confusing when the bride decides to retain her maiden name or use some hyphenated form of both her and her husband's name. If you decide to go the nontraditional route, you'll need to let others know. Some commonsense ways to notify friends and relatives: on your wedding website, on stationery or in the return address on thank-you-note envelopes, in newspaper wedding announcements, on "at home" cards enclosed in wedding announcements, or on Facebook. If you need to correct someone, do so kindly.

What to Call Your Same-Sex Partner

The traditional *fiancé* or *fiancée* is suitable during your engagement. After the ceremony, many couples introduce each other as "spouse" or "life partner." Regardless of how couples refer to their relationship, the etiquette point is to choose language that will be readily understood by others.

Changing Your Mind

If, at the time of the marriage, a bride does not change her name and later changes her mind, she can file a petition for change of name with the court. However, the marriage license and certificate cannot be changed to record the surname she decides to use after she is already married and registered with a different name.

Prenuptial and Postnuptial Contracts

The matter of formalizing financial and legal matters through a prenuptial contract or premarital agreement is a sensitive one for brides and grooms, many of whom consider doing so a crass form of hedging bets on the longevity of the marriage. It is certainly an issue that needs to be discussed early in the relationship— and not something you spring on your partner-to-be right before the ceremony.

What is a premarital agreement? Basically, a premarital agreement is a contract between two people that defines the rights and benefits that will exist during the marriage and after, in the event of divorce or death. It can expand or limit a person's right to property, life insurance benefits, or support payments. Usually, it addresses the rights to property that each brings to the marriage, retirement plan assets, and how money accumulated before the marriage will be distributed in the event of divorce or death. Without a premarital agreement, state laws define the rights and benefits of marriage. If the couple does not want to rely on state laws to determine their legal and fiscal fate, the premarital agreement allows them to make their own rules.

When is a prenuptial agreement used? Although anyone can have a premarital agreement, it is most often used when the bride or the groom or both bring assets to the marriage that they want to protect in the event of divorce or death. This is particularly true for people marrying for the second or third time who want to make sure that certain assets are passed on to their children from a previous marriage.

What is not covered in a prenup? Prenuptial contracts do not cover child custody and support. In the case of divorce, the courts will disregard the contract on this point and make a decision that is considered in the best interest of the child. The courts will also disregard a premarital agreement that, in essence, leaves one person destitute.

What is a postnuptial contract? A postnuptial contract is one made after a couple is married and can include the same considerations, usually having to do with property and money, as in a prenuptial contract. This contract is usually drawn up if the couple realizes that children from a previous marriage or other family members would be unprotected in the case of divorce or death.

What is meant by disclosure? Because one person is usually giving something up by agreeing to a prenuptial contract, both the bride and the groom must fully disclose their finances to each other in advance. Most states require that the premarital agreement include separate asset listings that describe and show the value of each person's assets. If the couple doesn't do this, each is preventing the other from knowing what he or she is losing by signing the contract—and this may constitute fraud, which makes the agreement unenforceable. Because of this, and to ensure that the agreement is written correctly and legally, it is a good idea for both the bride and the groom to seek the advice of their respective lawyers before entering into the agreement.

What is the form of the agreement? A prenuptial contract or premarital agreement must be in writing to be legally binding. It provides evidence of the terms of the agreement and demonstrates that both people understand and agree to the terms. It is generally legally binding as long as it is entered into voluntarily and without fraud and as long as it is reasonable and fair. It is not binding if a person is unfairly induced to sign the agreement or is coerced under excessive emotional pressure.

Wills and Finances

When there is no prenuptial or postnuptial contract, the bride and groom would be smart to put their wills and finances in order so that the disposition of their money and property is clear to each other or, should both die, to their families.

Changing beneficiaries. Insurance policies, annuities, and retirement plans have beneficiary provisions. Assuming the bride and groom want to make each other the beneficiary on any existing policies they own, the couple should call their respective brokers and talk to their payroll coordinators at work to see what documentation is required to make this change.

Decisions about bank accounts. How the couple will manage their finances is totally personal, but this is something to discuss well before the big day. Some couples decide to maintain separate accounts and open a joint household account or to pool all their finances into a joint account. Other couples maintain separate accounts and decide who pays which bills.

If the bride is changing her name, she'll need to take care of any paperwork for bank and investment accounts she retains in her name and, for direct deposit purposes, coordinate the account change at the same time as she changes her name at work.

Wedding Insurance

In many instances, the cost of a wedding is so astronomical that the additional cost of insurance is worth every penny if it protects such a large investment. Most homeowner policies cover liability for weddings hosted by you at another venue, so it's a good idea to check with your agent to see what your policy covers. If not, or if the coverage isn't sufficient, you can purchase additional liability insurance through your agent or a company that specializes in insurance for events. Liability insurance covers property damage to the venue or your home, bodily injury, and the host in the event of an alcohol-related accident.

Other insurance can cover you in the event the wedding must be canceled or postponed for reasons beyond anyone's control, such as a military deployment, serious illness, or natural disaster like a hurricane or serious storm. It can also cover the cost of rebooking elsewhere if a reception site suddenly cannot accommodate the party for reasons such as bankruptcy, fire damage, delayed opening because of incomplete renovations, or a health department quarantine. It can further cover vendor costs when a vendor fails to perform—the band you hired didn't show up or the photographer's digital storage device was damaged. A ruined wedding gown, stolen wedding gifts, a guest who damages the hotel carpet—consider every contingency when assessing the value and extent of the insurance you want. For a sampling of coverage and costs, visit www.wedsafe.com.

CHAPTER 4

TECHNOLOGY
AND SOCIAL MEDIA

The near universal use of computers, mobile devices, and the Internet has radically changed the way brides and grooms plan and experience their weddings. Twitter, Facebook, and email allow you to communicate instantaneously with anybody and everybody involved in your wedding. Wedding planning websites offer everything from advice on budgeting to personalized wedding webpages. There are planning apps for tablets and smartphones, too, and what busy bride doesn't love being able to use her phone to snap a picture of the dress she just found? Online gift registries come in all shapes and sizes, from the traditional to the avant-garde, such as honeymoon and charity registries. And now camera phones and social media have changed how guests experience wedding ceremonies and receptions, too.

As wonderfully convenient as they may be, these advances also bring their own unique etiquette challenges. Sending an inappropriate email, sharing overly personal information on your Facebook page, or trumpeting your registry information too prominently on your wedding website can backfire and come across as crass, greedy, or disrespectful. Mobile phones, for example, can be a great help in coordinating wedding planning and last-minute requests on the big day, but you won't want to walk down the aisle to a sea of camera phones instead of smiling faces or have your ceremony interrupted by the phone your groomsman forgot to turn off. (See page 55.)

No matter how new a technology may be, the basic principles of etiquette always apply in its use. Ask yourself these questions: How will my use of technology affect the people I'm communicating with? How does technology enable me to treat others considerately and respectfully—and how could it have the opposite effect? Think about the reactions of the people involved, not just the convenience factor. For example, texting with your mother-in-law-to-be might be easier for you than having a drawn-out phone call, but it can leave her feeling marginalized or like an afterthought.

One thing is certain: Technology itself is neither rude nor polite. It can trip you up, and it can bail you out of a tight spot when you forget your bouquet at home. The trick to using it well is all in how you go about it.

Communications and Planning

Couples getting married today communicate much differently than couples fifty years ago. Spreadsheets and electronic calendar reminders keep your to-do lists and your due dates in order. Facebook, Twitter, Pinterest, texts, and email connect you with your vendors, wedding party, parents, and invitees instantaneously and let these groups be more involved in every planning detail. The most important thing to remember about email, texts, Facebook posts, tweets, and other social media interactions is that just because you *can* doesn't mean you always *should*. The more formal the communication the more appropriate it is to use snail mail rather than email, text, Facebook, or Twitter. And sometimes, a good old-fashioned chat, either on the phone or in person, is just what the doctor ordered.

When Not to Use Email or Social Media

For wedding invitations. Emailing a wedding invitation, even to your closest friend or relative, generally is not appropriate. The wedding invitation serves to set the tone for the ceremony and reception to come in a way that an email just can't. Pinned on refrigerators or tucked on mantels, they also act as reminders and help build anticipation. Lastly, for many guests, they are keepsakes. (See also Chapter 8, page 99.) The only exception, and it's quite rare, is in the case of extremely rushed circumstances—if, for example, you and your fiancé(e) are moving overseas and you've decided at the last minute to get married before you leave. A good way to judge is that if the invitation is so hurried or informal that your only other option would be to invite someone over the phone, then using email to extend the invitation would be probably be fine.

SEEDS OF CHANGE

The environmentally conscious couple may balk at the idea of mailing out paper invitations, seeing it as wasteful. Consider using recycled and biodegradable materials, which can result in beautiful wedding invitations that are in keeping with your ideals. There are, also, invitation options that have seeds embedded in the paper, creating an entirely new kind of wedding keepsake when the invitation is planted.

For thank-you notes. For each wedding gift you receive, always pen a handwritten note and send it through the mail. No exceptions, unless you're shipwrecked on a desert island. (See also Chapter 14, page 177.) If you've fallen behind on your note writing, or know you can't write a note right away, you can send an email or private Facebook message as a stopgap measure to let the gift giver know you've received his or her gift and will be sending a formal thank-you soon. "So wonderful to see you at the wedding! We love the vase. Note to follow soon." Just remember this message doesn't replace the actual thank-you note.

When discussing personal or thorny issues. It's easy for communication over texting, Facebook, and email to be misconstrued, which can make working out compromises or resolving emotional conflicts difficult. You don't have tone of voice or body language to help interpret or smooth over a difference of opinion. Despite the fact that you wrote the words, it's also less personal than a direct conversation. If a tricky issue comes up, pick up the phone and call to talk it over, or arrange to meet face-to-face with those involved. It will get you back on the right track much more quickly than waiting for someone to reply.

When others need to know personally, privately, or ahead of time. Similarly, while it's extremely convenient to be able to send group messages about wedding-related plans ("As mother of the groom, I'm pleased to invite you to a bridal shower for my future daughter- in-law . . ."), it's still important to check your plans personally with other key people first. Otherwise, you run the risk of ruffling feathers ("Well! As mother of the bride, I thought we were going to host the shower together!") and putting a serious damper on the whole event.

When Email or Social Media Is Appropriate

Aside from the specific instances cited previously, email and social media are generally acceptable options for wedding-related communications—including the following:

"Save the Date" notices. Many couples, once they've pinned down their wedding day, choose to send out an early informal note alerting friends and family to put that date aside. It's perfectly fine to email this note.

Wedding RSVPs. When sending out your wedding invitations, it is acceptable to give your guests the option of emailing their RSVPs to you. Simply add a sentence at the bottom of your printed response card saying, "Replies also welcome at happycouple@rsvp.com by (date)." This is especially appropriate in the case of a short turnaround time for responses, if you are planning a relatively informal wedding, or if you are already in regular email contact with a majority of your invited guests.

Wedding announcements. Sure, lots of your friends in your Facebook world will know you got married, but you or your parents may have friends or more distant family who don't keep in touch through social media. Typically, printed announcements are mailed after the wedding itself to friends and family who weren't on the guest list as well as to acquaintances and business associates you think might wish to hear the news. (See Chapter 11, page 135.) While many couples and their parents still prefer this more formal way of sharing their happy news, it's also acceptable to send wedding announcements out via email—particularly if you and the recipient are on informal terms or if the wedding itself was informal. Use the bcc line on your email so that you don't share recipients' addresses, or use a service that gives you that option.

Invitations to informal or casual engagement parties, bridal showers, and other prewedding get-togethers. These are all extremely important occasions, and most couples and their families will

---

GROUP EMAIL ETIQUETTE

Begin any group emails to your guests with a general salutation—"Dear All"—and sign the email as you would on an individual message. To avoid annoying group "Reply All" messages and to respect guests' privacy, use the "bcc" (blind carbon copy) feature. Put your email address in the "To" line and add your other addresses to the "bcc" line. Your guests' email addresses will remain hidden and only your email will be available for a reply. Just be certain any guests who might not be online regularly receive the information they need in another form.

want to honor this fact by sending out printed invitations. Emailed invitations, or e-vitations, can be an acceptable alternative, however, particularly if you are planning an informal party or you're sure the people on your guest list are computer-friendly. This is not the time to create a Facebook event, though—each invitation should be sent to the intended recipient.

Information on lodging and destination. When sending out your wedding invitations, it's fine to include an enclosure containing a map and directions for out-of-town guests. To avoid overloading the mailing and detracting from the invitation itself, however, it may make sense to include any other material—including information on hotels, restaurants, and points of local interest—in a separate mailing. For those of your guests who are online, a group email is ideal for this purpose. It's also standard to include this information on a wedding website. (See also page 52.)

Wedding updates. Many couples enjoy keeping their family and friends updated on the progress of their wedding plans. Group emails, Facebook, and Twitter are perfect for this sort of informal communication. Again, though, this convenience factor makes it all the more important to use common sense and consid-

ASSEMBLING YOUR EMAIL LIST

It's not a bad idea to create an email list in your contacts for all of the wedding guests who have accepted your invitation. You may not need to use it, but if anything comes up at the last minute, such as a change in venue due to weather, it's a quick way to reach a large group at once. Just be sure to remember to phone any guests who might not use email regularly, if at all.

eration: Don't flood the in-boxes of your entire guest list with daily news flashes and don't share every tiny detail or development that are best saved for your closest friends. (See also page 54.) If you do decide to send out regular electronic updates, also send a printed copy to any friends and family who aren't connected through email, Facebook, or Twitter.

Planning and the Internet

The Internet has made it so much easier for couples to research almost every aspect of their wedding dreams, to use planning tools, and to communicate quickly and easily with vendors. Along with the convenience comes a few things to watch out for.

"Wed" Surfing on the Job

With honeymoon locales to research, webpages to update, emails to answer, and gift registries to create, the temptation to spend hours online tending to your wedding plans will be strong—especially when you're at work and your web browser is only a click away. Whether your company has policies and consequences regarding nonwork-related use of computers and Internet access or not, resist the urge to jump online when you should be working. Instead do the right thing, and conduct all wedding-related web-surfing on your personal time and using your own computer or mobile devices.

Pinning Sites

Image-pinning sites such as Pinterest and Loverly are a fantastic way to save, source, organize, and share wedding images and DIY projects. Pin to your heart's content, but keep a few things in mind:

Avoid overload. Limit the ability for these sites to automatically post to other social media sites, such as Facebook. Otherwise your Facebook friends may suffer from serious wedding fatigue before they even receive your invitations (and your friend list is likely big enough that many of them won't even be on the guest list).

Share and share alike. Pinning sites are all about sharing, so don't be surprised—or upset—if a friend pins your looks or even orders the bridesmaids' dress or wedding shoes you pinned. Just remember that imitation is the sincerest form of flattery!

Step away from the computer. Pinning sites are a treasure trove of ideas—and sometimes a bottomless one. It's easy to feel like you'll miss out on something great if you aren't constantly checking them, but there will always be more to see when you sign back in.

A Wedding in the Cloud

If you're like most people, you'll be using your home computer to enter and store your guest list, directions to the ceremony, a special poem you plan to read, and scores of other key documents related to your wedding. So heed this caution: Text can get typed over, files can get accidentally deleted, and hard drives can crash—and then you'll be up a creek, unless you've made a point of backing up your files. Ideally, you should back up your files on a daily or near-daily basis. If this seems like too much trouble, just imagine what it would be like to have your guest list vanish without a trace just as you were planning to send out invitations.

An external hard drive is one of the best ways to back up your files and a fairly inexpensive investment, but even those can get damaged or misplaced. Cloud computing has made storing your files securely online and accessing them from any mobile device worth considering. With Google Docs, for example, you can store documents and spreadsheets and even invite other people to collaborate on them. Once created, these files are accessible from anywhere you have Internet access on any mobile device.

It's also a good idea to keep a good old-fashioned manila (or plaid or Lily Pulitzer pink) folder handy containing hard copies of items such as your guest list, budget breakdown, contracts, directions, and lodging information. That way, if the worst happens and you lose every digital file, even the back ups, you'll be able to re-create them.

Bottom line: Back up often and in more than one location.

Creating Your Own Wedding Website

Because they are such a convenient way to create a central location for guests to access wedding information, most couples create their own personalized wedding webpages, sometimes referred to as "wed sites." Setting up a site is easy, and in most cases, free. Wedding-planning websites such as Wedding Channel (www.weddingchannel.com) and the Knot (www.theknot.com) provide step-by-step instructions for designing your own free webpage, reachable through their web addresses. Other services allow you to create a website with your own web address for a fee.

What to Post on Your Wedding Website

An effective wedding website will reflect who you are as a couple, convey the overall style and tone of your wedding, and be full of information that's useful for your guests to know. It's also a great place to share photos taken during your engagement. As you build your site, think about who will be using it. For example, you might consider including printable PDFs of maps and directions as well as links to sites such as Google Maps or MapQuest. Here are some suggested items and information to include:

- Date and time of your wedding ceremony and reception

- Location names, full address information (including zip codes), and phone numbers for ceremony and reception locations (handy for GPS entry)

- Directions to ceremony and reception (with web links and/or as a PDF document)

- Local airport(s), airlines that serve the region, and car rental companies

- Address and contact information for nearby hotels, inns, and B&Bs; their distance from ceremony/reception; and any discount arrangements ("Mention Smith–Jones wedding for a 15 percent room discount")

- Area map showing these locations

- Links to gift registries

- Option to RSVP

In addition, guests should be informed about the following:

- **Dress code:** While you can't dictate or micromanage what your guests wear, let them know ahead of time if they should wear particular clothing, such as a head covering or long sleeves, to your ceremony. Visual examples are especially helpful. You could even use a little humor. If, say, you're aiming for "dressy casual" at the reception you could "thumbs down" examples of guys in shorts and "thumbs up" guys in jackets, shirts, and slacks. It's okay to post "black tie requested" for a formal reception.

- **Special customs:** If a number of your guests aren't of your culture or religion, consider adding information they might need to know: the length of the ceremony, the meaning of certain customs or rituals, or any particular cultural etiquette that should be observed.

- **Schedule of events:** List time, location, and address for events surrounding the wedding that are open to all your guests, such as planned activities for out-of-town guests or a next-day brunch. Add the schedule for any shuttle services between hotels and wedding venues, too.

Wedding Website Guidelines

When designing your wedding website, keep these guidelines in mind:

Your webpage should be representative of who you are as a couple. Take the time to develop a design that you are both comfortable with—one that reflects your personal aesthetic and style. Be sure you both agree on the kind of content you include, and the tone.

If you plan to offer people the option of leaving an RSVP on your website, simply add the web address after the RSVP on your invitation or reply card: "Reply to happycouple.com by [date]."

List your website on your save-the-date card. Having your wedding date, the schedule of events as you know it, and travel and lodging information accessible on your website will help your core guests make their plans early.

Don't list your website on your actual invitation. There are plenty of other ways to let people know about the site, such as adding the web address to the response card, a separate enclosure, to other informational pieces enclosed with the invitation, or by group email to your guest list.

Don't overwhelm your visitors with content. A few well-designed pages covering important information guests will want to know is helpful; a daily update of your wedding planning progress or lots of polls on what kind of cake you should serve is not.

Don't include overly personal information. Some predesigned web templates prompt you to enter personal details such as when you shared your first kiss, what you did on your first date, and so on. This may be good fodder for a bachelor(ette) party, but there's no need to share so much with your entire guest list (and whoever else may be peering over their shoulders). Keep your postings tasteful and inclusive—remember, this is a space where you want every visitor to feel comfortable and welcome.

Don't overemphasize your gift registry links. It is perfectly fine to post links to your various online gift registries on your home page—in fact, these one-stop shopping links are now expected, if only because of their convenience. Still, it's important to strike a balance between discretion and your desire to make things easy for your guests. (Registry links should never be the only information provided on your wedding website.) Consider placing such links to the side of the page, in modestly sized type.

Don't overlook your offline guests. If you know that a certain invited guest is not connected to the web, be sure to send him or her hard copies of any important information posted on your webpage.

You can make good use of your website after the wedding as well, by posting pictures from the wedding and honeymoon along with any anecdotes you care to share and, most important, a heartfelt thank-you to everyone involved. (*But*: A group "thanks" doesn't replace individual, handwritten, mailed thank-you notes for gifts, special favors, or events hosted in your honor.)

Online Gift Registries

Almost all major American retailers have online gift registries for weddings and just about every other type of gift-giving occasion. It's no understatement to say that this advance has revolutionized the experience of giving and receiving gifts, especially wedding gifts. Guests can simply log on to a store's website, click on the "Gift Registry," type in the name of the couple, and have instant access to every item on the couple's list that is still available. Meanwhile, you—the couple—can log in anytime you wish to check on which items have been purchased.

As accessible as these online registries are, word of their existence should still be spread discreetly. If you have eclectic taste and desire gifts from a variety

---

SPREADSHEETS AND ELECTRONIC DOCUMENTS

So much wedding planning is done via electronic documents—spreadsheets for keeping track of budgets, guests, and gifts; PDFs of contracts and scans of important documents; and text files for composing your vows, toasts, ceremony program, and menu, to name a few. For tips on what to include on planning spreadsheets, see Chapter 3, page 29; Chapter 7, page 83; Chapter 13, page 161, as well as the Emily Post website (www.emilypost.com/weddings).

of online stores, Amazon offers a "universal wish list" that combines them all into one easily accessible list. (See also Chapter 13, page 161.)

Social Media and Mobile Manners

Weddings are fun and it's natural for guests to want to capture and share that excitement. Smartphones are ubiquitous these days, and while it's unlikely you can prevent guests from bringing them, you can set some guidelines for how and when they use them. There are also opportunities for technology to be the hero, such as video chats that allow special friends and loved ones who can't attend in person to join remotely.

A Device-Free Ceremony

Almost everyone at your ceremony (including the wedding party) will have a cell phone in his or her purse or pocket, and you certainly don't want someone's cell phone with a ring tone set to Beyoncé's "Single Ladies" going off just as you say "I do," nor do you want the ceremony interrupted by the chirps, beeps, and buzzes of text and email notifications. The wedding rehearsal is a good time to start reminding your wedding party to switch off their phones for the ceremony. Have the best man and maid of honor add that reminder to their final preprocession checklists for the next day.

As to guests, there are a few simple ways to remind them that it's time to stop texting or playing "Words with Friends" and give their full attention to the ceremony. You might post a "Please turn off all mobile devices" sign at the entry or by the guest book. If you are providing programs, you can add it there—most guests read the program cover to cover while they wait. If you don't think that any of those will do the trick, ask one of the groomsman to make an announcement just before the couple's parents are seated and the ceremony begins. Frankly, doing all three isn't a bad idea.

But calls and message alerts aren't the only potential trouble smartphones can cause. Many guests are excited and want to take pictures of their own of the ceremony. Whether it's because the couple would like to see their guests directly, without a camera phone hiding their faces or because they would prefer not to have photos of the ceremony, which many feel is private, uploaded to the Internet, it's fair to ask guests to put away their smartphones (something all good guests should do, but isn't always the case). Follow this up with a reminder before the processional begins.

Smartphones at the Reception

You could ask that guests refrain from using their smartphones at the reception, too, but it's less likely they'll comply. Once guests are at the reception, it's virtually guaranteed they will check their phones. They'll also take and post pictures of you, of their friends, of key moments like the cake cutting or toasts, and even of the food. Since there's no way you can police this without seeming like a party pooper, think of it as extra photo service and ask guests to share images while you're waiting for the formal ones from the photographer.

Video Chat

It's hard to imagine getting married without the people who mean the most to you, but sometimes due to circumstances outside your control, that's what happens. While a video chat isn't the same as having them there in person, it can bring them into your day in ways a phone call can't. If you have the capacity to do it and it won't be distracting to the ceremony, you could set them up to attend the service virtually. (Check with your officiant to be sure this is okay.) Otherwise, schedule five to ten minutes at your reception when you can slip away from the party and give your long-distance guest your full attention. Show them your dress, rings, bouquet—anything to help them feel as if they are there. You might even pan the camera around the reception site. If your guest is elderly, such as a grandparent, make sure you walk them (or someone who will be with them) through the video chat process in advance so you don't waste precious minutes on troubleshooting.

PART TWO

YOUR FAMILY, WEDDING PARTY, AND GUESTS

CHAPTER 5

WEDDING STARS

A short while ago you were plain old Kathy and Joe, maybe even KathyandJoe, but when Joe popped the question and Kathy said yes, the two of you were magically transformed into the fairy-tale land of fiancé and fiancée, bridal couple, the bride- and groom-to-be. Your feet barely touch the ground, everyone around you is smiling, you're the centers of attention, and everyone wants to do what they can to share in and make your happiness even greater.

As you make your way to the altar, you'll find you have many roles to play: host and hostess, honoree, planner, decision maker, diplomat. While the members of your wedding party have specific roles to play in your wedding, the other, unsung wedding stars are your parents. Together, you are the stars of the show, and you are the team that will plan and ensure that your wedding day is both joyful and enjoyable.

Team Wedding

The engagement is official, your parents have met each other and for the next *x* number of months of your engagement, you'll be operating as a team. Like any team, you'll need a training regimen to get yourselves in shape for the big event. Here are some things you as a couple and your parents can do to take some of the stress out of all the planning and to be and look your best for the wedding itself.

Get to know your teammates. While the parents of the groom and the parents of the bride may not develop a close relationship, the goal is to at least develop a friendly one. A good sign that you've accomplished that is when it's comfortable for all parties to be able to call or email each other.

STAR QUALITIES

- Willingness to communicate
- Diplomacy
- Tact
- Enthusiasm
- Graciousness
- Sense of humor
- Patience
- Flexibility

Set team meetings. In the first place, you'll want to keep everyone in the loop, and in the second, everyone will be getting the same information firsthand. Plan on talking soon after the big items have been settled (budget, date, location), and then it's up to you how often you get together to share wedding progress and information. Conference call (most smartphones can do that), iChat, Skype—there are lots of ways to get together.

Get to know the "new" family. Take some notes—mentally or on paper—of names and relationships: groom's older brother, Carl, in banking, married to Sara Jones, teacher, from Charleston, live in Winnetka, have 3 kids: Sean 7, Suzy 5, Joey 2. Not that there's going to be a quiz, but it's a way to familiarize yourselves with the people you may meet at showers or at the rehearsal dinner and wedding.

Hit the gym. Whether it's the gym itself, your favorite jogging path, or yoga studio, scheduling regular exercise into your routine will have a number of benefits. Not only will you look great for the wedding, exercise is a proven stress reliever as well.

Schedule wedding planning time. Most people's calendars are overpacked as it is. Add in a wedding, and there's a temptation to hit the panic button: How will you ever get it all done? While you're slotting in your exercise time, add in specific times to focus on your wedding responsibilities or assignments.

Take dance lessons. You'll have more fun and be more confident when it's time for your wedding solo. As the date approaches, you could include your parents to help them prep for their moment in the spotlight and to get a little extra time with them before the big day.

Make salon appointments. A little pampering won't hurt, and if you're thinking about a new look for the wedding, now's the time to test it out, not two weeks before the big event. Ladies, you may want to suggest that your significant other also make appointments for haircuts. They may want to indulge in a professional shave (no risk of nicks or missed stubble), and with all the handshaking, a manicure isn't a bad idea either.

Get together or call about nonwedding stuff, too. You'll need a break from all things *W*—a call or chance to have dinner with your parents without mentioning "wedding" is a good way to explore other aspects of your lives. Declare some nights "wedding free" in advance so you can relax and enjoy each other's company.

Your Roles as the Bridal Couple

Individually, you will each have lists of to-dos and parties to attend, but you have a role as a couple, too. From diplomats to honorees to just plain worker bees planning a major event, you will navigate these roles as partners.

Diplomats. One of your first roles is as diplomats to smooth the way for your two families to meet and get to know each other. (See also Chapter 1, page 7.) You'll want to share some basic information and answer any questions about your fiancé(e)'s parents ahead of that first meeting. It will help break the ice and, hopefully, suggest some topics of mutual interest. There's no reason not to expect the meeting to go well.

Throughout your engagement, you will each need to commit to getting to know each other's parents and family and to keep the interactions positive. Remember, this is a lot of change for everyone. Sure, there may be things your future father-in-law does or says that you don't agree with or find annoying, but try not to overreact or take it too seriously. Don't assume anything except good intentions. Not all of us are born diplomats—so take into account what's at the heart of something that may not have been expressed well. If there's something that really bothers you about the other's family, talk to each other, and together come up with approaches to handle sticky issues. While it's fine to be supportive of your particular parents, realize that the two of you are now a partnership, so resist taking sides.

One of the hardest things for brides and grooms to deal with is when conflict arises, sometimes seemingly out of nowhere. The sources of tension may be due to religious beliefs, generational differences, or other biases. Don't be surprised if these appear in places you didn't expect. Why is your grandmother so upset that you're not marrying in a church? It never occurred to you that your father, who is always so fair and reasonable, would be upset that you're marrying someone from a different background.

Reactions like these may feel confusing, frustrating, or hurtful, and it might take a huge effort on your part not to jump right in, defend your choice, and dig in your heels. Turn instead to your fiancé(e) for support and understanding. Work together on ways to allay concerns. Sometimes it just takes time for families or friends to accept an idea. Keep communication and doors open.

Honorees. Another role you'll take on is that of guests of honor at a number of social events, such as an engagement party, wedding shower, or rehearsal dinner. You'll want to be an enthusiastic, cheerful participant at any event in your honor. Even if you are hosting your own wedding, you are also the ones being celebrated.

Graciousness is the key here. As the guests of honor at any of these events, make sure that you spend time greeting or chatting with each guest, either individually or as a couple. Check in with each other, "Did you have a chance to say hi to Steve? If not, I'll go speak with him." For some couples not used to large parties, it can be tempting to stick to a couple of friends for the duration. But you are the reason all the guests are there, and you are the people the guests most want to see, so make an effort to branch out.

Get comfortable responding to compliments and congratulations—there will only be more to come. Have a few responses at the ready. A heartfelt "thank you" is usually all you need to say, or a "thank you, that's so kind." Then show your appreciation, both verbally and in writing to all the friends and family who host events or do special favors for you. (See Chapter 14, page 177.)

Planning committee. Whether or not the bride takes the reins on planning, there is still plenty to decide together, including the date and location, your contribution as a couple to the budget (if any), the guest list, and most likely the menu and music. Some grooms will make decisions with their brides every step of the way, right down to details such as which invitation paper to choose and what flowers would be best for center-pieces. Whatever the level of involvement, disagreement on some level will be inevitable, so be willing to talk, compromise, or even take a break when you don't see eye-to-eye.

Also, be sure to schedule yourselves regular nights off from planning. Use this time to reconnect on other aspects of your lives. You might opt for comfy favorites such as reservations at your favorite restaurant or dinner in. Or you can alternate surprise date nights, thinking up something the other might enjoy, like a new movie or wine or beer tasting. This is a good way to keep in the habit of thinking about what the other person might need or want. The whole point is to give yourselves room within all that planning to appreciate each other.

The Bride

No matter how low key you are, when you are the bride, you are the star of the show. Family and friends naturally want to shower you with congratulations, gifts, affection, and offers to "help in any way they can." No matter how much the groom's role has grown in the last decade or so, the tendency is still for it to be "all about you."

That can be a pretty heady experience: One day you're plain Jane CPA slogging through the daily grind; the next day you're radiant Princess Jane with an entire court at your beck and call. Please, dear princess bride, try not to take your status too literally, and maintain a sense of reality and a little humility. While the outrageous antics of brides behaving as demanding shrews—more over-the-top than anything Hollywood could write—let us gape and gasp in wonder, at heart we all know this is *not* the way to behave. Bridezilla fatigue has set in and not a moment too soon.

Your real role in the twenty-first-century wedding is to be the team leader. Whether you and your fiancé are planning and paying for your wedding on your own, or your respective parents are contributing financially, almost every wedding decision—big and small—will be run past you: Do you like roses or lilies? Do you want long dresses or short? Do you want beef or chicken? If your fiancé is equally interested in the planning, make sure that you include him and get the word out that you are coleaders.

Delegate. Most people need at least some help planning a wedding, and you'll also receive offers from friends and relatives who'd like to lend a hand. Your team—your fiancé, parents, and bridal party—are on tap to help as well. As you work on each part of your plan, mark items that you could delegate to others. For example, would your aunt who wants to help out be willing to house a bridesmaid or two, or would your neighbor be willing to deliver reception flowers to the local hospital the day after the wedding? Bridesmaids could assemble favors or help call guests who haven't replied to the invitation. Your fiancé could research and post restaurant recommendations, activities, and area attractions for the benefit of out-of-town guests. Keep track of who's doing what, not just so you can follow-up but also so that you'll be able to send the appropriate thanks, especially in the case of friends and relatives outside of your immediate wedding team.

Reality check. You've seen all the beautiful magazine spreads of gorgeous, fairy-tale weddings. And the text makes it sound as if all you have to do to make this your wedding is a little DIY and a magic wand. Keep the reality in mind: These are highly stylized, fussed-over photo shoots, and many of the elements are either donated or traded for designer or vendor magazine exposure. To re-create the photo in real life will take a large bank account behind that magic wand. Take these beautiful wedding scenes for what they are—inspiration.

Love every idea for five minutes. You will be amazed at how many people will make assumptions about your wedding. Your mom may have always dreamed that you'd wear her wedding dress, your grandmother envisions your reception at the Ritz, and two friends are equally convinced they'll be your maid of honor. Of course, you don't have to say yes to everyone else's idea of your wedding, but instead of rejecting these ideas out of hand, see if you can embrace them for a brief time: "Mom, I'm really touched by your offer. Let's try on the dress and see if it works for me." "Grandma, the Ritz would be amazing! I doubt we can afford it, but we'll make sure the Champagne makes you think you're there." "I don't know how I could ever choose between the two of you. Would you be willing to be co–maids of honor?" Giving each idea consideration will make it easier to either say no or to offer an alternative. And just as important, it will make the other feel included and heard.

Be enthusiastic. Your aunt Sandy is over the moon that she's throwing a shower for you. You've heard rumors that she has all sorts of corny games planned— and you hate these. This is the time to let go a little. As the gracious bride you are, it's your job to be enthusiastic about your aunt's party and to help make it a success by participating with a smile in everything she has planned.

Schedule dates. Don't let all the planning details get in the way of your romance with your fiancé. Schedule date nights, just as you did before you got engaged. Then, keep the wedding chat limited to the appetizer course or the drive to the movie.

Get to know his family. Do your best to keep in touch or visit with your fiancé's family. Now's the time to put effort into establishing a good rapport with them. If there are conflicts or sticking points, bring them to your fiancé and ask for his interpretation. Until you know his parents better, let him handle any big bumps—such as trimming his mom's guest list. It's better not to confront them on your own. If you do feel that there's a serious issue that needs addressing, speak to them together, as a couple. Then return the favor and be the guide, interpreter, and diplomat if he comes in conflict with your side of the family.

Keep calm and carry on. It's advice fit for a queen, and it can work for you, too!

The Groom

There's an old saying: "A man never knows how unimportant he is until he goes to his own wedding." Indeed, it wasn't so long ago that the groom's role was largely relegated to buying the ring, popping the question, selecting his groomsmen, planning the honeymoon, and making sure to show up on time on the scheduled day. Even the boutonniere—and sometimes the suit—he wore was someone else's choice.

These days, grooms are as likely as brides to be active participants in decision making and taking on wedding to-dos, from setting a budget to hiring caterers to writing thank-you notes. More and more, the marriage partnership actually begins in the joint planning of the celebration that will cement a couple's future lives together.

This heightened involvement has a lot to do with the fact that approximately 70 percent of engaged couples are paying for some or all of their own weddings. As a result, grooms are more invested in what they're paying for, and they want more say on where that investment goes. Grooms have embraced the trend toward more personalized weddings—ones that make a statement about who the couple is—which can make the day even more memorable for everyone involved. From choosing ceremony elements, writing vows, and designing the invitation, to building the registry, sampling menus, and creating a music playlist, there's probably no part of a modern wedding that hasn't seen the groom's touch.

Be a partner. Partnering to plan the wedding relieves your fiancée of the need to shoulder the bulk of the burden, when she may be just as busy in her day-to-day work life as you are. Sharing the duties is considerate—and a way to begin working together on important issues just as you will in the years to come.

It's her dream. You might want to be involved in all of the planning decisions, take on only the ones that interest you, or let her take the lead. No matter your level of involvement, keep one thing in mind: Your bride-to-be has been dreaming of her wedding since she was a young girl. If you have to do some reality-based bubble bursting, be gentle, offer alternatives, and be wiling to compromise. Bottom line? Listen.

Roll up your sleeves. Maybe you're not so interested in picking out flowers, or planning the menu. That's fine—but do take a proactive role in finding a few areas where you're willing to take the lead. Perhaps creating the wedding website is more up your alley, or researching photographers or musicians. You don't have to be involved in every decision to be an active, supportive part of the planning process. You can be helpful simply by being willing to lend a hand—and by staying on top of your share of the thank-you notes.

Keep your parents up-to-date. Without the responsibilities of wedding planning and hosting that typically fall to the parents of the bride, the groom's parents may feel left out of the loop. Keep your mom, especially, apprised of the latest details in the planning, and make sure she knows that her input and advice are not only welcome but also highly valued. Encourage your fiancée to do the same.

Practice your lines. Throughout your engagement, at some wedding parties, and at the wedding reception you'll be called on to make and respond to toasts. You'll be making toasts that thank her parents, your parents, and party hosts. You'll make a tribute toast to your bride, both at the rehearsal dinner and at the wedding reception itself. They don't need to be long, but write these out and practice them, out loud, ahead of time. Review, too, the etiquette of being toasted. (For more on toasts, see Chapter 26, page 349.)

You will also want to practice your vows, particularly if you have written them yourself. While couples don't say their actual vows during the wedding ceremony rehearsal, find a quiet moment to recite them a few times, either alone or with someone for an audience.

A Groom's Traditional Duties

The groom has always had a customary set of responsibilities to carry out before, during, and after the wedding. These traditional duties typically include:

- Selecting the engagement ring alone or with your fiancée-to-be

- Compiling your part of the guest list and making sure that your parents draw up their guest list

- Choosing your attendants: best man, groomsmen/ushers

- Choosing the attire for your attendants

- Selecting thank-you gifts for your attendants

- Arranging (and paying for) lodging for your attendants

- Selecting a gift for the bride (optional)

- Arranging the honeymoon (with your fiancée)

- Choosing wedding bands with your fiancée

- Planning the bachelor party or other event for groomsmen, if applicable. (The best man may also do this.)

- Obtaining the marriage license

- Arranging transportation from the ceremony site to the reception site for the groomsmen, if necessary, or asking the best man to do so

- Being dressed and ready for the ceremony or pictures a half-hour ahead of time

- Giving the wedding rings to the best man for safekeeping

- Preparing and delivering all fees for the ceremony, or delegating the best man to do so

- Standing in the receiving line (if there is one) or being sure—with the bride—to greet all guests during the reception

- Making toasts and responding to toasts at the rehearsal dinner and the reception

- Cutting the cake with the bride

- Dancing the first dance with the bride and dancing with your mother and mother-in-law and the maid/matron of honor

The Bride's Parents

It used to be that the bride's parents ran and paid for the entire show—and maybe that's how your daughter's wedding will go, too. However, statistics tell us that may not be the current reality. Your daughter and her fiancé may pay for and plan their wedding themselves—in which case you can relax, give advice when asked, and be honored guests. Or the groom's family may offer to contribute to the wedding, too. This has been a growing trend over the past two decades, and one that comes with a few etiquette minefields, the first of which might be having a delicate discussion of finances with people you barely know.

Dealing with finances. While it may be the trend for the groom's family to add to the wedding pot, don't assume or count on that being the case. In other words, it's both perfectly okay for them to offer to contribute and per-

fectly okay for them to remain silent on the matter. On your end, if the groom's parents do make an offer, it's fine for you to graciously accept and invite them to share in the wedding planning. On the other hand, if you are true traditionalists and believe the bride's parents alone should host and pay for her wedding, that is your prerogative. However, do try to think about the big picture, and first ask your daughter and her fiancé for their thoughts on the matter and how his parents would feel if their offer was turned down. Consulting with the couple will give you a better idea how to proceed.

Sharing responsibilities with the groom's family. If sharing expenses has been agreed to, it's a good idea to plan a finance meeting with everyone involved sometime soon after the first "meet and greet." (Don't have this conversation during your first meeting—it would be far too uncomfortable and create too much pressure.) Some families divide costs by choosing to pay for certain wedding elements directly—the flowers, the bar, the limos, the musicians. Others pool resources and then put the bride and groom in charge of how they wish to spend the total. This approach has a certain logic to it and minimizes the chance of one set of parents assuming control of guest list or menu decisions because "we're paying for it."

Getting to know his parents. Circumstances may have you living on opposite sides of the country, but do your best to establish a comfortable method of communication. Phone calls are best to discuss sticky issues, while email works well for short, factual exchanges of information. Be friendly and open, but don't expect to be instant best friends. It will take time to get to know each other. It's fine to ask your daughter questions about her new in-laws and use her as a sounding board for your interactions with them. When sharing wedding plans with the groom's parents, leave room for their feedback. Do this even if they're not contributing financially, especially on guest lists and seating arrangements.

Being good hosts. Whether your names lead the invitation or it's "together with their families," as the parents of the bride you will be hosts, cohosts, or "hosts of honor" at the reception. Greet guests you know and introduce yourself to those you don't, and make all guests feel welcome.

The Mother of the Bride

This is an exciting, emotional, and nostalgic time for you. As the mother of the bride, you have probably been dreaming of this day as long as she has and have lots of ideas and advice to make her day special. Be careful not to impose the vision of the wedding you had (or wished you'd had) on your daughter and her fiancé. Instead, embrace her ideas and let your wisdom and experience make her wedding a success.

Be a sounding board. No matter how involved (or not) you are in the planning, you can be a good sounding board for your daughter and her fiancé as they plan the ceremony and reception. Help them keep the big picture in mind, especially if decisions are trending in ways that might hurt long-term or family relationships.

Be a prewedding ambassador. Friends and family will be asking you all about your daughter's upcoming wedding. They'll want to know if they'll be invited, how they can help, if they can host a shower, what the couple would like for a wedding gift. Be ready for these questions, and don't commit to anything or anyone until you've cleared it with the couple: "We don't yet know the size of the wedding." "Thanks for

---

WHOSE PARTY IS THIS ANYWAY?

Not so long ago, as the holder of the purse strings, the parents of the bride usually had the final say on the guest list, the menu, the decor—you name it. Happily, as weddings have become more collaborative in nature, their focus has shifted to reflect the wishes of the couple marrying, rather than as a social event staged by parents. The guest list is one aspect of the wedding likely to cause conflict. No longer are they weighted in favor of the parents' friends and business associates, people the couple may barely know. (This is why dividing the guest list into allotments is a wise idea.) If there are any final decisions to be made on wedding guests, let them fall to the couple. Friends and business associates who didn't make the final list can always receive a printed wedding announcement.

---

your offer. I'll let Kathy know and get back to you." "A shower—how generous! Let me check with Kathy and Joe." "They're registered at weddinggifts.com, but I know they'll appreciate whatever you choose." And you'll need to be an advocate for their choices as well: "We're thrilled they've decided to marry in Italy!"

Share local knowledge. Be welcoming. If the wedding will take place in your neck of the woods, you might help the groom's parents find a location for the rehearsal dinner if they plan on hosting one and would like suggestions. Immediately after reserving blocks of rooms at local inns or hotels, give the groom's parents a rundown of what's available so they can make their own reservations for the wedding right away.

Share information about your outfit. Tradition says that the mother of the bride has first pick when it comes to choosing her wedding outfit, and that's still the case. Even so, it's gracious to let the mother of the groom know what you're wearing so she has enough time to choose her own outfit. Although not mandatory, it's often appreciated when the bride and her mother include the groom's mother in any shopping expeditions, say for the bride's dress or for their own respective outfits. (See also Chapter 19, page 251.)

The Father of the Bride

The father of the bride has his own traditional and often poignant roles to play at his daughter's wedding. With the mother of the bride, guests will look to you to be the wedding hosts, even if the entire wedding was planned and hosted by the couple.

Welcome guests. You'll be greeting, mingling with, and accepting congratulations from your reception guests. As best you can, familiarize yourself with the names on the guest list. Even if big social dos aren't your forte, you'll be expected to make introductions, engage in small talk, and respond to congratulations.

Practice your toasts. Throughout your daughter's engagement, you'll have the opportunity to make toasts to her, to her fiancé, and to his parents. It's a good idea to write these out ahead of time, and practice them out loud. The following are times when you may be called on to make a toast:

- **The engagement party.** When announcing the engagement, the toast will express your happiness for your daughter, welcome the groom and his family, and offer best wishes to the couple.

- **The rehearsal dinner.** Following the welcome toast by the groom's father, thank the groom's family for their hospitality.

- **The wedding reception.** After the best man gives his toast, the father of the bride welcomes all the guests and leads a toast to the couple. (See also Chapter 26, page 349.)

Walk your daughter down the aisle. Most dads say this is the most poignant, bittersweet moment of their daughter's wedding. No matter how well it goes at the rehearsal, you may get a bit misty-eyed when it's for real, and that's okay! (Pocket handkerchief to the rescue.) If your family is in a situation where there is a stepdad involved and he may be a possible candidate to escort your daughter, have this conversation with her early in the wedding planning—don't wait until the rehearsal. If she doesn't bring it up, you should. Be open to compromise and do your best to accept her decision graciously. (See Chapter 25, page 335.)

The father–daughter dance. This is another traditional tender moment between you and your daughter. She may be married, but she's still your little girl! Several weeks before the wedding, have fun choosing your music and practice dancing together. Again, if there is a stepdad involved, discuss dance options with your daughter well ahead of time.

Final wedding payments. Most final payments and tips for the catering, flowers, musicians, photographer, and venue are due just before or on the day of the wedding. Prepare these checks ahead of time and have them ready for delivery at the appropriate time. Even if the couple is responsible for the final payments, you can be a big help by taking on the responsibility of delivering them.

The Groom's Parents

The groom's parents used to have little role to play except welcoming the bride to their family and helping with the groom's expenses. Even hosting the rehearsal dinner is a comparatively new custom.

Your first job is to call the bride's parents a day or two after the engagement and make arrangements to meet in the not-too-distant future. If the bride's parents jump the gun, don't worry—the idea is to get the ball rolling. If you've never met before, the couple can facilitate or even host the get-together.

Sometime in the late 1950s and early '60s, it became popular for the groom's parents to host the rehearsal dinner, a more elaborate affair than the traditional refreshments served by the bride's family right after the wedding rehearsal. While it's not a requirement to host this party, it is now a typical component of the wedding experience. If you'd like to host this event, work with the couple or the bride's parents to find a location that's suitable and a time that's convenient. It's entirely your party to plan, but for a rundown of traditional guests, types of parties, and party elements, see Chapter 12, page 154.

In recent decades, it has become more common for the groom's family to contribute to wedding costs. Tread carefully here. If you want to take part in sponsoring the wedding, that's okay, but work it through the couple first to gauge how the offer will be received by the bride's parents. If the bride's parents want to go it alone, that's their prerogative.

Another recent trend is to include the groom's parents on the invitation as a courtesy, even when there is no financial contribution from them. However, don't take it as an insult if the bride's parents alone are paying for the wedding and decide to go the traditional route, listing only their names as hosts. This is perfectly okay. If you are added as honorary hosts, ask the couple and the bride's parents if there are any hosting duties you can help with or share in at the reception.

The Mother of the Groom

No longer do you have to wear beige and stay in the background! While you may have few assigned duties, it's fine to offer help with the planning or take on some of the details if you would like. Unless you're given carte blanche, run any decisions by the couple before going ahead. Even today, it's a wise mother of the groom who waits to give advice until asked.

Choose your dress. While the mother of the bride has the honor here, your goal is to choose a dress that makes you, as mother of the groom, feel and look gorgeous. If you haven't heard from the bride's mother soon after the bridesmaids' dresses are selected, give her a call to check in. While you don't want to jump the gun, it does take time to choose a dress and have it fitted. It's always nice when the two moms can coordinate. (See also Chapter 19, page 251.)

Get to know your son's fiancée. It can't be stressed enough how important it is to establish good communication and a good rapport early on. Getting to know someone takes time. If you have concerns about your relationship, talk them over with your son, and listen carefully to what he has to say. Assumptions and misunderstandings can cause grief, and your goal is for your son to have a happy marriage and for him and his bride to feel welcome in your home.

Prepare your guest list. The couple will let you know how many invitations are available to you. Even if the number is generous, you may need to make cuts. Once you've created your list, prioritize it so that making the final list will be simpler. (See Chapter 7, page 83.)

The Father of the Groom

As the father of the groom you have few specific duties, freeing you to lend support where you can. This may simply mean being a calm presence that helps the other trains run on time. Or perhaps you could invite your son and maybe the bride's father to go golfing, fishing, even bowling to get a break from all things wedding.

Specifically, the father of the groom may expect to stand in the receiving line (if there is one) to greet guests and to dance with the bride at some point after she has danced with the groom and with her father.

In addition, you will take the spotlight from time to time throughout your son's engagement to make toasts to him, to his fiancée, and to her parents. Jot a few notes and practice your toasts out loud, either alone or to an audience. The following are times when you may be called on to make a toast:

- **The engagement party.** Return the father of the bride's toast, expressing how happy you are for your son, welcoming the bride and his family into yours, and sharing your congratulations to the couple.

- **The rehearsal dinner.** Give the first toast, welcoming the guests and sharing your excitement for the wedding to come.

- **The wedding reception.** After the father of the bride toasts the couple, offer them one of your own. Discuss with your wife (or his mother, if not the same) whether or not she would like to join you in saying a few words. (See also Chapter 26, page 349.)

CHAPTER 6

YOUR WEDDING PARTY

Wedding attendants give help and support during the wedding preparations, serve as witnesses to a couple's marriage, and as ambassadors and assistants at the wedding reception. Including friends and loved ones in this happy milestone is one of the most cherished wedding customs.

For many couples, the choice of attendants is easy—sisters, brothers, and dearest friends—but if you have a large family or a wide circle of good friends, the decision can be quite hard. Asking siblings or your fiancé(e)'s siblings certainly promotes family unity, but it's not a requirement. As important as it is to honor family and friendship, you'll want to choose people who are supportive and on whom you can count.

Choosing Your Attendants

You have many options for choosing your attendants in both considerate and logical ways.

There is no required number of attendants. The average is four to six bridesmaids and a similar number of groomsmen or ushers, but you can include as many or as few as you like. Some couples have a large number of attendants, but even a formal wedding with just one or two attendants on each side is perfectly fine. Prince William of England and the Duchess of Cambridge each had one attendant for their marriage—a maid of honor and best man and several flower girls and pages.

It's not necessary to have an equal number of bridesmaids and groomsmen or ushers. Don't worry about pairing up. You can have more bridesmaids than groomsmen or vice versa. The goal is to avoid a wedding party so lopsided that the focus shifts from the couple and their vows to the eleven bridesmaids and two groomsmen flanking them. Just don't snub a good friend or family member or pull in someone you don't know as well for the sake of symmetry. One groomsman can easily escort two bridesmaids in the recessional, or bridesmaids can walk alone or in pairs.

You can have two maids of honor, a maid and a matron of honor, or two best men. If you don't want to choose between siblings or very close friends, have two principal attendants. The attendants can share the duties—and the fun! For example, one maid of honor holds the groom's ring, while the other takes the bridal bouquet. This arrangement has practical benefits, too.

If your matron of honor lives 300 miles away and has two young children, she can be your long-distance sounding board and can scour the Internet for wedding ideas; your sister who lives locally can go with you to shop for your dress.

Toss a coin or draw straws to decide who will be maid of honor or best man. When good friends are amenable to luck-of-the-draw decisions, leaving the choice up to fate eliminates any hint of preference or favoritism.

You can have pregnant bridesmaids. It's fine to ask a friend who is pregnant to be a bridesmaid. Just be considerate of her needs and capabilities, and make exceptions to bridesmaid attire or shoes when appropriate. You may want to have a chair placed nearby so that the mother-to-be can sit during a lengthy service; to excuse her from a formal receiving line; and to make sure that she doesn't go too long without eating or drinking at the reception. Don't be surprised if you're turned down, though, especially if the wedding date is within a month or two of her due date.

Brides and grooms can have attendants of the opposite sex. Accurate as *man of honor* and *best woman* are, *honor attendant* is another term for any attendant of the opposite sex. Many brides and grooms pay tribute to their closest friends or siblings by including them in the bridal party in this unique way. Honor attendants perform the same duties as the maid of honor, best man, bridesmaid, or groomsman position that they represent, although some responsibilities are altered as necessary—for example, a male honor attendant wouldn't help the bride get dressed. Adaptations and personal touches are fine as long as they

HOW NOT TO HURT FEELINGS

Q: I have several close friends and family members, but we have decided on a small wedding and can only select a few attendants. That means we're leaving someone out. How do you suggest we tactfully explain our choices to these dear friends?

A: Choosing siblings over friends needs no explanation. In your case, the desire for an intimate gathering necessitates a small number of attendants. If anyone asks, say, "Since we're having a small wedding, Tom and I have agreed to have only two attendants each. I hope you understand." But don't explain if you aren't asked—it only serves to highlight whom you didn't choose.

There are other ways to make friends feel like they are a part of the wedding. The most time-honored is to ask close friends or family to give a reading, a task often bestowed on those who are very special to the couple. You could also ask for help with small wedding planning jobs such as stuffing and addressing envelopes or putting together the favors, or solicit your friend's advice on destinations for the honeymoon.

are applied thoughtfully. The honor attendant should be completely comfortable with his or her role so that the special recognition their status is meant to convey is maintained.

Practicalities

While there may no longer be set rules regarding who can or cannot be an attendant, there are some practicalities to consider. Before you ask anyone to be an attendant, have a clear idea of the following:

Size and formality. The size and formality of your wedding can help determine the size of your wedding party. If you plan a small, intimate gathering, you won't want attendants outnumbering guests. If the ceremony site is small, you may have room for only one or two attendants. If you're planning a large, extravagant celebration, you may want an equally large wedding party. That said, there is nothing wrong with having 500 guests and no attendants at all.

Budget. The more attendants you have, the larger your expenses. The bride and groom are responsible for all bouquets, boutonnieres, and wedding-party gifts, as well as the attendants' accommodations if they don't live near the wedding's location. Also, the number of attendants will affect the cost of your rehearsal dinner and wedding reception because you are responsible for feeding and entertaining not only your attendants but your attendants' partners as well.

Religious restrictions. Some religions have strict rules regarding official witnesses. For example, for a traditional Jewish wedding, witnesses cannot be related by blood or marriage to the bride, groom, or each other.

Qualities to Look For in an Attendant

Participating in someone else's wedding is both a pleasure and a responsibility. When you consider which of your close relatives and friends to include, think about your expectations for their participation and how much you are likely to depend on your attendants—not just at the wedding but also throughout the planning and preparation as well.

Attendants have a special duty to assist the bride and groom and to see that the wedding and reception run smoothly. Consider these fundamental traits:

Reliability. An attendant should be a person you can count on to stay in touch in the weeks and months preceding the wedding, to follow up on requests without being reminded, to listen to instructions on the big day, and to be on time and ready for all events.

Consideration. Considerate attendants may offer suggestions but will understand that they aren't in charge. They will look for opportunities to be helpful but won't cause the couple stress with special demands or needless criticism.

SHOULD I ASK MY FIANCÉ'S SISTER TO BE MY BRIDESMAID?

Q: My fiancé has a sister whom I don't know well. Do I have to ask her to be one of my bridesmaids?

A: If you are considering skipping your future sister-in-law as a bridesmaid purely because you don't feel close to her, reconsider. She is about to become part of your family, and you of hers. Your invitation to be a member of the bridal party may open the door to a closer relationship. Your future in-laws would likely welcome such an inclusive gesture toward their daughter. While you are not obligated to include her, the long-term benefits to family harmony may outweigh the potential harm and hurt feelings you might cause by not asking. Plus it's a chance to get to know her better before the wedding.

Courtesy. In a sense, attendants are ambassadors for the bridal couple and their families. At prewedding events and during the wedding reception, they mix and mingle with guests, make introductions, look out for people with special needs, and can be counted on to behave appropriately.

Fun. Being a bridesmaid or groomsman isn't just about logistics; it's about having a great time planning with your closest friends. Choose friends who are drama-free, flexible, and upbeat. This isn't a military campaign, after all; it's a wedding!

Financial Obligations

Expenses for attendants can add up quickly, from travel to clothing to participation in parties and showers. The number of prewedding events requiring a financial contribution or gift seems to be on the rise—such as engagement parties, showers, and bachelor and bach-

elorette parties—and this can be a source of economic strain for attendants.

Attendants are expected to pay their own travel expenses for the wedding and wedding-related events. The bride and groom are responsible for covering the cost of their accommodations for the wedding or for making arrangements for friends and family to put up members of the wedding party. While not required, it's considerate when they can arrange lodging for attendants who travel for prewedding events such as an engagement party or shower.

People in their twenties and thirties may find themselves invited to attend or participate in several weddings in the same year. This can cause serious financial stress. Keep all of this in mind when you ask a friend or relative to be in your wedding.

For those who would find it a financial strain, you might thoughtfully ask them to participate in a differ-

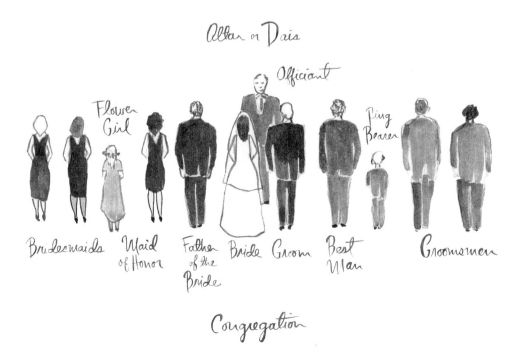

ent, less expensive way (see page 82). If cost is preventing a good friend from being an attendant and you can't imagine being married without that person by your side, you can certainly offer to pay his or her expenses. No one but you and your friend has to know of this special arrangement.

When to Ask

Once you've decided who you want in your wedding, give them as much advance notice as possible. Six months to a year before the wedding date is fairly standard, and most couples choose their attendants soon after they set the date for the wedding. This gives attendants time to organize their calendars, purchase clothing and have necessary alterations made, arrange transportation, and plan and host any parties they may wish to hold in your honor. If your schedule is very tight, you can find ways to cut a few corners (off-the-rack bridesmaid dresses rather than custom-ordered, a bridesmaids' luncheon and bachelor party but no shower or vice versa) to make things more enjoyable for you and your wedding party.

It's always nice to ask in person, but don't delay contacting someone who lives at a distance. A call is best as it's more personal, but by all means text or email your invitation if that's the easiest way to get in touch. Supply the wedding date even if you aren't sure of the time, the location, if travel will be required, and

WHO PAYS FOR THE BRIDESMAIDS' HAIR AND MAKEUP?

Q: I'd like my bridesmaids to have updos and am thinking of scheduling all of us at a salon the afternoon of the wedding. It would be a really nice way for us to spend time together before the wedding. I'm just not sure if I should pay for all of them, or if each bridesmaid should pay for her own services.

A: Good question, as there is a lot of gray area here. Usually, bridesmaids take care of their own hair and makeup and it is up to each individual whether she does it herself or goes to a salon. If she chooses the salon, she pays. However, you mention that you would like your bridesmaids to wear a particular hairstyle. This tips the balance in favor of you paying for the salon.

By the way, there's no "rule" that says all your bridesmaids must wear the same hairstyle or even the same dress. Your bridesmaids will want to look their best, and you wouldn't want to insist on a style that makes one of them uncomfortable, so check in well in advance to be sure that everyone is comfortable with your request.

The group outing to the salon for hair, nails, and makeup is increasingly popular, and it's a fun way for the bride and her bridesmaids to be together as "just the girls." But before you pick up the phone and make a booking, think about your bridesmaids' budgets. Dress, alterations, shoes, accessories, travel, shower and wedding gifts can add up to a big number quickly. An updo and makeup plus tip could easily run $100–$150 per person or more. Ask the salon to give you an estimate, then talk to your maid of honor and ask her to poll the bridesmaids. If even one says "Gosh, I'd love to but . . ." then I'd say drop the idea, or if you can afford it, treat them to the salon.

some sense of the formality of the event. Your friend
may accept immediately, but don't push for an instant
reply. Even your closest friend may need a day or two
to consider.

It's a great honor to be asked to be in a wedding,
but people have other obligations and accepting may
not be possible. Don't be offended or expect a detailed
explanation if your invitation is turned down. A refusal
is often based on important family, job, or financial concerns, so be sensitive. Express your disappointment
without any hint of disapproval. Rather than jeopardize
a friendship, assume that the person has made a con-
scientious decision and is doing what he or she thinks
is best for everyone.

Keeping Everyone Up to Speed

From the time your attendants accept your invitation,
it's your responsibility to keep them informed. Communication is essential to a well-planned wedding, and all
the members of your wedding party need updates—
especially about any changes that will affect them.
Maintain regular contact and be particularly attentive
to wedding-party members who live elsewhere. (For
more on emailing and texting with your wedding party,
see also Chapter 4, page 47.) Keeping your attendants
informed helps everyone stay organized. It also allows
members of the wedding party who may not know
each other to become informally acquainted. Share
information, such as:

- A list of names, email addresses, and phone
  numbers of the wedding party

- The dates and times of parties and showers
  attendants will be invited to

- The rehearsal time and place, and directions to the
  location

- Rehearsal dinner arrangements

- Where they will stay

- The dress code for different wedding events

- Reminders to bridesmaids and ushers to break in
  their shoes (!)

- Any plans for breakfast, lunch, or any other get-
  together before or after the wedding

- Where they will dress and receive their bouquets
  and boutonnieres

- The time and place for any prewedding photos

- Transportation arrangements to the ceremony and reception

Attendants' Duties and Financial Responsibilities

In addition to being generally helpful and gracious, attendants have some particular duties and financial responsibilities. Although these duties will vary based on the size and style of the event, there are elements common to most weddings. Here is a list below of the basic duties and financial responsibilities of adult attendants:

- Pay for their wedding attire and any alterations, shoes, hair, makeup, and accessories (excluding flowers).

- Arrange and pay for their own transportation, unless provided by the wedding couple.

ARE ATTENDANTS REQUIRED TO HOST A PARTY FOR THE COUPLE?

Hosting or cohosting a prewedding party, such as a bachelor or bachelorette party or shower, is nice but *by no means mandatory*. The bridesmaids often want to host a shower (and it might make the most sense for them to do so), but they should talk about this collaboratively rather than see it as an obligation. In no way should the couple pressure their respective attendants to host or pay for an event in the couple's honor. (For more on parties hosted by attendants, see Chapter 12, page 141.)

YOUR PRESENCE IS YOUR PRESENT

There's no question that being a bridesmaid or a groomsman can put a dent in one's bank account. When considering all that their attendants contribute in terms of time, talent, and expense, brides and grooms can ease the burden by telling their attendants that their participation in their wedding is their most cherished gift of all and no other gift is necessary. This is completely optional, but if you like the idea it's up to you to tell your bridal party; otherwise, they will either organize a group gift or purchase individual gifts.

- Attend the rehearsal and the rehearsal dinner.

- Attend other prewedding events when possible.

- Give an individual wedding gift to the couple or contribute to a joint gift from all the attendants if being in the wedding is not considered their wedding gift. (See above; and Chapter 13, page 171.)

- Arrive on time for all wedding-related events and follow instructions.

- Understand the specific responsibilities of their particular role.

- Assist the bride and groom with wedding preparations and at the wedding itself.

- Be attentive to other guests at the wedding and reception.

Attendants have a special duty to see that the wedding and the reception run smoothly. They are expected to be gracious and visit with guests, to assist the elderly and anyone else who needs help, to be attentive to young children in the wedding party, to be available for picture taking, and generally to help out whenever needed. If there's a formal receiving line, all bridesmaids may be asked to participate or only the maid/matron of honor.

Specific Attendant Responsibilities

MAID OR MATRON OF HONOR

- Helps the bride select the bridesmaids' attire

- Is available to be the bride's "right hand," helping with communication with other attendants and with wedding professionals if requested

- Helps address invitations and place cards

- Coordinates a shower or bachelorette party if the bridesmaids decide to host one

- Organizes the bridesmaids' gift to the bride (if one is given) and (optionally) the bridesmaids' luncheon or bachelorette party if there is one

- Holds the groom's wedding ring and the bride's bouquet during the ceremony

- Witnesses the signing of the marriage certificate

- Helps the bride during the reception (gathering guests for the cake cutting, dancing, the bouquet toss)

- Helps the bride change into her going-away clothes and takes care of the bride's wedding dress and accessories after the reception

BRIDESMAID

- Attends the rehearsal, rehearsal dinner, and the bridesmaids' luncheon if there is one

- Attends other prewedding parties when possible

- Supervises the children in the wedding party during the ceremony if asked

- Assists the bride at the reception as requested

- Participates in activities such as the receiving line and bouquet toss

- Gives an individual gift to the couple or contributes to a group gift from the bridesmaids or attendants

BEST MAN

- Organizes the bachelor party for the groom if there is one

- Coordinates the groomsmen's gift to the groom (if one is given) or gives an individual gift to the couple

- Makes sure that the groom's wedding-related payments are prepared, and delivers them to officiants, musicians, and singers after the ceremony

- Sees that the groomsmen and ushers are properly groomed and attired and arrive on time

- Instructs the ushers in the correct seating of guests (if there is no head usher)

- Keeps the bride's wedding ring and hands it to the groom during the ceremony

- Witnesses the signing of the marriage certificate

- Drives the bride and groom to the reception if there's no hired driver; has a car ready for the couple to leave after the reception and may drive them to their next destination

- Offers the first toast to the bride and groom at the reception; dances with the bride, the couple's mothers, the maid of honor, the bridesmaids, and single female guests

- Gathers and takes care of the groom's wedding clothes, returning rental items on the next business day

GROOMSMEN AND USHERS

- Attend the rehearsal, rehearsal dinner, and bachelor party if there is one

- Give an individual gift to the couple or contribute to a group gift from the groomsmen/ushers or attendants

- Know the seating order; and review special seating arrangements prior to the ceremony

- Greet guests and escort them to their seats

- Hand each guest a program if programs are provided

- Lay the aisle runner if one is used

- Tidy up after the ceremony: removing pew ribbons, closing windows, and retrieving any programs or articles left behind

- Help guests who need directions to the reception site

- Dance with the bride, the couple's mothers, the maid of honor, the bridesmaids, and single female guests

- Coordinate the return of rental clothing with the best man

Groomsmen stand with the groom during the ceremony. Ushers help prepare the wedding site for the ceremony and escort guests to their seats before the ceremony. Groomsmen may also serve as ushers, and this is fairly common at small- to medium-sized weddings (less than approximately 125 guests).

At large weddings or when the bridegroom has only a best man and perhaps one other attendant, additional ushers are often needed. As a general guideline, plan to have one usher for every fifty guests. When this is the case, these ushers do not join the groomsmen for the ceremony but take seats in the congregation.

An older friend or family member might be asked to serve as head usher. His duties include supervising the ushers, seeing that all preceremony and postceremony tasks are completed, and managing late arrivals. The head usher or best man will instruct the ushers in seating guests and the correct order for seating family members before the processional.

Children as Attendants

Children can add a special charm to a wedding, and many couples ask young helpers such as nieces and nephews to join the bridal party. They'll see your wedding as a huge occasion in their lives, and most take their role as flower girl or ring bearer very seriously. For a child whose parent is marrying for a second time, being included in the wedding can be just the ticket to help them adjust to a new situation.

Whether to include children in the wedding party is a personal decision for the couple. You have no obligation to do so, so don't yield to pressure if you want to limit your attendants just to adults. By their nature, young children are unpredictable. They can be utterly adorable and steal the show, but their charms can wear thin if they become tired or overwhelmed. Consider the time of day that your wedding takes place: Young children may find an evening wedding challenging and preschoolers who miss a nap may not be at their best for an afternoon wedding. No matter how often they've rehearsed their part in the ceremony, younger children may need prompting or a watchful eye. While a bridesmaid may take the little ones under her wing just before and during the ceremony, it's wise to arrange for a parent, babysitter, or another willing volunteer to supervise them afterward.

When you do want to give children a role in your ceremony aim at the older end of the age range. Children of school age are better able to follow instructions and wait patiently during the ceremony than preschoolers. Usually, very young attendants aren't invited to prenuptial parties and events unless their parents are included and other children attend. (See also Chapter 12, page 155.)

JUNIOR BRIDESMAID

Junior bridesmaids are between eight and fourteen years old. They serve as a bridesmaid but they have fewer responsibilities than adult attendants. They attend the rehearsal and, depending on the individual's age and maturity, the rehearsal dinner and other prewedding parties, such as a shower or a bridesmaids' luncheon. Her parents pay for her dress and accessories (excluding flowers). Other than participating in the ceremony, junior bridesmaids have no further obligations, but if asked, they should be in the receiving line. A junior bridesmaid may give a separate gift to the couple, be included in a group gift from the bridesmaids or attendants, or be included in her parents' gift if they are invited.

FLOWER GIRL

Flower girls are usually between the ages of three and seven and are often relatives of the bride or groom. There may be more than one flower girl, and this is a nice way to include children of close friends or relatives.

It is a charming idea to have the bride walk to the altar on rose petals, so the flower girl precedes the bride down the aisle carrying a basket of petals, which she scatters before the bride. However, real rose petals can be slippery when stepped on, and some venues don't want the trouble of cleaning up paper or silk petals. When this is the case, the flower girl can carry a tiny nosegay of flowers similar to those carried by the bridesmaids or a small basket of flowers.

During the ceremony, the flower girl stands with the bridesmaids or sits with her parents in the congregation. In the recessional, the flower girl walks with the ring bearer (if there is one), directly behind the couple.

A flower girl's parents pay for her dress and accessories (excluding flowers). She attends the rehearsal and is invited with her parents to the rehearsal dinner.

RING BEARER

The ring bearer, a three- to seven-year-old boy, walks down the aisle before the flower girl and carries the wedding rings on a small cushion, often pinned to prevent them from slipping off. (If there's worry that the rings could get lost, the best man holds the actual rings and the ring bearer carries token rings.) He stands with the groomsmen or may sit with his parents or other adults during the service.

In the processional, the ring bearer usually enters after the maid or matron of honor, and is followed by the flower girl. But a very young boy and girl may enter together. The children exit together immediately after the bride and groom, but if a child has fallen asleep, has wandered back to his parents, or is in any way reluctant, it's fine to dispense with the recessional walk. His parents purchase his outfit; he attends the rehearsal and is invited with his parents to the rehearsal dinner.

WHAT TO DO IF AN ATTENDANT BACKS OUT

Q: One of my attendants had to back out of my wedding because of her job. I'm getting married in less than three weeks! Should I try to find a replacement?

A: At three weeks out it wouldn't be a good idea to ask someone else to fill in at the last minute—it carries the obvious whiff of second choice. Think, too, of what you would be asking your new bridesmaid to do: rearrange her schedule and possibly her travel plans for your wedding, purchase clothing and accessories, get up to speed with the other bridesmaids. It's a lot to ask, even of a friend. If you're worried that you won't have an even number of bridesmaids and groomsmen, don't be. There's no need for them to pair up, and no one need know that you're a bridesmaid short. If her name is listed in the program and it's already been printed, don't worry about it. After all, she was part of your original team and will be with you in spirit.

If this had happened earlier in your planning, it would have been fine to ask another friend or relative to be your attendant. There would have been plenty of time to make arrangements and order clothes, and the invitation wouldn't seem forced or last minute.

TRAIN BEARERS AND PAGES

These young attendants hold and carry the bride's train and may assist with arranging it when she reaches the altar. They are rarely included except in the most elaborate formal, state, or royal weddings.

SPECIAL HONOREES

Some couples ask close family members and friends to assist at the wedding and the reception. Though not strictly members of the wedding party, these honorees may hand out programs or oversee the signing of a guest book, or perform special functions such as participating in the ceremony as readers, soloists, cantors, or altar assistants. At a home or church reception, their duties, or "honor roles," might include serving cake, pouring tea and coffee, and greeting guests. These honorees are usually given corsages and boutonnieres in the wedding colors. They are included in some wedding photographs, and their names and responsibilities are often listed in ceremony programs. It's nice to thank them with gifts, such as framed wedding photos, and notes of appreciation.

CHAPTER 7

CREATING YOUR GUEST LIST

Lists become second nature to brides—highly organized lists of gifts, quickly jotted lists of favorite flowers, carefully scheduled lists of planning appointments, and all sorts of to-do lists that somehow never seem to be complete. But there is one list that tops them all: the guest list for your wedding. For some couples, it's a breeze to piece this list together. For others, it's a struggle to find the right balance between inclusion and intimacy, new friends and old, budget and blowout. And that's before moms and dads toss in their two cents—and their two hundred guests. At heart, the guest list is a snapshot of all the special people in your life and it is well worth the care and effort it takes to create.

Creating the Guest List

As you build your list, you need to know how large it can be. The ideal guest list consists of a magical number of family and friends that:

❧ Suits the size of your ceremony and reception sites.

❧ Corresponds with the level of intimacy you would like your wedding to have.

❧ Can be accommodated within your wedding budget—an important reality.

Be on the lookout for factors that limit or define the "magic number." Are these factors consistent with the wedding you want? It might not make sense to book a reception location that seats 250 if your guest list is only 75. If you're dreaming of a formal five-course meal but have a limited budget, you'll have to plan on a fairly small guest list.

You'll soon see that your budget and the size of the guest list are symbiotic. For most couples, the budget will be the prime factor affecting the number of guests who can be invited. As food and drink can account for as much as 45–50 percent of the reception budget, limiting the guest list is one of the smartest ways to keep the budget under control. (See Chapter 3, page 29.)

Establish Neutral Dividing Lines

While there has never been any official rule about how to divvy up the guest list, traditionally each family was allotted half of the total guest count, and parents' guests often outnumbered the couples'. Today, the pie may be sliced quite differently. Remember that as you build the guest list, the couple and their respective parents will need to work together, with no one group trumping another. Here are two popular ways to start the process:

- ❧ Divide the list into equal thirds with the couple, the bride's parents, and the groom's parents each inviting one third of the guests.

- ❧ The bride and groom reserve half the list for themselves, with the other half divided equally between their parents.

Of course these are just two ideas for how to go about it. If the bride and groom are hosting the wedding themselves, their list may far outweigh those of their parents. Or if the groom's family consists of an uncle, aunt, and two cousins and the bride's is what could only be called a clan, an equal division isn't a practical solution. These suggestions are only guidelines—tested to be sure—so develop your list in a way that makes sense for your wedding and your family and friends. For example, your "magic number" may be 125, with 75 guests allotted to you and your fiancé and 25 to each set of parents.

Whatever numbers you choose, aim for neutral dividing lines and allocations that suit your situation. When set in place before the fate of any one guest is up for debate, these parameters can keep the elimination process from getting too challenging or personal.

GUEST LIST SURVIVAL GUIDE

Here are some big picture thoughts that might help you navigate the process of creating your guest list.

Realize that you have choices to make. Some will be easier than others, but in the end, you, your fiancé(e) and your parents (or any other wedding hosts) need to be in accord. Work on ways to prioritize your lists and use logical guidelines when making decisions.

Aim for harmony. When you disagree on a potential guest, think carefully before insisting that someone stay on the list or go. Here's a time to look at the big picture, and pick your battles. If your parents or fiancé(e) seem truly committed to someone you don't really know or you aren't a fan of, go for maintaining harmony.

Remember: It's your wedding. On the other hand, don't automatically agree that cousins you've never met or Mom's office colleagues take precedence over your own good friends. Many couples use "only people we have met" as a primary guest list criterion.

In for a penny, in for a pound. Unless it's the custom in your culture or congregation, inviting a large number of guests to the ceremony but only a small number to the reception is no solution at all. It would be insulting to send a formal ceremony invitation to many and a reception invitation to a favored few.

Once each group has completed their list, combine them, check for duplicates, cross your fingers and hope that your guest total is close to your target num-

Generally, guests for prewedding parties, such as an engagement party, shower, or rehearsal dinner are drawn from the master wedding guest list. Sometimes an engagement party or shower might be hosted before that list is finalized. If that's the case, make sure that these guests are also on your wedding invitation list. Under most circumstances, anyone invited to one of these parties should also receive a wedding invitation. There are a few exceptions, such as a shower hosted by coworkers, or a special gathering of your parents' hometown friends who would love to be a part of the festivities, but wouldn't be able to travel to the wedding. Still, it's wise for the couple to review guest lists for these parties with the hosts to avoid a potentially awkward situation later. (This is one reason surprise showers aren't a good idea—surprise, these guests are all now also wedding guests!)

ber. If it's not, tweak from there. This will be the basis of your master list.

The Must List

In addition to those nearest and dearest to you, there are some "hidden" guests who, out of courtesy, must also be added to your list.

- ❖ The spouse, fiancé(e), or live-in partner of each invited guest—even if you've never met or they are not your favorite people. Your guest is part of a package deal.

- ❖ The person who performs the ceremony and his or her spouse or significant other.

- ❖ The parents of ring bearers and flower girls, and of junior bridesmaids and ushers, if these younger attendants are too young to attend on their own.

Start thinking about whether to allow single guests to bring a date or guest. It's a nice thing to do if your budget and head count allow, but you're not obligated to invite "plus-ones." Many a romance has blossomed when two singles met at a wedding. Save this decision until you have your core list solidified. One or two single guests with a plus-one likely won't break the bank, but twenty might. (See also page 88.)

Categorizing the Guest List

It is helpful to have those who made the lists categorize them for you, as you may not be aware of all the relationship nuances between hosts and prospective guests. While it may not solve every "to invite or not to invite" dilemma, having clear distinctions will help keep tough choices to a minimum if (and likely when) the guest list requires a trim. As most couples want to guarantee that closest family and friends are on the list, ask each family to identify their lists in the following way:

First tier: immediate family (parents, siblings, grandparents, the couple's own children)

Second tier: extended family members (aunts, uncles, cousins, nieces, nephews)

Third tier: family friends (parents' close friends; longtime friends and neighbors; childhood friends and their parents, if close to you; longtime household employees)

Fourth tier: bride and groom's friends, broken into subgroups (childhood friends, high school and college friends, mentors, work friends, new friends)

Fifth tier: parents' or couple's colleagues (associates, employers, employees)

Of course, these guidelines should be based on what makes sense in your case, and any plan can be adapted to your situation. For example, the bride and groom's friends might take priority over parents' friends and be the third or, in the case of a small wedding, even the second tier. The point is to devise a method that helps you to prioritize and make decisions.

Counting on Regrets

Some wedding industry experts predict that 15–20 percent of invited guests send regrets, but most people are more comfortable estimating a 10 percent margin. That means if your magic guest number is 150, you can invite an additional 15 guests for a total of 165. Prior commitments, illness, and unseen circumstances will likely prevent more people from attending than you expect. Talk to your reception site manager to ensure that a few additional guests can be accommodated if more than 150 actually accept. This approach is far better than creating A and B lists of guests, the B-list invitations being those that are sent only after those on the

---

WHAT'S THE ETIQUETTE OF A STANDBY GUEST LIST?

Q: My future mother-in-law says it's appropriate to have a standby guest list ready when guests from the main list decline. Is this proper?

A: While not "improper," a standby guest list is a very risky proposition. If a guest perceives even a hint of B-list status it can cause hurt feelings and destroy friendships. It may seem that a standby list does provide a practical solution to controlling the numbers and budget, but we are hesitant to encourage you to go this route.

It's far better to invite your entire guest list from the start. You can always choose a simpler or less expensive menu or venue to accommodate all the guests you wish to invite. When the guest list is carefully planned, and when you consider the likelihood that typically 10–20 percent of invited guests send regrets—this approach is more straightforward and less deceptive than employing a standby list.

If, despite your best efforts to avoid it, you and your fiancé decide to take the standby list approach, be very discreet. Your standby list is for your eyes only. Guests must not have even the slightest idea that they are your second choice. For example, don't gush, "Oh, I was hoping I would be able to invite you and now that we have extra room, I can!" Keep the alternate list small and put people in logical categories. For example, "first cousins" could move or stay as an entire group.

Try to send secondary invitations within a week or two of the original invitation. This may mean mailing your original invitations two to three weeks earlier than planned. A last-minute invitation or one that comes with a tight RSVP date is a sure sign that the invitee was an afterthought.

A list send regrets. The potential for people discovering this and feeling hurt is too great.

Trimming an Overambitious Guest List

You've combined your lists, crossed off the duplicates, and . . . your guest list is worthy of a royal wedding! At this point, you can say, "These are our nearest and dearest and we can't imagine getting married without them," in which case, unless you have a royal budget, you'll need to rethink your reception plans. Cake and punch is a fine wedding tradition, as any Jane Austen fan will testify, but most couples opt to trim the list.

When it's time to prune, eliminating a whole group—high school friends, second cousins, work colleagues—is the most neutral option and keeps any explanations from becoming personal. Saying to a colleague "I'm not able to invite work friends" is a lot easier to swallow than "I had to cut *you*." Here are some suggestions for thoughtful ways to pare down your list:

Make across-the-board, clear-cut distinctions. To avoid hurt feelings, subdivide the groupings across the board. For example, if numbers are limited, you could invite all aunts and uncles and forgo cousins. Then stick to or eliminate the same categories across all the lists. It's far easier to say "No cousins" than to invite some cousins and not others in a way that seems arbitrary and could potentially lead to hurt feelings.

Leave out work associates—all or some. When space is absolutely at a premium, some couples skip work associates entirely. This can reduce the list considerably while also keeping the wedding more personal. Or perhaps you invite only your boss and your respective assistants, or just your immediate team. Your other coworkers will clearly understand that you had to make a cutoff.

Beware parental paybacks. This is not the time for parents to insist on reciprocity for all the gifts they've given and weddings they've attended in the past, nor does your wedding need to be the occasion for them to fulfill their own social obligations.

Beware parental pay-fors. Sometimes parents who are unwilling to cut their guest list offer to pay for their extra guests. As a couple, decide how you would like to handle this possibility before it arises. Even with financial help, not all couples want a larger wedding. Think, too, about what this may mean if applied to potential guests you would prefer not to have at your wedding.

Special Guests and Situations

Your guest list is coming together. Now it's time to address some of the stickier issues and round out the list. Inevitably the question of inviting children and plus-ones—guests of guests—will come up. Also, there are some considerations to weigh before you finalize your guest list for a destination wedding or encore wedding.

Inviting Children

One of the most hotly debated issues when planning a wedding is whether or not to invite children. From an etiquette point of view, whatever you as a couple decide is fine. Some people can't imagine a wedding celebration without children, from infants to teens. Others feel that having children at a wedding, other than a flower girl or a ring bearer, can be a distraction for guests intent on participating in and honoring a very grown-up ritual. If you already have children, it's likely they will be participating in or attending your wedding. It's a nice idea if you can invite a few of their friends as well.

In families with dozens of cousins, nieces, and nephews, the extended family may feel strongly that children be included, but the costs of inviting them all may be prohibitive. One option is to set an age limit— inviting children ten and older, for example. Other ideas include inviting only the children of close family members, such as siblings, and/or children of the wedding party. Either way, once you've made your decision, make no exceptions, since doing so can cause more hurt feelings than standing firm. (For more on how to invite children, see Chapter 10, page 124.)

Inviting Plus-Ones

The classic wedding of old was seen as a prime opportunity for singles to meet. After all, if you were a friend of the bride or groom, chances were pretty good that you might find a soul mate from among their friends. Plenty of romances that started at a wedding ended up at the altar. Today's etiquette says that you should invite the spouse, partner, fiancé(e), or significant other of any guest in a serious or exclusive relationship, even if you don't know or care for this person. After that, it's up to the hosts to decide if singles may have the option of inviting a guest.

Some of the plus-one considerations involve deciding just how many your budget can handle. It's hard to give some singles a plus-one and not others unless you have some sort of clear criteria, such as giving the option only to your single attendants. Otherwise, unless you let all your single guests bring a guest, you can risk hurt feelings.

When you offer a guest a plus-one, it doesn't mean that he or she must bring a romantic date. Your guest might bring a friend of either gender or a sibling. If your guest doesn't list his or her plus-one's name on the reply card, give a call to find it out. You'll want this information for seating charts, place cards, and to greet your guest personally. (For more on how to invite plus-ones, see Chapter 10, page 123.)

Destination Wedding Guests

A destination wedding requires that you establish your guest list very early in your planning. Because you are choosing to marry in a place to which guests will have to travel, the sooner you can share your plans with them, the better. A telephone call, an email, or a "save the date" notice is all your guests need to begin planning; you can wait to send the printed invitation closer to the date. A long lead time allows guests to get better deals on transportation, to arrange for time off from work, or perhaps even plan a family vacation around the wedding. So guests have an idea about cost, include or send information on the resort or other area accommodations.

Because it can be more difficult and costly for people to attend a destination wedding, your guest list will likely be limited to immediate family and closest friends. Even then, some may not be able to attend. Here's a case where you want to think carefully about who receives invitations. For example, there may be no way your eighty-nine-year-old grandparents would be able to make the trip to Bali, but as your grandparents they should receive an invitation anyway.

Another matter you and your fiancé should discuss before issuing any invitation or save-the-date notice is how you will handle travel and lodging costs for attendants or guests. Typically, you would pay for lodging, but not transportation, for the bridal party. But if your maid of honor or a close friend or relative truly can't afford the trip, would you be willing to pay for some or all of their travel costs? The answer may be no, which is okay, but it means you may be disappointed that a favorite person won't be at your wedding.

Encore Wedding Guests

Many brides marrying for a second (or even third) time ask, "Should the guest list for an encore wedding be kept small?" Not necessarily. It's fine to have a big wedding if that's what you would like. Some encore couples prefer to limit the guest list at the ceremony and reception to close family and friends and enjoy a later, larger get-together with their wider circle of friends. As a general guideline, invite those you couldn't imagine getting married without.

Guests with Whom You're on the Outs

Good friends and relatives don't always see eye-to-eye all of the time. Even though your relationship will last a lifetime, it can be tricky if you're on the outs with a good friend or relative at the time your wedding rolls around. The toughest of these scenarios is when a parent or sibling isn't on speaking terms with the bride or groom. Weddings and holidays are precedent-setting events. Opting for exclusion can calcify the situation, making it harder to extend an olive branch in the future. But, from a position of anger and hurt, it's so easy to say, "Well, if that's the way it is, then I don't want you at my wedding."

That truly may be the case, and of course you wouldn't want someone who wishes you ill or who might bring his or her anger to take away from the joy of your wedding day. Still, keep the long term in mind and don't be the one to slam the door. Do what you can to try to patch things up before the wedding. Then take the high road and leave the door to your relationship open. Send an invitation or, at the very least, make sure that the person knows where and when your wedding will take place and that you hope that he or she will attend.

Guests Who Can't Attend

Apply careful thought. In most cases, invitations aren't sent to those friends and acquaintances you know won't be able to attend the celebration. Since an invitation to a wedding carries an obligation to send a gift, inviting someone who can't possibly attend makes it look as if you are inviting those friends in order to receive one. Also, people with whom your only communication for the past several years has been Facebook updates or holiday cards at the most are generally not included on the invitation list either. Any of the above could receive a wedding announcement sent after the wedding, which carries no gift obligation whatsoever (see Chapter 11, page 135).

There is a flip side to this dilemma. Some good friends or family members who live far away might actually be hurt if you don't send invitations, even if your intent was to spare them from feeling obliged to send a gift for a wedding so far away. If a friend informs you of a conflict after receiving the save-the-date notice, you can always invite him and let him know you wanted him to have the invitation but don't want him to feel pressured to give a gift. This makes the gesture about honoring the relationship and in no way confuses a desire for gifts as the motive. In general, always invite truly good friends—even if they live far away.

Organizing a Carefully Planned Master Guest List

A beautifully organized and orchestrated wedding, most brides will tell you, is the happy result of single-minded attention to lists. The master guest list—the finalized combination of everyone's lists—is one of the most important documents of your wedding planning. You will depend on this list as the weeks go by—to address invitations; determine who needs maps and directions, who gets a save the date and

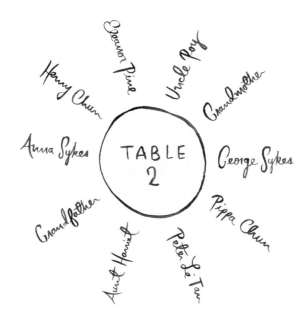

who will get wedding announcements; check off acceptances and regrets; note the names of single guest's plus-ones; and record gifts received and thank-you notes written. You will also use this list to count heads, create seating charts and even print place cards. Most likely, you will keep this list on your computer, as a database or as a subset of your address book. The master guest list is the foundation of your wedding plans. A savvy guest list includes not just names but also:

Contact information. Each guest's full name, address, phone number, and email. A "Note" field is useful for including information such as the guest's relationship to the bride or groom: Mike's aunt (mother's sister), Abby's senior year roommate from LSU, Mike's boss.

RSVPs. A space to indicate acceptances and regrets as well as how many members of the family or party will attend and to add the name of a guest's spouse, fiancé(e), or date so you can personalize their table assignment or place card.

Gifts. A description of any gift received, the date you received it, the registry or store it came from, and the date a thank-you note was sent.

Out-of-towners. Indicate if the guest is coming from out of town, so that you can send information on lodging and directions and invite him or her to any parties being thrown for out-of-town guests.

Extra information: Note special needs, such as food allergies or required access for those with disabilities, which will be helpful to know as you choose the ceremony and reception sites and plan your reception menu.

Dealing with Guest Dilemmas

As tricky as it can be to craft your guest list, you will need to use tact and diplomacy to deal with sticky guest situations after you mail your invitations, too. Here are some common dilemmas and suggestions for dealing with them:

It's three weeks before the wedding and I haven't heard from a number of our guests. Pick up your phone pronto! It's perfectly okay to call and ask (politely, of course) each tardy guest for a reply: "We hope you received our wedding invitation for the 24th and that you can join us." If you get voice mail, add a time by which you need to hear back. No matter what reply method you requested on your invitation, or how simple you tried to make it for guests to respond, failure to RSVP is epidemic. As annoying as it is, resist the urge to chew out the invitee—nothing will be gained. Stay focused on your goal: You want this guest at your wedding. So be as gracious as you can and consider this part and parcel of normal wedding planning.

A couple just replied and noted that they are bringing their child and au pair, neither of whom we invited. This couple may not be the last to respond that they're bringing the kids, so it's good to work out a script to cover this eventuality. Your goal is to clear things up firmly and quickly, as the longer you wait, the more awkward the situation becomes. You, or the wedding hosts, should speak to the couple personally—this conversation is too sensitive for email. Make a big effort to overlook their cluelessness. In a calm, friendly tone, stick to the facts: "We're delighted you can join us at our wedding, but there seems to be a mixup since your response card includes the names of your daughter and au pair. We're sorry we can't accommodate any extras—our guest list is very tight. We hope you and Jeff understand and can still attend."

Be prepared for any possible reply. They might graciously accept the reality (phew!) or they might become huffy and even try to bully you into inviting their child. Take a deep breath, and continue: "I know Suzie is a peach, but we can't make an exception. It wouldn't be fair to other guests who also have kids." It's important on your end not to make any exceptions for exactly this reason. Some may take the ultimate umbrage and threaten not to come at all. So be it—the rudeness is theirs, not yours. "Sorry it doesn't work for you; I know it can be hard to leave one's kids at home."

A single friend replied that he's bringing an uninvited plus-one. This one can be tough to deal with as well. See if you can get a little background info through a mutual friend. "Is Mark in a serious relationship?" If he is, you might try to accommodate his guest, even though he was wrong to include her. Usually, you invite people in a serious relationship as a couple. When it's news to you that a guest is now in that relationship, do what you can to include his or her partner. If that's not the case, and you really don't have the room, call him and have a conversation: "Mark, I'm so glad you can come to our wedding, but I'm afraid our list is tight and as much as we would have loved to give all our single friends a plus-one, we just couldn't." Use an approach similar to the one above in the extra child situation.

A guest calls and changes a no to a yes at the last minute. Just when you had your guest list finalized! Do your best to accommodate your guest—after all,

he was on your list. Most caterers keep the head count open up to seventy-two hours ahead of the event. Even if the list is closed, adding one more guest probably isn't a big deal. If there's absolutely no way he, or a couple, can fit, then do your best to let him know gently: "Oh, Sam, what rotten timing. We would love to have you with us, but I'm afraid the caterer has closed the list. I'll give you a call soon after the wedding so we can get together."

A guest responds with a note, "BTW, I'm a vegan." You don't have to create a special meal, but check in with the caterer to see what menu items will be suitable, or if any simple adaptations can be made—say, using vegetable instead of chicken broth. I wouldn't worry too much about it. People on restrictive diets know how to work their way around a meal or buffet that wasn't planned with their needs in mind. You can always give your friend a heads-up about your planned menu.

An uninvited guest shows up at the wedding. Ah, the wedding crasher. Don't let it ruin your day. Have a plan in mind for handling this situation well before your wedding so you don't have to expend any mental energy dealing with it. Assign a groomsman and instruct him on how to proceed. When the crasher is someone you know, options include trying to make accommodations or politely asking the person to leave—trickier because it could cause a scene. If the crasher is a complete stranger, the groomsman should contact the venue manager who should be able to have the person removed, hopefully without much fuss.

PART THREE

INVITATIONS AND STATIONERY

CHAPTER 8

WEDDING INVITATIONS

Sitting on each of our desks is a pile of all the wedding invitations we've ever received. They are beautiful reminders of friends whose lives we are honored to be a part of, as well as keepsakes from the terrific weddings we've attended. We are struck by how unique each invitation is and how much each one reflects the personality of the couple. Many are heavy with the weight of fine paper and assorted enclosures; some have ribbons, appliqués, or stunning envelope liners. All of them display the great thought and care that went into their selection.

Invitations should convey a sense of what the event will be like, and they reflect the couple's style and personality as well. Your invitation is the first glimpse your guests receive of the style and tone of your journey to the altar.

Recent years have seen a dramatic shift in the interest for unique and stylish wedding invitations. Modern invitations, with exotic typefaces, colors, and designs are a beautiful way to proclaim both the occasion and your style. Tradition holds strong, too, with classic, formally worded invitations engraved on heavyweight cream paper finding their way to mailboxes across the country. The special world of wedding stationery is waiting for you to explore.

Not only will you be designing your invitation, you'll also be choosing a wardrobe of stationery, which might include thank-you notes, save-the-date cards, announcements, and place cards (see Chapter 11, page 131) and invitation enclosures such as reply cards or pew cards (see Chapter 10, page 121). You'll spend a good deal of time getting the wording of your invitation just right, and you'll find wording for almost every situation covered in Chapter 9, page 107. And what about the envelopes? Chapter 10 will guide you through the process from addressing to assembling.

In this chapter we'll look at types of paper, invitation styles, and printing methods. But let's start with timing!

Timing for Ordering and Mailing

The timeline for selecting, ordering, addressing, and mailing your wedding invitation is carefully coordinated counting backward from the date of your wedding—a formula that may sound easy at first but can quickly seem more complex than theoretical physics. Not to worry, once you've established a schedule, it's just a matter of sticking to it. To start:

❖ Set your wedding date.

❖ Plan to mail your invitations about eight weeks (never less than six weeks at a minimum) before the wedding. You want to give guests enough time to respond, but you'll want those responses early enough to chase down any negligent guests and to give vendors a final head count.

❖ Schedule at least two weeks to address and assemble your invitations once you receive your order. If possible, add a few "just in case" days into your ordering and addressing schedule—just in case something unexpected delays your preparations. Count back *at least* two weeks from mailing day—more if you think necessary for contingencies—as this is when you want your order to arrive.

You might want to have your envelopes arrive well ahead of the rest of your order so that you or your calligrapher will have plenty of time to hand address them. (See Chapter 10, page 122.) Once the envelopes are addressed, this step becomes a question of how much time you would like to have to stuff and mail the invitations.

❖ To place your invitation order in time, count backward two to three months from the date that you want to start assembling and addressing your invitations. Plan on at least two to three months for printing and delivery of engraved invitations, enclosures, and envelopes. The wait may be less for nontraditional invitations—three to six weeks—but ask your stationer or supplier to be sure. The turnaround for flat or laser printing may be a week or less.

❖ It's important to see a proof of your invitation. This will add time to the ordering process (depending on the vendor you work with, this could be as fast as forty-eight hours or as long as another week or two), but you want to be sure that your invitation is letter perfect. Mistakes can happen—misspelled names, correct day but incorrect date—even with the most experienced stationers. Count back two days to two weeks from your order date; this is the date you want to have your final invitation selection and wording ready to submit.

❖ Plan for time to visit different stationers and review design and wording options. This step will vary in terms of timing; just don't expect to walk in and take care of everything in one visit.

So, if we do the math, from selection day to wedding day can be anywhere from twelve to twenty-four weeks or 3 to 5½ months! (These scheduled deadlines are the perfect use for electronic calendar reminders.) Now add in time to explore your design options and you can see that six months before the wedding is not too early to get started. Even if you decide to laser-print or handwrite your invitations, you'll still need time to select attractive papers and envelopes and to develop your design.

Does that mean that you can't have a beautiful invitation if you have a short engagement? Not at all, and a good stationer will steer you in the direction of options that fit your time frame. A local printer or online vendor may be able to turn a job around in less than a week, but beware that jobs like these may incur a rush charge, and that not all printing options, such as engraving, may be available to you.

SAMPLE TIMELINE FOR MAILING INVITATIONS
8 WEEKS BEFORE THE WEDDING DATE

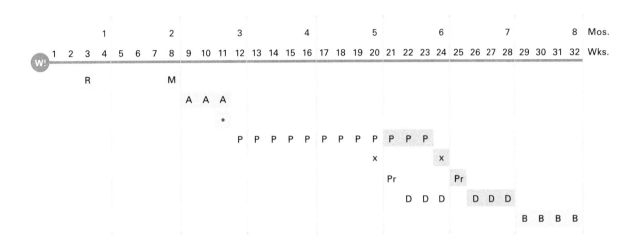

| | | | | | | | | | | 1 | | | | 2 | | | | 3 | | | | 4 | | | | 5 | | | | 6 | | | | 7 | | | | 8 | Mos. |

Plan on:

	W!	Wedding Day!
3 weeks out	R	RSVP by date
8 weeks out	M	mail invitations
2–3 weeks	A	address invitations
	*	invitations arrive
3-month turnaround	P	printing 3 months
2-month turnaround	P	printing 2 months
	x	invitation order date
1 week	Pr	proofing
3 weeks	D	design/wording
2–4 weeks	B	browsing/choosing

Use the *Plan on* guidelines above to create your own timetable to match your invitation mailing date.

How Many to Order

Now's the time to pull up your guest list spreadsheet and add in a column labeled "# of invites." Here's how to figure how many you'll need:

❖ Married couples, or couples living at the same address receive one invitation.

❖ Single guests each receive their own invitations.

❖ Family units—parent(s) and child(ren)—receive one invitation. However, teens should receive their own

---

WEDDING E-VITATIONS

They sound so practical, thrifty, and green—and they are. If those were the only criteria for sending electronic wedding invitations, they would be used by more couples and recommended by more wedding planners. We don't recommend them for the following reasons:

❖ **Email isn't personal or special.** A wedding invitation is one of the most personal invitations issued, and an electronic version may not convey that sentiment. Its ephemeral nature doesn't give it keepsake status.

❖ **Not everyone uses email or checks it regularly.** This may not be true for your peers, but perhaps it's the case for your great-aunt Sadie. Some services also require Internet access to view and respond to the invitation. You may end up having to print some invitations and mail them, which could cut down on the convenience factor.

❖ **It may not get delivered.** While posted snail mail has been known to go astray, emails can fall victim to misspelled addresses and spam blockers.

❖ **It does not facilitate or guarantee an RSVP.** The good guest will respond right away, no matter how the invitation is issued. But for the rest of the world, unless you set up reminders (and don't set them for two days before the wedding!), once the email notice falls below the screen it may be out of sight, out of mind. Follow-up phone calls are likely.

E-vitations can be whimsical and fun, and could suit an occasion with a smaller, more homogeneous guest list, such as a bachelorette party or shower. Even then, consider the above criteria before opting for an electronic invitation.

invitations. Usually, the cut-off age is thirteen, but it's fine to raise it if it makes sense for the families you are inviting to receive just one invitation. By eighteen, though, individual invitations are the way to go, even if the young adult is still living at home.

- Plus-ones are usually included with the invitation to the guest you know.

- If you have a B list (see Chapter 7, page 86), you will need to order an invitation for each individual or household on the list.

- Add in extra invitations for keepsakes, and definitely order one to two dozen extra envelopes in case of addressing mistakes.

The Wonderful World of Wedding Invitations

These days, the range of invitations is practically infinite. Shop around before making a final decision. Local stationers have a wealth of sample books and catalogs on hand. These run from the traditional engraved invitation on heavy cream-colored stock to creative letterpress and modern, colorful designs from boutique studios. They are a great place to browse and most offer personal design services, guiding you

through selection and wording, and overseeing the order through to delivery.

You can also visit the websites of many wedding stationery companies and download brochures. You can shop for and complete your entire order online, or do your browsing and then place your order through a local store.

The Key Design Elements of a Wedding Invitation

The most important elements to consider when choosing invitations are paper size, shape, weight, type (what it's made of), and color as well as typeface and ink color. The printing method you choose is important to the look of the invitation and may guide some of these decisions. It will also affect your budget. Together, these elements determine the overall look and feel of your invitation.

Size and shape. While the traditional wedding invitation used to be a 5½-by-7½ portrait rectangle, modern styles include landscape rectangles and squares.

- **Folded sheet:** Also called a wedding sheet, this is an 11-by-7½-inch sheet folded on the left edge to 5½ by 7½. This is the classic, formal invitation. The invitation is printed on the top sheet; nothing is printed inside.

- **Flat card:** The flat card is made of heavier card stock and is usually 5½ by 7½ inches, printed either portrait or landscaped. This is usually the most economical choice, and is less expensive than the folded wedding sheet. Larger 6³⁄₁₆-by-8⅞-inch cards are also available. While their weight makes them an excellent choice for formal invitations, choosing a

colored card stock transforms them into a fun, modern variation.

- **Square card:** Made of card stock, usually 5 by 5 or 6¾ by 6¾ inches, square cards have a truly modern look and feel. Mailing costs may be higher because the USPS charges more for nonstandard-sized mail.

- **Trifold:** Another modern addition to the wedding invitation family, these combine invitation, pocket for enclosures, and envelope all in one.

Color. The classic paper shades for the most formal and traditional wedding invitations are ivory, soft cream, and white. Modern invitations might use a colored paper chosen to complement colors featured in the wedding. Just be sure there is enough contrast between ink and paper color so the invitation is easily readable.

Paper. The heaviest-weight paper in these shades may cost a bit more, but its appearance and feel are substantial and bespeak formality. More important is to choose a paper that complements the printing style. You may want your paper flat or prefer a raised plate mark or margin.

Typeface. After choosing paper shade and weight, you should select a typeface. For formal invitations, shaded and antique roman faces are traditional choices. Simple styles are easier to read than ornate scripts, though scripted typefaces can add elegance and romance. Some couples opt for a more formal typeface for their invitation and response card, and use a simpler, complementary font for enclosures, programs, and table or place cards. Make sure the first letters of your names look good and are readable. In some typefaces the letter *T* can look like a *J* or an *I*, for example.

Ink color. While black is the classic choice for formal invitations, use any color in the rainbow if it pleases you. To make sure that the ink shows well against the paper, ask for a proof. What looks terrific on a computer screen doesn't always translate well to actual ink on paper. Be especially conscious of this when using paper or ink that has a shimmer or sheen to it.

Designs, borders, backings, die cuts, fold-overs, and bows. Once you've made the basic decisions about paper, format, color, and font, you can add flourishes to complete your design. The choices are endless: colored or raised borders, colored or patterned backing sheets, vellum and die or laser-cut overlays, fold-over elements, ribbons, bows, duograms (the couple's first name initials), or a single decorative element. If your wedding has a theme, you can start out by applying it to your invitations: a scallop shell motif for a Cape Cod wedding or a mistletoe sprig for a Christmas wedding. Some couples choose their first name initials combined into a duogram, or their names are featured as part of the design. A truly formal invitation has no ornamentation except for a family crest if the bride's family has one. If that's the case, it may be blind embossed at the top center of the invitation.

Envelopes. You can complete a classic look by choosing plain cream or white inner and outer envelopes. Colored envelopes make sense to complement and pull together more contemporary invitations. There are also limitless envelope liner choices, from colors and patterns to metallic or textured papers. (Just bear in mind that this is a fleeting experience for guests; if you're on a tight budget, you might omit the liner and let your money have more impact elsewhere. (For more on envelopes, see Chapter 10, page 121.)

Printing Options

In general, the more formal the wedding, the more formal the printing style. The joy of creating modern invitations is that couples aren't limited just to engraving, and there are techniques from the popular letterpress to thermography and laser printing to suit every style and budget. The quality of any printing is directly related to the quality of the paper, so it's smart to work with an experienced stationer or printer to put together the right combination.

Engraving. Engraved invitations are the most traditional printing style for formal invitations. It is a centuries-old technique and begins with making a copper plate of the invitation, etching the words in reverse. The plate is inked and pressed onto the paper, one at a time, resulting in raised letters on the front, and an indentation or "bruise" on the back. It is expensive and time-consuming—creating the plate, proofs, and final printing can take up to eight weeks. Still, the results are elegant and timeless. Using colored ink or paper is one way to achieve a softer, more modern look while still being formal. Cotton paper, because of its softness

---

THE CLASSIC
WEDDING INVITATION

The iconic formal wedding invitation is engraved on ivory, soft cream, or white stock, usually 5½ by 7½ inches, either as a flat single card on heavy stock or a wedding sheet that folds on the left and opens like a book, with the text on the outside right-hand side. The ink is black and the lettering is classic and conservative, such as a Roman serif, Copperplate, or Bank script.

and absorptive qualities, gives the best results. Most engraved invitations need to be booked through a stationer or directly with a stationery supplier.

Letterpress. Letterpress uses raised type or designs on wooden or plastic blocks to press ink into the surface of the paper, leaving an indentation. Letterpress can be as expensive and time-consuming as engraving. This old-fashioned printing method (it's the same movable type invented by Johannes Gutenberg) is enjoying a fashionable comeback. Cotton paper is also a good choice for letterpress printing,

Thermography. Less expensive than engraving, thermography uses heat to affix ink to the page. The lettering is raised above the paper. The results are similar to engraving except that there is no indentation on the back of the paper. Turnaround time is much less than for engraving or letterpress.

Lithography. Also called flat printing, lithography applies ink directly and flatly to the paper. It's what most print shops use today and results in a crisp look. It is less costly than engraving, letterpress, or thermography.

Laser. Good laser printing looks similar to lithography. It's the least expensive option, has the fastest turnaround time, and is well suited for less formal invitations and peripheral enclosures. Blank invitation forms are available online, at print shops, stationers, and at office supply stores.

SOME INVITATION TIPS

Here are some good ideas that can help the invitation process proceed smoothly:

- Order extras both as keepsakes and in case of damage (think spilled coffee!). At the very least, order extra envelopes.

- Make sure that your supplier can deliver invitation envelopes to you as early as possible, so you can get a head start addressing them.

- Allow plenty of time to address, assemble, and mail the invitations, whether you do this yourself or hire a calligrapher (See Chapter 10, page 122.)

- For addressing, you'll need the full names and titles for all guests. Be certain that spellings are correct and make note of relationships ("Kevin's mom's best friend," "Keisha's fiancé") as you assemble your guest list. These details will also be helpful to you later on when you arrange table seating for the reception, greet guests whom you don't know personally, and write your thank-you notes. (For how to address the envelopes, see Chapter 10, page 122.)

- Triple-check the spelling and correct address for the ceremony and reception sites. Triple-check the date, both the numerical day and the day of the week.

- Check the postage. Take an assembled invitation to the post office and have it weighed. If you are sending different sets of invitations—say, one with directions and one without—take an assembled set of each kind for weighing. Then note which postage to put on which set.

Embossing. Often used for monograms, crests, and symbols, embossing uses a plate into which the image is cut. When pressed onto paper, the image is raised above the surface, creating a three-dimensional look. In blind embossing, no ink is applied; in debossing, the image is depressed below the paper's surface.

Handwritten. A handwritten invitation on lovely stationery is the most personal wedding invitation of all. However, it is a practical option only for a very small wedding. (See Chapter 9, page 110.)

Ordering Your Invitations

Most invitations are sold as a four-piece set consisting of the invitation, the reply card, and their respective envelopes. All other pieces such as reception cards and pew cards are usually priced separately. Prices vary widely from a few dollars per set to well over $100 for one-of-a-kind, elaborately constructed masterpieces.

Before you finalize your order, make sure to ask for a proof. Designers may provide proofs as part of their service, but for the most part there's a charge, whether you order online or through a stationer. Is it worth it? Definitely! This is your opportunity to see if the robin's egg blue ink shows up well on the deep cream paper, or if the ribbon is "over the top." It's also your last chance to proofread. Once you place your final order, you are responsible for what you've asked the printer to print, errors and all. Reprinting your invitations because your fiancé's name was spelled "Grieco" instead of "Greico" is a costly hassle.

If you discover that all the extra enclosures are breaking your budget, it's fine to use a less expensive printing method for these pieces. A local printer can set them using the same or a very similar font, ink color, and paper for less cost.

Double check your guest list to give a final count to the stationer or printer, and don't forget to factor in the extras mentioned above. (See page 98.) It's also the time to tally enclosures. While some pieces like a map or reception card may go to all your guests, others such as a pew card may go to a select group.

A Change in Plans

Even the best-laid plans can go awry. A hurricane, an illness or death in the family, a military deployment, a serious business crisis, a disaster at the reception venue—these are all circumstances that could force a change of wedding date or venue after invitations have been printed. A true cancellation is more serious and usually hinges on a complete change of heart or other extreme circumstances. Whatever the situation, once the decision to postpone or cancel has been made, you will need to inform guests and anyone involved in the ceremony and reception right away.

When the Wedding Date, Time, or Venue Is Changed

When a new wedding date or venue is decided on after the invitations have been printed but before they are mailed, it's not necessary to order new invitations. Reprinting invitations is costly and might not be able to happen in time. If there's no time, you can draw a single line through the incorrect information on the invitation and neatly write the new date, time, or venue in ink. If there is time, or you can get a printer to do an overnight job, a better option is to include a small printed or handwritten card with the message "The date/time/place of the wedding has been changed from _____ to _____."

If the invitations have already been mailed, then guests should be notified right away by telephone or email as discussed below.

When the Wedding Is Postponed

When the wedding is postponed, announcements can be sent to all the guests if they will arrive within two weeks of the wedding. The most formal way of handling the situation is to recall the invitation and then send a new invitation if the wedding is rescheduled at a later date:

Doctor and Mrs. James Stuart Evans, Jr.
regret that
the invitation to their daughter's wedding
on Saturday, June twentieth
must be recalled

That level of formality is rare these days, and the following is more the norm:

Doctor and Mrs. James Stuart Evans, Jr.
announce that
the marriage of their daughter
Katherine Leigh
to
Mr. Brian Charles Jamison
has been postponed

If a new date has been chosen, then add: "has been postponed / to October twenty-fourth / [etc.]" This saves having to print a second invitation. If there is no time to have a card printed, then inform guests by telephone or email, as discussed below.

When the Wedding Is Canceled

If the decision to cancel the wedding is a last-minute one, phone everyone on your guest list as quickly as possible. It's a good idea to have a prepared message: "I'm sorry to have to tell you that Kate and Brian's wedding has been called off." It isn't necessary to go into details. Members of the wedding party, family, and good friends can make these calls to spare the couple and their families from having to explain again and again. If in the horrible event the cancellation is caused by the death of one of the couple, this is one detail that should be shared, as the people being called may not have yet heard the sad news.

When phoning, don't rely on just leaving a voice-mail message. Either request a call back, or keep calling until you speak to the guest. You wouldn't want a guest flying 3,000 miles because they didn't check voice mail. It's okay to send texts and emails, too, but ask for a reply to be sure the message was received, and then call anyone who doesn't text or email back.

If there is time, say, three to four weeks before the wedding date, the family can send printed cards. Cancellation notices should be sent to all invitees whether they have responded to the wedding invitation or not.

Doctor and Mrs. James Stuart Evans, Jr.
announce that
the marriage of their daughter
Katherine Leigh
to
Mr. Brian Charles Jamison
will not take place

This saves the bride, groom, and their families from having to answer questions when they are undoubtedly upset. Given time and circumstances, it might not be possible to hand-address the envelopes. It's fine to print out address labels, both for the recipient and return addresses.

If the decision to cancel is made before the invitations have been mailed, be sure to inform anyone who received a save-the-date card. Then inform family and friends as soon and as best as you can.

CHAPTER 9

INVITATION WORDING

For more than a hundred years, the wording of the wedding invitation has followed the same form. Born of necessity—engravers charged by the letter—a style developed that it is clear, concise, and elegant, conveying both the special nature of the occasion and exactly what a guest needs to know. Its "plug and play" nature makes it simple and guarantees success.

Manners, the *way* we do things, may change over time, but the underlying etiquette remains the same. Whether you choose the traditional tried-and-true form or opt for a more uniquely worded invitation, be sure that your phrasing conveys the essentials of an invitation.

Invitation Essentials

No matter the form in which it is written, the underlying etiquette of the invitation lets a guest know:

- ❖ Who is hosting: the parents of the bride or couple, the couple themselves, or others
- ❖ The purpose of the event: a marriage, commitment ceremony, or renewal of vows
- ❖ Who is being honored: the names of the couple
- ❖ When the event will take place: the date and time
- ❖ Where the event will take place: a house of worship or other location

Additionally, when everyone invited to the wedding is also invited to the reception, reception information can be included as well, along with an RSVP or request for reply.

Traditional Formal Wedding Invitation Wording

Third-person wording is the rule for formal invitations. This example invites all guests to the ceremony and the reception:

DOCTOR AND MRS. JAMES STUART EVANS, JR.
REQUEST THE HONOUR OF YOUR PRESENCE
AT THE MARRIAGE OF THEIR DAUGHTER
KATHERINE LEIGH
TO
MR. BRIAN CHARLES JAMISON
SATURDAY, THE TWENTIETH OF JUNE
(TWO THOUSAND FIFTEEN)
AT HALF AFTER THREE O'CLOCK
FIRST CONGREGATIONAL CHURCH
SPRING HILL, MINNESOTA
AND AFTERWARD AT THE RECEPTION
SPRING HILL GOLF CLUB
425 OAK DRIVE
RSVP

The wording and spelling follow these conventions.

❖ The wording is centered on the invitation, except for the RSVP, which is flush left.

❖ The hosts of the wedding are listed first. When there are multiple hosts, as when the bride and groom's parents host together, or divorced parents or divorced and remarried parents host, each is listed on separate lines with their names and titles in the following order, regardless of the amount of their financial contribution:

  • The bride's mother (and spouse)

  • The bride's father (and spouse)

  • The groom's mother (and spouse)

  • The groom's father (and spouse)

❖ No punctuation is used except for the abbreviations Mr., Mrs., Ms., Jr., or Sr. or when a phrase requiring a comma occurs on the same line, as in the date: "Saturday, the twentieth of June."

❖ Abbreviations aren't used, except for social titles: Mr., Mrs., Ms.

  • Jr. and Sr. may be abbreviated; more formally they are written out in lower case (junior, senior). Both forms are preceded by a comma.

  • Doctor is preferably written out unless the person's name is particularly long and wouldn't fit on one line.

  • Military titles are not abbreviated.

❖ Full names and titles are always used on formal invitations. It's okay to omit a middle name by choice or if the name is too long for one line, but don't use an initial.

❖ Purists will use the British spellings for *honour* and *favour* in the phrases "the honour of your presence" and "the favour of a reply." It's fine to use the American spellings; just be consistent.

❖ When the ceremony is in a house of worship, use the phrase "request the hono(u)r of your presence." Otherwise, "request the pleasure of your company" is the correct form for a civil or nonreligious ceremony or a religious ceremony performed outside of a house of worship.

❖ When a Roman Catholic Mass is part of the ceremony, use the phrasing "request the hono(u)r of your presence / at the Nuptial Mass uniting their daughter / Katherine Leigh / and / Mr. Brian Charles Jamison."

❖ The bride is listed without her title or last name, unless her last name is different from the hosts'.

❖ The groom's full name and title is used.

❖ For Jewish weddings, use *and* instead of *to* to connect the names of the bride and groom.

❖ Numbers in the date and time are spelled out: "the twentieth of June," "three o'clock."

❖ Including the year on the invitation is optional. If you choose to do so, spell it out using lowercase: "two thousand (and) fifteen." (The *and* is optional, but grammarians would prefer you omit it.)

❖ Half hours are written as "half after three o'clock" (not "half past three or "three thirty").

❖ Don't include the phrase "in the morning/afternoon/ evening."

- One-word numbers in an address are spelled out: Thirty Oak Drive; otherwise use numerals: 425 Oak Drive.

- When asking for a reply, "RSVP," "R.S.V.P.," "R.s.v.p," or "The favo(u)r of a reply is requested" are all correct.

RSVP QUICK TIPS

Here are some pointers on using an RSVP correctly:

- An RSVP is added to invitations to the reception only or when the invitation to the ceremony and the reception is combined, as in the example on page 107.

- An RSVP is *not* added to an invitation to the ceremony only.

- The RSVP is placed on the left, not centered.

- If you do not include a reply card with a preaddressed envelope, it means you expect guests to send handwritten replies to the return address on the invitation envelope. (See page 112 for a sample of a handwritten reply.)

- If you'd like replies sent elsewhere, or to be phoned or emailed, add this information below the RSVP:

  RSVP
  sara@mywedding.com

- Add a "reply by" date, if you wish—usually three to four weeks before the wedding date.

A MATTER OF TIME

Q: What time should I put on the invitation: the time guests are expected to arrive or the time the ceremony will start?

A: Just like other invitations, a wedding invitation states the start time for the event. Guests know, or should know, to arrive early enough to allow them to be seated before the ceremony starts. You don't want to inconvenience guests who arrive on time by making them wait an additional fifteen or twenty minutes so you can accommodate latecomers. Instead, assign someone to handle stragglers and start your procession at the time stated on the invitation.

When the couple issue their own formal invitation. In this case, the bride and groom's titles are used. Here are two examples of formal, third-person wording:

THE HONOUR OF YOUR PRESENCE IS REQUESTED
(THE PLEASURE OF YOUR COMPANY IS REQUESTED)
AT THE MARRIAGE OF
MS. KATHERINE LEIGH EVANS
TO
MR. BRIAN CHARLES JAMISON

— or —

MS. KATHERINE LEIGH EVANS
AND
MR. BRIAN CHARLES JAMISON
REQUEST THE HONOUR OF YOUR PRESENCE
(REQUEST THE PLEASURE OF YOUR COMPANY)
AT THEIR MARRIAGE
[etc.]

Invitations to the Ceremony, Reception, or Both?

To the ceremony and the reception. When all the guests are invited to both the wedding ceremony and the reception, the invitations can be combined as in the example on page 107. The reception information follows the ceremony address, and because hosts will want to know how many people to expect at the reception, an RSVP is added, too. (See also page 111.)

Instead of combining the ceremony and reception invitations, some couples prefer to enclose a *separate* invitation on a **reception card.** The RSVP goes on the reception card, not the wedding invitation:

Since the town and state are listed on the accompanying wedding invitation, there's no need to repeat that information on the reception card.

To the reception only. Sometimes a couple will invite a select number of guests to a small, private wedding ceremony and then invite a larger group to the reception. When that's the case, two invitations are needed, one for each event. The invitation to the wedding may be printed or engraved, or if the guest list is very small, it may be delivered personally or by note. A separate, printed or engraved invitation is sent to the reception guests. Here is an example of traditional wording for an invitation to the reception only:

SATURDAY, THE TWENTIETH OF JUNE

(TWO THOUSAND FIFTEEN)

AT SEVEN O'CLOCK

SPRING HILL GOLF CLUB

425 OAK DRIVE

SPRING HILL, MINNESOTA

RSVP

When the reception is at a later date, such as following a destination wedding, the wording is changed slightly. Be sure to list the couple as they wish to be addressed. For example, note if they are Mr. and Mrs., or if the bride is keeping her maiden name:

THE PLEASURE OF YOUR COMPANY IS REQUESTED

AT A RECEPTION

IN HONOR OF

MR. AND MRS. BRIAN JAMISON / MS. KATHERINE

EVANS AND MR. BRIAN JAMISON

[LESS FORMALLY: Kathy and Brian Jamison / Kathy Evans and Brian Jamison]

While the type of reception is up to the hosts and the couple, guests do need to have a clear idea of what to expect. If the reception falls during a mealtime but you aren't serving one, be sure guests understand that. The place to do so is on the invitation to the reception. Where you would normally print "Reception to follow," be more explicit. "Cocktail reception to follow," "Champagne and cake to follow"—or whatever the option may be—lets guests know not to expect a full meal and to plan accordingly. This is also the case if local custom equates wedding receptions with serving just cake and refreshments or, as in the South, cocktails and substantial hors d'oeuvres. Let your invitation give a heads-up to out-of-town guests who may not be in the know.

RSVP Etiquette

RSVP is an abbreviation for the French phrase *Répondez s'il vous plaît*, meaning "please respond." An RSVP or the phrase "The favour of a reply is requested" asks invitees to accept or regret an invitation.

As you plan the wording of your invitation, think about where, when, and how replies should be sent. The default is for a guest to send a written reply to the host's address on the outer envelope. If you wish to have replies sent elsewhere—say, to the couple (if they're not hosting) or to a wedding coordinator—add this address below the RSVP or use it as the address for the response card. Adding an email address or telephone number for replies is another option, in which case replies by phone or email only are fine.

It's also a wise idea to add a reply-by date, usually three to four weeks before the wedding date. That gives you enough time to track down stragglers and finalize your reception plans. "RSVP by May third" or "Please reply by May 3" are both good options.

Most hosts choose to add a response card with a preaddressed, stamped envelope to save their guests the trouble of scrambling to find stationery and hand writing a formal reply worded like this:

Ms. Sara Elizabeth Jenkins
accepts with pleasure / regrets she is unable to accept
the kind invitation of
Doctor and Mrs. James Stuart Evans, Jr.
for
Saturday, the twentieth of June

Unless it's issued by personal note, it's not necessary for a guest to reply to an invitation to the ceremony only. (See also page 109.)

Contemporary Invitations

Many couples opt for wedding invitations outside of the classic white or ecru engraved ones. These can be just as formal or elegant but reflect more of the couple's personality and the style of the wedding. Stationery manufacturers now offer a wide variety of color schemes, borders, designs, colored inks and backings, envelope liners, and contemporary typefaces to choose from. Many contemporary invitations feature the couple's names in larger type, which may necessitate combining two or more lines.

Couples might choose a formal look but use less formal wording or use the classic third-person wording with a uniquely designed invitation. It's your choice, as long as you cover the invitation essentials (see page 107) and respect the important nature of the ceremony.

Here are some examples of contemporary wedding invitation wording:

From the bride's parents. In this example, titles are omitted and first names are used. The groom's title is also optional.

GEORGES AND MARTHE DEMARAIS
INVITE YOU TO SHARE OUR JOY AT THE MARRIAGE OF
OUR DAUGHTER
CAROLE RENÉE
TO
(MR.) DOMENICK MASULLO
ON SATURDAY, THE FIFTH OF JUNE
[etc.]

From the couple with their parents. Less formally, couples may prefer to send out wedding invitations in their own names and not use social titles:

TOGETHER WITH THEIR PARENTS/FAMILIES
JULIA SHAW AND THOMAS WILLIAMS
INVITE YOU TO JOIN THEM AS THEY CELEBRATE THEIR
MARRIAGE
SATURDAY, DECEMBER SEVENTH
[etc.]

From both sets of parents. When both sets of parents issue the invitation, the bride's parents are listed first.

CHARLOTTE AND JIM MORSE

TOGETHER WITH

LILAH AND FRANK MEYER

WOULD BE HONORED TO HAVE YOU SHARE IN THE JOY

OF THE MARRIAGE OF THEIR CHILDREN

ALEXA

AND

DAVID

SATURDAY, JULY 7, 2015

[etc.]

Wedding invitations don't need to follow the traditional form; they may be as original as the couple and/or the bride's parents wish, as long as the invitations are dignified and sincerely reflect the sentiments of the bride and groom and their families. Among the loveliest and most meaningful is the following example, written as a letter from the bride's parents:

> *Our daughter, Lisa, will be married to Frank Adams O'Gorman, on Saturday, February 5th, at 7:30 in the evening at St. John's Lutheran Church, Mamaroneck, New York.*
>
> *We invite you to worship with us, witness their vows, and be our guest at the reception and buffet which follow at the Beach and Tennis Club, New Rochelle.*
>
> *If you are unable to attend, we ask your presence in thought and prayer.*
>
> *Helen and Davis Wilson*

Same-Sex Unions

Same-sex unions can take various forms, and your invitation should reflect the nature of the ceremony, whether it is a marriage ceremony, civil union, or commitment ceremony. Other choices to describe commitment ceremonies include affirmation ceremony, celebration of commitment, rite of blessing, relationship covenant, and union ceremony. Beyond the essentials of who, what, when, and where, the invitation style and wording is up to you. Some couples adapt traditional formats, as illustrated below; others opt for a blend of old and new styles. Or you may want to create an invitation that is uniquely yours. Although couples today are likely to issue their own invitations, parents, grown children, or other family members can certainly serve as hosts, and their names on the invitation are a loving way to demonstrate that they support the union.

Here is an example of an invitation to a gay or lesbian commitment ceremony issued by the couple themselves:

THE PLEASURE OF YOUR COMPANY IS REQUESTED

AT THE COMMITMENT CEREMONY OF

SUSAN BETH GIBSON

AND

GEORGIA LEE O'DELL

[etc.]

If both sets of parents (or other family) appear on the invitation as hosts, there is no etiquette as to which set of names appears first. You might decide alphabetically or flip a coin. Either way, list the couple's names respectively to the parents':

MR. AND MRS. FRANKLIN JOHNSON

AND

MR. AND MRS. JASON BOLIVIA

REQUEST THE HONOUR OF YOUR PRESENCE

AT THE MARRIAGE OF THEIR SONS

VICTOR KENNETH JOHNSON

AND

MARC WILLIAM BOLIVIA

[etc.]

Here's an example of less formal wording:

LUCIUS GRISHAM

AND

WILLIAM RYAN BARKER

INVITE YOU TO SHARE OUR JOY

AT THE CELEBRATION OF OUR CIVIL UNION

SATURDAY, THE TWENTY-SEVENTH OF MARCH

AT HALF AFTER ELEVEN O'CLOCK

756 ORIOLE COURT

WESTHAVEN, CONNECTICUT

AND AFTERWARD FOR BRUNCH

RSVP

Wording for Special Situations

Etiquette accommodates almost any circumstance with grace. A growing number of wedding invitations issued today reflect the often-complicated makeup of modern families. A bride may have two divorced and remarried sets of parents hosting her wedding. A groom may have the approval of one divorced parent but not the other. Birth mothers of adopted children may be involved. Or the bride might have recently lost her father with whom she was very close. For brides and grooms in these situations, there's no need to panic. These sample invitations are just a few that cover a variety of complex situations gracefully:

When the Bride Has One Living Parent

The invitation is issued only in the name of the living parent:

MR. [MRS.] DANIEL WATSON DRISCOLL

REQUESTS THE HONOUR OF YOUR PRESENCE

AT THE MARRIAGE OF HIS [HER] DAUGHTER

SUSAN PATRICIA

TO

MR. DREW RANDOLPH DONNEY

[etc.]

If the bride very much wants to include the name of her deceased parent, it's important not to use wording that implies that the deceased is issuing the invitation. The special wording of this type of invitation takes precedence over any question of who is actually hosting the wedding:

DIANE JUNE TIERNEY

DAUGHTER OF MARY ANN TIERNEY

AND THE LATE WILLIAM TIERNEY

AND

JAMES THOMAS DUFFY

SON OF MR. AND MRS. SAMUEL DAVID DUFFY

REQUEST THE HONOUR OF YOUR PRESENCE

AT THEIR MARRIAGE

SATURDAY, THE FIFTH OF OCTOBER

[etc.]

The same form is used if the groom wishes to acknowledge his deceased parent on the invitation: ". . . James Thomas Duffy / son of Mr. Samuel Duffy and the late Mrs. Duffy (Jennifer Duffy) . . ."

SIX INVITATION MISTAKES TO AVOID

Before you okay your proofs or send your invitations to the printer, review them for the following:

- Check, double-check, and then have others check the wording. Be particularly attentive to spelling, the correct names and addresses of ceremony and reception sites, and the correct date and time.

- Avoid any mention of gifts or listing of gift registries. Also, don't include a notation such as "No gifts, please," tempting as it may be. This keeps the entire focus of the invitation on the person you are inviting, not on any implied obligation to bring a gift. You can put registry or charitable-giving information on your website, or have family members and attendants help spread the word. (See also Chapter 13, page 161.)

- Don't write "Adults only" or "No children" on the invitation. If you aren't inviting children to your ceremony or reception, then simply don't list their names on the inner envelope (or outer, if there is only one) of their parents' invitation.

- Dress notations aren't included on invitations to the ceremony, unless the ceremony and reception invitations are combined. If it's essential to indicate "black tie" or the rare "white tie," add the notation to the reception invitation in the lower right corner.

- References to alcohol service aren't included on invitations, although menu choices may be listed on reply cards.

- Don't use stick-on labels to address your invitations; they are far too impersonal. Plan ahead and take the time to hand-address your invitations, or hire a calligrapher or someone with good handwriting to do it for you.

When the Bride's Parents Are Divorced
It is important to list the parents on separate lines, so as not to indicate they are still married.

When the bride's mother hosts on her own, she uses her first and last names:

(MRS.) ANN SYVERSON
REQUESTS THE HONOUR OF YOUR PRESENCE
AT THE MARRIAGE OF HER DAUGHTER
[etc.]

When divorced parents act as cohosts, the invitation is issued in both names. The bride's mother's name (and her current husband's if she has remarried) appears first, followed by the bride's father (with new spouse, if applicable). The bride is identified by her full name:

MR. AND MRS. SHELBY GOLDRING
AND
MR. MICHAEL LEVY
REQUEST THE HONOUR OF YOUR PRESENCE
AT THE MARRIAGE OF THEIR DAUGHTER
RACHEL LYNN LEVY
[etc.]

When the Bride Has Stepparents

When the bride has been raised by a parent and stepparent, and her other biological parent is not cohosting the wedding, use the following wording and note the bride's full name if her last name is different from her stepfather's:

Mr. and Mrs. Kenneth Cummings

REQUEST THE HONOUR OF YOUR PRESENCE

AT THE MARRIAGE OF HIS/HER DAUGHTER

[or: Mrs. Cummings' daughter]

Olivia Carol (Marsh)

[etc.]

When the bride has been legally adopted by a stepparent or she regards the stepparent as if he or she were a biological parent, the invitation reads "their daughter."

When Other Relatives Issue Invitations

If the bride's siblings or other relatives are giving the wedding, then the invitations are sent in their names. If her parents are no longer living, then the bride's title, "Ms." or "Mrs.," is used before her name.

Mr. and Mrs. Paul John Carey

REQUEST THE HONOUR OF YOUR PRESENCE

AT THE MARRIAGE OF THEIR NIECE

Ms. Rosemary Gelbach

TO

Mr. Karl Andrew Rauch

[etc.]

When a bride and groom's grown children are giving their parents' wedding, the invitation is issued with the bride's children listed before the groom's. When several children are involved, their names are given in the order of their age, from the oldest to the youngest in each family. For example, when the bride's married son and the groom's single daughter and married son are giving the wedding together, the invitation reads:

Mr. and Mrs. Brendan Shine

Ms. Christine Barrett

Mr. and Mrs. Jerome Barrett, junior

REQUEST THE HONOUR OF YOUR PRESENCE

AT THE MARRIAGE OF THEIR PARENTS

Madelyn Whitefield Shine

AND

Jerome Wallis Barrett

[etc.]

When the Bride Is a Widow or Divorcée

The parents of a widow or divorcée may issue the invitation for her second wedding just as they did for her first. The only difference is that the bride's name is the one she currently uses. If she has reverted to her maiden name, then her last name is omitted; otherwise, include her current last name:

Doctor and Mrs. Daniel Thomas McCann

REQUEST THE HONOUR OF YOUR PRESENCE

AT THE MARRIAGE OF THEIR DAUGHTER

Sheila McCann O'Neill

[etc.]

In any of the above situations it is also fine for the couple to issue the invitation themselves.

When the Groom's Family Gives the Wedding

MR. AND MRS. WENDELL WILLIAM ORR
REQUEST THE HONOUR OF YOUR PRESENCE
AT THE MARRIAGE OF
MS. SARAH JANE ANDERSON
TO THEIR SON
JOSHUA ALLEN ORR
[etc.]

Including the Groom's Parents in the Invitation

Increasingly, couples wish to include the groom's parents on the wedding invitation, either as a courtesy, a sign of family unity, or because the groom's parents are sharing in the hosting of the wedding, financially or otherwise.

When the groom's parents are included as a courtesy, the following wording does the job nicely:

MR. AND MRS. DAVID ZIMMERLI
REQUEST THE HONOUR OF YOUR PRESENCE
AT THE MARRIAGE OF THEIR DAUGHTER
CYNTHIA ANN
AND
MR. JOHN HOWARD GONZALEZ, JR.
SON OF
CAPTAIN AND MRS. JOHN GONZALEZ
[etc.]

When the parents are cohosting, the bride's parents are listed first:

MR. AND MRS. DAVID ZIMMERLI
AND
CAPTAIN AND MRS. JOHN GONZALEZ
REQUEST THE HONOUR OF YOUR PRESENCE
AT THE MARRIAGE OF
CYNTHIA ANN ZIMMERLI
AND
JOHN HOWARD GONZALEZ, JR.
[etc.]

A form followed in some countries provides for a double invitation with the bride's family's invitation on the left and the groom's family's invitation on the right:

MR. AND MRS. ARTURO MENDEL	MR. AND MRS. ROBERT PEREZ
REQUEST THE HONOUR OF YOUR PRESENCE	REQUEST THE HONOUR OF YOUR PRESENCE
AT THE MARRIAGE OF THEIR DAUGHTER	AT THE MARRIAGE OF THEIR SON
ANGELINA RUTH	EDUARDO ROBERT
TO	TO
MR. EDUARDO PEREZ	MS. ANGELINA MENDEL
[etc.]	[etc.]

When both the bride's and the groom's parents have been divorced and have remarried, and all are participating in giving the wedding and hosting the reception, it's not unusual for all their names to appear on the invitation. In this instance, the bride's mother and her husband would appear first, the bride's father and his wife second, the groom's mother and her husband third, and the groom's father and his wife fourth (see also page 108):

MR. AND MRS. MICHAEL HANNIGAN
[BRIDE'S MOTHER AND SPOUSE]

MR. AND MRS. LAWRENCE ANVIK
[BRIDE'S FATHER AND SPOUSE]

DOCTOR AND MRS. RUSSELL HEALY
[GROOM'S MOTHER AND SPOUSE]

MR. AND MRS. JEFFREY JACOBS
[GROOM'S FATHER AND SPOUSE]

REQUEST THE HONOUR OF YOUR PRESENCE

AT THE MARRIAGE OF

LINDSAY CATHERINE ANVIK

TO

MR. ANDREW LLOYD JACOBS

[etc.]

However, it may be simpler (and less expensive) to use the following:

TOGETHER WITH THEIR FAMILIES
(MS.) LINDSAY CATHERINE ANVIK
AND
(MR.) ANDREW LLOYD JACOBS
REQUEST THE HONOUR OF YOUR PRESENCE
[etc.]

For a Wedding at Someone's Home

When the wedding and reception will be held at a friend or relative's house, the invitations are still written in the name of the bride's parents or sponsors, the parents' of the couple, or in the name of the bride and groom:

DOCTOR AND MRS. JAMES STUART EVANS, JR.
REQUEST THE HONOUR OF YOUR PRESENCE
AT THE MARRIAGE OF THEIR DAUGHTER
KATHERINE LEIGH
TO
MR. BRIAN CHARLES JAMISON
SATURDAY, THE TWENTIETH OF JUNE
TWO THOUSAND FIFTEEN
AT HALF AFTER THREE O'CLOCK
AT THE RESIDENCE OF MR. AND MRS. ROBERT COZZA
124 TALL OAKS DRIVE
KANSAS CITY, MISSOURI
RSVP

All About Titles

It is customary to use social titles on formal wedding invitations, wedding announcements, and also when addressing the envelopes. Medical doctors, dentists, veterinarians, clergymen, judges, those in the military, and all others customarily called by their professional titles should have those titles included on their own wedding invitations and on the invitations to their daughters' or sons' weddings. When used, titles such as "Doctor" are written in full, but it's okay to use an abbreviation if the title makes the line too long to fit the person's name.

- Physicians, veterinarians, and dentists use "Doctor," and clergy use their religious titles.

- Professional certifications (CPA) and business titles, such as Esquire, aren't used in wedding invitations and announcements; social titles (Mr., Mrs., Ms.) are used instead.

- Educational degrees (PhD) aren't used, but if the person is known by "Doctor" then it's fine to use the title: Doctor John Smith, not John Smith, PhD.

- People who are customarily addressed by titles in their daily lives may also use them in invitations—Judge or Justice Judith Wade, Mayor Angelo Bentonni, or Senator Rachel Waggoner.

- A person who may be referred to as "the Honorable" doesn't use the title to refer to himself: "The Honorable John Jacobs and Mrs. Jacobs / request the honour . . ." is incorrect. Instead he or she uses a social title or the title of their office.

- Man or woman, the person with the title is listed first: "Senator/Doctor/Reverend/Judge/Colonel Marilyn Simpson Wentworth and Mr. Russell Loren Wentworth." Because of the length of title and name, you'll probably need to use two lines. Use the first line for the person with the title; the spouse's name goes on the second line, preceded by *and*:

DOCTOR MARILYN SIMPSON WENTWORTH
AND MR. RUSSELL LOREN WENTWORTH

- If both parents are doctors, use "The Doctors Wentworth" or "Doctor Russell Loren Wentworth / and Doctor Marilyn Simpson Wentworth."

(For specifics on using titles when addressing invitation envelopes, see page 122.)

MISS OR MS.?

Not so long ago, formal invitations listed the bride as "Miss Katherine Leigh." Today, most young girls make the switch from "Miss" to "Ms." between the ages of sixteen and eighteen. Unless it's your preference, or considered de rigueur in your part of the country, "Ms." is the preferred contemporary social title before a bride's name.

Military Titles

When the bride, groom, or one or both of their parents are members of the armed services or serving on active duty in the reserve forces, their military rank or rating is used in invitations. All military titles are written in full—never abbreviated—on invitations and announcements, and for mailing addresses.

When the Groom Is in the Military

For officers ranked captain or higher in the army, air force, and marines, or lieutenant, senior grade or higher, in the navy, the rank appears on the same line as the name, with the service branch below:

COLONEL GRAHAM O'GORMAN
UNITED STATES ARMY

Members of the reserve forces on active duty only follow the same rules regarding listing their rank and rating but add *reserve* to the second line: United States Army / Naval / Air Force Reserve.

High-ranking officers of the regular armed forces should continue to use their titles, followed by their branch of service, even after retirement, with *Retired* following the branch of service:

GENERAL GEORGE HARMON
UNITED STATES ARMY, RETIRED

For junior personnel, rank and branch of service are printed below their names:

JOHN MCMAHON
ENSIGN, UNITED STATES NAVY

Some military personnel, if they prefer, may use their titles (chaplain, doctor) instead of rank or rating on social invitations with no indication of service branch:

DOCTOR MICHAEL MARTIN ORTIZ

In the army, use just *Lieutenant* when the officer is a first or second lieutenant.

When the Bride Is in the Military

When the bride is on active duty, both her rank or rating and the branch of the military are included in the invitation. Her first and middle name appear on one line with her rank or rating and service branch on a separate line following:

MARRIAGE OF THEIR DAUGHTER
MARIE CLAIRE
LIEUTENANT, UNITED STATES NAVY

If her parents are issuing the invitation and her last name differs from theirs, then her last name is added:

MARIE CLAIRE ROSWELL

When One or Both Parents Are in the Military

When a parent is a member of the armed forces, either on active duty, a retired officer, or retired after many years of service, the military rank and rating may be used. The service branch or *retired* isn't used since a civilian spouse cannot be included in a military designation:

COLONEL AND MRS. JAMES OAKS

If both parents are in the military, the higher ranked officer is listed first:

COMMANDER JAMES OAKS AND MAJOR BRENDA OAKS
REQUEST THE HONOUR . . .

CHAPTER 10
ENVELOPES
AND ENCLOSURES

Now that you've designed your invitation and gotten the wording just right, it's time to look at envelopes and enclosures. This chapter addresses the issue of using one envelope or two and the conventions for addressing the inner and outer envelope. Most wedding invitations today include a reply card with a preaddressed, stamped return envelope. In an effort to convey information efficiently, you might include other enclosures, such as pew cards for special guests, rain cards for an outdoor wedding, or maps and directions, to name a few of your options. Let's start with envelopes.

Envelopes
One or Two Envelopes?

Formal third-person invitations are traditionally inserted into two envelopes, an inner envelope and an outer envelope. The outer envelope is the one that is addressed using the guest's full name and address and is stamped, whereas the inner envelope bears only the guests' names. The inner envelope is another holdover from the past, but unlike tissues (see page 127), this one continues to serve a real purpose.

Imagine New York City in the early 1900s—horse and carriage transportation, streets and sidewalks that were less than clean. There was a good chance that an envelope arrived at its destination in less than pristine condition. So, for this most special of invitations, the custom was to use a second, interior envelope to enclose a wedding invitation. Because the inner envelope didn't go through the post, it was left unsealed, the address information was omitted, and the guest's name abbreviated to title and last name.

Today, couples use an inner envelope because they like the tradition or because they want to be very specific as to who is invited. It's the most gracious way to communicate that a guest may bring a plus-one, and it's also the best way to communicate which young children (if any) are invited by listing their names individually below their parents' (or not).

This tradition may seem redundant or wasteful of paper to you. It's fine to dispense with the custom of the inner envelope altogether if you wish.

Addressing Outer Envelopes

Because the event is so special, most wedding invitations are still addressed using a formal style. That's why you want to collect detailed name and address information when you assemble your address list. Here are the general conventions for addressing the outer envelope:

- Use your guest's full name and title: Mr. and Mrs. Ashok Singh; Doctor Susan Bartlett and Mr. Henry Bartlett.

- Mr. and Mrs. are abbreviated; Dr. and Rev. may be abbreviated if there isn't enough room on the line. Military titles are not abbreviated.

- It's fine to use middle names, but don't use an initial: Mr. George Arthur Harris or Mr. George Harris, but not Mr. George A. Harris.

- In the address lines, words like *Street*, *Avenue*, *Boulevard*, and *Post Office Box* are fully written out.

- Either write out the state name—most formal—or use the two-letter postal code abbreviation: Vermont or VT.

- The return address can be embossed or printed on the back flap, or in the upper left corner of the front of the envelope (the location preferred by the U.S. Postal Service). Names aren't used, but do use the address where you would like guests to send replies and gifts.

DO I NEED TO HIRE A CALLIGRAPHER?

Because of their personal nature, wedding invitations are hand-addressed. Some couples hire a calligrapher (most stationers will be able to recommend one) to set a special tone for their invitation before guests even open them. No piece of junk mail here! The results can be mini works of art and are certainly a special way to herald your news. Confirm with the calligrapher the time needed to do the job, and order your outer (and inner) envelopes to arrive early so he or she can get a head start, even if your invitations haven't yet arrived.

If a calligrapher isn't in your budget, handwrite your envelopes as clearly as you can, or enlist the aid of a relative or member of your wedding party who has good handwriting. Plan about a week or two to address all your envelopes, setting a daily goal, and be sure that you're done well ahead of your mailing date.

Since you probably have your guest list in a database, it might be really tempting to print stick-on labels. Resist this; it's just too impersonal and implies "mass mailing." If you want to save time, you could have your envelopes laser-printed, using a font that complements the invitation inside. A local printer can use your list and guarantee better results than if you try to do it yourself on a home printer. Just be sure that your list is 100 percent accurate—what you send is exactly what will be printed. Check that names and addresses—and their spellings—are correct and make changes such as "St." to "Street" and "Dr." to "Doctor." (See above and page 123.)

The Finer Points of Addressing Outer Envelopes

Just as there are conventions regarding the way you address the envelope, there are also conventions in the way you address your guests:

Married couples. Wedding invitations are always addressed to both members of a married couple, even though the bride may only know one of them or knows that only one will attend.

A married woman who uses her maiden name. These days, either name can be written first, but old-schoolers will list the gentleman first:

Mr. John Henry Harris and Ms. Elizabeth Angier Riggs

If the names are too long for one line, put the first name on the first line, and the second on the next line, indented and starting with *and*:

Mr. John Henry Harris
and Ms. Elizabeth Angier Riggs

Guests with titles. Use titles for members of the clergy, the medical professions, the military, or for those who hold government office. These titles should be written out, but may be abbreviated if length is an issue. Military titles are not abbreviated.

- ❧ Always list the person with the official or professional title first.

- ❧ If a woman uses her maiden name, it is "Doctor (Dr.) Barbara Hanson and Mr. James Werner."

- ❧ If both are doctors, the address is either "The Doctors Werner," "The Drs. Werner," "Drs. Barbara and Robert Werner," or "Doctors Barbara and Robert

Werner." The same format is followed if the woman were a reverend, or if both she and her husband were reverends.

Unmarried couples living together. In the past, it seemed important to distinguish between married couples and those just living together. Today, invitations to committed, established but unmarried couples who live together at the same address are written on one line following the same conventions as for married couples:

Mr. Scott Daniel Posig and Ms. Anne-Marie Heller

List gay couples the same way; either name can come first, or go in alphabetical order:

Mr. Sydney Francis Foote and Mr. James Kevin Taylor

Plus-ones. When you know the name of a guest's plus-one, but he or she doesn't live at the same address, send the invitation to the person you know at his or her address, but list the plus-one as an individual on a separate, indented line:

Mr. Scott Daniel Posig
Ms. Anne-Marie Heller
425 South Street, [etc.]

One of the purposes of using an inner envelope is to let a guest know in a more private and personal way that he or she may bring a plus-one of their choosing. When you don't know the name of an invitee's plus-one, the outer envelope is addressed to the guest you know and the inner envelope to your invitee "and Guest." It's a more formal and personal way to extend the invitation. Today, because of cost or preference, many couples don't use an inner envelope. When this is the case, it has become both practical and acceptable to address the outer envelope to "Ms. Penelope Denise McKay and Guest." Or, if you prefer, an elegant alternative is to address the outer envelope to your invitee, and convey the message to bring a guest by including a separate note, jotting a note on the reply card, or by a personal phone call.

Children. By age thirteen children should, if possible, receive separate invitations—certainly by the time they are eighteen years old. Use "Miss" for girls sixteen to eighteen and "Master" for boys seven and younger; no title is used for boys age eight and up until they turn eighteen, when they are "Mr." Sisters and brothers may be sent a joint invitation when all are invited, addressed to "The Misses Smith" or "The Messrs. Jones." (*Messrs.* is an abbreviation of the French *messieurs*, meaning "misters." It's very formal and somewhat archaic, so it's fine to write "The Misters" instead.) If there are both boys and girls, use two lines:

The Messrs. Jones
The Misses Jones

If you choose to use inner envelopes, the outer envelope may be addressed to the parents only, and the children's names written below their parents' names on the inner envelope. (For more on addressing inner envelopes, see below.)

Families. When relationships are so complicated or children so numerous, it may seem simpler to address the envelope "Mr. and Mrs. Anthony Williams and Family." Unfortunately, this type of invitation can be misconstrued. Consider this option only if the situation meets the following criteria:

1. It is clear that you are inviting just the people living under that roof, not the aunt and uncle down the street as well.

2. The children are young (adult relatives who reside in the household should receive their own invitations).

3. Every person living under the same roof is intended to be included in the invitation.

Addressing Inner Envelopes

If you have chosen to use inner envelopes, they have some etiquette fine points all their own. They are addressed differently than outer envelopes; in most cases, you use titles and surnames only: *Mr. and Mrs. Singh; Doctor and Mr. Bartlett.* Here's how to handle addressing the inner envelope to various guests.

Close family and friends. It's fine to address inner envelopes with familiar names and titles for close family members and good friends: *Aunt Virginia and Uncle Mac, Gran and Pops, Lexie.*

Couples with young children. While you address the outer envelope to the parents only, add the children's first or full names (without titles) below their parents' on the inner envelope. This is important if you are inviting only some children in a family, say those over the age of ten:

Mr. and Mrs. Adair
   Lisa and Bobby

— or —

   Lisa Adair
   Bobby Adair

When you are inviting all the siblings in the same household, you can address the sisters as "The Misses Adair" and the brothers as "The Messrs. Adair."

Teenagers at home. Children age thirteen and over generally receive their own invitations (by eighteen years old at the very latest), but if this isn't possible, then include them in their parents' invitation as above. When courtesy titles are used, teenage girls are "Miss" before age eighteen; afterward, use "Ms." Teenage boys use no title until they turn eighteen, when they are "Mr."

Couples who live together. Address the inner envelope to "Ms. Rasmussen and Mr. Colwell," or "Ms. Davis and Ms. Lucas."

An invitee and guest. Using an inner envelope is a gracious way to communicate to an invitee that he or she may bring a guest. In this case, address the outer envelope to your invitee only, and write "Ms. McKay and Guest" (or the guest's name if you know it) on the inner envelope.

People with military and professional titles. On inner envelopes, treat military and professional titles as you would social titles, but don't use abbreviations: *Admiral and Mrs. Jernigan; Judge Sims and Mr. Sims.*

Enclosures

In addition to the invitation(s) to the ceremony and reception, you might want to include a response card, directions, or other information for your guests. Perhaps you'd like to inform guests the ceremony will be at another location if it rains, or let your aunt to know there's a place reserved for her in the third pew. All of this information can be included with your invitation on various insertions, also called enclosures.

Response or Reply Cards

Although handwritten replies are always correct, printed reply cards and envelopes are now the norm. Reply cards are actually just for the reception—to give you an accurate guest count—not for the ceremony. They're engraved or printed in the same style as your invitation, but using a small card and envelope, and may be included as part of an invitation set.

Reply cards should have a space for invitees to write their names and a space to indicate whether they will or will not attend. It's always a good idea to include the date by which you'd like to receive replies. For invitations sent eight weeks ahead, a standard reply-by date is four weeks out; three weeks for invitations sent six weeks ahead of the wedding date.

M_____

_____ ACCEPT(S) [*or* WILL ATTEND]

_____ REGRET(S) [*or* WILL NOT ATTEND]

THE FAVOUR OF YOUR REPLY IS
REQUESTED BY JULY 26

The *M* precedes the space where the guest writes his or her social title and name, as in "*M*s. Phyllis Reynolds" or "*M*r. and Mrs. Joseph Iorio." Guests can also use the card to write the names of any invited children and whether they will attend or not. The same is true for plus-ones: guests can write in the name of their plus-one—a great help when you go to make table or place cards.

Generally, a response card shouldn't include the phrase "number of persons." It's confusing to invitees who may think that other members of the family are invited to attend, even if their names weren't listed on the outer or inner envelope.

Another contemporary option is a card printed solely with "Please reply by ____" at the top. Guests use that card to write a short note to accept or regret—a more personal response than a checked box or formal handwritten reply.

Since a reply card is meant to be a convenience, make it as simple and easy to use as possible. Whichever style you choose, include a preaddressed, stamped envelope so that all the guest has to do is write in his, her, or their names, check "accepts" or "regrets," seal the card in the envelope, and drop it in the mail. It's a smart idea to take one of your response cards and its envelope to the post office to check for correct postage before sending.

Reception Cards

When the invitation to the reception is separate from the invitation to the wedding, it's often printed on a smaller reception card. The reception card is placed in the envelope in front of the invitation to the wedding ceremony. (See page 128.)

Pew Cards

Small cards printed with "Pew Number ____" or "Within the Ribbon" are sometimes included in invitations to family and friends who are to be seated in reserved areas. Guests with cards simply take them to the ceremony and show them to the ushers. The

ushers will make sure they're seated in the correct place. Within the Ribbon cards indicate that pews or seats marked with ribbons have been set aside for special guests. Ushers escort guests presenting these cards to a row and guests can sit anywhere within these seats.

Pew or Within the Ribbon cards can also be sent separately after acceptances or regrets are received, when the bride knows how many reserved seats are needed.

Admission Cards

Admission cards are necessary only when a wedding is held in a popular church or cathedral, such as St. Patrick's Cathedral in New York City, which attracts sightseers and is open to the public. To ensure seating in the rows set aside for the ceremony, each guest is asked to present his or her admission card at the entrance. It is generally engraved or printed in the same style as the invitation and reads:

PLEASE PRESENT THIS CARD

AT

ST. PATRICK'S CATHEDRAL

SATURDAY, THE TWELFTH OF JUNE

At-Home Cards

Adding an "at home" card to the wedding invitation packet or wedding announcement lets friends know what the bride and groom's new address will be if they did not previously live together. The date indicates their return from the honeymoon (or from the wedding if the honeymoon is delayed). At-home cards are also a great way to communicate whether or not the bride will keep her maiden name:

MR. AND MRS. BRUCE ROWE /
BRUCE ROWE AND LORI GRISWALD
WILL BE AT HOME
AFTER JULY SECOND
3842 GRAND AVENUE
HOUSTON, TEXAS 77001
(898) 555-4321

Rain Cards

These are a "Plan B" defense strategy if bad weather means moving your ceremony or reception to another location. For example, "In case of rain, the ceremony and reception will take place at 33 Elm Street, Traverse City."

Tissues

The delicate tissues that are sometimes included in a wedding invitation are optional today. Once they had a real function: to keep the oils from the ink on engraved invitations from smudging as they slowly dried. Improved printing and engraving techniques have made tissues unnecessary for decades, but their use continues as a bow to tradition. If you decide to use them, place the tissue on top of your invitation when you put it in the envelope. Enclosures are stacked on top of the tissue.

Maps, Directions, and Other Guest Information

Some couples like to include all the relevant wedding information with their invitation, creating a wedding packet. Maps and directions to the ceremony and reception, contact information for local hotels or where blocks of rooms have been reserved, area transportation options, information on local area attractions, and

INVITATIONS TO OTHER EVENTS

While it may seem efficient to include invitations to a rehearsal dinner, after party, or day-after brunch with the wedding invitation, in most cases it's better to send them separately. For example, people other than the couple or the bride's parents might host these events, and therefore the invitation should come directly from the host. Additionally, different guests may be invited to different prewedding and postwedding events. There's a chance a mistake could be made when assembling the invitation packets and a rehearsal dinner guest invited instead only to a brunch or a guest being left out completely. However, if all wedding guests are invited to a particular event before or after the wedding, and the hosts are in agreement, it's fine to include the invitation with the wedding invitation package.

restaurants. This can get pricey, both in terms of printing and postage, and too many enclosures can also take attention away from the invitation. Here are some alternative ways to cut costs or share information:

- A local flat or laser printer might be able to print these pieces for less, using similar paper, ink color, and font.

- Wait until you have received all your replies, and then print and mail information only to your yeses.

- Create PDF files and email the information to your guests, or send links to an online map service, such as Google Maps. (Keep in mind you will still need to communicate this information to guests who don't use a computer.)

- Put this information on your wedding website. Include your website address on a separate business card–sized enclosure with your invitation. (Again, provide this information another way to non-Internet-using guests. See also Chapter 4, page 54.)

Stuffing the Envelopes

Use the following guidelines to put each item in its correct place. The idea is that when the outer envelope is opened, the guest can read his or her name on the inner envelope, and when the inner envelope is opened the guest can read the invitation or the enclosures stacked on top of it.

Using an Inner and an Outer Envelope

1. Insert the invitation printed side up and folded edge first if not a flat card.

2. Slip the reply card under the flap of its envelope so the card is faceup and the addressed side of the reply envelope is facedown.

3. Stack the enclosures—reception or ceremony card, directions or other information, and reply card with stamped, addressed envelope—faceup, in size order, largest piece on the bottom.

4. Insert all the enclosures, faceup, on top of the invitation and slide the whole package into the inner envelope. If using tissues, place them between the invitation and the enclosures. In the case of a folded invitation, insertions are placed in the same order but within the fold, faceup.

5. The inner envelope is not sealed, nor is the flap tucked in. Turn it address side up, and place it in the outer envelope so the name of the invitee is visible when the invitation is opened (the flap of the inner envelope will be against the addressed side of the outer envelope).

Using an Outer Envelope Only

If you only use one envelope, follow the above directions through step 4 and insert all the pieces faceup, into the outer envelope, and then seal it.

CHAPTER 11

MORE FROM THE STATIONER

You've had a busy day at the stationer's: choosing your invitations and envelopes, crafting the wording, and making decisions about enclosures. That may be enough for one day, but you're not done yet! If you can't decide another thing, make a date soon to complete your wedding stationery order. At the very least, you may want to order personal stationery for thank-you notes. Save-the-date cards and wedding announcements are also options. Stationers offer place and table cards and often carry guest books, printable favors, and accessories. If you want your entire wedding suite to match, think about placing an order for your wedding program as well, although many couples design and print these on a home computer.

Another DIY project for the bride and groom is creating a welcome letter and schedule of wedding events to be delivered to out-of-town guests when they check in at their various lodgings. Kick it up a notch by putting together welcome bags—also available through your stationer—stocked with a few comfort items for their stay.

Personal Stationery

It may seem as if you've ordered more paper than you ever used in college, but don't forget to order stationery for your thank-you notes, too. Fold-over note cards, correspondence cards, and single sheets are perfect for this purpose and can be printed with your monogram or name on the front. Remember: The groom can also write thank-you notes. You might want to order "his" and "hers" stationery to use before you are married. At the same time order stationery to use after you are married: Stationery with both of your first names, your duogram, or a monogram of just the initial of your last name can be used by both of you.

You might also create note cards with a recent picture of the two of you on them to use for notes before the wedding. This is another great opportunity to use photos from an engagement shoot. You could use a wedding photo for any cards sent after the big day, though you would need to get the photo and have the notes made quickly.

Save-the-Date Cards

Save-the-date cards, giving advance notice of an upcoming wedding, can be very helpful to guests who will need to make travel plans or when the wedding will be held at a time when there may be travel or hotel booking conflicts, such as on major holiday weekends. They are especially helpful for alerting guests about a destination wedding.

Save-the-date cards have become wildly popular. While they may be formal printed cards, they are far more likely to be fun, casual, and creative, running the gamut from paper cards to fridge magnets, calendar stickers, postcards, or note cards featuring a photo of the couple. When possible, it's a great idea to include travel or lodging suggestions so that out-of-town or destination wedding guests can start arranging for plane tickets and hotels.

Save-the-date cards are usually mailed from four to eight months prior to the wedding, but may be sent even a year earlier for a destination wedding at a distant location.

Everyone who receives a save-the-date card must receive an invitation. Chances are you may have your date and location long before you have constructed a guest list. Unless you know your final guest list, only send save-the-dates to the guests who are closest to you, the friends and family you are certain you will invite. Other guests can just receive an invitation. This way, you haven't committed yourself to any but your core guests, as there is no way you can "uninvite" a guest who received a save-the-date. (For more on determining who should receive a save-the-date, see Chapter 7, page 83.)

Here is wording for a typical save-the-date card:

Please save the date
for the wedding of
Kate Evans and Brian Jamison
[full names for a formal card]
Saturday, June 20, 2015
[for a formal card: Saturday, the twentieth of June /
two thousand fifteen]
Spring Hill, Minnesota
Invitation to follow [this line optional]

A more informal save-the-date card might read:

Kate and Brian are getting hitched!
Saturday, June 20, 2015
Spring Hill, Minnesota

Welcome Letters and Information for Guests

You can set a gracious tone the minute your out-of-town guests arrive at their lodging (hotel or residence of a local friend or family member) by presenting them

Dear friends and family,

Welcome! We're excited and honored that you're here to celebrate our wedding with us. Richmond is an exciting city and we hope you have a chance to enjoy your visit here as well. If you have any questions you can call or text Josh Hamlin (Lila's brother and our point person) at 888-555-1234. We're looking forward to seeing you at the wedding.

Much love,
Lila and Scott

with a letter of welcome and a schedule of wedding events.

About a month before the wedding—before your schedule gets crowded with final wedding details—write a short note saying how excited you are for your big day and how much you appreciate having your friends and family celebrate with you. Then, as soon as your wedding schedule is finalized, create a schedule for your guests. (See a sample below.) Include a timetable of events, relevant addresses for venues, links to online map sites, telephone numbers, and any information about transportation schedules if you are providing bus or trolley service.

Depending on your budget, you can have these pieces printed professionally, or you can do it yourselves on your home printer.

SAMPLE SCHEDULE OF EVENTS FOR GUESTS

HAMLIN-FLYNN WEDDING
SCHEDULE OF EVENTS FOR GUESTS

The wedding and reception will be at:

Middlesex Farms
406 Chestnut Lane
Middlesex, VT 05602

802-555-5555

Note to guests: Parking is extremely limited at the wedding venue—please use the shuttle service.

Saturday, May 14, 2016

4:15	Shuttle bus #1 departs Hampton Inn for the Farm Barn, Middlesex Farms
4:30	Shuttle bus #2 departs Hampton Inn for the Farm Barn, Middlesex Farms
5:00	Ceremony begins
5:45	Reception begins
9:30	Shuttle bus departs Middlesex Farms for Hampton Inn
10:30	Shuttle bus departs Middlesex Farms for Hampton Inn
11:00	Reception ends
11:30	Last shuttle bus departs Middlesex Farms for Hampton Inn

Sunday, May 15, 2016

9:00–11:00 AM   Brunch at the Hampton Inn

Ceremony Programs

Programs have become increasingly popular and have grown beyond the outline of a religious service. They are an opportunity for the couple and their families to send a personal message to their guests as well as to explain religious or cultural customs that may not be familiar to all guests.

In addition, programs usually include a "who's who" of the wedding party; the names of immediate family of the bride and groom; the officiant(s), reader(s), soloist(s), and anyone else participating in the ceremony. The order of the ceremony is listed, including the music (with composer) and any readings as well as any prayers, hymns, lyrics, or responses expected from the guests, so that all may join in. Programs are also a convenient place to reiterate directions or a map to the reception venue if different from the ceremony location.

Some couples include the story of how they met, share inspirational quotations or poems that have meaning to them, or take the opportunity to thank their families and guests. The wedding program is also a good place to share a remembrance of a deceased loved one, such as a parent, grandparent, or sibling.

Many guests keep programs as souvenirs, but that doesn't mean you have to go all out on the design and printing. Some houses of worship will print them for you if you provide the text, or you can print them yourself at home or use a local print shop.

If you plan on having programs at your ceremony, think about how you would like guests to receive them. Ushers can hand programs to guests as they seat them, or children or the flower girls and/or ring bearers can hand them out as guests arrive. Programs can also be placed in pews or on chairs or in baskets by the door.

Place Cards and Table Cards

While the use and placement of place cards and table cards is discussed in Chapter 16, page 225, they are mentioned here because they are often ordered with other wedding enclosures. Wedding stationers include them as another element in the suite of wedding papers so their design will match that of the invitation. However, simple fold-over cards are widely available at office supply stores and will do the job just as well. Because they will all be presented together on one table, they should have a uniform look, either handwritten by a calligrapher (or someone with good handwriting), or printed. There are programs available online for creating seating plans that also have the capability to print the place cards or table cards. (See Chapter 16, page 223.)

Printed Accessories and Favors

If you would like to have personalized cocktail napkins, matchbooks, coasters, or other mementos at your reception, see if the stationer or printer who is handling your invitations, announcements, and other inserts can do them. Sometimes you can get a better price when ordering everything from one source.

Guest Books

Wedding guest books are another popular but completely optional item. They used to be fairly plain vanilla—a leather or silk cover embossed or stamped with the couple's initials or "Will and Susan / July 20, 2016" and lined pages where guests could sign their names and perhaps add a message. Now couples can use online services to create their own books that include photographs (perhaps taken during their engagement or at prewedding parties), poems, or quotations interspersed with blank pages for guests to sign. If you had

an engagement photo shoot, either with your wedding photographer or another photographer, consider using these for your guest book.

Wedding Announcements

Most couples and their families will want to share the happy news of the marriage with friends and business associates who, for one reason or another, were not invited to the wedding or the reception. After the wedding, many couples share the news online through their social network. Others may choose a more traditional route and send printed announcements, or even do both.

Announcements are by no means obligatory. If you are considering them, keep in mind it may be convenient to include your announcement order while you are planning and placing the order for your wedding invitations, enclosures, and personal stationery, though you can always do so later.

Recipients

You can send an announcement to anyone you think might be interested in hearing the news. A wedding

announcement comes with no implied gift obligation—although some recipients may send cards, notes, or gifts to congratulate and wish you well. Announcements aren't sent to those who received a wedding invitation, even if they sent regrets.

Of course, this means creating another list. You'll probably already have the names and addresses of those who didn't make the final guest list, but it's a good idea to go through your contact lists once more in case you missed someone and ask your parents to do the same.

NEWSPAPER WEDDING NOTICE

If you'd like your wedding announced in your local or regional paper, you'll need to plan ahead, since newspapers often receive more wedding announcements than they can print. It's possible that they will post your announcement online as well. Call or check your paper's website; most have a form that can be downloaded or filled out online. Many papers now accept photos as well, and today you are more likely to see an informal picture of the couple instead of a headshot of the bride in her wedding dress and veil. If you do want to be in wedding attire, you'll have to work out when to take the photo or be willing to postpone publication until you have reviewed your wedding photos. (See also Chapter 22, page 302.) While each newspaper may use its own style, most ask for biographical information about the bride, groom, and their parents (and possibly grandparents) as well as details about the wedding and reception, the bridal party, the bride's gown, where the couple will honeymoon, and where they plan to live.

Design

You can take the traditional route and match the style of your announcement to your wedding invitation, or take it in a different direction. Either way, it's nice to get the wording and proofreading done at the same time you create your invitation and any enclosures.

Wording

Like the formal wedding invitation, a formal wedding announcement is sent in the names of the bride's parents. The format and wording follow the same conventions as for wedding invitations. That's one more reason why it may be a good idea to take care of the wording for your invitation and announcement at the same time. Announcements always include the year and where the wedding took place. Here's an example:

DR. AND MRS. JAMES STUART EVANS, JR.
HAVE THE HONOUR OF ANNOUNCING
THE MARRIAGE OF THEIR DAUGHTER
KATHERINE LEIGH
TO
MR. BRIAN CHARLES JAMISON
SATURDAY, THE TWENTIETH OF JUNE
TWO THOUSAND FIFTEEN
THE FIRST CONGREGATIONAL CHURCH
SPRING HILL, MINNESOTA

There's always room for creativity and personal choice. You may use "have the honour / honor to announce" or merely "announce." Today, with the emphasis on marriage as a "joining" rather than a "giving" of a woman to a man, and with the groom's family presumably proud and happy to share the news as well, announcements often go out in both families' names:

Dr. and Mrs. James Stuart Evans, Jr.

and

Mr. and Mrs. Charles Dewey Jamison

announce

the marriage of

Katherine Leigh Evans

and

Mr. Brian Charles Jamison

Saturday

the twentieth of June

two thousand fifteen

[etc.]

The couple may make the announcement themselves:

Katherine Leigh Evans

and

Brian Charles Jamison

are pleased to announce

their marriage

[etc.]

Or simply:

Kathy and Brian tied the knot!

June 20, 2015

Spring Hill, Minnesota

Mailing

Ideally, announcements are dropped in the mail the day after the wedding, but if that isn't possible, then try to send them off within a few weeks of the wedding. (We know one couple who received an announcement seven months after a wedding, and mistook it for a save-the-date for a wedding to come!) As with wedding invitations, hand-address (or laser-print) the envelopes. (For address styling, see Chapter 10, pages 122 and 123.)

WEDDING STATIONERY CHECKLIST

The Basics:

- ☐ Wedding Invitations
- ☐ Envelopes (1 or 2)
- ☐ Personal stationery choices:
  - ☐ Bride, prewedding
  - ☐ Groom
  - ☐ Bride, postwedding
  - ☐ Couple, postwedding

Enclosure Options:

- ☐ Reply cards and envelopes
- ☐ Reception cards
- ☐ Tissues
- ☐ Admission cards
- ☐ Pew cards
- ☐ Rain/Change of Venue cards
- ☐ At Home cards
- ☐ Maps, Directions: A printed card for out-of-town guests

Extras and Other Options:

- ☐ Save-the-date cards (and envelopes)
- ☐ Ceremony programs
- ☐ Wedding announcements and envelopes
- ☐ Place cards / table cards
- ☐ Menu cards
- ☐ Personalized favors
- ☐ Guest book
- ☐ Welcome notes, schedules, etc. for hotel welcome bags

PART FOUR

PARTIES, PRESENTS, AND THANKS

CHAPTER 12

PARTIES AND CELEBRATIONS

As soon as your engagement is announced, friends and family may begin asking how they can entertain for you. Everyone connected with you will want to celebrate you in some way, and special parties have become a much-beloved part of the wedding experience. These aren't everyday parties, and each has a different purpose and particular etiquette. Engagement parties (see Chapter 1, page 13) celebrate a couple's decision to marry; showers help the couple establish their new home together; bachelor and bachelorette parties mark the end of single lives; the rehearsal dinner gives the groom's family a chance to entertain; a farewell brunch can wrap up a wedding weekend; and good friends might host out-of-town guests while the wedding party is at the rehearsal.

Do you have to have all of these parties? No, none of these parties are "musts" or "have-tos," but they are fun and a true sign of the affection of your friends and family. The weeks and months following the engagement party are usually taken up with a dizzying amount of wedding planning details. Fortunately, just when it all might start to seem overwhelming, tradition throws you a couple of lifelines—parties that let you catch your breath and enjoy yourself with your closest friends. Prewedding parties don't have to be gift-giving occasions and it's fine for the couple to suggest a "gift free" gathering when someone offers to host a party for them.

So let's make the rounds!

Wedding Showers

Legend has it that long ago in Holland, a young Dutch girl fell in love with a poor miller. Her wealthy father opposed the match and threatened to withhold her dowry if she went through with the wedding. The couple married anyway, but her lack of dowry left them penniless. The townsfolk took pity on the miller, who had always been kind to them, and his young bride, and they came to the mill with gifts for the couple's household. The bride's father was so ashamed when he saw this outpouring of kindness and generosity that his heart melted. He bought them a house and hosted a feast so everyone could celebrate their marriage. Of course, they lived happily ever after.

DO THE BRIDESMAIDS HOST A SHOWER?

Contrary to popular belief, bridesmaids aren't required to host a shower, so, dear bride, please don't insist that they do. It's really up to the group to decide. It may not be possible for them to make an extra trip for a party, or, given their other wedding expenses—outfits, accessories, shoes, travel, and gifts—budgets may be too strained. The group may prefer to have a more low-key, gift-free gathering a day or two before the wedding to spend time with the bride.

If together the bridesmaids do want to plan a shower, it's very important that they are all in agreement. It's unfair for the maid of honor to take it upon herself to organize a party and then expect all the others to split the cost. It's also unfair to bully a bridesmaid into contributing if she cannot afford to do so.

The bridal shower may be the ultimate "girl" moment of the prewedding season—tea sandwiches, punch, ribbons, and bows—but coed "Jack and Jill" showers are also very popular. A shower may have a theme that indicates the type of gifts expected. Opening the presents is usually the high point of the party, but equally important is bringing good friends together to celebrate an upcoming marriage.

The party timeline. Ideally, showers are held after the couple has firm wedding plans, anywhere from two to four months before the wedding. Any closer to the big day and it can stress an already packed preparation schedule—and the busy bride. Further out, the couple may not know what they need, and the party won't build momentum toward the wedding. When a wedding is arranged on short notice, it's okay to hold a shower fairly soon after the wedding day. Weekday or weekend, whatever suits the host, the honoree, and the convenience of the guests is fine.

Who hosts? While an engaged couple shouldn't throw themselves a shower—a direct "ask" for gifts—it's fine for anyone else to host. Friends of the couple or of the couple's parents are the traditional shower hosts, as are more distant relatives such as aunts and cousins. Typically, mothers or grandmothers of the bride didn't used to host showers (it, too, could look like an "ask" for gifts), but there may be circumstances today that make it practical for them to do so. The groom's mother may want to host a bridal shower, engagement party, or reception to introduce her future daughter-in-law to hometown friends and family. Sometimes several of the brides' friends or relatives host the shower together, or coworkers host a workplace shower.

What kind of party? A shower can be in any form the host chooses—a brunch or supper, an afternoon tea, an evening get-together—and is more often casual than formal these days. Unless the shower is a surprise, the bride is consulted about the date, time, theme, and guest list, but party planning is up to the host.

Who is invited? A shower guest list usually includes close friends, attendants, and family members. The days of the strictly all-female wedding shower are gone, and while brides often like to keep it an all-girl event, more and more, grooms-to-be and their male friends are included on the shower guest list. The host decides the number of guests since he or she is footing the bill and providing the space.

The host should always consult the bride about the guest list, as invitees are chosen from her wedding guest list. When the party is a surprise, the host should check with the mother of the bride or the attendants instead. With very few exceptions, shower guests are wedding guests. However, when the couple is having a very small or destination wedding, friends may want to host a shower knowing the couple is unable to invite them all to the wedding. Another exception is a workplace shower—in this case, wedding invitations aren't expected.

Showers are intimate gatherings for people you know very well—not excuses to haul in more gifts. Large-group showers can get tedious for the bride and the guests. There's a rush to get all the gifts opened, and guests can feel as if the gift they spent so much time choosing and wrapping is quickly set aside to "keep the party moving." A smaller group allows the bride to focus on each present she unwraps and to show her sincere appreciation to the giver.

How many showers? There is no specific rule here, but common sense and consideration should guide you. Multiple showers are fine, but invite different guests to each party. Parents, close family members, and wedding attendants will most likely be invited to multiple showers, but they're not expected to bring presents to each. Some choose to bring small or homemade gifts, such as a collection of favorite recipes. Brides, if you have a guest in this position, it's nice to mention their previous gift at a subsequent shower, so it's clear to other guests that a gift has been given.

How are invitations issued? Shower invitations are usually informal, so notes, preprinted fill-ins, or blank invitations that can be printed at home or through a stationer are standard. It's also fine to invite by phone, email, or e-vitation. (See also Chapter 4, page 49.)

Invitations should include the theme of the shower (if there is one) and any pertinent information, such as the couple's color preferences in the case of kitchen, bath, and linen showers. It's fine for the hostess to include a separate card with gift registry sources but never specific requests or suggestions.

Showers for encore couples. It's fine to have a shower as an encore bride (or groom). It used to be that a second-time bride wouldn't have a shower thrown for her, or if one was, it would be very small. The idea was in part that she didn't need to build a household as she had already done so, but mostly it was about not taxing the goodwill and wallets of guests who had given a shower gift at a previous wedding and were now being asked to do so again.

Today, close friends and family will most likely want to celebrate this marriage just as much as any previous one. As a shower shouldn't be a huge affair with all wedding guests invited in the first place, showers for second-time brides shouldn't be a problem. In many cases, guest lists may have subtly shifted, with new friends entering the lists.

Bottom line, no bride should feel slighted or apologetic for marrying again. If a shower guest feels put out by the thought of attending a shower for a second wedding, he or she can simply choose not to attend. As with any shower, keep the spirit of the guest list about celebrating the bride's happiness, not about receiving gifts, and all will be well.

Showers for same-sex couples. Whether a couple is planning a life commitment, civil union, or marriage, friends and family may throw them a shower to celebrate and help prepare for their life together. The choice of whether to have a shower, and whether to have one together or individually, is up to the couple and the prospective host.

Registering is helpful and will let guests know what you and your partner would like. Many retailers have gotten beyond the "bride" and "groom" awkwardness, which might have been a turn-off to same-sex couples and now ask for the "registrant" and "co-registrant."

SHOWERS ON A SHOESTRING

Conscious of the financial burden that shower gifts plus wedding gifts can place on friends, many couples and shower hosts today are coming up with considerate, clever, low-cost ideas like the following:

- **Stock the bar.** A great idea for a shower held as a cocktail party, gifts might be bottles of wine, liquors or liqueurs, wine or cocktail glasses, tumblers, shakers, mixers, garnishes, swizzle sticks, coasters, bar tools, bar towels, or cocktail napkins.

- **Book and music showers.** Reading and music make great themes for showers for couples. A DVD shower might be perfect for movie lovers.

- **Recipe showers.** In this popular revival of an old custom, the presents are favorite recipes, written on standard recipe cards and collected in recipe boxes or albums. Send recipe cards with the invitation so guests can fill them out ahead, and ask them to write a little note about why it's their favorite: grandmother's apple pie, the simplest dinner ever, perfect chocolate cake.

- **Pantry showers.** For couples who already have well-equipped kitchens, guests bring useful and often exotic pantry supplies—spices, condiments and jams, rubs, coffees and teas, dried pastas, fancy nuts and dried fruits, special baking supplies, and the like.

- **Best-wishes showers.** Instead of things, guests bring sentiments—original writings, favorite quotations, humorous sayings. These expressions can be written on pages supplied by the hostess before the party, read aloud at the party, and then collected in an attractive notebook for the couple.

- **Handmade.** This shower has a very personal touch, while helping to keep gift budgets low. Gifts can be anything as long as it's made by the guest—not a professional wood carver!

- **Labor-of-love shower.** Promises, not gifts, are brought to this shower, where friends pledge to paint, wallpaper, garden, wash the couple's car, or donate their talents in any number of ways.

Surprise showers. Surprise parties can be risky. Suppose the bride has something come up at the last minute, or she isn't dressed appropriately? Or what if people are invited who she wasn't planning on inviting to the wedding? Even worse, what if she didn't really want a shower at all? Unless you're absolutely sure that springing a surprise shower will be an unquestionable hit, opt for some sort of smaller surprise at the shower instead—such as:

- A special guest from out of town (just be sure it's someone on the wedding guest list) or her fiancé

- Crowd-appropriate photos from the bride's (or groom's) past

- An arrangement of her favorite flowers that she can take home with her

Theme Showers

A shower needs no theme other than to celebrate the upcoming marriage of a couple, but sometimes a hostess narrows or custom-designs the focus of the shower after discussions with the bride regarding the wedding couple's needs. Guests are then expected to bring gifts related to that theme, and the hostess may even provide theme-related food and decorations. Ideas for themes are limitless. Choices include:

KITCHEN SHOWER

Suggested gifts: Glasses, knives, wooden salad bowls or cutting boards, linens, utensils, small appliances, cookware

SPA SHOWER

Suggested gifts: Massage certificates, aromatherapy oils, candles, robes, slippers

HENS AND CHICKS

One of the best showers I ever attended was given for my friend Melissa by her sisters. Melissa is a serious cook and a passionate baker with a sideline hobby of raising chickens. Baking was the shower theme and the entertainment. Her sisters hired a baker to teach us all how to make ricotta apple cake from scratch. When we arrived, they presented us with homemade aprons—stenciled with hens and chicks. Then we teamed up in groups of three to sour the milk for the ricotta, sieve the curds, pare and slice the apples, sift the flour, and mix the batter under the direction of our chef for the day. While the cakes were in the oven, mimosas were sipped and baking- and chicken-themed presents opened. And finally, our dessert—scrumptious apple cake! —ANNA

LINGERIE SHOWER

Suggested gifts: Lingerie, camisoles, nightgowns, pajamas, robes, slippers

GOURMET COOK SHOWER

Suggested gifts: Gourmet foods and wines, utensils, cookbooks, cooking lessons

THE GREAT OUTDOORS SHOWER

Suggested gifts: Badminton set, flower seeds and gardening tools, picnic basket, Japanese lanterns, croquet or bocce set

HAPPY HOLIDAYS SHOWER

Suggested gifts: Decorations for every holiday of the year

Suggested gifts: 8 AM guests might give a set of egg cups or a juicer, while 8 PM guests might give a mix of dinner music or set of candlesticks for the dinner table

Suggested gifts: Monogrammed luggage tags, note cards, bath or beach towels, sheets, key rings, canvas totes. (The host should check with the bride on what monogram she plans to use; see Chapter 13, page 172.)

The Etiquette of Shower Gifts

Showers are the one prewedding event where gifts are expected. After all, giving gifts is largely the purpose of showers. In general, shower gifts should be relatively inexpensive. People who can't attend are not obliged to send a shower gift, though sometimes close friends and relatives do. Here are some guidelines on sharing information about and selecting shower gifts:

- A group gift, often organized by the hostess, is a popular way to give a more elaborate or expensive present, such as a food processor or high-end espresso machine. No one should be pressured to participate, and no other present is expected from people who do contribute.

- Any shower theme (kitchen, bath, bar) should be noted on the invitation. For kitchen or bathroom showers, note the couple's color preferences on an insert that can be included in the envelope with the invitation.

- Don't include registry information on the invitation itself. It's fine to enclose a list of locations where the couple is registered on a separate sheet inserted into the invitation envelope. The hostess can also compile a list of specific gifts that the couple needs and make *recommendations* to *people who ask* for gift suggestions. (See also Chapter 13, page 164.)

- For a lingerie shower, don't put the bride's sizes on the invitation. Instead let respondents know when they accept.

Jack and Jill Showers

"Jack and Jill," or coed, showers are basically the same as a traditional shower except they include the groom and his guy friends, too. Most of the themes described above can be easily modified for both the bride and groom. But a word of advice, here: Skip the lingerie party. At first glance, the concept might seem amusing and even provocative, but this party is very bride-oriented, and if the groom's friends are there, too, it could get uncomfortable for everyone fast.

Jack and Jill showers really get fun when it comes time for the games. These usually involve asking the couple questions that center on "How well do you *really* know your spouse-to-be?" This requires a little preparation, since someone will have to ask both the bride and the groom a number of questions in advance and keep track of the answers. "What's his favorite movie?" "Who was her best friend in kindergarten?" "Where did you share your first kiss?" Keep the questions light and focus on subjects that can withstand a little teasing, in case one of them gives a wrong answer.

GAMES AND TRADITIONS

Party games for bridal showers are greeted with groans or giggles. It's all in good fun, and even if party games aren't your thing, as the guest of honor, be a good sport and go along with what your hosts have planned. Here are some of the more popular, time-tested traditions and entertainments.

THE RIBBON BOUQUET

The bridesmaids collect all the ribbons from the bride's shower presents and gather them into a bouquet for the bride to carry at the wedding rehearsal. (My grandmother remembers doing this at her bridal showers!)

FORBIDDEN WORDS

Arriving shower guests receive a clothespin or safety pin to attach to her clothing. If a guest mentions any of a list of words having to do with a wedding—church, marriage, bride, groom's name—another quick-witted guest "steals" her pin. The guest with the most pins at the end of the party wins a prize.

SHOWER GIFT BINGO

Each guest is given a bingo card, printed with a blank 5x5 grid, and a pencil. Guests fill in the blanks with gifts they think the bride will receive at her shower. The middle spot is "free" and of course a guest can fill in her own gift. As the bride opens her gifts, players cross them off the card. The first to have five in a row across, vertically, or diagonally, wins a prize.

WHAT THE BRIDE SAID

Put a guest in charge of writing down all the comments the bride makes (shh . . . don't tell her!) as she opens her gifts: "Oh, it's adorable!" "My mom has one of those, and I always wanted one." "How do you wear this?" After all the gifts are opened, have someone read them aloud (or take turns), telling the bride these are comments she'll make on her wedding night.

THE BRIDE AND ME

Have each guest bring a photo of herself with the bride. Provide a blank album as each guest puts her photo in it, she tells the story behind the photo. A twist on this game is for guests to tell a story about the bride and/or groom, say something from childhood, or share something guests might not know about the bride and her fiancé.

MARRIAGE RECIPES

Give guests recipe cards and ask them to write their recipe for a good marriage. The bride reads them aloud and tries to guess who wrote what.

WEDDING PICTIONARY

Divide guests into two teams. Provide a large drawing pad, perhaps on an easel. One person draws while her team tries to guess a wedding-related word or phrase: "honeymoon," "elope," "pop the question." Have prizes for the winning team.

TOILET TISSUE WEDDING GOWN

Divide the group into two teams, and give each team four rolls of toilet tissue. Pick two people, say the mother of the bride and mother of the groom, to be "models." Using only the tissue, the teams design and then dress the models in a wedding gown. The bride chooses the winning dress. Or forget the contest and just dress the bride.

Q: I've been to many showers and I think they're really deadly—all that sitting around watching someone open presents. Now I'm the bride-to-be and I don't want to subject my guests to this ritual. Can I open the presents at home?

A: It can be hard to be the center of attention, but it really wouldn't be fun for the other guests if you just collect all the gifts and stash them in your car. The whole point of the shower is for guests to see the gifts and for you to show your appreciation and enthusiasm as you open them. But that doesn't mean it has to be a marathon opening session.

Encourage your hostess to keep the guest list small. The more guests there are, the longer it will take to open the gifts. You also don't have to open all the gifts at once. Perhaps split the session to before and after refreshments.

It's fun to receive presents—especially when they are for you! So we encourage you to get in the spirit of the event, open your gifts with enthusiasm, and graciously thank the givers.

Party Particulars

Fun, games, gifts, and refreshments are the focus of a wedding shower, but here are some other important party elements to plan for, too.

- Gifts are generally opened after refreshments have been served. The guests gather around while the bride (or the bride and groom together if it is a joint shower) opens the presents one by one and thanks each giver.

- Someone—often one of the bridesmaids—is designated official note taker. The note taker sits beside the bride and makes a list of the gifts and who gave them, making sure the gift cards are kept with their respective gifts.

- Gifts are passed around the room so that everyone can see them. Make sure there's enough time so everyone has a chance to have their gift opened, appreciated, and fully oohed and ahhed over.

SAYING THANK YOU

Showers are special parties because they are so personal. Hosts tend to go all out, coming up with themes, games, and refreshments to please the bride. Guests put a lot of creative energy into choosing and wrapping their gifts. For these reasons, it's particularly important for the honorees to show their appreciation in a gracious and tangible way.

Q: One of my shower guests gave me note cards with my married initials on them. Should I use these to write thank-you notes for my shower gifts or should I wait until I'm married and use something else in the meantime?

A: Wait until you're married before you break out the stationery monogrammed with your married initials. Fold-over note cards are fine to use for shower thank-yous, or you can use your monogrammed maiden-name stationery.

- The bride (and groom, too, if honored at a shower) must send a thank-you note for each shower gift. Even if you've thanked the giver in person, it's important to take a moment of your personal time and show your appreciation to those who attended your shower and brought gifts. Don't forget to write thank-you notes to those who were unable to attend the shower but sent gifts. (See also Chapter 14, page 177.)

- *Do not*, under any circumstances, ask guests to fill out envelopes with their addresses at the shower. Hostesses think it's a convenience for the bride when she writes thank-you notes, but it implies laziness and an assembly-line approach to what should be a personal communication in response to a guest's personal gesture. Instead, the hostess should provide the bride with a list of names and addresses of the guests. If the invitations were sent via email or e-vitation and the bride is concerned she doesn't have all of the guests mailing addresses, it's fine to place out a guest book. Ask guests to sign with a message to the bride and their mailing address.

- Show your appreciation to anyone who hosts a shower or other prewedding party for you with a small gift, a phone call, and a handwritten note. Flowers come to mind as a classic thank-you gift. They can serve as decoration for the party when sent beforehand, or for the host to enjoy when sent afterward.

Office Shower Etiquette

Since many of us spend so much time with our colleagues at work, an office shower is a great way to celebrate your upcoming wedding with your workmates, without necessarily inviting them to the wedding itself.

IS IT OKAY TO HOST A SHOWER FOR AN ABSENTEE BRIDE?

Q: My son is marrying a wonderful woman who lives a long way away from here. Her work prevents her from coming to town for a shower before the wedding. We have lots of friends and relatives who can't make the wedding but who would love to honor the couple. Can I give the bride and groom a wedding shower without them present?

A: Certainly you can! Throw the bride and groom a "proxy" shower, a shower for a bride who cannot attend or lives far away. The hostess is responsible for sending the gifts to the bride. One idea is to have the hostess ask guests to bring their gifts unwrapped so that everyone can see them. She then provides a variety of wrapping paper and ribbons for the guests to wrap their gifts during the shower so that they can be packed into large cartons and mailed to the bride. At most proxy showers, a telephone or video call is made to the bride or the couple so that they can thank their friends in the moment (thank-you notes should still be sent to each guest).

An office shower is never something that the bride or couple requests; it happens when colleagues offer to throw one for the bride, groom, or couple. Since most offices are coed, it's nice to include both the bride- and groom-to-be in the event if schedules allow. Depending on the office, the shower might be held during office hours, or scheduled off the clock, usually after work or during the lunch hour as opposed to the weekend, though that would be fine if it was the only option.

If the office staff is small, be sure everyone is invited. If it's large, use good judgment, perhaps limiting the invited guests to the bride's department, floor, or team. Printed invitations aren't necessary; an email, phone call, or personally delivered message with the details is fine.

At most office showers, colleagues all chip in together for a gift. Fund collecting needs to be handled carefully: It's best to let people know there's a collection envelope at a designated person's desk rather than going around from person to person, which could really put someone on the spot. While a suggested amount is fine, keep it low and never make it mandatory that someone contributes in order to attend the shower. The main point is to wish your soon-to-be-married colleague well. No one should ever be given a hard time for donating less than others or nothing at all. In fact,

the "designated collector" should never mention how much each person gave.

If you are the honoree, write personal thanks to anyone who gives you an individual gift. Otherwise, write a heartfelt note of thanks to the group, deliver it to the shower organizer, and request that it be passed around or posted where all the attendees can see it. In addition, a group email is a nice way to share your thanks.

Bachelor and Bachelorette Parties

These parties good humoredly celebrate (and mourn) the bride and groom's farewell to their single life. Once just the purview of men and their legendary last sowing of wild oats, the past twenty years have seen women adopt and adapt it as well, and it's become a staple in the wedding party panoply—one that's often

---

BRIDAL SHOWER DOS AND DON'TS

Do include registry information on a separate enclosure with the invitation—but not on the invitation itself.

Do provide a copy of the guest list (names and mailing addresses) to the bride or couple.

Do send thank-you notes to all shower guests—even if you thanked them in person at the shower.

Do send a thank-you note and a gift to anyone who hosts a shower for you.

Don't coerce anyone—especially bridesmaids—to host a shower for you. It can be expensive and not everyone may be able to take it on.

Don't invite anyone to a shower who won't be invited to the wedding. (Exceptions might be when guests already know they won't be invited to the wedding, as when a destination wedding is planned or when coworkers throw a shower for an office mate.)

Don't invite guests to more than one shower. (Exceptions might be attendants and close family members.)

Don't ask guests to address their own thank-you notes.

tamer for both men and women than its old reputation suggests. Bachelor and bachelorette parties run the gamut from the iconic weekend in Vegas to fishing trips or a steak-brandy-and-cigars dinner for the guys to a spa weekend or drinks and dinner out for the girls. It could just as easily be combined with a trip to a concert or sports event, a brewery or winery tour, or a group activity such as bowling, sailing, or golf. Anything that involves spending some quality time with the bride's and groom's best friends is on the table.

Party timeline. Bachelor and bachelorette parties are usually held anywhere from two months to a week before the wedding. The extra lead time is both in case a little recovery time is needed, and also because the week before the wedding is sure to be jam packed with last-minute details and preparations.

Some couples double the fun by scheduling a shower and the bachelor or bachelorette party over the same weekend so that out-of-town friends can participate without having to arrange and pay for two trips.

The basic idea for these events is to treat the groom or bride to one last night out as a single person. The guests are good friends, the atmosphere is relaxed, and there's no reason not to have a great time—as long as everyone is willing to exercise self-control.

Who hosts? The best man and maid or matron of honor lead the other attendants in organizing their respective parties. Good friends could also throw this party, as long as they clear it with the bride or groom.

Who pays? Most bachelor and bachelorette party costs are split among the guests, with all the guests pitching in to cover the bride's or groom's expenses. Any arrangement is fine—just be sure that it's clear before the festivities begin.

BACHELOR AND BACHELORETTE PARTIES: THE FINE PRINT

⁘ Bachelor and bachelorette celebrations are by no means necessary. No one should be guilted into organizing or hosting one. Some brides and grooms prefer to skip it altogether, and good friends should honor the couples' wishes.

⁘ It's okay for encore brides and grooms to have bachelor(ette) parties.

⁘ If alcohol will be served, appoint a designated driver or make arrangements for taxi or limo service.

⁘ Generally, anyone invited to the bachelor(ette) party is also invited to the wedding.

⁘ Whatever entertainment is planned, it should not embarrass, humiliate, or endanger the honoree or any of the guests.

⁘ It's wise to hold a bachelor or bachelorette party a week or more before the wedding, so everyone can rest after what will probably be a late night.

⁘ If gifts are given, they're usually inexpensive and often humorous. Look for items that are both funny and in reasonably good taste. It's popular to give the bride or groom a humorous, inexpensive little something to commemorate the event, like a T-shirt saying "Taken."

Who's invited? For the men, the best man, the groomsmen, and the groom's closest friends and relatives form the core guest list, and sometimes the father of the groom and the father of the bride are included in part or all of the celebration. It's a similar scenario for the women: the maid of honor, the bridesmaids, and the bride's close female friends and relatives (usually those near her in age—though mothers and aunts have been known to make an appearance). That said, there's no rule that says the party can't be a coed event, start to finish. Since the night is all about celebrating with closest friends, the guest list is kept to about a dozen or so.

How does a bachelorette party differ from a bridesmaids' luncheon? The bride's female friends give the bachelorette party. It is different from the bridesmaids' luncheon in that it is often held at night and may include toasts and a dinner, similar to the bachelor party. The guest list for the bridesmaids' luncheon usually includes the attendants and the bride and groom's closest female relatives, but the bachelorette party may also include other of the bride's female friends. The bridesmaids' luncheon is often held closer to the wedding, perhaps in the days just before.

Wedding Week Parties

More and more, the week before the wedding is becoming an opportunity for extra events, as close family, the wedding party, and perhaps even some guests start arriving early. All of these parties are optional and are meant to be casual, relaxed get-togethers. Scheduling some downtime in between last-minute fittings and checking final details is a great way to keep everyone fresh and ready to smile on the big day. Wedding-week parties offer a wonderful opportunity to spend some special time with the people who mean the most to you.

When to hold them? These parties can occur anytime during the week or so before the wedding, except the night before—that's usually reserved for the rehearsal dinner.

Who hosts? While some parties have traditional hosts, any close friends or family might offer to host given how busy the couple and their parents will be in the days leading up to the wedding. For example the bride's aunt might host the bridesmaids' party, and good friends of the couple's families could entertain out-of-town guests while the wedding party is at the rehearsal dinner.

Who is invited? The members of the wedding party are on the guest list for the rehearsal dinner and the attendants' parties, but it's up to the couple to help determine additional guests, which may depend in large part on who's already in town and what kind of event it is. If any of these events are planned, it's a good idea to give the attendants a heads-up well in advance—say, when the wedding invitations go out—so appropriate travel arrangements can be made. The actual invitations are sent about a month ahead.

Are these gift-giving events? No, not in themselves, but the rehearsal dinner, bridesmaids' party, and groom's dinner are good opportunities for the bride and groom to exchange any gifts they might be giving to their attendants.

Bridesmaids' Luncheon or Party

The bridesmaids' party is usually held either a day or two before the wedding, once all the bridesmaids have arrived for the wedding, or on the morning of the wedding itself—in which case it might become a trip to the salon or a visit from a makeup artist and/or hairdresser. It's one last chance for the bride, her mother, and her attendants to have some girl time before the wedding.

Who hosts? This is a very adaptable event. The bride can host the party as a thank-you to the bridesmaids for all their hard work and support. Alternatively, an aunt, grandmother, or good friends of the bride's mother can host so the bride, her mom, and the bridesmaids don't have any entertaining duties so close to the wedding.

What type of party? A luncheon, brunch, or afternoon tea is traditional, but a dinner or cocktail party is equally nice, either at home or at a restaurant. It could just as easily be a visit to a day spa, a golf outing, a hike, or an afternoon of croquet—any event in which all can participate. The bridesmaids' party is an ideal time for the bride to exchange any gifts with her attendants.

Who is invited? The bridesmaids, the bride, and her mother form the core group, but it's also nice to include the mother of the groom and any of his sisters, if they aren't already in the wedding party, and the couple's grandmothers. Junior bridesmaids and flower girls are also invited—a point to keep in mind when planning the event.

Are gifts given? "No gifts" is generally the rule, unless the attendants or bride use this party to exchange their general wedding gifts with one another.

Groom's Dinner

Along a similar concept to the bridesmaid's luncheon, this event is hosted by the groom for his groomsmen and ushers or by the groomsmen for the groom. And while tradition calls for the event to be a formal dinner, any celebration is fine, including a lunch, barbecue, or even meeting for beers at a local pub. When hosted by the groomsmen, the best man usually organizes the event and schedules it in the days immediately preceding the wedding. The guest list can include the couple's fathers, grandfathers, and brothers who aren't groomsmen or ushers. It's also a good opportunity for exchanging any gifts between the groom and his groomsmen.

Parties for Out-of-Town Guests

A party for out-of-town guests and early-arriving wedding attendants is a lovely gift for the couple from relatives or friends. This, too, relieves the bride's parents of extra work before the wedding and gives guests a chance to spend time together in an informal atmosphere.

Invitations should be sent well in advance so that guests can plan their travel itinerary accordingly. Often the party is given by multiple hosts, who share the expenses and work. These parties may be held at home or in a club or restaurant. In addition to out-of-towners, guests could include the attendants, the couple's families, their close friends, and friends of their parents. Alternatively, the party can take place at the same time as the rehearsal dinner and focus on entertaining just the out-of-town guests.

Outings, too, can be arranged rather than parties—bowling, miniature golf, hiking, the beach, visits to local tourist attractions. These often work well on the morning of the wedding, especially when the ceremony is scheduled to start later in the afternoon. It's a great way for visitors to relax and explore the area before the wedding while their hosts are busy getting ready.

The Rehearsal Dinner

The rehearsal dinner has become a popular tradition of the wedding-party weekend—and is nearly as festive as the wedding reception. Many people say it's their favorite part of a wedding. It's a time to celebrate the upcoming wedding in a relaxed atmosphere, without the pomp and ceremony reserved for the wedding day. Everyone is arriving fresh and excited, and since rehearsal dinners are almost always limited to the couple's closest friends and family, the atmosphere is more personal and private than the wedding reception.

Like all wedding-related parties, the rehearsal dinner is completely optional. If for any reason the couple doesn't wish to have one, their choice should be respected. Still, it's a rare wedding that doesn't feature some sort of dinner for close family and friends the night before.

Party timeline. It almost always makes the most sense to hold the rehearsal dinner the night before the wedding. Not only is this convenient for everyone, but it also builds momentum to the wedding ceremony and reception the next day.

Who hosts? It has become customary, though not obligatory, for the groom's family to host the rehearsal dinner, and they should always be given first crack at taking charge of the event. This night is their chance to make a contribution to the tone of the wedding, provided they don't upstage the ceremony and reception.

WHEN SOMEONE ELSE HOSTS

Typically the groom's family chooses to host the rehearsal dinner or at least to take on the lion's share of the planning and the bill. Still, it's fine to have a rehearsal dinner if the groom's family can't or chooses not to host one. The couple can host the dinner themselves, the bride's family can host, or another relative or good friend can. Or it could be a group effort involving a combination of any of the above.

Often, the groom's parents aren't from the town or city where the wedding will take place. The couple can be a link between the two families, and help out by arranging a time for everyone to talk about rehearsal plans in person or over the phone. Specifically, the groom's family will need to know:

- ❖ The style of the reception, including size and level of formality

- ❖ Recommendations for appropriate places in town to host the dinner (preferably close to the rehearsal site)

- ❖ The time and location of the rehearsal

- ❖ The names and mailing addresses of wedding guests who will be on the rehearsal dinner guest list

These conversations are opportunities for the two families to get to know each other better. The groom's family can help by being open to suggestions and advice; the bride's family can return the favor by offering to assist with local details and by remembering that ultimately the groom's family is in charge of this event.

Discussions about hosting and about who may be paying for what should be honest and straightforward and should be respectful of people's limitations.

What kind of party? You are only limited by your budget and imagination. It could be a picnic, barbecue, clambake, buffet, or formal dinner. Given that the groom's family may not be from the area, rehearsal dinners are often held in restaurants, clubs, or private dining rooms at hotels rather than in a private home. The bride's family can help by offering ideas about suitable venues. The only guide: Don't outshine the wedding reception to come.

Who is invited? Since the purpose of the party was generated by the wedding rehearsal, the guest list focuses on those who will be participating in the ceremony, plus some close relatives:

- ❖ The bride and groom

- ❖ Members of the wedding party—and their spouses, partners, or significant others

- ❖ The officiant—and his or her spouse, partner, or significant other

- The parents, siblings, and grandparents of the bride and groom

- Any children of the bride and groom from a previous marriage unless their parents think they are too young

It's a courtesy to invite the flower girl, ring bearer, and their parents to the rehearsal dinner, but it's not mandatory for them to attend. If it's going to be a late night, parents may choose to decline the invitation or let the children attend for a short while and then depart for an early bedtime. Either way, the goal is to have the children well rested for the wedding.

Stepparents of the bride or groom are invited with their current spouses, but the hosts should avoid seating them next to their former spouses.

The wedding party's spouses, fiancé(e)s, and live-in companions are also invited. If an attendant has a guest who doesn't fit this bill, while *technically* they don't have to be invited, it's considerate and gracious to include them rather than leaving them on their own.

INVITING YOUR OFFICIANT

If the rehearsal dinner is supposed to be for the wedding party and close family, it may seem counterintuitive to invite a minister or officiant who you may hardly know. It's more than just a courtesy. If nothing else, you'll be more comfortable with him or her the next day, having spent some time socializing. And, as this is the person joining you to your true love for life, returning the favor with a nice dinner isn't a bad way to say "thank you."

After that, any number of people may be invited, and the choice is up to the hosts. Most couples include very close relatives and friends, such as aunts and uncles or godparents. In some cases, such as a destination wedding or when the wedding guest list is very small, all the wedding guests are also invited to the rehearsal dinner.

Invitations. Invitations can be written on fill-in cards, printed on blank cards, or telephoned. E-mailed invitations aren't recommended: They don't have enough oomph for the event and could easily go astray in cyberspace. If a good number of out-of-town guests are being invited, the written invitation is the best way to go; it serves as a tangible reminder of the date, time, and address of the party. Send out rehearsal dinner invitations with, at the same time as, or just after the wedding invitations have been mailed, so that guests can plan their travel accordingly.

Gifts. Guests at a rehearsal dinner don't honor the couple with gifts, but it can be the perfect occasion for the presentation of attendants' gifts, whether from the couple to the bridesmaids and groomsmen or from the attendants to the bride and groom. If being given, the attendants' gifts to the bride and groom are presented by the maid of honor and the best man, respectively or together, accompanied by a short speech or toast.

Toasts. Toasts are the main feature of the rehearsal dinner. To keep the event from going on all night, it's wise to encourage the majority of toasts during dinner, not after. The host—often the groom's father—makes the first toast, welcoming the guests and expressing his pleasure about the forthcoming marriage. He is

A JOB FOR THE BRIDE AND GROOM

The main focus of the rehearsal dinner is about bringing two families together, and often they are meeting the more extended family for the first time. The best thing the couple can do to help smooth the way is to be sure that everyone is introduced to each other. Since you'll be busy chatting with all the guests, remember to give a little help here and there with introductions.

Mixing up the families a little bit when arranging the table seating can also help; just be considerate of who you pair up with whom. If you're using place cards, consider writing names on both sides of the card. You could also add the relationship to the bride or groom: Lana Taylor, Jamie's aunt. It makes it easier for those across the table to get to know names and relationships.

SHOULD WE INVITE OUT-OF-TOWN GUESTS TO THE REHEARSAL DINNER?

Q: My fiancé's parents say we should invite all out-of-town guests to the rehearsal dinner. Is this true?

A: It's a nice gesture to include out-of-towners if your budget allows, but it's by no means a must. Many couples like to keep the rehearsal dinner a more intimate affair. Most out-of-town guests don't expect to be entertained for the entire wedding weekend, but it's a good idea to at least provide them with detailed information on local area restaurants, attractions, and activities. It's very helpful to have this information posted on your wedding website so guests can plan ahead, as well as in a prepared welcome packet at their hotel. Family friends who live in the area could host an informal dinner for out-of-town guests while the family and wedding party are at the rehearsal dinner—a lovely gift to the couple.

If you do decide to invite out-of-town guests to the rehearsal dinner, be sure to invite them all. Inviting some friends but not others or a couple of cousins but not all could easily cause hurt feelings. The same is true if you arrange another type of gathering or if someone is hosting for you.

Sit down with your fiancé and his parents and discuss their concerns and wishes, and see what options will work for you both. Many couples strike a happy compromise by keeping the rehearsal dinner small but letting other guests know they will meet them at the hotel bar or other suitable location to say hello afterward.

generally followed with a return toast by the bride's father or stepfather and then with toasts from groomsmen, bridesmaids, and anyone else who wishes to say something.

Unlike toasts at the wedding reception, which should be short and sweet, the rehearsal toasts, while sentimental to some extent, are often filled with anecdotes, jokes, and poems regaling guests with tales from the bride and groom's past. Sometimes the bride and groom stand and speak; even if they don't, they generally end the toasting by proposing a toast first to their respective parents and then to all their friends and relatives in attendance. (See also Chapter 26, page 349.)

. . . And Even More Parties

When out-of-town guests are staying overnight on the day of the wedding, the last thing the parents of the bride may want to do is entertain, but often the afterglow of the wedding carries over to an impromptu gathering with friends. Any postwedding entertainment, which can also be hosted by a close friend or relative, can be as simple as take-out pizza offered to guests who have changed into comfortable clothes or as elaborate as a next-day brunch—or both!

The fun of the gathering is in hearing and sharing postwedding stories and impressions. Often the couple and their parents are so busy and swept up in the emotion of the occasion that they miss some of the details.

The After-Party

More dancing and midnight food can follow a late-afternoon or evening wedding, especially if the bride and groom aren't leaving for their honeymoon after the reception. While all the wedding guests are invited, it's likely that the older set will say their good-byes at the end of the reception or after the wedding cake is cut. The party can continue at the reception location or move to a hotel, restaurant or bar, or a private home or beach. After-parties can be great fun—less formal than the reception and a chance to just party! The bridal party might change out of their wedding attire into more casual or party clothes. Most serve some sort of late-night comfort food, such as sliders, pizza, fried chicken, or mac and cheese.

A few things to keep in mind:

- Be respectful of neighbors, noise ordinances, and closing times.
- Limit or cut off the alcohol.
- Arrange taxis or limos to take guests home.

The Postwedding Brunch

At many weddings, this is the final, wrap-up event—a chance for family and guests to gather, relive wedding highlights, and say farewells. When many people have often traveled from a distance, it's nice to maximize time together. It's usually a very casual, drop-in type of event, say from 9 or 10 AM until noon or 1 PM. No one is expected to dress up.

Almost anyone can host—the bride's or groom's parents, other relatives, or friends. Plan on a convenient location, either someone's home or a nearby restaurant or hotel so that guests can drop by on their way home. Invitations should be sent soon after the wedding invitation is mailed. If all the guests are invited, then it's fine to post this information on the couple's wedding website or in the wedding program.

Food can be as simple as bagels, juice, and coffee or a smorgasbord of hot and cold dishes and Bloody Marys or mimosas.

A Belated Reception

When a small, private, or destination wedding has taken place, some couples decide to give a party in the weeks following the ceremony to share their happiness with friends and family.

The couple may host their own wedding party, or the bride's or groom's family can host a wedding reception for the couple.

This celebration may include all the components of any wedding reception and can be as formal or as infor-

WELCOME TO OUR FAMILY!

If the bride and groom were married in her hometown or elsewhere, and the friends of the groom and his family live too far away to attend, his parents might host a reception for them before the wedding or the first time they come to visit after the honeymoon. In some regions, this is a very typical and traditional wedding party.

Invitations can be printed or fill-in cards that say "To meet Priscilla Holmes" (before the wedding) or "In honor of Priscilla and James" (after the wedding). They should be mailed four to six weeks before the party.

This party does not try to anticipate or replicate the couple's wedding reception: There is no wedding cake, and the couple don't wear their wedding clothes. However, if the wedding has already taken place, a display of some wedding photos, especially of the bride in her wedding dress, is a nice touch.

Usually, the party is an afternoon tea or cocktail buffet and, since the whole point is to meet the bride or greet the newlyweds, an informal receiving line is called for. The host and hostess stand with the newlyweds and introduce them to everyone who has not met them. The bride's parents are invited as well, but they certainly don't have to attend if travel is an issue. Gifts are optional, as close friends and family may have already sent or intend to send wedding gifts.

mal as the couple wants. If she wishes, the bride may wear her wedding dress again at the reception party and can even have a wedding cake ready to be cut and served to guests.

Invitations. Depending on the formality of the reception, fill-in cards or printed invitations can be sent four to six weeks in advance. Here's an example of a formal invitation from the bride's parents:

MR. AND MRS. WILLIAM DEROSA
REQUEST THE PLEASURE OF YOUR COMPANY
AT A RECEPTION
IN HONOR OF
MR. AND MRS. JOHN NELSON
[etc.]

Less formally:

BILL AND PAT DEROSA
INVITE YOU TO CELEBRATE THE MARRIAGE OF
JOHN AND NANCY NELSON
[etc.]

Gifts. Because guests didn't attend the actual wedding, no gifts are expected, so don't be offended if guests don't bring or send them. However, some guests, especially good friends and close relatives, may choose to send or bring gifts. Open any gifts after the party, and send prompt thank-you notes.

CHAPTER 13

GIFTS

Wedding gifts conjure images of thick cream ribbons, carefully wrapped packages, and notes of love and best wishes. They can also bring to mind classic china, fancy silverware, and monogrammed linens—the "good stuff" most couples don't have the kind of budget to buy for themselves. But wedding gifts can also mean a fancy coffee grinder, power tool, or apple tree from the local nursery. Those classics were only classic because they were what couples wanted and felt they needed; most couples want more practical or "exciting" items today. Let your registry reflect what matters to you while following a few simple guidelines. You'll turn opening gifts from "Great, another fork" to "Yes! Someone got us a pasta maker!" (Guests will likely be more enthused as well.)

Wedding gifts have a long history. In ancient cultures, whole communities celebrated weddings as times of renewal and hope for the future. Each union was greeted as the beginning of a new family, and families ensured the survival of the community. Wedding couples were showered with symbols of fidelity, fertility, and prosperity as well as household items to help them establish their home and prepare for children. Since the bride and groom would have lived with their respective families prior to marrying, they would have needed everything—literally.

The idea behind wedding gifts is a sweet one, and showering gifts on the bridal couple is a tradition that seems to become only more deeply ingrained with time. Gifts are a tangible representation of the love and support of friends and family, and are a generous way to help young newlyweds get a head start in their lives together. Wedding gifts may be practical or fanciful, inexpensive or extravagant, but each one represents the giver's happiness for the bride and groom.

The etiquette surrounding engagement and shower gifts, gifts between the couple and their wedding party, the dos and don'ts of gift registries and the guidelines for alternative registries such as honeymoon and charitable-gift registries are all very important. You'll need to tactfully communicate your gift suggestions to your guests, and to keep track of the gifts you receive. Finally, no gift is complete without heartfelt written thanks and appreciation. (See Chapter 14, page 177.)

Gift Registries

Gift registries have been around for nearly a century as a means of helping guests select gifts that the bride and groom will enjoy. Throughout most of the twentieth century, brides typically registered with only one or two stores for traditional household gifts, listing their chosen patterns for fine and everyday china, crystal, silverware, and linens. Wedding guests could select a place setting or serving piece from a couple's pattern, and salespeople kept track of what was purchased. This kind of in-store registry with personalized service is still around, but it's a rarity.

With more than 2 million marriages performed each year, wedding-gift giving has also become big business, and almost every retailer with an online presence promotes a gift registry. And it's not just stores featuring the traditional household linens, kitchenware, flatware, stemware, and fine china; any retailer with a service or product that might be of the slightest interest to a bride and groom makes sure to feature a registry as well. National chains and catalogers can track gift purchases at all their outlets and online so that a couple's registry is always up-to-date. (See also Chapter 4, page 54.)

More and more, couples are suggesting other types of gifts—particularly when merging established households. Couples can now register with stores specializing in hardware, garden supplies, and sporting goods, to name a few, or go the honeymoon or charitable-giving route. Grooms continue to be involved in setting up the couple's wish lists, especially at kitchen stores and major home and appliance centers, which tend to have items better suited to their interests.

Today's gift registries are an even greater convenience for guests, especially those who don't know a couple's tastes, have little time for shopping, or live at a distance and can't shop at local stores. Online ordering also takes care of wrapping and delivering gifts. But many guests enjoy shopping for gifts and take pleasure in selecting "just the right thing," and no one is ever obligated to select an item from a couple's gift registry.

When, What, and How to Register

If you plan to register, do it sooner rather than later. Most couples set up their registries early in the planning process shortly after they become engaged, and complete their registries before wedding invitations are sent. Register even if you're marrying in a short time frame, so guests can shop after the wedding.

Retailers offer comprehensive checklists of suggested household items, down to the tiniest measuring spoon. By no means does this mean you need to sign up for each and every item! The following suggestions can help you select registry items wisely and with consideration for your guests:

Think about what you need. A registry is a "wish list" based on your real needs and lifestyle. If your style is casual, you may not be interested in fine china or silver. On the other hand, you may look forward to the time when your life is more formal and want to register for these more traditional gifts.

Register as a couple. Registering can be a fun and effective way to plan together for your home. In fact, it's not just brides who choose the china pattern anymore; many grooms play an active role in selecting registry items as well. Whatever you select, be sure that you and your spouse-to-be agree on the choices. You may need to compromise here and there, but there is usually room on the list to accommodate your individual choices and tastes.

Register for "couple" gifts. While there is no rule that says you can't register for an electric razor or an iPad, these are usually considered personal items and don't make for good registry gifts. That's what birthdays and holidays are for; your registry is for your new household and married life together.

Leave the choice of gifts to your guests. It's a guest's prerogative to choose your wedding gift, and they don't have to select a gift from your registry. In fact, surprises are often the best gifts of all.

Register for items in a variety of price ranges. Just as guests have varying budgets, your list should contain items in different price ranges. Also, it's a good idea to include choices for more moderately priced shower gifts.

GIFTS AU NATUREL

Some registries give you the environmentally friendly option of suggesting that guests skip the gift wrap. It is absolutely okay to check the box and save a tree!

Register with national chains and/or catalog services when possible. This makes gift selection easier, especially for out-of-town guests. They can order through catalogs, local stores, or use a chain's website or toll-free number.

Multiple registries are okay. It's fine to register with more than one store or website. Two, or three at the most, should give you plenty of variety.

Don't register for the same items at different stores. Since retailers don't coordinate information with other retailers, you might receive many more of an item than you want.

Monitor your registry. Most guests select gifts in the week or two just before the wedding day. As your day approaches, check your registries to make sure that there are still a variety of items on the lists. Add choices in varying price ranges, as necessary, so your guests who shop at the last minute have something to choose from other than one washcloth or an expensive grill.

Registry Alternatives

Not every couple is comfortable registering, and not everyone needs or wants tangible items. Alternatives, like the following, can fulfill your wishes, help your guests with gift selections, and may even spread your happiness in unexpected directions.

No registry. Couples don't have to register for gifts. If you plan a small wedding or your guests are all family and friends who know your tastes and needs, there may be no reason to register. You also simply don't have to if it doesn't feel right for you.

Charitable gifts. Couples who don't want gifts might steer guests to charities or nonprofits that are near and dear to their hearts. Share this wish on your wedding website, and give close family and friends the name(s) of one or two causes you consider worthwhile. Ask them to inform other guests to donate in your name. You could also encourage guests to give to their favorite charities in your name in lieu of their gifts to you. (Asking guests to give in your name isn't egotistical; it's important for purposes of thanking: Established charities will notify you of donations made in your name so you can write a thank-you note to the donor.)

You can also set up a "registry" to track donations at websites like www.idofoundation.org. It's advisable to avoid political or highly controversial causes. Also, some people may not hear about your desire or may prefer to give a tangible gift, so be gracious if you receive traditional items.

Note, too, that since you aren't requesting a traditional gift, some guests might consider your request to donate to a charity "in lieu of gifts" as an optional alternative to "no gifts." Don't be surprised or offended if some guests don't donate or give a gift if you have gone this route.

Combination gift and charity registries. This creative type of gift registry is offered by some stores, which donate a percentage of the value of each gift you receive to one or more charities of your choice. Couples can do this at www.idofoundation.org/welcome/registries/giftregistry.html, or you can link to the foundation through www.weddingchannel.com.

Financial registries. Check with your bank or investment house about financial gifts; some now have registries for savings accounts, stocks, bonds, and other investment vehicles. There are even registries for couples who are saving for down payments on houses or cars.

Cash and checks. Cash gifts are perfectly acceptable *if* the guest feels comfortable with the idea. Although cash gifts are traditional in some areas and cultures, some people just don't like to give money, and that's their prerogative.

Honeymoon registries. Now available through many travel companies and agents, these registries allow guests to contribute to a couple's honeymoon-trip fund. Make sure the service has a system for advising you of each person's gift.

Getting the Word Out

Word of mouth is the tried-and-true polite method of telling people about your gift registry, but increasingly, guests turn to a couple's wedding website to find out registry information and/or link directly to the registry. Once you've registered, provide your parents, siblings, and your wedding party with a list of your registry sources because these are the people who guests will usually ask. Guests may also ask you directly, or check your wedding website.

Do not include any gift registry information in your wedding invitation. Some retailers encourage couples to send registry lists or an enclosure saying where they're registered with their invitations (these enclosures are sometimes provided by retailers for "convenience"). Although this may seem practical, their real purpose is as a marketing tool for the retailer. Mentions of registries and enclosures such as these easily offend recipients by putting the emphasis on gifts instead of on the invitation to join you on your wedding day. Don't do it. This is also the reason to even avoid the phrase "No gifts, please." While the message is different and meant well, it still draws attention to the question of gifts instead of to guests.

If asked, it's okay to tell guests where you're registered. As long as you're not the one to bring up the subject of gifts with a guest, it's fine to respond to their questions. If asked directly, a courteous response not only includes retailer names but also a kind addition such as: "Whatever you choose would be special. Thanks for thinking of us!"

GIFTS FROM THE GUESTS' PERSPECTIVE

It's important to know the gift etiquette for guests so that you can understand and appreciate their choices.

- The choice of what to buy or give you is always up to the guest, even if you have a registry or have expressed a preference for an alternative. Period.

- There is no minimum (or maximum) amount guests should spend.

- Families living under one roof, couples, or guests with plus-ones give gifts jointly.

- While becoming more popular, engagement gifts aren't always given.

- Guests attending a shower bring a gift (in the spirit of the theme, if there is one). If a guest cannot attend the shower, he or she may send a gift but is not obligated to do so.

- Guests invited to a wedding ceremony, whether or not they can attend, should send or bring a gift.

- Following on this idea, guests invited to a destination wedding, whether they attend or not, should send a gift instead of bringing one, as it requires the couple to coordinate shipping them home. However, as the costs of attending destination weddings are often high, it's gracious of the couple to spread the word that "your presence is your present."

- Guests invited just to a reception (the same day or a belated one) may give a gift if they wish but aren't required to do so.

- Technically, no additional gifts are required from bridesmaids and groomsmen other than their wedding gift (and shower gift, should they attend one). Again, given the cost of being a member of the wedding party, many couple's consider their attendants' participation as their gift. (See also page 171.)

Share unconventional gift requests diplomatically. As with registries, give this information out by word of mouth when asked, "Of course we would love anything you give us, but we could really use help with the honeymoon / a down payment on our first home / etc." It's okay to say "cash," but if that makes you uncomfortable, "donation" "help," or "contribution" are all good substitutes. It's also sometimes more comfortable for a guest to give money when they know what it is going toward—a car rental on the honeymoon, your future backyard orchard, and so on. Lastly, always include a comment letting them know that any gift will be appreciated so they will feel at ease choosing a more traditional gift if that's more comfortable for them.

Do include registry information on your wedding website. It's convenient for guests, and many wedding guests now expect to find gift registry links there. Just make sure the links aren't the first (or worse, only!) things a guest sees when visiting your wedding website. It could appear tacky—that you're more interested in gifts than in sharing your wedding news.

It's okay to include registry information with shower invitations. While you won't be sending these invitations yourself, anyone hosting a shower for you will want to inform shower guests where you're registered, so they can include a note *with*, not *on*, the invitation. Why is this okay? Unlike a wedding, the purpose of a shower is to "shower" the honoree with gifts, and this is a convenience for guests. The separate note may seem like splitting hairs, but it's a gracious nod to keeping the focus on their attendance, not their gift.

All About Wedding Gifts

A gift is, by definition, voluntary. Although gifts are customarily expected for some occasions, including weddings, this is a matter of social convention, and no one should regard a gift as an entitlement. Local and cultural traditions may influence gift choices and methods of delivery or presentation, but the following guidelines will help couples know when gifts are considered appropriate, what types suit specific occasions, and how to receive every gift with grace and gratitude.

Engagement Gifts

Unless it's customary in your area or part of your culture, engagement gifts aren't expected, regardless of whether there's an engagement party. If given, engagement gifts tend to be tokens of affection and aren't very expensive. Classic engagement gifts run along the lines of a picture frame, a guest book or photo album, a bottle of good wine, or a set of guest towels. Some traditionalists give gifts just to the bride—little luxuries for her engagement such as closet or drawer sachets, pretty slippers, or elegant note cards.

If some guests bring presents to an engagement party, open the gifts later so that guests who didn't bring gifts aren't embarrassed. Never make a guest feel as if they were in error by not bringing a gift. Only if *everyone* brings gifts to an engagement party (and in some locales that is the norm) is it okay for the couple to open them at the gathering. No matter when you open the gifts, or if you thanked the giver in person, send a handwritten thank-you note.

Shower Gifts

While showers are by no means mandatory, most brides or couples will have one, or possibly more, thrown in their honor. Unless it's a surprise, the host of the party will consult with the bride or the couple about the guest list (shower guests are almost always wedding guests) and the type of shower, say a kitchen shower, hour-of-the-day shower, or letter-of-the-alphabet shower. Years ago, shower gifts were handmade for the occasion, and while such gifts are still treasured, most shower guests buy their gifts these days. Conscious of the financial burden that shower gifts, plus wedding gifts, can place on friends, considerate couples and shower hosts may choose a clever low-cost themed event such as a recipe shower or a best-wishes shower.

Guests who attend a shower for you will bring an individual gift or might contribute to a group gift. Guests who can't attend may or may not send a gift—either is entirely correct and up to the individual. Also, guests who have already attended one shower for you—perhaps your bridesmaids or an aunt or two—don't need to bring a gift to subsequent showers. Or they might bring a simple, inexpensive one. You might consider mentioning any previous gifts at subsequent showers so the other guests understand.

Since presents are the point of the shower, it's important that you open each gift with enthusiasm. That means saying something complimentary and positive about the gift—"These towels are the perfect color for our guest bath"—and thanking the giver—"Thank you, Alex, I appreciate that you went to the trouble to have them monogrammed so beautifully."

Shortly before the shower, ask your host for a list of anticipated guests and collect any addresses that you don't have. If the invitations were sent by email, you could also put out a guest book, asking guests to leave their address along with a message. But by all means, *don't* ask the guests to address their own envelopes to save you time (the promise of using them to draw door prizes does not mitigate the problem)—this is for you to do. If you catch wind of your host planning to do this, gently but firmly dissuade her, "Pam, I know it sounds helpful, but I'm much happier addressing them myself. I really don't want your guests to have to go to that effort on my behalf."

Even when you've expressed your thanks personally, follow up with a handwritten note within a few days. Most people go to a good bit of effort selecting and wrapping their shower gifts, so you'll want to go the extra mile to show your appreciation, too. Write to each person who participated in a group gift or, as in the case of a gift from a large group of coworkers, write to the organizer and ask that the note be shared. (Here's a case when an email group thank-you is also appropriate.) (See also Chapter 14, page 177; and Chapter 12, page 149.)

Your Wedding Gifts

Most of us like the thrill of opening a gift, especially when we don't already know what's inside. It's especially delightful when couples open their gifts together, but circumstances don't always cooperate, such as when you and your fiancé(e) live some distance apart. Don't put off opening gifts; delays will hold up your thank-you notes and may cause red faces when you run into a friend whose unopened package you've stashed away. Being organized about receiving and acknowledging gifts is critical to helping you show your appreciation—and to keep the process from becoming stressful.

THE GIFT OF FRIENDSHIP

Q: My wife and I have been married for three months. A handful of guests, mostly my friends, have not given us gifts yet. Is it still the case that you have one year to give a gift? If we do not receive a gift, what is a proper way to remind them?

A: There is a world of difference between what a guest should do and what you are owed (or can "remind" about). While it's customary for a wedding guest to give a gift to the bride and groom, the couple shouldn't view the custom as an entitlement. (Incidentally, the one-year time frame has always been a loose myth. Ideally, a gift is sent sometime close to the date of the wedding.)

The answer: Be kind. Be patient. Give the benefit of the doubt. If a gift never arrives, let it go. It's far better to focus on appreciating the gifts you did receive than to head down the awkward path of confronting guests who didn't pony up. You'll only end up embarrassing and shaming those guests rather than engendering feelings of generosity and affection. To stay mad about not receiving a gift suggests you care more about the gift than the friend. Chalk it up to their forgetfulness, cluelessness, or hard times. Friendships are fundamentally based on much more than gifts.

Is a wedding gift expected? Yes. Following long-established tradition, everyone who receives a wedding invitation should send a gift—whether they attend the wedding or not. There are a few exceptions: If you send invitations to very casual acquaintances, business associates you don't know well, or people you haven't seen in years and they don't attend the festivities, then gifts aren't expected. It would be more appropriate to send these people wedding announcements instead of invitations.

Married couples and nuclear families generally send one gift, as do people invited as a couple. When you invite someone "and Guest," the person you invite is responsible for a gift, but the guest or date isn't. Group giving, when guests pool their resources to purchase a more elaborate gift, is fine.

How much should guests spend on gifts? A wedding gift is a social obligation, but the choice of the gift is based on the giver's affection for and relationship to the couple and their families and on their personal budget. It's a complete myth that a guest should spend an amount that is equal to the per-person amount spent on a guest at the reception. (How would they know that anyway?) Expecting this kind of quid pro quo exchange is impractical and thoughtless.

You can also expect that your wedding gifts may take many forms: housing for some of the bridal party; a party for out-of-town guests; a heartfelt letter of good wishes from a favorite professor who can't attend; a homemade pottery vase; an heirloom passed along by your great aunt. Be gracious and always show appreciation as much for the thought behind it as for the gift itself.

When are gifts sent? Be prepared. Gifts may be sent as soon as the wedding invitation arrives, and some may come earlier if people know for certain that they'll be invited (like your grandmother). Most guests send gifts before the wedding, but gifts may arrive afterward, particularly when the wedding is held on short notice. In some cultures and communities, gifts are brought to the wedding itself. Circumstances such as an invitee's illness or personal troubles may cause a delay, and couples shouldn't question a late arrival. Modern etiquette advice says wedding gifts should be sent close to the wedding date or within three months after. Still, you might have a guest or two operating on the erroneous "one year" timetable.

How are gifts delivered? Gifts are usually sent by mail or delivery service to the return or RSVP address on the wedding invitations, so when you craft your invitation, be sure that this address is where you want both your replies and your gifts delivered. If ordering through an online or in-store registry that offers shipping, gifts will be sent to whatever address you provide. After the wedding, guests usually send gifts to your home address, so set a reminder to update your registry shipping information if this address changes.

If it's customary for guests to bring their gifts to the wedding ceremony or reception, then you should plan to have a table set up for them. You're not expected to open the gifts during the reception, but you will have to arrange to have someone oversee the packages and transport them to a safe place afterward. It's also a nice idea to have a pretty box or basket to collect cards and notes brought by guests.

How are gifts acknowledged? When gifts are mailed or shipped a quick call or email to let the giver know that the item arrived is thoughtful. Regardless of whether you thank the person verbally, *every wedding gift must be acknowledged with a handwritten personal thank-you note.* A guest who doesn't receive a thank-you note after a reasonable time—usually three months after sending the gift—may (rightly)

contact you (or your mother!) to learn if the gift was delivered. (See also Chapter 14, page 177.)

What about wedding gifts for encore couples? Guests who have attended a prior wedding of the bride or groom and given a gift have no obligation to give another. Still, there will be close friends and relatives of couples who want to give a present anyway to share in the couple's happiness. New friends who had not attended a first wedding for either member of the couple would give a gift as at any other wedding, unless the word has been spread that the couple requested no gifts be given. (See also Chapter 18, page 247.)

Will belated reception guests give gifts? When the reception takes place sometime after the wedding ceremony, guests may very likely give a gift to share their excitement for you. There is no obligation for them to do so when invited to the reception but not the actual ceremony, regardless of whether the reception is held on the same day as the ceremony or at a later date. (See also Chapter 12, page 158.)

A WEDDING ANNOUNCEMENT HAS NO ATTACHED GIFT OBLIGATION

Wedding announcements, sent soon after the wedding to people who weren't on the final guest list or far-flung friends or business associates who might be interested in your news, are a courtesy. Like birth and graduation announcements, they carry no obligation to send a gift. While some recipients may send you a card or a present, you shouldn't expect them.

Keeping Track of Your Gifts

There's no question that you'll need a simple but comprehensive system to keep track of your wedding gifts and to check off when you acknowledged them. Gift tags can easily be lost or mixed up, and it's hard to remember who gave what. Keeping a record helps you associate specific gifts with the givers, so you can say something complimentary when you next see your guests and personalize your thank-you note. A detailed list also serves as a record for insurance purposes.

Most couples keep a written log or computer file, recording information as soon as gifts arrive. (See also Chapter 4, page 47.) This information should include:

* **The date the gift is received.** To make sure a thank-you note is sent within a reasonable time and in case you need to contact the seller.

* **A clear description of the item or items.** Writing "platter" won't help much if you receive three or four. Be specific: "18-inch pottery platter, sunflower design." Include the quantities of multiple items (e.g., "four monogrammed pillowcases, pale blue").

* **The source of the gift and shipping method.** Store, catalog service, and so forth, if known. Also note how it was shipped (USPS, UPS, FedEx, etc.) in case there is damage or breakage.

* **The name and address of the giver or givers.** Save gift tags or cards to double-check spellings.

* **The date you sent your thank-you note.** A record that your note was mailed.

It's also a good idea to number the gifts in your log and attach the corresponding number to each gift.

#	Name	Address
1	M/M Harry V. Smith	555 Ridgewood Ave Essex Fells, NJ 07021

Gift	Date Recieved
Silver Revere Bowl	05/01/15

From	Shipping
Tiffany's	UPS

TY Note: 5/4/15

Notes: monogrammed "P"

Gifts for the Wedding Party

Gifts are often exchanged among members of the wedding party, and gifts from the bride and groom to their attendants are considered especially important.

Bride and groom's gifts. It's traditional for the bride and groom to give a special gift of appreciation to each attendant. Usually the bride chooses the gift for her bridesmaids and the groom for his groomsmen and/or ushers. Some brides give their attendants the jewelry—a necklace or earrings, for example—that they'll wear on the day. Grooms might give groomsmen cuff links, tie clips, or the tie itself. Alternatively, a couple might give the same gift to everyone. Glassware (such as etched wine or pilsner glasses), picture frames, and gadgets such as iPods are typical of gifts that cross gender lines. Gifts need not be expensive but should be a meaningful or fun commemoration of the occasion.

If you have children in your wedding party, personal and age-appropriate gifts will be a special treat for each young participant.

Gifts to the wedding party are usually presented at the rehearsal dinner, at the rehearsal if there is no dinner, or at bridesmaids' and groomsmen's parties. Sometimes gifts are presented at the wedding, but there's always the risk they could be lost.

Attendants' gifts. Wedding attendants often present gifts to the bride and groom, though this isn't an absolute. The expense of being in a wedding can put a serious strain on an attendant's budget, so couples need to be sensitive. If attendants host a prewedding party or give shower presents in addition to their individual wedding gift, a considerate couple will make it clear that no other gifts are expected. Although costly gifts shouldn't be expected in any case, a group gift— bridesmaids to the bride, groomsmen / ushers to the groom, or the entire wedding party to the couple—can be the ideal way to express love and best wishes at the least expense for each attendant.

Attendants' gifts are usually presented at bridesmaids' and groomsmen's parties, the rehearsal, or the rehearsal dinner.

Gifts to each other. Though not essential, couples often give each other personal engagement and wedding gifts in addition to their rings. Gifts can range from jewelry engraved with the wedding date or a special sentiment to fun items to share in your new life together.

Gifts for family. Though not expected, gifts for parents, stepparents, and grandparents are a lovely tribute to the people who have cherished and supported you both through thick and thin. Expense isn't the issue: A family gift can be as simple as roses and a loving notes placed on their seats at the ceremony or a small book of verse or meditations with a special personal inscription.

Gifts are very important for the young and teenage children of either or both members of the couple. (For ideas for making children feel special at an encore wedding, along with gift suggestions, see Chapter 18, page 244.)

All About Monogramming

A personal monogram consists of three initials (first, middle, last) or uses the last name initial only. The initial of a nickname is not normally included in a monogram. Traditionally, married couples use his and her first initials plus their last name initial or, more simply, just their last name initial. For their personal monograms, a husband's initials don't change unless the couple uses a hyphenated last name; and a wife generally uses her maiden name as her middle name if she takes her husband's name, though in some regions a newly married woman will keep her given middle name and drop her maiden name. But today, with some couples using both last names and some wives keeping their maiden names, monograms can be a bit more complicated.

CREATING A MONOGRAM

This chart will help you choose the right monogram. The order of initials depends on whether the letters are of the same size or the initial of the last name is larger, in which case it's centered.

	WHEN INITIALS ARE THE SAME SIZE	WHEN CENTER INITIAL IS LARGER	SINGLE INITIAL
For a couple named Jane Anne Bowen and Thomas Ryan Nelson:			
Single woman (used for personal items and stationery before marriage)	first, middle, last *JAB*	first, last, middle *JBA*	last *B*
Single man (used for personal items and stationery before and after marriage)	first, middle, last *TRN*	first, last, middle *TNR*	last *N*
Married couple		wife's first name, married/last name, husband's first name *JNT*	married/last name *N*
Married woman (for personal items and stationery)	first, maiden name, married/last name *JBN*	first, married/last name, maiden name *JNB*	married/last name *N*

	WHEN INITIALS ARE THE SAME SIZE	WHEN CENTER INITIAL IS LARGER	SINGLE INITIAL
Married couple with a hyphenated last name		wife's first name, hyphenated married name, husband's first name *JB-NT*	hyphenated last name *B-N*
Married woman or man with a hyphenated married/last name uses the same form)	first, middle, hyphenated last name *JAB-N* *TRB-N* (or) first, hyphenated last name *JB-N* *TB-N*	first, hyphenated last name, middle *JB-NA* *TB-NR*	hyphenated last name *B-N* *B-N*
Married couple when wife keeps her maiden name	wife's maiden name and husband's last name initials separated by a dot, diamond shape, or other design *B*N*		

For Lynn Carter-James and John Lewis-Wiesner:

	WHEN INITIALS ARE THE SAME SIZE	WHEN CENTER INITIAL IS LARGER	SINGLE INITIAL
Married couple when wife keeps her maiden name and both wife and husband come with hyphenated last names	same as above, or *C-J*L-W*		

For Anna Smith Von Haegel; for Anna and Carl Von Haegel:

	WHEN INITIALS ARE THE SAME SIZE	WHEN CENTER INITIAL IS LARGER	SINGLE INITIAL
Individual or married couple when the last name includes a capitalized article, making it two words: Von, Van, Du, etc.	*ASVH*	*AVHC*	*VH*

For Peter James O'Neil; for Leslie and Peter O'Neil:

	WHEN INITIALS ARE THE SAME SIZE	WHEN CENTER INITIAL IS LARGER	SINGLE INITIAL
Individual or married couple when the last name begins with Mc, Mac or O', but is only one word	*PJO*	*LOP*	*O*

Some guests may want to have some items like bath towels, dinner napkins, or a serving piece monogrammed for you, and they'll want to know the correct initials or form to use. Let your parents and attendants know your preference in case a guest asks.

Here are ways some typical wedding gifts are monogrammed:

Linens. Many people today prefer the single last name initial or hyphenated initials, but the other monogram forms on the chart on pages 172–173 are also appropriate.

Towels are marked at the center of one end. Top sheets are monogrammed so that when the sheet is folded down, someone standing at the foot of the bed can read the letters. Pillowcase monograms are centered approximately two inches above the opening's hem. Rectangular tablecloths are monogrammed at the center of each long side, and square cloths at one corner. Dinner napkins are marked diagonally at one corner.

Flatware. The choice of monogram is usually determined by the shape of the flatware handle. The last initial or hyphenated last initials are often used. In some cases, a couple's initials are stacked in an inverted triangle, with the couple's first-name initials on top and the last initial below:

$$J \quad T$$
$$N$$

Clothing and other personal items. Generally, use the individual's personal monogram or the married/last name initial (single or hyphenated).

Exchanging and Returning Gifts

Handling gift glitches gracefully can be tricky. From a purely practical standpoint it is reasonable to replace a gift that arrived damaged or mismarked ("Sarah" when you spell your name "Sara"). As you decide how you'll handle your sticky gift situation, keep consideration of the giver foremost in your thoughts. When you come up with your answer, ask yourself, "How would I feel had this been my gift?" Here are some suggestions for handling some common gift dilemmas.

What do we do with duplicate presents? You may discreetly exchange duplicate presents. If friends who have given a gift realize that you have more than one, they should encourage you to exchange theirs for something else.

What about unwanted gifts? If a gift isn't a duplicate but rather something you neither like nor need, you may exchange it—but take care before you do. Would your close friend be hurt if she knew you returned her gift for something else? Don't exchange the presents chosen for you by your own families unless you are specifically told to do so. Nor should you discard a gift that was made especially for you.

Should I let the giver know I exchanged his or her gift? When you write a thank-you note for a duplicate gift that you have exchanged, simply thank the giver for the present with enthusiasm. You don't have to explain that you exchanged the gift for something else.

What do I do if a gift arrives broken? If a gift that was sent directly from the giver arrives broken, check to see if the package was insured. If so, notify the per-son who sent it immediately so that he or she can collect the insurance and replace it. If the package wasn't insured, you may not want to mention that it arrived broken; otherwise the person who gave it may feel obligated to replace it.

When a broken gift arrives directly from a store or online service, simply take it back or contact the service for a replacement without mentioning a thing to the donor. Any reputable store will replace merchandise that arrives damaged.

Is it okay to regift? Regifting is generally better avoided whenever possible, and that goes double for wedding gifts, which are so personal (and often expensive). Would the giver be hurt if he found out? If there's any chance of that, don't do it. (There's more than one story of a couple who regifted a wedding present being outed when the new recipient discovers a numbered sticker used by the couple to keep track of who had given it still attached!)

CHAPTER 14

THE IMPORTANCE
OF "THANK YOU"

There are two fundamentals of expressing gratitude. First, every gift—whether a tangible item, money, a social event in your honor, or a gift of time or talent—should be acknowledged in writing. And second, your acknowledgment should be prompt.

Personal, handwritten thank-yous remain the gold standard of courtesy in this age of texting, email, and instant messaging. Written notes demonstrate that the writer cares enough about the giver to compose an individualized message and put the words on paper.

How to Thank

When it comes to thanking, it's not just that you do it; it's also how you do it that matters.

Respond in a timely fashion. Ideally, you'll write within a few days of receiving a wedding gift. If you put off all note writing until after the wedding, it can truly become a chore. For couples stymied by the large number of notes to be written, set a daily goal. Completing three or four notes each day doesn't seem nearly so impossible as writing a hundred notes within a month.

Follow the accepted standard. Your thank-you notes should be written and sent *within three months* of the receipt of each gift, not the mythic year.

Share the responsibility. The days when thank-yous were the sole duty of the bride are over. Today's brides and grooms share the responsibility, which greatly decreases the time involved. Often, each writes to the people he or she knows best. This makes it easier to tailor notes to the individual givers.

> ### NO THANKS
>
> The number one complaint from wedding guests is the lack of a thank-you note for a gift. Here's how they'll handle it: They'll either call your mother, who will then be on your case, or they'll think you have bad manners. It's the type of thing people don't seem to be able to let go of: "Alex and Sam? We sent them a really nice (read 'expensive') decanter and never heard a word from them."

WHAT KIND OF STATIONERY?

There's no single stationery required for thank-you notes, though you'll probably use a single-fold note card, correspondence card, or single sheet and matching envelope. The paper can be plain or bordered, white, ecru, ivory, or a pastel color. Use ink that's easy to read; black is always legible.

Notepapers printed with "Thank You" or a short quotation or verse are fine as long as you add your own note; it's not acceptable to just sign a card with a preprinted message. Some photographers offer note cards printed with a photo from your wedding or engagement shoot. These can be great souvenirs for guests, but if using a wedding photo don't delay note writing while you wait for these cards to arrive.

Monogrammed notes sent by the bride before the wedding have her maiden name initials; post-wedding notes have her married initials (if she changed her name) or the couple's last-name initial. When husbands and wives share monogrammed stationery, the last / married-name initial, hyphenated initial, or double last-name initials (when the wife retains her maiden name) can also be used. (See also Chapter 13, page 172.)

Include your fiancé/fiancée or new spouse in the thanks. Your message expresses gratitude from both of you. Traditionally, you alone would sign the note you pen. Many couples now both sign thank-you notes, regardless of who wrote them. There may be exceptions to the joint note (such as when someone does a favor or entertains specifically for you), but in general people are giving to you as a couple. (See also page 180.)

Don't take shortcuts. Simply signing store-bought cards shows very little consideration and is tantamount to a brush-off. Likewise, writing virtually the same message to everyone is mechanical, and people quickly recognize a "fill in the blank"–type note. You might post a general thanks on your wedding website or Facebook page to everyone for sharing your special day, but this doesn't replace the need to send personal notes.

Whom to Thank

As you write notes, remember that not all gifts come wrapped in pretty paper. The following categories include both gift givers and the people who make a wedding special through their efforts and goodwill.

Everyone who gives you a wedding present. This includes people who literally hand you a present, no matter how effusively you thank them in person. You should write to each person or couple who contributed to a group gift. The one exception is a group gift from more than four or five coworkers, in which case you can write one note to be shared among them.

Thank-you notes are expected for shower gifts even though you thanked the givers in person when presents were opened. Written notes must also be sent to anyone who couldn't attend the shower but sent a gift.

Everyone who gives you money. This includes cash, checks, contributions to savings and investment accounts, and donations to designated charities. You can mention amounts if you want, and doing so assures givers their gift arrived intact. Always include some indication of how you plan to use a monetary gift. (See also page 181.)

Your attendants. In addition to thank-you notes for wedding presents, be sure to attach a card or note with a personal sentiment to the gifts you give your attendants: "Thanks for everything, baby brother. You really are the *best* best man I could ask for. Love, Mitch."

People who entertain for you. When there's more than one host for a shower or party, write to each person or couple. These notes should go out no later than two days after the event. The one exception is when a large number of people in your office or workplace host a shower or party in your honor and give a group gift. It is fine to write a group note and post it in a common area and/or send a group email thanking everyone involved. If your coworkers give individual presents to you, write and mail or deliver individual handwritten notes of thanks.

People who house and/or entertain your guests. When family and friends invite out-of-town guests or attendants to stay in their homes, write notes to the hosts and send thank-you gifts (those staying with them should do the same). The gift, with your card or note attached, might be an item for their home such as a potted plant, a basket of soaps, or a book by their favorite author. Friends who entertain your visitors—inviting them to dinner, taking them shopping, showing them the sights—deserve a note from you, too.

People who do kindnesses for you. The neighbor who accepts delivery of your gifts when you're at work, the cousin who supervises guest parking at your reception—anyone who assists you during your preparations, the wedding itself, and after the big event should be graciously thanked. It's also nice to send notes to your officiant and others (the organist or music director, for instance) who worked with you on the ceremony, even if you've paid them a fee.

Suppliers and vendors. You don't have to write everyone you hire for services, but anyone who exceeds your expectations will appreciate a warm note of thanks. (See also Chapter 2, page 36–37.)

The A+ Thank-You Note

While there's no formula for the perfect thank-you note, the notes people remember are the ones that express real feeling. Think about the people you're thanking before you write anything. How would you say it if you were thanking them in person? Another hint: Look at the gift when you prepare to write; it may provide inspiration.

The first two examples below illustrate the difference between a note that gets the job done adequately and one that expresses thanks for a gift and real interest in the givers. While there is nothing wrong with the first note, the extra effort in the second is well worth it.

A simple note:

Dear Mr. and Mrs. Gresham,

Thank you so much for the lovely silver candy dish. It was so nice of you to think of Phil and me on our wedding day. I'm sorry you couldn't be with us, but we hope to be back in St. Paul during the holidays and maybe we can all get together then.

Thanks again for thinking of us in such a nice way.

Love,
Courtney

A more personal note:

Dear Mr. and Mrs. Gresham,

I'm looking right now at the lovely silver candy dish you sent and imagining how pretty it will be on our Thanksgiving table next month. (We're hosting Phil's family for the first time!) It really is one of our favorite things, and Phil and I are so grateful to you.

We were both sorry that you couldn't come to the wedding, but I know your trip to New Zealand must have been amazing. If all goes according to plan, we will be in St. Paul for Christmas, and we'd love to see you and the girls and hear about your travels.

Again, thank you so much for the candy dish and for the beautiful thoughts in your note.

Love from both of us,
Courtney

There's no reason for a note to be stuffy and formal. Write from your heart and the words will come—as they did in this warm and humorous example:

Dear Uncle Jim,

Well, you really saved the day—the Big Day—when my car conked out. If it weren't for you, I'd probably still be standing in front of Bartlett's, hanging on to my tux bag and trying to hail a cab in that downpour. Meg considers you our personal guardian angel. First you get me to the church on time, and then we arrive in Antigua and discover that you've treated us to three days of our trip! I'm enclosing a photo so you can see the incredible view of the ocean from our hotel.

We can't thank you enough for everything you've done. And I promise never to leave home without my jumper cables again.

Much love from your grateful,
if forgetful, nephew,
Peter

Thanks for the Money

Thanking someone for a monetary gift can seem awkward, especially as most of us have been taught that it's not polite to talk about money. While you can dance

around the subject, the fact is that you were given money in some form, and the giver should be thanked just as directly for his or her gift as someone who gave you a teapot. Mentioning the amount is optional. (See also page 178.)

Dear Mr. and Mrs. Abel,

Chris and I were delighted and touched by your generous gift of $500 / your generous check (for $500) / the two shares of Apple stock / the ($500) Treasury bond. We have started a house fund, and this will make a big dent in the down payment.

We were so glad you were able to make it to our wedding. You've been my parent's friends for as long as I can remember, and it meant so much to me to have you there.

Chris and I are planning to be back in Dayton for Thanksgiving, and I'm sure we'll see you then.

Love,
Sophie

PART FIVE

PLANNING THE BIG DAY

CHAPTER 15

PLANNING YOUR CEREMONY

A wedding isn't a wedding without the "I dos," and for all of the planning that goes into the reception, your ceremony is the jewel in the crown of all your wedding events, and as such deserves careful thought and planning by you and your fiancé(e). The ceremony, more so than the reception, is often influenced by family and cultural traditions—such as your or your parents' religious preferences; your church, temple, or other affiliation; and the customs of your culture or community. Adhering to traditional ceremonial customs is a way to honor your families and cultural heritage. It can provide a spiritual connection to the generations that have gone before and infuse the ceremony with meaning.

There is a considerable amount for you to research and plan early on. Certain faiths have requirements regarding prewedding counseling or limitations as to how much of the ceremony can be personalized. There are legalities to confirm: Not all religious officiants have the legal authority to perform marriages and you may need to have a civil ceremony as well.

Now is a good time to take a look at Chapter 25, page 329, to get an overview of how the service flows. You'll want to use it to start making notes about schedules, delegating tasks, and ceremony checklists. Some of the details of the ceremony, such as the choice of readings and music, can wait, but other decisions—the day and time, location, and officiant—should be among the very first planning tasks to check off the list. Here's a look at what to think about as you plan your ceremony as well as a look at different religious and secular wedding ceremonies.

First-Level Decisions

There are three integral decisions regarding your ceremony—the site, the officiant, and the date and time. One decision often impacts the others, so think about which is your top priority. It may be a desire to be married by an officiant whom you've known all your life. In turn, that may dictate the ceremony site, and his or her availability may determine the date and time of the wedding. Or you may want to be married in the synagogue where you grew up because of its significance in your life. Some couples have a special date in mind—and make decisions about location and officiant based on date availability.

If you have a special person in mind to perform your marriage ceremony, check out http://www.ordainmeplease.com/Wedding_Officiant_Laws.html to be clear on the legalities in your state and county. There are several organizations that offer ordination in a recognized religion through their websites. The Universal Life Church (www.ulc.net) has been ordaining ministers who can legally perform marriages since 1977. Many states also provide other means of obtaining a license to sign marriage certificates. For example, California gives a "Deputy Commissioner of Marriage" a one-day authorization to perform a marriage.

1. Choose your ceremony site. Traditional venues include a house of worship, a wedding facility, or the bride's home. (See also Chapter 2, page 20.)

2. Decide on the date and time of your ceremony. If your ceremony and reception will be held at different locations, you will need to coordinate accordingly. The ideal is to have the two events scheduled with about forty-five minutes to an hour in between the end of the ceremony and the beginning of the reception. (See also Chapter 16, page 210.)

3. Choose an officiant. For some couples, the choice of an officiant is easy. They marry in the bride's or groom's hometown in a ceremony officiated by the clergyperson they've known for years. Other couples plan to marry in a community, location, or country where they have no religious associations or affiliations. If this is the case, start by speaking with the wedding coordinator at your site. Ask for recommendations of officiants who have done other ceremonies there.

In most states, judges, justices of the peace, and ordained clergy can perform marriages; in others the privilege is extended to other civil servants as well. Search online to find the requirements for the state or country where you are marrying. If you would like a friend or relative to marry you, you'll need to make the arrangements to have that person authorized to do so. (See above.)

Make an appointment to meet with your top choice(s)—typically officiants won't be available to meet on the spot.

Doing Your Homework

The number of questions to ask your officiant about your ceremony and your site coordinator about the facility may seem daunting, but the more you know now, the sooner you can get on to the actual planning and avoid any surprises down the road.

Questions to Ask at the Ceremony Site

When you visit a potential ceremony site, you'll need to learn what's permitted as well as any restrictions—religious or otherwise—that may exist. From photography and attire to decor and flowers, it's important to find out from the officiant or ceremony site manager what is customary, as the answers will likely inform other decisions. Get all the details when you meet, using this list of questions as your guide. The information you learn will need to be shared with other wedding vendors. It's likely that the answers to some significant questions may lead you to choose one venue over another.

CEREMONY SITE SPECIFICS AT A HOUSE OF WORSHIP

❖ How many guests can be accommodated comfortably?

❖ Are any other weddings or ceremonies planned on the same day as your wedding? Does that give you a time restriction? You may be able to share flowers—and floral costs—with another bridal party.

❖ Some religious sites request that ceremony flowers be left behind as a courtesy or donation. Is that the case for this for this ceremony site?

❖ How does the site accommodate guests with disabilities?

❖ Does the site have appropriate temperature control? Ask about heat, air-conditioning, fans, and if windows may be opened.

❖ Is there a room where the bride and her attendants may dress or wait unseen prior to the service?

❖ Is there a way to ensure that space is left vacant for the cars that will carry the bride and her attendants to the front of the building?

  • Is there enough space on the street that a traffic jam won't occur when the wedding takes place?

  • If not, are the services of a traffic officer or an off-duty police officer to direct traffic recommended?

❖ What fees or recommended donations are required for the use of the facility, the officiant, the organist or additional musicians, the cantor, soloist or choir, and/or the sexton?

❖ If there will be other service participants such as altar boys or acolytes, is it the officiant's duty to arrange for them to be there?

  • Should they be paid, and if so, how much?

  • Should they attend the rehearsal?

❖ When should fees be delivered, and to whom?

❖ Can a receiving line be formed at the ceremony site, if desired? (In some instances, there may be another ceremony following yours or there may not be enough room for a receiving line.)

❖ Who should your other wedding vendors contact if they have questions?

FLOWERS AND DECOR

While this list of questions aims primarily to avoid any surprises at a house of worship, it's a good idea to pose them to the site manager of any wedding facility you are considering.

❖ Are there any decorating restrictions or rules, and what kinds of floral arrangements and decorations are permitted?

❖ At what time may decorations be delivered, and how does the florist gain access to decorate?

❖ Is there a policy on removing the flowers after the ceremony? You may wish to use flowers as reception decorations; to deliver them to area hospitals or nursing homes; or to give them to friends.

❖ Are lighted candles permitted as decorations, other than within the sanctuary?

❖ Does the ceremony site provide an aisle runner? (Many now prohibit them altogether.)

- For a Jewish ceremony: Who will provide the chuppah, and may it be decorated with flowers?

- Can the flower girl scatter flower petals? Can they be real or should they be silk?

- Is throwing rose petals, confetti, or birdseed outside the building permitted?

ATTIRE

- Are there restrictions concerning dress for the wedding party, such as bare shoulders or arms, and are head coverings required for men or women?

- Are there attire guidelines for guests?

PHOTOGRAPHY

- Are photography and filming allowed? If so, when: before, during, and/or after the ceremony?

- What are site rules on lighting and the use of a flash?

MUSIC

Some religious sites stipulate that any musician performing in a wedding ceremony must be engaged through the in-house music department, most likely headed by a music director or organist. Some religions forbid secular music altogether.

- Are there restrictions on the type of music, musical instruments, or whether or not music is played with a microphone?

- Are there any restrictions on recorded music? If not, what audio equipment is available and in what format should the music be delivered?

- Are secular, classical, or popular selections permitted, or are you restricted to sacred music?

- Are there certain hymns or secular songs that can or can't be sung at the ceremony?

- Can additional music be inserted in the ceremony—such as a solo by a flutist, a trumpeter, a guitar player, or a vocalist, and if so, where?

- Is there sound-recording equipment, and can the ceremony be recorded as a memento? If so, in what format?

Things to Discuss with Your Officiant

As much as you need to know about the ins and outs of the ceremony site, the officiant will want to know about you as well. This is the person who will perform your marriage, a seminal event for you and your fiancé(e). Even if this is an officiant who you've known since childhood, he will want to get to know you as a couple and learn your thoughts on marriage and on your ceremony.

If your chosen officiant is a priest, rabbi, or minister, let him or her know if yours is an interfaith marriage or if neither of you is a practicing member of that particular faith. Each religion has different standards, rules, and restrictions. Also discuss whether you plan to marry in a house of worship or at a secular site. Clergy may have restrictions on whom they can marry and where they can marry them.

- Reconfirm the date and time of your ceremony.

- Discuss any issues or concerns you may have as well as any ways you might like to personalize the ceremony. (See also page 189.)

- Ask if there's any leeway in the way you are pronounced "married." Some clergy persons are still saying "man and wife." If you prefer, ask to be pronounced as "husband and wife."

- Discuss the length of the ceremony. A Roman Catholic wedding that includes a Mass with communion can take at least an hour, but the Mass is not obligatory.

- If you haven't already done so, be sure to make a *reservation for the wedding rehearsal* at this meeting. You should do so as soon as possible—a venue that is heavily booked on your wedding day is likely to be equally tight on the day before, the traditional time to hold the rehearsal. (See also Chapter 24, page 325.)

  - Are there restrictions or rules for the rehearsal, such as clothing regulations, or guidelines on who may attend?

  - How long will the rehearsal run? You might want to know this if the rehearsal dinner follows the rehearsal. You may want to include extra time in the schedule in case the rehearsal runs over.

  - Are there any fees for the rehearsal?

- Arrange appointments for premarital counseling if required by your religion.

- Provide the officiant with the names you'll use in the ceremony (Elizabeth/Beth, James Matthew / Matt). Also mention whether or not you will be taking the groom's last name.

WHEN A RELIGIOUS CEREMONY IS AT A SECULAR LOCATION

If you plan to have a religious service at a site that is not a house of worship, ask these additional questions:

- Can you have a religious ceremony at a secular site? (Some religions don't allow it.)

- What are the officiant's travel needs?

  - Would he or she prefer to come in a hired car?

  - Can you reimburse him or her for time, gas, and mileage?

- Will you need to provide an altar, an altar cloth, a kneeling bench or cushions, candles, or any other liturgical items?

  - If the answer to any of these questions is yes, ask for the names of resources that provide them, or if the venue is a popular wedding location, you may find that these items are already available.

PERSONALIZING A RELIGIOUS CEREMONY

Some couples find all the meaning and symbolism they need in the words of a traditional marriage ceremony, whereas others like to include personal readings, musical interludes, or self-penned vows. (See pages 191 and 193.) If you are having a secular ceremony, you can design it as you wish. That may not be the case if you are having a religious ceremony. For example, a particular liturgy may offer three options for a psalm reading, but your choice is limited to those three.

From a practical standpoint, whether you design your own ceremony, or alter or add to a traditional form, keep the overall length of your service in mind.

Here are some issues to discuss with your officiant:

❖ What latitude do you have in altering the ceremony?

❖ Can you write your own vows or make any alterations to the traditional wording?

❖ Can you choose your own readings or substitute or add secular readings? Can the officiant provide a list of approved choices?

❖ Does the officiant need to review your additions or alterations to the service?

HOW TO ARRANGE FOR A VISITING CLERGY TO PERFORM THE CEREMONY

Q: I'd like to have my hometown minister marry us in the church where my fiancé and I are now members. What is the protocol for inviting him? I don't want to upset our current minister.

A: This isn't such an unusual request, but the first step is to talk to the minister at your ceremony location. Explain that you're hoping that your hometown clergyman, an old friend, can be involved in your wedding. In some cases, it's required that the local officiant be present and lead or participate in the service as well as the visiting clergy. In others, there is no such requirement, and the visiting clergy may have the use of the church or synagogue. These steps can ensure that all goes smoothly:

❖ Check with your local church about their policies before asking the out-of-town officiant to perform all or part of the ceremony.

❖ Get permission to use the house of worship.

❖ Invite your officiant by handwritten note.

❖ Coordinate the communication between the out-of-town officiant and his or her contact person at your local house of worship.

❖ Make sure legalities are covered. For example, does the out-of-town clergy need to provide documentation proving that he or she can perform a marriage?

❖ If the out-of-town officiant will be the sole clergy, ask for a list of ceremony needs ahead of time.

❖ Pay the travel, lodging, and meal expenses of any clergyperson (and his or her spouse) you invite from out of town.

❖ Remember an honorarium for each clergyperson. If your out-of-town officiant is the sole officiant, make a donation to your local house of worship as well to cover the use of the site and the assistance of personnel.

❖ Invite each officiant participating in your ceremony (and spouse) to the rehearsal dinner and reception.

❖ Discuss the inclusion of rituals or readings from other religions or cultural traditions, such as lighting a unity candle or a sand-blending ceremony. If they are not permissible during the standard liturgy, can they be performed after the conclusion of the ceremony and before the recessional?

If you are allowed to personalize your wedding service, ask for a copy of the liturgy for the wedding ceremony and mark those places where you may make changes or additions.

Adding Personal Touches and Cultural Traditions

When you are not limited by religious constraints, your options are many—unity candles, religious customs such as the Greek Orthodox wedding crowns, secular readings, musical mixes, jumping the broom, handfasting, and the shared cup are just a few elements that can be added to your ceremony to make it personal and unique. Just be sure they are meaningful to you as a couple or to your families. (For more information on religious rituals and cultural traditions to personalize your ceremony, see Chapter 17, page 229.)

Writing Your Own Vows

Your wedding vows are the expression of your personal commitment to each other. Most clergy are willing to allow certain adaptations of traditional vows as long as the basic tenets of those vows are expressed in one form or another: promises to be true to each other in good times and in bad and in sickness and in health and to love and honor each other "until death do you

---

THE TRADITIONAL ORDER OF THE WEDDING CEREMONY

While individual clergy members may proscribe specific procedures and may require a certain processional, order of service, and recessional, most Christian and many secular wedding ceremonies follow this order:

1. Prelude music is played.

2. Honored guests are ushered to their seats.

3. The processional music begins (followed by separate music for the bride).

4. The wedding party processes, followed by the bride (and her father).

5. The officiant offers greetings, opening remarks, or prayers.

6. The couple declare their intent to marry and exchange vows and rings.

7. The officiant proclaims the couple married.

8. The couple kiss.

9. The couple recess, followed by the wedding party, accompanied by the recessional music.

---

part." Vows may also include pledges to cherish and respect each other.

Read the marriage service carefully, as many couples today disagree with the idea of a woman being "given" or that she vows to "Love, honor, and *obey*." Your objections won't be the first, and most officiants can offer alternative wording that's more in tune with the nature of a couple's relationship in a marriage today.

If you decide to write your own vows, keep in mind the following tips:

- Start writing your vows early; don't leave it to the last days—or hours!—before the wedding.

- Keep them brief—about one minute at most. Simplicity and brevity can be far more eloquent than long-winded, overblown metaphors.

- You may write your vows together, but if you are writing separately, agree on length and general content so they sound balanced.

- Make sure your vows express who you are, reflecting your beliefs and sensibilities. If you decide to personalize your vows, avoid sweeping generalizations and clichés—make your words personally meaningful.

- You are writing your vows for each other as a couple, but remember that you have an audience. Avoid inside jokes or straying onto personal subjects not appropriate for a public audience.

- If you come from two different cultures or two different faiths, vows that commit to building bridges of understanding and honoring each other's traditions can be particularly meaningful.

- Don't put too much pressure on yourself to be overly profound or poetic. Be honest, and focus on telling your future spouse you will love and be there for him or her.

- If you plan to memorize your vows, make sure you or the officiant has a written copy in case you go blank and forget what comes next. (It's been known to happen!)

- Practice, practice, practice—out loud. You'll want to have a strong, steady voice so the congregation can hear you. If you don't want to say your vows at the wedding rehearsal, bring something else to read so you can get feedback on how loud your voice needs to be.

Honoring the Deceased

It is very appropriate to honor deceased family members, either privately or publicly, at a wedding ceremony. It's important to let the remembrance be a part of, but not overshadow, the happy event you and your families are celebrating.

If you decide to include a tribute in your ceremony, be sure that it is neither morbid nor lengthy. A simple declaration of love, a moment of silence, or the lighting of a candle may be the most eloquent commemoration. A large photo of the deceased by the altar or a long speech will quickly turn a wedding into a memorial. The program is always a good place to write a short piece or dedicate a poem in honor of the deceased, or to explain any symbolic remembrances: "The flowers on the altar are in honor of Justin." Sometimes couples make their memorials private by offering a silent prayer, wearing something that belonged to the person

---

HONORING FRIENDS AND FAMILY

Not everyone can be in your bridal party, and you may have more family or friends than there is room for at the altar. Consider asking them to be ushers, give a reading, or if they have musical talent, perform as a soloist.

who has died, or laying a bouquet of flowers on the front pew or by the altar.

Alternatively, the remembrance could be at the reception—a small table with photos of the deceased or a mention in a toast is also appropriate. While there may be sadness in the happiest of occasions, however you choose to honor your loved one try to keep the focus on the joy of your wedding day.

Readings for Your Ceremony

Readings included in the ceremony are generally taken from three categories: those that are scriptural and are about marriage, love, and the nature of joy; those that are classical poetry or prose and similar in theme to the scriptural readings; and those that are original poetry or prose. You may have a favorite poem or song lyric that expresses what you feel about love, marriage, or your love for each other.

Following are excerpts from selections that are popular with brides and grooms:

SCRIPTURAL

TRADITIONAL CHRISTIAN

Love is patient and kind; love is not jealous or boastful; it is not arrogant or rude. Love does not insist on its own way; it is not irritable or resentful; it does not rejoice at wrong, but rejoices in the right. Love bears all things, believes all things, hopes all things, endures all things.

Love never ends; . . . So faith, hope, love abide, these three, but the greatest of these is love.

—I CORINTHIANS 13:4–8, 13

Two are better than one, because they have a good reward for their labor. For if they fall, one will lift up his fellow; but woe to him who is alone when he falls and has not another to lift him up.

—ECCLESIASTES 4:9–10

I am my beloved and my beloved is mine.

—SONG OF SOLOMON 6:2–3

Set me as a seal upon thine heart, as a seal upon thine arm: for love is as strong as death.

—SONG OF SOLOMON 8:6–7

Beloved, let us love one another, because love is of God.

—JOHN 4:7–12

But Ruth said, "Do not urge me to leave you or to return from following you. For where you go I will go, and where you lodge I will lodge."

—RUTH 1:16–17

Therefore a man shall leave his father and his mother and hold fast to his wife, and they shall become one flesh.

—GENESIS 2:18–24

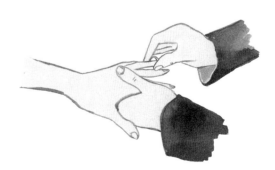

TRADITIONAL JEWISH

Blessed are You, Adonai our God, King of the Universe, Creator of the fruit of the vine.

Blessed are You, Adonai, our God, King of the universe, Who has created everything for your glory.

Blessed are You, Adonai, our God, King of the universe, Creator of Human Beings.

Blessed are You, Adonai, our God, King of the universe, Who has fashioned human beings in your image, according to your likeness and has fashioned from it a lasting mold. Blessed are You Adonai, Creator of Human Beings.

Bring intense joy and exultation to the barren one (Jerusalem) through the ingathering of her children amidst her in gladness. Blessed are You, Adonai, Who gladdens Zion through her children.

Gladden the beloved companions as You gladdened Your creatures in the garden of Eden. Blessed are You, Adonai, Who gladdens groom and bride.

Blessed are You, Adonai, our God, King of the universe, Who created joy and gladness, groom and bride, mirth, glad song, pleasure, delight, love, brotherhood, peace, and companionship. Adonai, our God, let there soon be heard in the cities of Judah and the streets of Jerusalem the sound of joy and the sound of gladness, the voice of the groom and the voice of the bride, the sound of the grooms' jubilance from their canopies and of the youths from their song-filled feasts. Blessed are You Who causes the groom to rejoice with his bride.

—SHEVA BRACHOT [THE SEVEN BLESSINGS]

Your rabbi may also suggest selections from the Song of Solomon or other readings from the Torah.

SECULAR

Let me not to the marriage of true minds
Admit impediments. Love is not love
Which alters when it alteration finds,
Or bends with the remover to remove:
O no! it is an ever-fixed mark
That looks on tempests and is never shaken;
It is the star to every wandering bark,
Whose worth's unknown, although his height be taken.
Love's not Time's fool, though rosy lips and cheeks
Within his bending sickle's compass come:
Love alters not with his brief hours and weeks,
But bears it out even to the edge of doom.
*   If this be error and upon me proved,*
*   I never writ, nor no man ever loved.*

—WILLIAM SHAKESPEARE, SONNET 116

Love is something you and I must have. We must have it because our spirit feeds upon it. . . . With it we are creative. With it we march tirelessly. With it, and with it alone, we are able to sacrifice for others.

—CHIEF DAN GEORGE

You have become mine forever.
Yes, we have become partners.
I have become yours.
Hereafter, I cannot live without you.
Do not live without me.
Let us share the joys.
We are word and meaning, unite.
You are thought and I am sound.
May the nights be honey-sweet for us.
May the mornings be honey-sweet for us.
May the plants be honey-sweet for us.
May the earth be honey-sweet for us.

—HINDU MARRIAGE POEM

Now you will feel no rain, for each of you will be
shelter to each other.
Now you will feel no cold, for each of you will be
warmth to the other.
Now there is no more loneliness, for each of you
will be companion to the other. Now you are two
bodies, but there is only one life before you.
You will now go to your dwelling place to enter unto
the days of your togetherness.
And may your days be good and long upon the earth.

—COMMONLY REFERRED TO AS THE
"APACHE WEDDING PRAYER," WRITTEN
BY SCREENWRITER ALBERT MALTZ
FOR THE MOVIE *BROKEN ARROW*

How do I love thee? Let me count the ways . . .
I love thee to the depth and breadth and height
My soul can reach, when feeling out of sight
For the ends of Being and ideal Grace.
I love thee to the level of every day's
Most quiet need, by sun and candlelight.
I love thee freely, as men strive for Right;
I love thee purely, as they turn from Praise.
I love thee with a passion put to use
In my old griefs, and with my childhood's faith.
I love thee with a love I seemed to lose
With my lost saints,—I love thee with the breath,
Smiles, tears, of all my life!—and, if God choose,
I shall but love thee better after death.

—ELIZABETH BARRETT BROWNING

Throw things away and love will bring them back,
again, and again, and again.
But most of all, love needs love, lots of it.
And in return, love loves you and never stops.

—TAYLOR MALI, "HOW FALLING
IN LOVE IS LIKE OWNING A DOG"

An Overview of Religious Ceremonies

Even with so many different religious rituals and cultural traditions being used in weddings today, there is generally one common thread: A marriage is a joyous occasion worthy of high celebration.

Mainstream Protestant Ceremonies

The wedding ceremonies of Baptist, Lutheran, and Presbyterian churches are familiar to many and, in general, are quite similar. They are the ceremonies most frequently portrayed in movies and television shows. Marriage is not a sacrament, but it is considered holy.

Interfaith marriages are permitted and co-officiants welcomed, although the more conservative synods or branches may not permit a co-officiated Christian or non-Christian marriage. Premarital counseling is customary, usually conducted in a series of private meetings with the minister who will conduct the ceremony.

Holy Communion may be part of the ceremony if the bride and groom wish. The bride and groom may add readings and music to the ceremony and may write their own vows to replace the ones included in the church's worship book.

THE SERVICE

The service, without additional readings and music or communion, can take as little as fifteen minutes. The service consists of three parts:

1. The welcome and introduction by the minister

2. The exchange of vows and rings

3. The final blessing

Episcopal

The Episcopal Church considers marriage a sacrament and requires that at least one partner be a baptized Christian. Interfaith marriage is accepted, and Episcopal priests are usually willing to co-officiate with other clergy if the couple wishes. Premarital counseling with the priest who will marry you is customary. If either the bride or the groom has been divorced, she or he must receive a dispensation to marry again from the area bishop.

The bride and groom may choose to follow the wedding ceremony with the celebration of the Eucharist. All baptized Christians are welcome to receive communion. With communion the ceremony takes about forty-five minutes to an hour; without communion, the service is about twenty minutes long.

THE SERVICE

The Episcopal ceremony, the Celebration and Blessing of a Marriage, is taken from the Book of Common Prayer and has four parts, which follow the processional of the bride and her attendants:

1. The priest begins with the call to worship: "Dearly Beloved, we have come together in the presence of God to witness and bless the joining together of this man and this woman in Holy Matrimony."

2. It is followed by the declaration of consent: "Will you have this man/woman . . ."

3. The Ministry of the Word follows, using one or more scriptural passages.

4. This is followed by the exchange of vows and the blessing of the rings, and then by the blessing of the marriage.

INTERFAITH MARRIAGES

Whether yours will be a marriage of mixed faiths, one that integrates age-old traditions and rituals into a modern ceremony, or one that follows religious tradition to the letter, your officiant can best help you choose the right ceremony rites for you. Using happiness as the common denominator, today's brides and grooms from different religious and cultural backgrounds are able to blend the traditions of one with the rituals of the other by weaving those aspects that matter most to them and their families into their wedding ceremony and reception.

Deciding on a ceremony can be an interesting challenge, especially when families and friends have a wide range of practices and beliefs. There will be decisions to make and traditions to consider. With the help of your clergyperson, provide a wedding program that explains the symbolic meaning of different parts of the ceremony so that guests can follow along. Programs can also provide translations if parts of the ceremony are in another language.

If your faiths don't allow interfaith marriage and offer no way for you to incorporate the two faiths in one ceremony, you may have to be married in a civil ceremony, or marry in one faith first and follow with a separate ceremony for the second. You can schedule the two ceremonies on the same day or hold them on separate days. Guests may attend both, or one ceremony may be private with guests invited to the second.

Roman Catholic

Marriage is one of the seven sacraments of the Roman Catholic Church. For such a serious step, the church requires a prescribed series of religious and personal counseling sessions, called Pre-Cana counseling, for both the bride and the groom, even if one of them is not Catholic. Interfaith marriage is accepted as long as the partner of another faith complies with counseling requirements, and most priests will co-officiate with the clergy of the non-Catholic half of the couple.

Divorce is not recognized, so a bride or groom whose previous marriage did not end in annulment but rather in divorce is not permitted to be married in the Catholic church if their former partner is still living.

Couples may opt to have a nuptial Mass following the exchange of vows. The mass plus wedding ceremony takes approximately one hour; the wedding ceremony itself is approximately twenty minutes to a half hour. Only Roman Catholic guests may receive Holy Communion. Generally, the service must take place in a church unless special permission is granted by the local bishop to hold the service elsewhere.

THE SERVICE

The ceremony without a nuptial Mass consists of four parts:

1. The Introductory Rite consists of the entrance music, a greeting, and opening prayer

2. The Liturgy of the Word includes readings from the Old and New Testaments, the reading of the Gospel, and the homily.

3. The Rite of Marriage begins with the statement of intention and declaration that the couple is free to marry, followed by their consent to marry and the exchange of vows. The rings are blessed and exchanged and the celebrant offers a nuptial blessing.

4. Concluding Rites consist of the Lord's Prayer, concluding prayers, blessings, and recessional music.

When a nuptial Mass is celebrated, it begins after the Rite of Marriage.

Eastern Orthodox

Marriage is a sacrament in Eastern Orthodox congregations, which can be Greek, Russian, Serbian, Syrian, Polish, or Yugoslavian depending on the nation of origin. The ceremony is filled with symbolism, beginning outside the church doors with the betrothal, when the rings are blessed and exchanged. The couple is then led by the priest into the church to stand on a white cloth in front of a wedding platform. A wedding icon is carried in the processional, and the couple is given lighted candles, which they hold during the service.

Much of the symbolism of the service, which can last up to one hour, is represented by threes:

1. During the betrothal, the priest asks God's blessings upon the rings and then blesses the groom and the bride with the rings. He does this three times. He then places the rings on the ring fingers of the right hands of the couple, and the rings are exchanged three times.

2. The betrothal and blessing of the rings is followed by the sacrament of Holy Matrimony, which is followed by three prayers.

3. During the service, no vows are exchanges. Crowns or garlands joined by a white ribbon, symbolizing that the two are now one, are exchanged three times over the couple. The crowns have several meanings, of which these two are most important: God bestows his blessing upon his children in the form of crowns; and the identification of the bride and the groom as the beginning of a new kingdom.

4. The service continues with readings, with the presentation of the common cup to the bride and groom to symbolize that from that moment on they will share the same cup of life and that whatever life has in store for them they will share equally and with the expression of joy.

5. The priest takes the arm of the bridegroom and leads him and the bride around the table three times as an expression of joy.

Jewish Ceremonies

Jewish weddings may take place anywhere that a canopy, or chuppah, can be erected and often the reception follows in the same location. The chuppah symbolizes both the tents of ancient ancestors and the formation of the new home of the family being created beneath it. The chuppah can be decorated with flowers and constructed in a fixed position or held by special attendants. The ceremony may be conducted in Hebrew, or a combination of Hebrew and English.

Interfaith marriage is not encouraged but nonetheless occurs, usually with a Reform rabbi presiding. Some Reform rabbis will also permit a co-officiant of another faith, but Orthodox and Conservative rabbis, as a rule, will not. Even in a Reform congregation, a divorced woman cannot be remarried without a *get*, an official rabbinical document of divorce.

The wedding ceremony is in two parts. It begins in private with the signing of the *ketubah,* or marriage contract. This beautiful, ornately decorated document is traditionally written in Aramaic and is a record of the promises the groom makes to his bride. It is signed by the groom before the marriage ceremony and is given to the bride. It will hang in a place of honor in the couple's home. Today, the *ketubah* may include promises made by both the bride and groom, and may be signed by them or by two witnesses, depending on the tradition followed.

The signing of the *ketubah* may be followed by the *bedeken*, or veiling of the bride. Before the ceremony begins, the groom places the bride's veil over her face. The custom recalls the biblical story of Jacob, who was tricked into marrying the elder veiled Leah, thinking her to be the younger Rachel.

Then the public ceremony begins:

1. The bride and groom are escorted by their parents in the procession and gather, with the attendants, under the chuppah.

2. The first part of the service is the betrothal, or *erusin*. It begins with the reciting of a blessing, after which the bride and groom drink from the same cup of wine, symbolizing that they will share everything that life brings them. The groom places the wedding ring—a simple band in precious metal, usually gold, with no stones, piercings, or engravings—on the bride's right forefinger, the finger believed to have the most direct line to the heart. The *ketubah* is read aloud and presented to the couple.

3. Then follows the *nisuin*, or nuptials. This is the actual wedding ceremony, which begins with the chanting of *Sheva Brachot,* or the Seven Blessings, after which the bride and groom again take a sip of wine, this time symbolizing the commitment of the marriage. At this point, the bride may give the groom a ring.

4. The ceremony ends with the groom stomping a glass (wrapped carefully in a cloth to prevent shards flying) while guests cry, "Mazel tov!"— good luck and congratulations. The breaking of the glass represents the destruction of the Temple in Jerusalem and is a reminder that even on such a joyous occasion it is important to remember that others may not be so fortunate.

5. The service ends with the recessional, led by the bride and groom and followed by the bride's parents, the groom's parents, the attendants, the rabbi, and the cantor if one is participating.

6. In conservative communities, the bride and groom retire to a private room for several minutes before they join the reception. This lovely tradition is known as *yichud*, or "seclusion." These few minutes give the couple a brief time to be alone before the excitement of the rest of the day. It symbolizes the couple's right to privacy. Tradition also says that the couple is to share their first meal together, so they are often brought a small plate of their favorite foods.

7. Now the celebration, or *simcha*, begins. Tradition says that the bride and groom are king and queen on their wedding day. Their guests celebrate them with food and dancing to bring them joy. The reception often begins with a blessing of the challah, a loaf of braided bread that here symbolizes the sharing of families and friends. The meal often concludes with a blessing and seven special benedictions, sung in Hebrew.

Mormon Ceremonies

Members of the Church of Jesus Christ of Latter-day Saints (Mormons) may be married in one of two ways: in either a marriage ceremony or a civil ceremony. The marriage ceremony, or "sealing ordinance," is for couples of great faith. This sacred ceremony is always held in one of the church's dedicated temples. Members of the Mormon faith believe that when they are married (sealed) in a temple by proper priesthood authority, their union continues forever, even after death. Only faithful members, recommended by their temple, may be participants in—and guests at—a temple wedding; non-Mormons may not attend.

Mormons not eligible for a sealing ceremony or marriage in a temple have a civil ceremony in a church or a home. This ceremony may be attended by anyone, Mormon and non-Mormon. Bishops from the church are authorized to perform civil ceremonies but receive no pay for conducting such services.

Islamic Ceremonies

Marriage is a holy and desirable union under Islamic law and a sacred contract.

There is no objection to interfaith union, but there may be objection to intercultural marriage, another issue entirely. Prior to the religious ceremony, the bride and groom are required to undertake civil preliminaries and may be required to go through a civil ceremony in addition to their religious ceremony.

The marriage ceremony usually takes place in a mosque or at the bride's home.

THE SERVICE

1. When the groom, who is attended by a *serbala* (the youngest boy in his family, usually the son of a sister), arrives at the ceremony, he and his *serbala* are given floral garlands in welcome.

2. The ceremony is conducted by an imam. The bride, who is heavily veiled, and the groom are seated apart during their wedding, often on opposite sides of the room.

3. The bride's father and two witnesses ask the bride if she has agreed to the marriage, and the imam asks the groom if he has agreed. Assuming they have both agreed, the imam completes the marriage certificate and reads from the Qur'an.

4. A meal is served after this ceremony, with the bride and groom still separated, each sitting with their own families.

5. After the meal, the bride leaves, puts on all the jewelry she has been given for her wedding, and returns to sit next to the groom. Her veil is lifted.

Hindu Ceremonies

Marriage, *vivah Sanskar*, is one of a series of holy sacraments in the Hindu faith, and believed to have a purifying quality. There are many variations based on regional, caste, and ethnic differences. In the United States, it is possible that a civil ceremony may be required in addition to the Hindu ceremony to make the marriage legal. Since the requirements for civil and religious ceremonies are separate, the civil ceremony may take place first, but the couple is not deemed married by the Hindu community until they have had a religious ceremony. Interfaith marriages are accepted.

In India, the Hindu wedding ceremony, which is conducted by a priest, or pandit, can last all day. In the United States, the Hindu ceremony has been shortened to about ninety minutes, although cultural traditions surrounding the wedding can last several days. It does not have to be performed in a temple and in fact is often conducted in the bride's home.

Throughout the ceremony, regardless of the duration, the couple is instructed in lessons for married life. There is frequent chanting of mantras, or prayers in Sanskrit, which ask for blessings on the union. A traditional Hindu mantra is "I am the word and you are the melody. I am the melody and you are the word."

The bride usually wears a sari made of a single piece of red fabric embroidered in gold. She is also adorned with 24-karat-gold jewelry, presented to her by the groom's family. The groom wears white trousers, a tunic, and a ceremonial hat.

1. At the beginning of the ceremony, the bride and groom, usually seated under a decorated canopy called a *mandaps*, may exchange garlands of flowers.

2. After emphasizing the importance of marriage, the priest ties the couple's right hands together with cord and sprinkles holy water over them.

3. The bride's father then gives his daughter to the groom.

4. A sacred flame is lit, and the bride and groom make an offering of rice to symbolize their hope of fertility.

5. The most important part of the ceremony is the Seven Steps, and until this rite is completed, the couple is not married. The Seven Steps symbolize food, strength, wealth, fortune, children, happy seasons, and friendships. The groom's scarf is tied to the bride's sari. Together, the bride and groom either take seven steps around the sacred flame or walk around it seven times.

6. Now married, the bride and groom feed each other five times with little bits of sweet food, and the ceremony ends with prayers and readings.

Sikh Ceremonies

The Sikh wedding ceremony is called Anand Karaj, which means "the ceremony of bliss." It solemnizes the union of the couple's souls and seals their religious, moral, and legal obligations. A civil ceremony may be required to legalize the union.

The ceremony may be performed in a *gurdwara*, or temple, or, most often, in the bride's home. It almost always takes place before noon, believed by Sikhs to be the happiest time of day.

The bride wears either red trousers and a tunic or a red sari made from a single piece of cloth, a red headscarf, and all the jewelry the groom's family has given her. The groom wears a white brocade suit, a scarf, and a turban, or he may wear Western dress.

Wherever the ceremony is performed, a central platform is used, on which the *Guru Granth Sahib*, the Holy Book, is displayed by the person who conducts the ceremony. It is not necessary for a priest to be present; any Sikh may be in charge of the ceremony as long as both families agree. Guests sit on the floor around the platform, with men to the right of the Holy Book and women to the left.

1. Flower garlands play a role, as they do in Muslim and Hindu weddings, beginning when the parents of the bride welcome the groom and his parents by placing garlands around their necks. The bride is brought to greet the groom, and they exchange garlands.

2. The couple stands before the priest and the Holy Book, and the bride's father hands one end of a sash to the groom and the other end to the bride. This symbolizes giving her away.

3. The wedding ceremony comprises four verses from the Holy Book that explain the obligations of married life. Each verse is read and then it is sung. During the singing of each verse, the groom leads the bride around the Holy Book one time, sometimes with the help of guests to symbolize their support. After they have walked around four times, they are married.

4. A prayer and a short hymn follow, and the sharing of a sweet food by all the guests is symbolic

of God's blessing on the marriage. Guests place garlands around the necks of the couple or throw flower petals, a symbol of happiness.

Unitarian-Universalist Ceremonies

The roots of this society are Judeo-Christian, making it a pluralistic religion. It is not a church with ecclesiastical rules or rituals, so wedding ceremonies may be personalized and individualized, and couples are encouraged to design their own service from a combination of religious, spiritual, or other traditions that are meaningful to them.

Quaker (Society of Friends) Ceremonies

A Quaker wedding is the simplest of all Christian marriages, for it has no music or set order of service. Couples who wish to marry in a Quaker meetinghouse must apply for permission in writing, often two to three months in advance. Several levels of approval are required for the marriage to take place, including an interview by members of the meeting, not unlike the counseling required by other religions. The bride and groom pledge their lifelong love and loyalty to each other but do not exchange rings during the ceremony, as it is believed that the words of the pledge are sufficient. Rings may be exchanged after if the couple wishes.

The marriage takes place during a regular Quaker meeting, which is mostly conducted in silence. The couple speak their vows to each other when they feel ready—at no particular time and in no particular order.

At the end, everyone in the meeting signs the marriage certificate, an ornate document that also pledges the community's support should the couple need it. Depending on the state, a civil marriage may be necessary as well.

Same-Sex Weddings and Commitment Ceremonies

Gay and lesbian couples who wish to form life-long partnerships have several options today, including civil union and marriage. State law governs the type of ceremony you may have.

Because many churches don't sanction a gay or lesbian union through wedding liturgy, most gay couples design their own ceremonies and write their own vows, drawing on religious and secular sources, customs, and traditions as they wish. In thinking about how to structure a ceremony of commitment, couples generally follow the standard order and format of Jewish or Christian ceremonies. Others, according to Steven Petrow, author of *Steven Petrow's Complete Gay & Lesbian Manners*, take a more political stance and reject the rites of a heterosexual tradition that has excluded them for so long. Instead, they create events that focus more on the reception or celebration than on the ceremony itself.

Although there is no set structure for a commitment ceremony, it often includes the following:

1. The introduction includes a processional, a gathering together and welcome, and an invocation. Some couples want a statement made about being gay because they feel that their sexuality is so integral to their being and their relationship that they wouldn't think of not addressing it. Others choose to focus on love and commitment.

2. The service can consist of prayers, songs, readings, a homily, and an address by the officiant. Some couples like to read from the book of Samuel, specifically Chapter 18, verses 1–5, and

Chapter 20, verses 16–17. Lesbian couples often select readings from the book of Ruth, Chapter 1, verses 16–17.

3. The vows can be borrowed from any service book ("I, Jane, take you, Beth"), or the couple can write their own vows to be read by an officiant, or declare to each other with no prompting.

4. The exchange of rings may be preceded by a blessing of the rings.

5. The pronouncement is the public proclamation by the officiant that the couple is recognized as united or married. This part of the ceremony can be worded several ways, such as "Since you have consented to join together in the bond of matrimony and have pledged yourselves to each other in the presence of this company, I now pronounce you married"; "I pronounce you partners in life"; or "Because you have pledged to one another your vows of commitment, we recognize you as married."

6. The closing can consist of the kiss, the blessing of the union, and a recessional.

Military Weddings

A military wedding ceremony is conducted by a secular officiant or according to the religion and traditions of the bride and the groom. It differs in that it also includes military etiquette and traditions. For example, the American flag and the standard of the groom and/or bride's unit is displayed near the altar or dais.

In general, brides and grooms in the service may wear either civilian clothes or their uniforms, as may their colleagues who serve as attendants. Depend-

---

THE ARCH OF STEEL

Undoubtedly the most romantic sight at a military wedding is the raising of sabers or cutlasses to form an arch under which a couple passes at the end of the service. The formation varies slightly by service branch and is a tradition rich in history and meaning, symbolizing the couple's safe entry into their new life together. It may be performed inside or outside the ceremony site, sometimes both. Whether formed by commissioned officers who are members of the wedding party or a special honor guard, a command will be given: "Draw swords" or "Arch sabers." Only the couple participate. All other military guests should stand at attention, and civilian guests honor the tradition by standing still and holding their applause until the couple emerges from the arch.

---

ing on the formality of the occasion, everyday and dress uniforms are equally correct, since young and noncareer personnel often don't have dress uniforms. For commissioned officers, evening dress uniforms are the equivalent of civilian white tie (the most formal), and dinner or mess dress is the same formality as a tuxedo, or black tie. Noncommissioned officers can wear dress or everyday uniforms for formal and informal ceremonies.

Regulations vary by service branch, but as a rule, only commissioned officers in full uniform wear swords or sabers. Hats and caps are carried during an indoor ceremony, and saber or cutlass bearers always wear gloves. Flowers are never worn on uniforms, so men in uniform don't wear boutonnieres and women do not wear corsages. Brides in uniform may carry a bridal bouquet. Service members not in uniform and nonmilitary members of the wedding party dress as they would for any wedding service. (For information on military forms of address, see Chapter 9, page 119; and Chapter 10, page 122–123.)

Civil Ceremonies

When time is of the essence, couples may head to their local city hall or a Las Vegas wedding chapel and have a civil wedding ceremony. Haste may be the reason when one or both of a couple is facing military deployment. For some couples city hall is neutral ground when families with differing backgrounds or faiths cannot come to agreement regarding the wedding ceremony. Others simply prefer to skip the attention brought by a larger wedding.

The ceremony itself is simple and brief and is performed by a person invested with civil authority to perform a marriage, such as a judge or justice of the peace. The only things necessary are to fulfill the legal requirements, obtain a license, and often provide two witnesses. Check the town, city, or state offices or websites for requirements, which could also include a blood test, a waiting period, or providing documentation such as a birth certificate.

Not all civil weddings take place at city hall. A civil ceremony can also take place at another site, such as the bride's home, a garden, or a rented facility. You should make the same type of arrangements for their officiant as for a religious ceremony, which could include covering travel expenses and including him or her (and his or her spouse) as a guest at the rehearsal dinner and reception.

A civil service doesn't need to be cut-and-dried, limited to a statement of intent to marry, vows, an exchange of rings, and pronouncement of marriage. If you wish to personalize the order of a civil ceremony, arrange to meet with your officiant to discuss the length of the service, any requirements, and a list of elements that could be added to the service. Having a friend or relative who is authorized to perform marriages can be the most personal and meaningful of all. Check the laws of the state, county, or country where you will marry to find out who can be authorized to legally marry you and what is required of that person to become authorized.

Church Blessing After a Civil Ceremony

Couples who did not have a religious wedding originally can usually get approval from their church for a church or chapel ceremony at a later date to bless the marriage, but check with your own church to be sure. There is such a service in the Book of Common Worship. This widely used Presbyterian service book follows the traditional marriage service, except that the minister says, "Do you acknowledge [rather than take] this woman . . ." and makes other similar changes. No one gives the bride away, nor does the

groom give the bride her ring again because this is a blessing and not a new celebration of the marriage. Couples may invite guests to the service or have a private ceremony.

Reaffirmation of Vows

Couples who would like to reaffirm their vows often do so on a big anniversary, say, their twenty-fifth or higher, but there's no reason why couples can't recommit to one another at any time during their marriage. Most clergy will perform a blessing for a couple who renew their marriage vows. The form of the service varies, depending on the officiant or the tenets of the religion, and it can occur during a regular service or at a separate time. A vow renewal is not a re-creation of the original marriage ceremony, but the couple can invite members of their original wedding party to be with them. In a secular setting, the couple can repeat their vows to each other in front of their children, family, and friends, or say them privately to each other in a ceremony of their own creation.

Many couples host a party or reception following the reaffirmation, especially if they didn't have the chance to celebrate after the original wedding. Others make a reaffirmation of vows a destination affair, inviting family (and perhaps close friends) to a vacation location for both the ceremony and the party.

CHAPTER 16

PLANNING
YOUR RECEPTION

A couple's wedding is their big day, and just as important, it's their big day to share with their friends and families. Wedding guests aren't merely a backdrop or admiring audience for all of the effort and beautiful details a couple puts into the event. Their comfort and enjoyment are as much a planning consideration as the bride and groom's personal dreams for the wedding. The good news is that one doesn't come at the expense of the other. By using some consideration and keeping guest comfort in mind, you can have your cake and eat it, too. Whether you plan a grand affair with elegant food and white-glove service or prefer a barefoot clambake under the stars, your reception should be a reflection of your personality.

A reception typically lasts from three to five hours. It sounds like a long time, but trust me, it will go by very quickly. Jump ahead to Chapter 26, page 345, for an overview of the traditional events and activities. It will help you anticipate what you'll need to create schedules and reception planning checklists.

Reception Decisions

There are many decisions to be made about the reception. Here's a review of the major ones you'll need to make that are covered in this chapter:

- Choosing a venue
- Choosing a caterer
- Planning your food service and menu
- Planning beverage service
- Mapping the seating arrangements
- Organizing transportation and parking

Finding the Perfect Place

Finding a reception locale is a top-priority decision, a process that begins once you have determined the size of your guest list—and the size of your budget. Your choice may affect the style of wedding you have, the food you serve, and the entertainment you choose.

time and style of your reception. Many facilities have a minimum number of guests for larger spaces or main ballrooms. When you visit, have the wedding coordinator or catering manager show you where cocktails will be served; how the room is set up for table service, buffets, or stations; the location of the bar(s) and the dance floor and where the band or DJ sets up. Ask how best to decorate the room and what restrictions there may be. For example, some places don't allow lit candles.

Sites that offer only space. The reception areas of most houses of worship, private meeting halls, civic sites, public parks, historic sites, galleries, museums, and private homes are examples of places that generally provide physical space only. You must take care of everything else, such as a tent, restroom facilities, catering and staff, dance floor, tables, chairs, tableware and linens, and also arrange access for your suppliers and vendors. Find out from the administrator or wedding coordinator exactly what's allowed and what's not. For example, are there spaces such as corridors that are off limits, or do you need to cover an antique floor for dancing? Try to imagine how you would set up the space for your wedding, and if there will be enough space not just for tables but for food service, mingling, and dancing, too.

Restaurants. A restaurant reception is a kind of hybrid. Some restaurants offer a full array of services, but most provide only the space, food and beverages, waitstaff, and cleanup. It may be possible to rent the entire restaurant or a private party room.

A restaurant reception is a smart choice for the busy couple who has little time to plan but prefers a more intimate setting than a hotel or club. It's all there in one place: food, service, ambience, and a built-in cleanup

Ask to see photos of how other couples have arranged and decorated the spaces you consider. There are three main types of reception sites.

Hotels, private clubs, and reception halls. Generally, these sites do weddings on a regular basis and provide food, beverages, and service. The location may offer complete wedding packages, leaving you with little to do but select the menu and color table linens you prefer. Wedding packages may vary according to the crew. A restaurant is a great choice for lunch or dinner after a ceremony with a small guest list.

Unless you are inviting guests to order off the restaurant menu, the food and choice of beverages are ordered ahead of time. (To be clear: There is no way to invite guests and ask them to pay for their own meal.) Having a set menu—whether served by waiters at a sit-down meal or offered buffet-style—is often the most economical choice and is more in keeping with a reception. It also eliminates any complications in paying the check. Many larger restaurants have party-menu choices and even reception consultants to help out. The focus is on the food, beverages, and service but not necessarily other reception elements such as dancing, music, flowers, photography, and the cake. If these are important to you, check with the manager to see what's possible.

Site Considerations

Be thorough in selecting just the right space. Most sites require hefty deposits the day you reserve them and have equally steep cancellation fees. In addition to cost, there are a few other important considerations in selecting a reception site. These include:

Size and comfort. You may fall in love with a space the first time you see it, but until you determine its comfort capacity—not its standing-room-only capacity—refrain from booking it. No matter how lovely it may be, your guests will be uncomfortable if they have no room to move. Look for potential bottlenecks: The entrance and coat check, for example, should be spaced so that guests won't have to wait in line. Consider the flow of the space, making sure aisles and hallways aren't cluttered and won't cause traffic jams.

If the guest list for your reception is small, don't pick too spacious a venue unless the site manager or wedding planner can create a smaller "room within a room." Otherwise, tables could be miles apart, and the room will feel cavernous and empty. If you plan on hours of dancing, you will want a dance floor large enough to accommodate guests. Make sure guest tables are spaced far enough from the food stations or buffet line that guests can move and those in line won't bump into guests seated at the tables.

Other comfort factors to scope out include:

- Sufficient restrooms and a place for coats

- Plenty of chairs, even if you're having an afternoon tea or a cocktail reception where guests will stand more than they sit

- Good acoustics so that your music is neither too low nor too deafening

- Good air circulation. The church hall may be a perfect space to decorate, but if it has few windows or no air-conditioning, it may need extra fans to provide better air circulation.

Time availability. You need to check availability not just for the date of your wedding but for the start time of your reception as well. The lag time—the time between the end of the wedding ceremony and the beginning of the reception—depends on several factors: whether formal photographs of the wedding party will be taken after the ceremony; whether there's a receiving line at the ceremony site; the distance from the ceremony site to the reception site; and the amount of available time you have at both spaces.

The ideal lag time is thirty to forty-five minutes. While that may not be possible, aim for as short a lag time as possible and avoid keeping reception guests

waiting. If you have more than a one-hour break between the two events and your heart is set on the two sites, you'll need to come up with some creative ways to keep your guests occupied in the meantime.

The level of formality. Both the time of day of your wedding and the environment you choose for the reception influence the degree of your celebration's formality. Generally speaking, the later in the day the wedding is, the more formal it is, though evening weddings don't have to be formal. Certain spaces, by virtue of their casual ambience, are unlikely choices for formal weddings. No matter how you decorate, casual spaces such as a rustic lodge or a tent on a beach will never look like a ballroom in a country club or hotel.

Accessibility. When scouting sites, think about how your guests will get there. If access is difficult, consider hiring shuttle vans or a bus to transport guests to and from the reception. (Be sure to clear it with the ceremony site that cars may be left there, or arrange alternate parking.) If the parking lot at the reception site is a distance from the entrance, arrange valet parking (the tab and tips are on you), so that guests don't have to walk far in high heels or in rain, snow, or heat. Also check for access for those with disabilities. Most sites that cater to events will be wheelchair accessible, but older venues may not be.

TAKE A TOUR

Before you sign a contract and formalize your plans, meet with the reception site manager. Whatever site you select, have at least one guided tour before signing an agreement. Look at the place from a practical point of view, and check the lighting, electrical supply, and food preparation areas, too.

- How easily can tables be set up?

- How big will the bridal table need to be and where will it be situated?

- Where will the band/DJ/music player and speakers be located?

- Is there room for a table where guests may pick up their seating assignments and space for a table for gifts in case guests bring them to the reception?

- Is there a place to have a receiving line?

- Is there a separate room or space for children to play?

- Is there a coatroom, or will you need to set aside a space?

- Is there easy access to restrooms?

Most sites have guidelines as well as restrictions that you and your vendors will need to follow. Have the details spelled out before signing a contract. You'll

---

HIDDEN CONSIDERATIONS FOR AN AT-HOME WEDDING

Many brides dream of getting married at their family home, and no other site could be more personal. You'll have your choice of dates because you're not competing with other couples for reception venues, and in most cases you can even have the marriage service performed at home, too. However, it doesn't necessarily mean that you'll be saving money. All of the amenities that are typically supplied and covered by the reception site will have to be supplied by you, including:

- Tent, generators, dance floor, lighting, heaters, fans

- Tables, chairs, linens, glassware, china

- Portable restrooms

- Maintenance, such as sprucing up gardens, lawns, landscaping, and painting the house

- Parking, possibly including shuttle transportation from parking to site, permits for street parking, parking attendants, security guard or off-duty policeman

- Garage space or a separate tent for caterers to set up a kitchen

- Extra liability insurance

Most family homes aren't large enough to handle a seated meal for a large number of guests, so you might plan on a reception that features substantial hors d'oeuvres or finger foods. If you do plan on a served meal, you may have to move to the backyard, and that will involve a tent large enough for table seating and dancing in case of rain.

It's a tall order to take on, and often couples or their parents hire an experienced wedding coordinator to organize and take charge of all these details. (Make sure someone alerts the neighbors—you don't want anyone calling in a noise complaint just as the band gets swinging!) The good news is that because you're not dealing with the markup charged by a reception site, you can save on buying liquor from a local supplier or discount house.

want to ensure that all your vendors will have access to the space to do their work. You'll need to communicate specific details to the site manager, such as the final guest count. Before the wedding, make arrangements for outside vendors to inspect the site. Later you may need to set up delivery times; make sure parking spaces are available for vendors (such as the band, the florist, and the photographer).

Questions to Ask the Site Manager

Here is a list of important questions to ask the site manager before signing a contract:

- What policies and restrictions does the site have for food, beverages, music, flowers, and decor? Are there restrictions on the use of candles? Are there restrictions on photography or videography lighting?

- What are the laws in the state regarding the serving of alcohol? Does the site have a liquor license?

- Who assumes liability if a guest becomes inebriated and has an accident?

- How large a band or orchestra is recommended?

- Are there sufficient outlets for a sound system and speakers, or would the band or DJ have to bring extra power cords and power strips?

- Are there any restrictions on floral decorations? (Some reception halls, for example, aren't keen on having flower garlands twined around statuary and staircases or have restrictions on moving furniture to make room for, say, potted plants or carpet runners.)

- At what time may decorations be delivered and what access will the florist be given for putting them in place?

- Is there a place for the wedding party to change clothes, if necessary?

- Does the site provide babysitting services? Is there a place where a children's room can be set up, with a television and DVD player, if necessary?

- What is the level of access for those who use a wheelchair or walker or who have mobility issues?

Outdoor Ceremonies and Receptions

An outdoor service and/or reception might be held at home; at a club, restaurant, reception hall, or house of worship with outdoor facilities; at a favorite natural spot like a park or beach; or at a historic site that is available for entertaining. When weather cooperates, the great outdoors and all that Mother Nature has on display can be unparalleled and romantic. But think about some of the less romantic aspects: Unshaded lawns on a hot afternoon can equal sunburn or heatstroke, and wooded clearings can be rife with mosquitoes. Tents, sunscreen, parasols, and a basket of insect repellent go a long way to keeping guests comfortable. Here are some other things to consider:

Be weather-conscious. Whatever the general climate, the weather on your wedding day is the great unknown. Rain is the typical spoiler, but factor in heat, cold, wind, and even insects. Check historical weather trends for the area.

Have a Plan B. You might feel as if you're planning two weddings, but you must have a fallback plan. This will include an alternate indoor site or tent and a plan to notify guests if your backup is at another location entirely. (You can prepare "just in case" phone, text, and email lists and provide these to attendants and family members.) Be ready to make a quick decision as early as possible if the weather doesn't cooperate.

Check on fees, permits, and restrictions. Some sites, such as public parks or beaches, may charge a fee or require a permit. Before choosing, be sure any restrictions on hours of operation, vehicle access, consumption of alcohol, or use of fire (candles, campfires, cooking) won't affect your plans. Consider purchasing insurance.

Think about access to the site. Caterers, florists, and other vendors will need access for their vehicles. Where will guests park? Will walking to, from, or at the site be difficult? How might rain or snow change the scene for arriving and departing guests? An uneven lawn or a rocky path to a ceremony site can turn an idyllic setting into an insurmountable challenge for guests who aren't steady on their feet. In some instances, a car or golf cart shuttle, temporary walkway, or even extra chairs can help.

Provide directions. If the site is off the beaten track, include maps and detailed directions in your wedding invitations and on your wedding website, as well as signage to the location.

Working with a Caterer

In general, hiring a caterer is recommended for a reception of more than twenty-five guests. Depending on the catering company, they can provide just the food or the works: food, beverages, the wedding cake, the serving staff, tableware, tables, chairs, and linens. Some larger outfits even provide tents, dance floors, and party decorations—or can recommend reliable suppliers and vendors.

ALL ABOUT TENTS

Tents today run the gamut from simple to palatial. There are arched entryways, bridges and pathways, parquet floors, stained-glass panels, and chandeliers. You can get a colored tent that matches your wedding theme or a climatized tent, with generators for heating or cooling and ceiling fans to keep air circulating.

Because the choices vary so widely, it's a good idea to get a referral from a caterer or club manager for reputable suppliers. You'll want recommendations as there can be a big discrepancy in costs from one tent supplier to another. Don't order a tent over the phone—go in person to see what you are paying for.

In general, for dinner and dancing you'll need at least one 60-by-60-foot or 40-by-100-foot tent per 200 people. If you want restrooms or plan on having a cocktail hour, count on adding extra footage. You may also need sound system hookups, a generator and a backup generator, ground cover, a dance floor, any permits required by local ordinance, and whatever supervisory and other personnel are required for tent installation and maintenance. Your tent may be up for several days prior to and following your wedding, so make sure that's okay, whether the site is at home or at another facility.

Before you enter an agreement, check the caterer's references. Friends are a good source for recommendations, but it's essential to talk with people, especially other couples, who have actually hired the caterer you're considering.

You may choose to use the on-site caterer at your reception location. Banquet facilities often offer wedding packages that include onsite catering. It's a convenient and cost-efficient alternative to renting a space and hiring independent vendors.

Meet with your caterer or the site manager before proceeding too far into your planning. A caterer's experience can be extremely valuable in assessing how well equipped the site is, deciding where to place tables, determining how many guests can be accommodated comfortably, how much staff will be required, and addressing any number of other details essential to the perfect reception.

Selecting the Caterer for You

Food and food service are among the most important elements of your wedding celebration, so if you've decided to use a caterer, finding the right person or company will be one of the most important goals of your wedding planning. When you start to interview caterers, consider the following criteria:

Portfolio. Some caterers keep albums containing photographs of previous receptions. Look for creative presentation touches: how the food is arranged; color schemes and variations in texture; a variety of dishes; well-organized and attractive presentations if you're considering a buffet. In other words, the food should be attractive enough to stand on its own.

Creativity and variety. The catering menu reflects the chef's breadth of preparation know-how and awareness of food trends. If a menu seems fussy and complicated, the chef may be overreaching—especially problematic when you consider the challenges of serving large groups of people efficiently. On the other hand, if the menu appears uninspired, offering the same old standards prepared the same old ways, then that's exactly what you are likely to get.

Flexibility. Most caterers have menus with a number of selections to choose from in each category—hors d'oeuvres, first course, main course, and dessert. The best caterers are happy to accommodate special requests or tailor the menu to your needs. Any caterer who is adamant about not veering from his or her patented script is one you probably don't want to work with.

Service. The kitchen and the front of the house—the waitstaff, manager, and bartenders—are two parts of the same team, and you'll want to make sure there is good communication between the two so service goes smoothly, something you can observe during a tasting (see "Tips on Tastings" below). Ask how the caterer plans to time each presentation or course.

Tips on Tastings

Most caterers will offer a food-tasting session for a fee. Tastings are a great way for you to evaluate the caterer's attention to fresh, quality ingredients. Ask to sample a variety of dishes, from hors d'oeuvres to a main course to a dessert. If you have hired a wedding planner or consultant, you should include him or her in the tasting; it's the wedding planner's job to be the clear-eyed troubleshooter, and to make sure you get the service you want. Here are some tips on things to watch for during your tasting:

❖ **Look for signs of good-quality foods and ingredients.** Is the food plated attractively? Are the vegetables brightly colored and not soggy and is the salad fresh and not wilting? Are meat and fish tender and not hidden under a blanket of gravy or sauce? If it's important to you, ask if the caterer uses local, organic, or farm-to-table ingredients.

❖ **Notice the attentiveness of the staff.** At a buffet tasting, note whether food is allowed to sit out for long periods without being replenished. The caterer should have sufficient staff to keep the presentation as fresh looking at the end of service as it was at the beginning.

WHAT DO CATERERS COST?

Q: How much will we need to budget for catering?

A: Caterers generally set prices based on a per-person figure. That figure varies from region to region, state to state, and urban area to rural area. Costs are dependent on other factors as well: the formality of the occasion, the time of day, the day of the week, the number of guests, what kind of food service you choose, how you choose to serve alcohol and other beverages, and the number of service people needed for the job.

Generally, couples allocate 40–50 percent of the reception budget for food. Costs can run from $25 per person for an informal party to $350 per person for a grand, served dinner in a major city. Having an open bar at $10 per mixed drink (city prices) can add $20–$30 or more per person to the total cost. Don't forget to figure in gratuities and taxes; they can add an additional 25 percent or more to the total bill.

Once you and your caterer have toured the reception site and agreed on arrangements, be absolutely sure that every service and item to be provided down to the last canapé is listed in an itemized contract. Check for the following:

❖ Per person cost and a list of all food items

❖ Alcohol charges, and what wines, beers, Champagnes, and liquor will be served

❖ Charges for staffing: servers, bartenders, chefs on stations, restroom and coat check attendants

Ask about the following:

❖ Is breakage insurance included or extra?

❖ Are gratuities and taxes included in the caterer's estimate?

❖ How will you be charged for any overtime?

* **Ask if it's possible to meet the chef at your tasting.** Be sure to thank the chef and offer positive feedback. Once you empower a chef with your attention and confidence, the results can be amazing.

Helping the Caterer Help You

The caterer is an important member of your wedding team. It is the caterer's job to tailor his or her skills to meet your needs and wishes. You can make your caterer's job easier by viewing the relationship as a collaboration working toward a common goal: the success of the occasion. Here are suggestions and advice on ways to make working with a caterer a positive, fun, enjoyable experience for all involved:

* Come prepared for your meeting with the information your caterer needs to know:

  * Approximate number of people to be served: guests, wedding party, children, musicians and photographers

  * The date, time, and style of your reception

  * Location details including the size of the space, kitchen facilities, and site restrictions

  * Your vision and food preferences: be ready to articulate your goals

  * Your budget

* Recognize the strengths of your caterer. Ask what the company's signature and most popular dishes are.

* Just as it's helpful to say up front if there is something you really want on the menu, it's also invaluable to specify any food you don't want. This is especially important if you're aware of allergies of any of your guests, for example, or if there are certain religious restrictions regarding foods. No one wants to have to handle special food needs on the day of the wedding.

* If you want a variation made or have a special request, say so.

* If the menu you envision is a budget buster, trust your caterer to come up with an interesting menu that is along similar lines but more cost effective.

Questions for the Caterer

When you interview a caterer, take a list with you of the nuts-and-bolts questions you'll need answered. Consider the following:

* What is the timing of service? For example, will there be Champagne or drinks ready for arriving guests? How soon will appetizers be introduced (ideally fifteen to twenty minutes after the drinks are served)? How will switching from serving hors d'oeuvres to serving dinner be coordinated? Run through the timing for your type of reception.

* What is the ratio of serving staff to guests? For high-end service, that ratio is generally one server to ten guests, or 1½ tables per waiter. For more modest receptions, the ratio is more like one server to twenty guests.)

* What are the components of a place setting?

* What are the selections of table linen colors? Are there choices for china, silver, and crystal? Can tables and chairs be provided if necessary? What about tents, heaters, portable toilets, and other miscellaneous items?

- Is insurance against china and crystal breakage included in the costs? If not, what are additional insurance costs?

- How are meals for the band, DJ, photographers, and/or videographers, charged? (Remember to plan a space for them to eat, too.)

- Is it possible to have a separate children's menu, and at what cost?

- Can the cake be provided and served? Does the caterer have a cake portfolio?

- What is the price difference between brand-name liquors and house brands?

- What is the price difference between an open bar just for the cocktail hour and an open bar throughout the reception? Between a consumption bar (where drinks are charged on a per-drink basis), and an open bar? What about a soft bar?

- At what time do servers go on overtime pay? What would the overtime charges be?

- Are gratuities and taxes included in the total bill? What about delivery charges? Are the fees for setup and cleanup included in the total bill?

ADDITIONAL QUESTIONS TO ASK ON-SITE CATERERS

- Is it possible to see a book of on-site wedding cakes and to sample a selection? Is it possible to provide your own wedding cake at no extra cost? If not, what is the extra cost? Can arrangements be made for your baker to finish decorating the cake on premise? Is there a slicing charge?

- Will a manager be on-site during the reception to oversee the event?

Planning the Wedding Feast

For many couples, the menu is at the heart of their reception and is the most fun to plan. With the renewed interest in food, caterers have expanded their repertoires far beyond the once expected "wedding creamed chicken." What's in? Seasonal foods with farm-to-table menus and regional cooking from barbecues to crawfish boils.

You'll want to create a menu to please most guests, but in doing so you don't have to settle for bland or boring—just don't force a quirky or trendy menu on them either. You can find foods that will excite your guests, that perfectly fit the season and the setting, *and* that are a meaningful expression of your personality.

Before you decide on the menu, consider logistics. There will be many different factors in determining the final menu—the size of your guest list, the type of food service (discussed below), the season, the time of day, the formality of the occasion, and your budget.

Types of Receptions

Meal options for receptions can run the gamut from breakfast to lunch, afternoon tea to dinner, and cocktails with hors d'oeuvres to Champagne and cake. What you serve depends primarily on your spending limit and the time of day of your reception.

If cost is a key concern, then breakfast, brunch, afternoon tea, or early-evening cocktail receptions are all excellent, affordable options. However, if your reception falls during a meal hour—say, from noon to 1 PM or 6:30 PM and beyond—then lunch, dinner, or other substantial fare is called for. Here are different types of receptions with appropriate meal options around the clock.

Sunrise. Sunrise services can be followed by simple bagels and danishes accompanied by a mimosa toast or a proper tuck-in complete with eggs and bacon.

Midmorning. This is the traditional British time for weddings to take place, followed by a wedding breakfast or brunch. Queen Elizabeth treated the morning wedding guests of Prince William and the Duchess of Cambridge to a reception that featured substantial hot and cold passed hors d'oeuvres and Champagne.

Midday. If a midday ceremony caused your reception to fall during lunchtime—between 11 AM and 1 PM—plan on serving either a brunch or luncheon.

Midafternoon. For a reception between 1 PM and 4 PM, lighter fare is the rule. Champagne with cake, afternoon tea with mini sandwiches and pastries, or early cocktails with hors d'oeuvres all work nicely.

Early evening. If the ceremony is at 5 PM, it's fine to plan a cocktail reception at 6 PM with heavy hors d'oeuvres. Events occurring any later encroach on the dinner hour, so think carefully about your guests and how long your reception will last when planning what type of food to serve.

If the reception falls during a mealtime and you aren't serving one, give your guests a heads up in the wording of your reception invitation. Rather than writing "Reception to follow," be more specific: "Cocktails and hors d'oeuvres to follow," for example. This is also true if local custom dictates lighter fare at a wedding reception. (See also Chapter 9, page 111.)

Types of Reception Service

SIT-DOWN OR SEATED MEAL

At a traditional seated dinner or luncheon, guests are usually assigned places at dining tables and are served by waitstaff. At a large reception, tables are numbered, and the individual place cards indicate a guest's table assignment. Place cards can either be laid out alphabetically on a separate table where guests pick them up early in the reception, or set on the tables themselves—in which case you will need additional table cards or a printed, alphabetized list to let guests know where they are seated. (See also page 225.)

Generally, a seated wedding meal comprises three courses—soup, salad, or appetizer; entrée (or entrée choices) with vegetables; and dessert—but can be more lavish. Whether or not you offer a choice of entrées, the food items are predetermined, so it's easier to estimate quantities than for a buffet. Per-person cost may actually be less than for a buffet, but the primary deciding factors will be the food itself (lobster will obviously be more expensive than chicken) and the number of waitstaff required.

There are several variations on the method of service, including:

Plated service. The food is already arranged on the plates when they are set before the guests at the table.

Russian service. Empty plates are on the tables, and the waitstaff serve each course from platters. There may be more than one waiter; one serves the meats, another the vegetables, and a third might serve salad.

French service. One waiter holds the serving platter while another serves the plates. French service can be very efficient when guests are offered a choice of entrées.

You can also mix these styles—perhaps having plated salad and dessert courses and Russian or French service for the main course.

BUFFET

Buffet service adapts to any wedding style and is particularly well suited for brunch and luncheon receptions. Whether a buffet is more or less expensive than a seated meal depends on the costs of the foods served, the number of service staff required, and the amount of food likely to be consumed. Though a buffet doesn't involve additional food courses, guests are welcome to return to the buffet for second helpings, so people tend to eat more. The advantage of a buffet is that you can serve a varied menu from which most people will find things they like.

Self-service is one option, but you may want waiters to serve at the buffet table, especially if the menu includes items such as large roasts that are carved on the spot or sauced dishes that can easily be spilled or dripped. It's simpler for guests to manage their plate if they are served. Servers can also keep dishes refreshed and impose a bit of portion control.

Guests sit at dining tables, which may or may not have assigned places. Normally, places are set with tableware, glasses, and napkins, but guests might pick up their own utensils and napkins at a casual buffet. Drinks can be served from a separate service table(s) or at the dining tables by waitstaff.

When guests return to the buffet, they leave their used plates on their tables and receive a clean plate at the buffet table. (Waiters remove the used plate.) At a small or very casual reception (such as an outdoor barbecue or a clambake), guests usually take their plates back to the buffet for another helping.

STATIONS

Stations can be an alternative to a buffet—think of them as several small buffets spread around the room. Each station features something particular, for example, a roast beef carving station, a pasta station, or one featuring regional or ethnic cuisine. They are also a great addition to passed-tray service at a cocktail reception. Stations featuring a raw bar, sushi, anything with an accompanying sauce or dip, or fruit and cheeses work particularly well.

A LITTLE BUFFET FOR LITTLE KIDS

If you plan to have children attend your wedding, one thoughtful way to serve them at the reception is to set up a separate children's buffet table—of kid-friendly height. Locate a low table, cover it with colorful linens or crayon-decorated butcher paper, and include such kid-pleasing foods as stacks of small sandwiches (but no peanut butter!), fish sticks and chicken fingers, mini raviolis, and brownies and cookies.

PASSED-TRAY SERVICE

Passed-tray service is ideal for afternoon and cocktail receptions when a full meal isn't provided. Waiters or servers circulate among the guests and offer hors d'oeuvres from trays. Finger foods are the general rule, and cocktail napkins are provided. Sometimes the food trays are supplemented with crudités, cheeses, and fruit served from a buffet table or tables. If sauced or dipping foods are served, see that trays have picks, napkins, and a receptacle for the used picks.

Determining costs for a passed-tray reception requires a reasonable estimate of quantities, and it's better to have too much than too little. Caterers and reception sites usually charge by the piece or by a per-person fee for hors d'oeuvres and can provide guidelines (say, six or seven servings per guest). Passed hors d'oeuvres may precede a full buffet or seated dinner that includes a cocktail hour. In this case, fewer servings are probably needed.

Menu Accommodations

With so many food allergies and dietary restrictions to consider today, menu planning is part art and part science. You don't have to call all of your guests and inquire about allergies—it's the guest's duty to inform the host when there's something that might prevent him or her from partaking in a meal. Think about a range of options so that all your guests will find something to eat. For example, a choice of meat, fish, or vegetable entrée is common. If you know a number of guests are vegetarian, consider requesting that side dishes be made without chicken stock, or, in the case of vegans, without butter, to keep another option open for those guests. There is a balance between being

---

GUEST COMFORT

The best hosts will keep the comfort and enjoyment of their guests high on their list of priorities. If there is a lag time between the ceremony and reception because of a receiving line or photography session, it's a good idea to offer a little refreshment to your guests while they are waiting. Begin by serving drinks, followed by food fifteen to twenty minutes later. Stations, buffets, and passed tray service are all good options for starting early with small bites. Mini danishes or smoothie shooters in the morning, or canapés and hors d'oeuvres in the afternoon or evening, can satisfy hungry guests until the couple arrives.

If you have invited children or elderly guests, remember their evening mealtime may be on the early side. Talk with your caterer to see what options are available to show consideration for these special attendees. Your hospitality will be much appreciated.

---

sure that every guest can eat everything and knowing that all guests can find enough to enjoy.

When it comes to allergies, some are simple to deal with—if raw tomatoes are the culprit, you can skip them in the salad course. Other conditions, such as nut or shellfish allergies, are more serious and pervasive, so ask your allergic guests about a solution that will keep them safe at your table. Whether or not you can accommodate their needs, pay them the courtesy of considering what those needs are.

If you do decide to provide a special meal, any extra costs fall to you, even if the guest offers to pay. Discuss any guest allergies or diet restrictions with your caterer, too; they're pros at accommodating all kinds of scenarios.

DESSERT BUFFET OR CAKE TABLE

If you're serving the traditional-style wedding cake, you may want to display your cake on a decorated table. Then, after the bride and groom cut the cake, it's usually returned to the kitchen to be cut and served to guests. Instead of (or in addition to) a wedding cake, you may prefer a dessert buffet. Guests can serve themselves from whatever desserts you choose to offer.

The Wedding Drinks

Think about providing a variety of beverages. You don't have to serve alcohol if you don't want to or if you have religious or moral reasons not to. Some couples and their families don't drink alcohol themselves but do provide alcoholic drinks for their guests. Others restrict alcohol to wine; wine and beer; or just Champagne for toasting. Budget is always a consideration, but these days, people are also limiting or eliminating liquor for health and safety reasons.

If you serve liquor, estimate the amount of alcoholic drinks likely to be consumed. If you serve a seated dinner, plan for drinks for the cocktail hour and the meal. Generally, caterers estimate consumption in two ways: Guests will drink approximately one beverage per hour, or count on two cocktails or two to three glasses of wine per person, plus one glass of Champagne for toasting. The methods of charging for beverage service include:

KEEP THE FIZZ; LOSE THE BUZZ

Whether for health or religious reasons, some guests may prefer an alternative to Champagne. While any beverage from fruit juice to water will do, it's more fun if the beverage has some sparkle. Here are some options:

Ginger ale or other pale soda
Sparking cider
Sparkling white grape juice
Seltzer water, plain or flavored
Fruit juice spritzers

ARE CASH BARS ACCEPTABLE?

Q: My fiancé really wants to serve alcohol at our wedding reception, but it would put a big crimp on our budget. Someone suggested a cash bar. What are your thoughts?

A: You wouldn't think of asking someone to pay for a cocktail in your home, so don't have a cash bar at your reception. When you invite guests to your reception, they are just that—your guests. If a full bar is not in your budget, serve soft drinks, a signature cocktail, wine, beer, or just Champagne for toasting instead. Perhaps you'll cut back on the size of your guest list and serve a full array of drinks. Just don't let a hotel, club, or reception-site manager talk you into selling tickets for drinks or having guests pay their way!

Open bar. The hosts pay a flat fee for drinks served during a specific time period—either during the cocktail hour or for the entire event.

Consumption bar. Drinks are charged at a per-drink rate, and a running tab is kept for the time the bar is open. The hosts are charged for what is actually served.

Soft bar. There is no alcohol, so ask how you will be charged.

The word *bar* doesn't have to be taken literally. Whether you offer liquor or not, beverage service may mean that drinks are passed on trays, served at drink stations, or from the buffet table. At a seated dinner and often at a buffet, wine is poured at the dining tables. For a very casual outdoor reception, drinks might be kept in ice coolers so guests can serve themselves.

You have many nonalcoholic beverage options and it's a good idea to provide several choices. Any beverage can be substituted for Champagne toasts.

Working with the Bartender or Caterer

When you talk to your reception manager or caterer, ask if a bar set up is included or if you'll need to hire a bartender. If you do need a bartender, *hire one who has liability insurance.* Here are some points to discuss:

- How many bartenders will you need?

- When will the bar close? (It's a good idea to stop service about 45 minutes to an hour before the end of the reception.)

- How will you be charged for soft bar items, such as juice, soda, bottled water? Are these beverages included or charged as consumed?

CHEERS!
A CHAMPAGNE PRIMER

The very mention of the word evokes celebration, glamour, and joy. The term *Champagne* refers only to the sparking wine made in the Champagne region of France. All other bubblies are called sparking wines or noted as being produced by the *méthode champenoise.* True Champagne is made from a blend of Chardonnay, Pinot Noir, and Pinot Meunier grapes. Count on six flutes per 750ml bottle. Here's what the label is telling you:

Brut: Dry

Extra Dry: Sweet

Blanc de Blancs: Made entirely from Chardonnay grapes

Blanc de Noirs: Made from 100 percent Pinot Noir, Pinot Meunier, or a blend of the two

NV—Nonvintage: Made mostly from grapes grown in a particular year but may contain a percentage of grapes from previous years. The blending produces a very consistent style, replicable year to year. It's generally less expensive than vintage.

Vintage: Made from at least 85 percent of the grapes from the year it was harvested. A producer usually makes a vintage wine only in a great year. Because they're more rare, vintage wines are quite pricey.

- Will you have an open bar or a consumption bar? How will you be charged for open bottles of liquor if they're not completely consumed?

- How will the bar be set up, and what type of glassware will be used? Request glass rather than plastic—unless the reception is around a pool—and that guests be given a napkin with their glass. The bar should be draped so that no boxes of liquor, ice chests, or trash bins are visible.

- How does the bartender or venue handle guests who have had too much to drink?

- Do you need extra liability insurance yourself?

- If you are purchasing liquor and soft beverages yourself, ask if you can return unopened bottles—a big savings.

The Fine Art of Seating Arrangements: Who Sits Where?

At most sit-down dinners or formal buffet receptions, the bride and groom determine seating arrangements. Deciding who sits with whom requires tact, consideration, diplomacy, and a sense of fun, so it's smart to begin your plan once you've received most of the guest replies. Ask your reception site manager for an exact diagram of table placement. You may want to make copies as you're unlikely to nail the perfect seating plan on your first try. (See page 224.)

Types of Table Groupings

The bridal-party table. The bridal-party table is generally rectangular or U-shaped and set against one side or end of the room. The newlyweds sit at the center, facing all the guests, and no one is placed opposite them. The bride sits to the groom's right, the best man sits next to the bride, and the maid or matron of honor is seated next to the groom. Bridesmaids and groomsmen then alternate boy–girl down the table to either side. If there's enough room, spouses and partners of wedding party members can be included, as well as children or siblings of the bride or groom who weren't in the wedding party.

The "sweetheart" table. This variation has the bride and groom seated on their own at a table for two, separate from the rest of the bridal party. This can be charming and romantic and gives the newlyweds an opportunity to have some private conversation during their first meal together. However, some couples might find it awkward to be the center of attention while they are eating. They may prefer to be with their attendants and save "alone" time for later.

Parents' tables. Customarily, each set of parents has their own table, hosting family members, close friends or both. If the number of people involved is small, the bride's and the groom's families can be seated together. However, it's usually best to seat divorced parents and their families at different tables. The divorced parents may be amicable, but their separate entourages of family and friends are often too large for a single table.

Informal bridal-party seating. Some couples opt not to have a formal bridal table, choosing instead to move about the room and visit with guests during dinner. Still, a table should be reserved for them and their attendants, even though they may not all eat at the same time. At a buffet, the couple can go to a buffet table with their guests, or a waiter can bring filled plates to them whenever they sit.

Guest Tables

Your basic objective is to make each table as congenial as possible. Couples usually try to mix and match guests by interests and personalities.

❖ Married, engaged, and steady couples can sit at the same table, but to keep conversation flowing it's usually best not to put them next to each other.

❖ Try to make sure that a guest knows at least two or more other people at the table. Seating one stranger at a table where the rest of the guests are close friends can leave the person feeling like the odd man (or woman) out. However, if a guest knows no one else at the reception, seat him or her with those closest in age.

❖ Seating "his" friends with "her friends" is a good way for them to get to know each other, if they don't already.

❖ While it can be nice to mix generations, your twenty-something niece will have a better time if she's seated with the twenty-something medical student than with her great-aunt and -uncle.

❖ Younger children are usually seated with their parents. But older children and teens often enjoy not being with their parents. Take your cues from what you know about a young person's preferences.

❖ Some guests need special consideration. A person who has difficulty walking may need a table near the entrance or restrooms. A person with impaired sight or hearing might enjoy a place near the bridal table or away from the band. People in wheelchairs should have easy access to tables. No chair is set at their place.

Place Cards

Place cards are recommended for seated dinners and formal buffets with more than twenty guests. For small receptions with only a few tables, you can put a card at each guest's place. At larger receptions, tables are usually numbered. The number of each guest's table is then written on his or her card.

ASSIGNED TABLES

"Let's find our table" is one of the first things guests say as they arrive at the reception. Most couples opt for open seating at assigned tables, which offers some direction but lets tables organize themselves as they like. Delegate someone to arrange the cards in alphabetical order and to place them on a side table at the reception entrance. On entering the reception area or after going through the receiving line, guests pick up their cards. Sometimes, particularly at informal and casual receptions, couples use place cards only at the bridal-party and parents' tables, and other guests seat themselves as they wish.

ASSIGNED SEATS

There could be assigned seats in addition to assigned tables, designated with preset place cards. In this case, instead of picking up a place card when they enter the reception site, guests might simply see a list with their names and table number, directing them to the table where they will have a place card at their designated seat. While it's expected that guests will respect seating arrangements, don't correct guests who swap seats.

Planning Transportation

Unless the ceremony and reception are held at your home, getting from one place to another requires planning. It isn't necessary to hire limos; you might do nothing more than spruce up the family car or cars. Or a borrowed or rented vintage car might be more your style. What matters is that everyone involved in the wedding gets where they need to be on time.

Generally, the bride's family organizes transportation for the bridal attendants to the wedding and reception. The best man and/or head usher coordinates for the groomsmen and ushers. The best man usually drives the groom to the ceremony site, sometimes drives the newlyweds to the reception, and often organizes transportation for the couple when they leave the reception.

Attendants may arrange their own transportation, but they must know scheduled arrival times. If wedding participants drive themselves, you may need to reserve convenient parking for them—even for home weddings. Children in the wedding are usually brought to the ceremony site by their parents; they may go to the reception with the other attendants or the bride's parents, but it's fine if they want to ride with their families.

Hiring Limousines

Working with a limousine service doesn't necessarily mean you must hire stretch limos. You may want less dramatic vehicles that are attractive and roomy enough for the people you will transport. Roomy is important;

you'll need extra space to accommodate the gowns and outfits of the bride, her attendants, and the couple's mothers. Whatever your preference, begin interviewing reputable rental services once your ceremony and reception sites are confirmed—limousine companies are often booked many months in advance for peak times, which could include prom seasons, Christmas, New Year's, and Valentine's Day.

Transportation Needs and Considerations

Regardless of how you get to the ceremony and reception, consider the following issues when you choose your transportation:

Scout local transportation services. Your interview should cover the following issues and questions.

- Ask their advice on the number and size of cars you'll need for your wedding party.

- Do you have a choice in the types of cars?

- What is their minimum number of hours and what services are included in the rates?

- Discuss drivers' attire so that their style of dress will be in keeping with the occasion.

- Are extras, such as Champagne, included or an add-on?

- Is the tip included in the price of the hire?

- Can you decorate rented cars, and are there any restrictions?

Determine the number of cars you'll need. A typical wedding might include:

- A car to the ceremony site for the bride and her father or escort (if the bride won't be dressing at the site)

- Cars from the ceremony to the reception for:
  - The bride and groom
  - The bride's mother or both parents plus any children in the wedding party and/or bridesmaids
  - The rest of the bride's attendants

The groomsmen drive themselves or group together under the direction of the best man. You'll need more vehicles if you provide transportation for special guests, grandparents, and other family members. You may want only one limo for the newlywed's drive to the reception, and cars for the rest.

Don't try to cram the entire wedding party in with you on the way to the reception. Even if the car is a huge stretch limo, enjoy the luxury and the romance of having your spouse alone with you if only for a few minutes. This will very likely be the first time you have been alone all day and most probably the last time you will be alone until you leave the reception. Savor the moment.

Confirm directions and driving times. If you're not hiring a driver, drive the route ahead of time to get the timing down. When it comes to weddings, it's far better to be early than to keep everyone waiting. When you arrange rentals, be precise about locations. Determine exact times that drivers will be needed, and provide detailed directions to unfamiliar sites.

Hiring a shuttle service. Sometimes it's necessary to transport guests from parking areas to the ceremony and/or reception site. Vans, buses, trolleys, even golf carts, can do the job. Make these arrangements at the same time that you hire a limo service. You'll need to spell out the route, number of hours of service, frequency of the shuttle, and how tips are handled. Pay close attention to the qualifications of drivers.

Make sure the members of the wedding party have transportation home. If you won't be using the limousine service to transport the wedding party home after the reception, be sure your attendants know their transportation arrangements. Enlist the best man or reliable relatives to see that every attendant has a safe ride and to stop anyone (attendants and guests) who has overindulged from driving.

Parking

Adequate parking is a must for hired cars and guests both at the ceremony site and the reception. Ask your site manager and officiant for the particulars so you can convey them to any hired drivers. If there is infor-

mation about parking that your guests need to know, include this information in their wedding packet or on your wedding website.

If the ceremony and/or reception is at your home, check with your local police department about on-street parking, and scout out local garages. Discuss, too, whether you need to hire security or parking attendants to watch guests' cars. If you live in a more rural area, adjacent fields might fit the bill for parking, but a rainy day can quickly turn them from charming parking lot to a muddy bog full of stuck cars.

"JUST MARRIED"

Here are some fun alternatives to leaving by limo:

Antique or classic car
Bicycle built for two
Biplane
Convertible
Farm tractor
Golf cart
Horseback
Horse and buggy
Hot air balloon
Motorcycle with or without sidecar
Pedicab
Rowboat, sailboat, motorboat, canoe

CHAPTER 17

TRADITIONS AROUND THE WORLD

Love is a universal phenomenon, and the ceremonial commitment a couple makes to each other is an expression of a timeless trust. Each culture has its own special ways of celebrating and honoring the combining of two lives, many of them traditions that have been lovingly passed on for many generations.

That so many contemporary brides and grooms turn to these traditions is proof of their lasting power and significance—and attests to the desire of modern couples to invest their ceremonies with meaning and personal and historical context. It's a way to honor their heritage and personalize their ceremony. If the bride and groom come from different cultural backgrounds, incorporating different traditions into the wedding events can be a connective thread linking both families. In some cases, the couple has two ceremonies, one in each tradition, with guests coming to one or both. Personalization of both the ceremony and reception is a hallmark of contemporary weddings. With the freedom to fashion a wedding that is unique, you have the best of both worlds—new ideas reflecting your personal interests and values combined with timeless traditions. (See also Chapter 15, page 185.)

Traditions in New Contexts

Discuss the inclusion of any religious rituals and/or readings from other religious texts with your officiant. Some faiths do not allow deviation from their standard services, but it may be possible to include other rituals either before or after the ceremony or at the reception.

When you include elements that are unique to your heritage, life experience, or religion, the result should be a pleasant and inclusive experience for guests—not a shock. They will enjoy the ceremony even more if they know what to expect. Your wedding website can give your guests a heads-up regarding any aspects of your wedding that include customs, etiquette, or expectations with which they may not be familiar. For example, if it's considered respectful for women to wear long sleeves or a head covering, you can note that on a page devoted to "customs." Your website is also a good place to give an overview of your ceremony and its length, or a link to a website that does, so guests can familiarize themselves ahead of time.

The ceremony program is another good place to include explanations of customs and rituals that are likely to be unfamiliar. (It also makes for good reading while guests wait for your ceremony to begin.)

Let's take a look at some of the customs drawn from cultures and traditions all over the globe that couples today employ to personalize their weddings.

Unity candle. An eloquent and popular addition to many marriage services, the lighting of a single candle symbolizes a couple's unity. The ceremony can be performed before, after, or at some point during the wedding ceremony. The bride and groom each hold a lighted candle, and together light a third candle. The individual candles can then be extinguished, but some couples keep them lit throughout the service as a sign that they remain individuals within their union.

The unity candle ceremony is easily adapted. Family members may be included, and parents and stepparents can participate if everyone agrees. Sometimes the bride and groom's mothers light the candle. Lighting a unity candle is also a good way for an encore couple to involve their children in their wedding service. The ceremony can take place at any point in the service, but if more than the couple are involved, it's often staged after the exchange of vows.

FINDING INSPIRATION

Want to add some cultural touches but unsure where to look for ideas? Start at home by talking to your family members—parents, grandparents, aunts, and uncles. There may be traditions from their weddings that you can incorporate into your own. Check online for ideas as well. Try a search for "Latino wedding traditions." Or Russian, Italian, Greek—whatever your heritage or interest. A little research will likely yield interesting ideas.

Customs from other faiths and cultures. In religious and secular services, couples may adopt and adapt elements from faiths other than their own. For example, couples may have their mothers and fathers escort them in the processional or gather under a decorated canopy as in Jewish weddings. Some couples have adapted the Greek Orthodox crowning, or wreath, ceremony as a symbol of their unity. Another gracious addition to some American weddings is the Chinese tea ceremony, during which the couple offers cups of sweet tea to each other's families. Native American ceremonial sand painting has inspired sand-blending rituals to signify the mingling of two individuals and their families into a single family.

Secular readings. Including nonreligious poetry and prose readings in marriage ceremonies enables couples to express their commitment in words that have special significance for them—and also allows personalization of the service by couples who do not compose their own vows. Couples may ask family members and friends to be readers. Religious and secular officiants might suggest sources for readings, and an Internet search will yield many ideas. Appropriateness and brevity (readings are usually one to two minutes in length) are important, so discuss your options with the officiant early in the planning process. (See also Chapter 15, page 193.)

Musical mixes. Maybe you'd like your ceremony to open with the ringing of a Tibetan gong. Or walk up the aisle to the sound of Scottish bagpipes. Or include Balinese dancing at your reception. Music provides innumerable ways to personalize (and internationalize) wedding celebrations. Ask your officiant about any restrictions on secular music. In the ceremony program, you can add a brief explanation of any special musical selections from other traditions and their significance to you.

Jumping the broom. The broom has long played a symbolic role in weddings, most notably in Scotland, Wales, England, and in Romany culture. Walking over a piece of the flowering shrub called broom or a broom for sweeping "sealed" a common law marriage.

In the United States, "jumping the broom" is most often associated with African American weddings and honors slaves who were not allowed to marry legally. They did marry, in secret, by their own tradition and formed strong families. The ritual symbolizes the establishment of a new household and is usually performed just after the wedding service or at the reception. Tradition has it that the person who jumps the highest (or touches the ground first) rules the household. The broom (a regular house broom is fine) is decorated with ribbons, flowers, and perhaps special trinkets.

The broom is laid on the floor or held just above it, and guests gather round. On the count of three, the newlyweds, hand in hand, jump over the broom and into their new life as husband and wife.

Breaking the glass. In a traditional Jewish ceremony, the bride and groom stand beneath the chuppah, a wedding arch or canopy that's often adorned with flowers. Following the reading of the Seven Blessings, wine is poured into a new glass, and the bride and groom drink from it. The groom then places the glass, wrapped in cloth, on the ground and breaks it with his foot—an act symbolizing the destruction of the Temple in Jerusalem and meant to underscore the fragility of love.

Handfasting. A custom most associated with pagan Celtic tradition, handfasting is now included in some religious as well as secular services. During the service, the couple's hands are ceremonially tied with rope, cords, or ribbons to symbolize their union. Though the Celtic handfasting ceremony probably originated as a contract between a couple to stay together for a year and a day (if the arrangement worked, the contract was renewed), handfasting today signifies the enduring nature of the marriage commitment. It may be the source of the phrase "tying the knot."

The shared cup. In many traditions, both religious and secular, the bride and groom share a cup of wine during the wedding ceremony—a custom unrelated to Christian communion services. In Chinese tradition, the couple drink wine and honey from goblets tied together with red string. In Japan, couples who wed in the Shinto tradition take nine sips of sake, as do their parents, to symbolize the new bonds of family.

Q: My mother insists that I not see my husband-to-be on the day of the wedding until the ceremony. Is this still customary in today's weddings?

A: Most couples today disregard the old superstition of the bridegroom not seeing his bride before the ceremony on their wedding day. The custom stems from the days when marriages were arranged and the groom might never have seen the bride. There was the chance that he might take one look at her and bolt—so it was often safer for them to meet for the first time at the altar!

This custom certainly doesn't need to be followed these days unless it's something you both feel strongly about. It's also fallen victim to practicality. To avoid leaving guests in limbo while posed wedding pictures of the couple, attendants, and family members are being taken before or during the reception, many couples schedule this photo session a few hours before the ceremony. It's also an opportunity to get a really great "first look" photo, when the groom first sees his bride in all her glory.

Sharing a wedding cup is also a reception custom in many cultures. French couples drink wine from a *coupe de marriage*, or double-handled cup. Irish guests gather round the newlyweds, and toasts are made over cups of mead, a fermented drink made from honey, malt, and yeast.

More Wedding Traditions from Around the World

Included below are more ideas from around the globe for making your wedding day a unique expression of your heritage. Add your personal touch—through music, food, and drink, and even good-luck charms.

African Traditions

In addition to "jumping the broom" described above, some couples use fabric and color to highlight their African American heritage. Kente cloth, woven in a red, gold, and green design, is often used in African American weddings. This cloth reflects personal, societal, religious, and political culture. The traditional red, gold, and green repeated in the design are liberation colors recognized by people of African descent all over the world: red for the blood shed by millions in captivity, gold for Africa's mineral wealth (prosperity), and green for the vegetation of the land of Africa (home). Boxes arranged in an X shape in the fabric represent all ideas coming together at one point, symbolizing leadership, consensus, and the voice of the people. The stepped border motif symbolizes defense against assaults and obstacles encountered in the course of a lifetime. The traditional color of African royalty is purple, accented with gold. These color and fabric accents can be used in many ways—in invitations, as colors in clothing or accessories worn by the bridal party, on place cards, and in decorations.

British Traditions

If a couple marries in a church, banns—the announcement of the proposed wedding—are read aloud in the church for three consecutive Sundays before the wedding. It's unlucky for the bride and bridegroom to be present at the calling of the banns. The bride and groom and their wedding party often walk together to the church. Traditional weddings are held at noon, and afterward there is a seated luncheon, also known as a wedding breakfast. When the bride and groom enter and leave the church, bells are rung to scare off evil spirits. It's good luck for a chimney sweep to kiss the bride when she comes out of the church—still a sideline job for a sweep today.

A Victorian rhyme captures the customary bridal accoutrements: "Something old, something new, something borrowed, something blue, and a silver sixpence in her shoe." Orange blossoms, popularized by Queen Victoria's wedding, may be sprinkled on the ground in front of the bride. The bride carries or wears a small horseshoe for good luck, and the best man should see that the groom also has a good-luck charm in his pocket. The top layer of the wedding cake is called the christening cake; it's saved and served at the baptism of the first child.

Chinese Traditions

Red is the Chinese color for joy and luck—and can be integrated in wedding invitations, flowers, the aisle runner, candles, favors, tablecloths, napkins, and bridal clothing.

In Chinese culture, great importance is placed on dates and numbers. Auspicious days for marrying are determined by fortune-tellers and feng shui experts, who examine the Chinese almanac along with the day and hour of the bride and groom's birth.

Dowries for marriages are still honored in many families, whether in the form of a whole roasted pig, a live chicken, or some other symbolic swap. For the wedding banquet, the bride often changes from her wedding dress into a long red cheongsam, a traditional Chinese dress, which may be adorned with dragon and phoenix images, representing the union of man and woman.

The Chinese Historical and Cultural Project (www .chcp.org) is a great resource for couples wishing to learn about Chinese wedding customs. The wedding banquet revolves around a feast of elaborate courses, serving foods that have special symbolism, representing such attributes as prosperity, happiness, and long life. Eight courses are generally served—eight being considered a lucky number. Popular foods for Chinese wedding banquets include shark's fin soup, which represents prosperity (but today it's also controversial); "red" foods, such as lobster (another good-luck symbol); and noodles, which symbolize longevity. Lotus seeds, in soup or steamed bread, represent fertility. The Chinese symbol representing "double happiness" is often hung on the wall behind the bridal-party table.

Chinese couples traditionally honor their relatives and new family members with a tea ceremony—the couple kneels before older relatives and family friends and offers each of them a cup of tea as a gesture of respect. Each honoree hands the couple an envelope of money or gold jewelry in return.

French Traditions

Similar to British weddings, the bride, groom, and the wedding party walk to the church together. Children run to stand in front of the entrance with white ribbons that the bride cuts before entering the church. A silk wedding canopy is held over the couple to protect them from evil spirits during the ceremony. The bride and groom drink a reception toast from a *coupe de marriage*, a two-handled silver cup that is shaped like a small bowl on a pedestal. The bride drinks first, then the groom, and in so doing they seal their commitment to each other.

German Traditions

In Germany, a couple's silver marriage cup is made in the shape of a young girl wearing a full skirt, holding the cup over her head. The bride and groom drink from it at the same time to symbolize their joining together. Start your own marriage cup tradition at your wedding and save the cup for the next in the family to wed.

The night before the wedding there is a party, called *Polterbend* (rumbling night), at which the couple is teased and dishes are broken to dispel evil spirits. Friends and family, and even the couple, purchase cheap china for the event. Only the couple has the privilege of tossing the china down the stairs the night before the ceremony. The festivities continue until the early hours of the morning and may be followed by a breakfast at the bride's parents' home.

Another playful exchange occurs at the end of the ceremony, when guests "rope" the couple in with a barricade of ribbons and garlands of flowers. To get out, the couple has to promise the guests a party.

Greek Traditions

In ancient Greece, brides wore wedding veils of yellow or red, which represented fire. These brightly colored veils protected the bride from evil spirits and demons. A Greek bride may carry a lump of sugar on her wedding day to ensure she has a sweet life, or she might carry ivy, as a symbol of endless love. At the ceremony, the bride and groom are "crowned" by the best man to show that the couple are the king and queen of their union as man and wife. (See also Chapter 15, page 197.) The Greek tradition of the *kalamatiano*, the circle dance, is done at the reception. Candy-coated almonds are traditionally given to the guests as favors.

Hispanic American Traditions

Brides and grooms of Latino descent who are removed from their heritage by time and distance can reconnect by adding long-standing cultural traditions to their wedding.

The bride's traditional wedding dress is white, but the bride may sew colored ribbons into her lingerie: yellow for food, blue for money, and red for passion in her marriage. She also wears a mantilla, a chapel-length white lace veil, and she may carry a fan instead of flowers. Brides don't wear pearls; they symbolize bad luck. The groom wears a black bolero jacket and fitted pants similar to a matador's costume or, more casually, white drawstring pants and a Mexican wedding shirt.

In addition to the common customs of decorating the church with white roses and holding the Mass at nine o'clock in the evening, couples ask those closest to them to be *madrinas* and *padrinos*, sponsors or honorary godparents, giving a customary responsibility to each. One responsibility is to make three bouquets—one to place on the altar for the Virgin Mary, one to keep as a memento, and one for the bride to toss at the reception. Another godparent holds a dish with thirteen gold coins (*arras*) and rings: The groom takes the coins from the dish and hands them to the bride as a sign of giving her all his possessions; he also promises he will use all he possesses for her support. Two more godparents carry a very long rosary rope (*lazo*), which they drape around the bride and groom as the couple kneels at the altar.

At the reception, a mariachi band is most traditional, as is *la vibora*, a line dance performed by the single women. Mole, a dish featuring a sauce made of chiles, chocolate, and peanuts, is a staple at wedding feasts, so much so that "*va a haber mole*" (there's going to be mole) is an idiom meaning "someone is getting married." Flan is a traditional dessert, and *pastelitos de boda* (wedding cookies) can be served with dessert or given as favors.

HOW TO COMBINE TRADITIONS RESPECTFULLY

- Discuss your plans and ideas with your parents. Ideally, everyone will be supportive. If they have objections, listen carefully and see if you can make accommodations that will overcome them. For example, are there aspects or traditions, such as the Jewish breaking of the glass, which could be performed at the reception instead of at the ceremony?

- Speak to your officiants if you are of two faiths and planning on a religious ceremony. Depending on the orthodoxy of your officiant, church, or temple, you may be able to combine the ceremonies, if the core elements from each marriage service are included. If that's not possible, you should discuss the option of two separate ceremonies.

- Be respectful of any traditions that you "borrow." The elements you choose should have significance or meaning to you as a couple and relevance to your ceremony. A nondenominational ceremony packed with a smorgasbord of customs borrowed from a multitude of cultures and religions could appear to lack focus and sincerity.

- Educate your guests. Use your wedding website to familiarize your guests with the customs or traditions you will be observing. For example, guests will need to know if there are any expectations regarding dress for your ceremony and reception. You could also link them to websites that give a general overview of wedding customs in your cultures.

- Create a ceremony program. List the order of your service and add a description explaining the significance or history of the various elements, including nonreligious traditions you may have chosen such as handfasting, sand blending, or lighting a unity candle. This is particularly helpful if the ceremony is performed in another language, such as Hebrew, Spanish, or Hindi.

GOOD-LUCK CHARMS

Horseshoes. The Irish bride wears a little porcelain horseshoe on her wrist for good luck.

Coins in shoes. The Swedish bride places a gold coin from her mother in the right shoe and a silver coin from her father in the left shoe. The Irish bride puts an Irish penny in her bridal shoes for luck; the English bride, a silver sixpence.

Jordan almonds are given to guests at weddings in the Mediterranean countries, and are called *confetti* in Italian. They represent the bitter and the sweet sides of marriage.

The evil eye. Attendants in Greece wear a good-luck charm or pin in the shape of an eye to protect against evil spirits.

Plates are broken in Germany on the doorstep of the bride to drive away evil, and the remaining shards are considered good luck.

Lumps of iron are carried by the groom in his pocket for good luck.

Indian Traditions

Indian weddings are elaborate, lavish, and rich in regional, family, and religious traditions, a colorful, joyous celebration that can last five days. Marigold garlands are the most common decoration, and the *mandap*, or four-pillared canopy, where most of the wedding ceremony takes place, is decorated in shades of red, maroon, purple, orange, silver, and gold.

The Hindu bride usually wears a red and gold sari with lots of jewelry and a veil that covers her head. Prior to an Indian wedding, the bride's hands and feet are intricately decorated with elaborate flowery scrolls using henna, a practice known as *mehndi*. This ritual is also performed in Pakistan and many other Muslim countries and is meant to bring good luck to the bride.

The wedding day starts with the *baraat*, a joyous procession. The groom rides to the wedding venue on a white horse accompanied by the beat of a drum and friends and family who dance around him. Family members greet each other and exchange garlands and gifts. The bride and groom have a playful exchange of garlands in the *varmala* ceremony just before entering the *mandap*. When the groom finally puts the garland on the bride's neck, it symbolizes that she has accepted him. In another custom, the groom ties a *mangalsutra*, a black and gold beaded necklace with a gold or diamond pendant, around his bride's neck as a symbol of their marriage. (See also Chapter 15, pages 200 and 201.)

Irish Traditions

The traditional Irish bride carries a horseshoe for good luck. Today, a decorative porcelain version replaces the real horseshoes brides used to carry. According to legend, the chime of bells keeps away evil spirits and reminds the couple of their wedding vows, so a bell is a traditional Irish wedding gift. The Irish wedding blessing is a popular toast, no matter what your heritage: "May the road rise to meet you. May the wind always be at your back. May the sun shine warm upon your face, and the rains fall soft upon your fields."

The musical traditions of the Celtic world are naturally celebratory, perfectly suited to the joyous events surrounding a wedding. Irish *céilí* bands play toe-tapping music for dancing. Irish set dancing is an elaborate form of traditional dancing, practiced by four couples in a square, and many modern Irish weddings feature performances by hired set dancers.

Italian Traditions

An Italian wedding is rich in symbolism and tradition. On the day of the wedding, the bride doesn't wear any gold until after her wedding ring is slipped on; wearing gold before or during the wedding is considered bad luck. The groom carries a lump of iron in his pocket for good luck. Traditionally, the ceremony (*sposalizio*) is officiated by a priest or by civil authority. Old church traditions and folklore banned marriages during Lent and Advent. Religious custom held that weddings shouldn't be scheduled in May (dedicated to the veneration of the Virgin Mary) and August, which was considered bad luck. (Besides, everyone is on vacation in August in Italy!) Sunday is considered the luckiest day for Italians to marry.

Although she may pick the flowers and design, the groom delivers the bride's bouquet to her at home or at the church, his last gift to her before their marriage. Often, the couple walks to the church together, symbolizing their journey in life. The church is decorated with a white ribbon tied to the door, meaning a marriage is to take place. As the couple leaves the church or registry, guests throw rice or grains to symbolize fertility and doves are released, symbolizing love and happiness.

Most receptions are held at a restaurant, and no wonder, because there could be as many as fourteen courses. The reception starts with a cocktail hour, and guests are served aperitifs. About an hour later, after their wedding photos, the bride and groom make a grand entrance to great fanfare.

There's lots of toasting—*Per cent'anni* (For a hundred years) or *Evvivi gli sposi* (Hooray for the couple)—and whenever there's a lull, someone will demand the groom kiss the bride. At some point the groom stomps on a wineglass, and the number of shards indicate how many years the couple will be happily married.

All the men at the reception kiss the bride for good luck—and to make the groom jealous. One Italian custom, known as the *buste* (envelope), is still practiced at Italian weddings today. The bride carries a satin bag (*la borsa*) into which the male guests deposit envelopes containing their gift checks in exchange for a dance with the bride. In the past, the money helped the bride's family to defray the cost of the wedding, which was exclusively their financial responsibility. Today, the checks are the guests' wedding gifts to the couple.

Wedding knots, or *farfallette dolci*, made of twisted dough, are popular wedding treats in Italy. After the cake is cut, the bride and groom go from table to table and give tulle or lace bags of sugared almonds, called *confetti*, to their guests. Tradition calls for an odd number, say five or seven, for luck. Finally, guests receive a small favor, often a small silver or porcelain trinket. Everyone receives the same favor underscoring that no guest is considered more important than another.

Japanese Traditions

In choosing a wedding date, a Japanese couple looks for an auspicious day of good fortune. The predominant religion in Japan is Shinto, which means "the way of the gods or spirits." The traditional Japanese religious wedding ceremony is held in a Shinto shrine. Shinto wedding ceremonies are very private with only family and close friends in attendance.

Today, only 20 percent of couples in Japan marry in the traditional Shinto wedding ceremony. As part of the ceremony, the bride and groom partake in the sake ritual. They are served sake in three cups. They each take three sips from each cup, repeating this process three times, to complete what is known as the three-times-three ceremony (*san-san kudo*). Then their parents also take sips, cementing the bond between families. The ceremony ends with the offering of a sacred branch (*tamagushi*). The bride may change her dress several times during the reception, a Japanese wedding tradition dating from the fourteenth century called *oiro-naoshi* that signifies that she is prepared to return to everyday life.

The Japanese believe that guests bring so much luck with them that the bride and groom should thank them in return. Favors are always given to guests: a pair of chopsticks imprinted with the date and names of the bride and groom and tied with a ribbon; a collection of origami cranes; and a bag of candied almonds. Japanese brides and grooms sometimes give their wedding guests a special box with *kohaku manjyu*, a pair of round steamed buns—one red, one white—with sweet bean paste in the middle.

Korean Traditions

Before the wedding, a Korean groom gives his future mother-in-law a wild goose. Wild geese mate for life, and his gift symbolizes his promise to care for his future wife for her entire life. The traditional live goose is more likely to be a wooden goose today.

The wedding usually takes place at the bride's home. During the wedding ceremony, or *kunbere*, the bride and groom exchange vows and seal their marriage with sips of a special wine, drunk from a gourd grown by the bride's mother. A few days later the couple visit the groom's family for the *p'ye-back* ceremony. The bride gives dates and chestnuts—symbols of chil-

dren—to the groom's parents, who offer the couple wine or sake in return. Then the groom's parents throw the dates and chestnuts at the bride, who tries to catch them in her wedding skirt—presumably the more she catches, the more children the couple will have.

Polish Traditions

The night before her wedding, a Polish girl's mother and female relatives rebraid her hair from the one braid worn by a girl to the two braids worn by married women. In Poland, the wedding ceremony takes place in two parts, first at the magistrate's office and then at a church. Before the church ceremony, friends and family gather at the bride's home and accompany the couple to the church. At the church steps the couple thanks and is blessed by their parents before entering the church for the wedding ceremony. As they exit the church, guests shower the couple with rice or small coins.

The wedding reception can last for two days, with a "follow-up" party the second day at the home of the groom's family. The couple's parents greet them with bread sprinkled with salt and a glass of wine. The bread symbolizes the hope that the couple will never be hungry and the wine that they will never be thirsty. The salt is a reminder that life can be difficult or sorrowful, but that they will learn to cope with life's hardships.

A polka band and Polish specialties such as beet soup, pierogies, tortes, and fruit are standards at the wedding feast. The first toast and song to the newlyweds is "*Sto lat*" (One Hundred Years) of good health for the couple. It's traditional for the maid of honor to collect money and checks from guests who pay to dance with the bride. The money collected is given to the couple for their honeymoon. A highlight of a Polish wedding is the *oczepiny*, or unveiling ceremony. The women circle around the bride and her mother or maid of honor removes her veil, and it is given or tossed to the other single women, marking the bride's transition to married life.

Scottish Traditions

In Scotland, at the end of the wedding ceremony, the groom takes off his colorful tartan sash—often the tartan of his clan or family—and places it on his bride, whether gently over her head or on her shoulder, with the sash running diagonally across her gown. It symbolizes the welcoming of the bride into the family and the joining of two into one.

Scottish wedding receptions often feature music for dancing jigs and reels, keeping up the high-energy custom of Scottish wedding days of old, when pipers played all day in the fields and fiddlers played all day in the house. Bagpipes continue to be a popular instrument at both Scottish wedding ceremonies and receptions, announcing the entrance of the bride and other important events.

CHAPTER 18

REMARRIAGE: THE ENCORE WEDDING

It is estimated that more than 40 percent of all weddings in the United States are encore weddings—weddings in which one or both of the couple have been married before. The decision to marry again is a powerful commitment to the ideals and values of love and family, and it deserves to be celebrated.

An encore wedding is almost, but not quite, like a first wedding. Couples are no longer expected to celebrate second (or third or fourth, etc.) weddings with as little fanfare as possible. Today, remarrying brides and grooms celebrate their unions in whatever style they like, and their weddings range from the classic and traditional to highly personal and creative events. Encore brides and grooms have every wedding tradition option available to them. Many brides wear white and ask their fathers to walk them down the aisle. Encore couples register for gifts, have engagement parties and showers, and some ask attendants from a previous wedding to join them again at the altar.

By definition, the encore bride or groom—or both—is either divorced or widowed. They often have families from previous marriages to consider as they plan their wedding and new life together. These additional and sometimes more complex relationships can require a little extra attention, sensitivity, and even diplomacy as you make your wedding plans.

THE WIDOW WAIT PERIOD

Discussions about encore weddings tend to revolve around remarrying after a divorce, but that's not always the case. Widows and widowers also find themselves in the happy position of planning an encore wedding. It's natural to wonder if there is a "correct" period of time that must pass before a widow or widower should remarry. There is no set time frame, other than to go with what feels right to you—and to consider the feelings of children from your previous marriage, your in-laws, and other close family members. One year has generally been considered the appropriate waiting period. If you feel ready sooner and you have the support of your family, it's fine to consider a shorter time frame.

When one or both of the couple have children, the marriage is the joining not only of two people but also of preexisting nuclear families. The wedding marks the beginning of a new family and brings changes to the children's established relationships and routines. Other family members, former spouses, and former in-laws will also be affected.

This time around, an encore couple is likely to be wholly responsible for wedding planning and expenses. Encore brides and grooms have certain advantages based on the perspective gained through past experiences. Having been through it all before, they're usually familiar with some of the essentials of wedding etiquette and are often better prepared to anticipate the decisions they need to make and to take any glitches in stride.

Start Spreading the News

Tell your children first. Before telling anyone else that you're getting married, inform your children from previous marriages—whatever their ages. Ideally, each parent will talk with his or her own children privately and in person (or via phone, as necessary). Your one-on-one talks can give your children the opportunity to be candid and also give you insights into any concerns they might have.

In some families, the news of the remarriage is good news from the start for all involved, without fear or worry. But the news might be unsettling, particularly for younger children and teenagers. No matter how fond they are of a future stepparent, children often feel torn, seeing the remarriage as a test of their loyalty to their other biological parent. They may be sad that

there's an end to any hope they may have had that their parents would reunite.

They may also worry about how their new family will function, especially sharing their parent with step-siblings, and how much control the new stepparent will have over their lives. Very young children may not know how to react and will need your help to understand what's happening.

No matter how your children take the news of your remarriage, the engagement period is a great opportunity to lay the solid foundations of mutual respect, understanding, and affection on which to construct your new family.

When divorced couples are on reasonably good terms, the first concern should be helping their children adjust to the new family arrangement. So be sure to tell your former spouse the news, especially if he or she is a custodial parent. You might want to inform your ex before talking with your children, so he or she can be prepared to react appropriately with the kids.

Telling your families and others. After you've shared the news with your children, it's time to inform your parents, siblings, and other close relatives. Though you may no longer be dependent on the people who raised you, make the effort to tell them of your plans before they hear it from someone else.

Now, too, is the moment to inform your in-laws, if you are a widow or widower, or former in-laws if you are divorced and on speaking terms. Depending on your relationship with them, share the news either in person, via phone, or in a personal note.

Once your families have been informed it's time to tell your friends and coworkers and to post it on Facebook.

Your Guest List

Who to invite. The guest list may be especially significant in determining the size and style of your encore wedding. The number of guests is up to you (and your budget). But who to invite can get tricky if a previous marriage ended in discord and you retain mutual friends with your former spouse. If friends think that attending your wedding means choosing sides between you and an ex-spouse, they may legitimately feel trapped between a rock and a hard place. In this instance, you might decide on an intimate wedding with only your closest family and friends in attendance. Another option might be a small ceremony and a larger, informal reception.

If you include guests who attended your first (or most recent) wedding, it's best to plan a ceremony and reception that won't lead to comparisons.

Your former spouse and in-laws. It's usually not a good idea to invite your former spouse or in-laws to your encore wedding. Your family and friends could feel awkward celebrating your new marriage when they are there. Most important, consider your new spouse and

---

TEN GUIDELINES FOR ENCORE WEDDINGS

The following list can help couples plan and stage encore weddings that become happy memories for the bride, groom, and those they care about. While many of these basics apply to any wedding, some are specific to encore weddings.

1. Work together. The decisions about your wedding should be shared.

2. Don't let the details take over. It's just as easy to become overwhelmed planning an encore wedding as planning a first.

3. If you have children, tell them first—no matter what their ages.

4. Be realistic about your budget—in all likelihood, it's just the two of you footing the bill.

5. Plan your celebration around traditions and themes that are significant to you and have positive associations for your children, family, and friends.

6. Talk with your officiant about ways to include your families, especially children. Review the wording of traditional services and texts for appropriateness.

7. Make sure that you have put closure to your first marriage legally, financially, and emotionally. Put away engagement and wedding rings from past marriages; you can save them for the next generation or have stones reset into other jewelry.

8. Register for gifts if you want. Even if you don't expect gifts, many guests will want to give them. Be sure to register in a range of prices.

9. Thank-you notes never go out of style. Send a written note within three months for every gift you've received. And remember: Grooms can write notes, too!

10. Thank everyone—in person or by note—who helped make the wedding a success.

any children you both bring to your marriage. It can be difficult and confusing for them to celebrate your new family if your ex is there.

Even if you and your ex are friendly, it's generally best to leave him or her out of the festivities, but circumstances vary. Let your particular situation be your ultimate guide as to whether to invite your ex and/or former in-laws. If you and your fiancé(e) both feel good about doing so, you may certainly bend the general rule.

If you are widowed and have remained close to your former spouse's parents, it's likely that you'll want to invite them. Just be conscious of their feelings; your new marriage may be bittersweet for them. It's a good idea to talk with them personally and tell them how much you would like them to attend. But also let them know that you understand if they choose not to.

Invitations

Just as for first-time weddings, invitations to encore weddings reflect the nature of the occasion—formal, informal, or casual. Invitations to especially small weddings might be made by phone calls or personal notes.

Who issues the invitation? When the couple has been living independently, they usually issue the invitation themselves. But parents may issue the invitation, especially if the bride is young; or the invitation could be sent in the names of both the bride's and the groom's parents, with the bride's family listed first. These options are correct even if parents aren't paying for the wedding. (For examples of wedding invitation wording, see Chapter 9, page 107.)

When adult children host. It's particularly meaningful when grown children host their parents' wedding and/or reception. On the invitation, the children (and their respective spouses) are listed as hosts with the bride's children named first. Each set of children is listed according to age, from eldest to youngest.

A Family Event

The following are some ways that today's encore couples are reaching out to make their weddings into genuine family affairs.

Children's participation. Asking your children to be attendants in your wedding is a great idea, especially if they are happy about the marriage. Most important: Ask the children if they want to be included, and give them room to say no.

There are various roles they can choose from. Some couples ask their children to be bridesmaids or groomsmen or, if they're young, flower girls or ring bearers. An encore bride might ask a son or daughter (or both) to walk her down the aisle. Instead of "giving the bride away," the child is participating in forming a new family. It's a wonderful, personal touch to hear the officiant ask "Who will support this new family?" and hear a child's voice happily answering "I do."

Older children can present readings if they are comfortable in front of an audience. Or you could ask some of them—girls as well as boys—to serve as ushers. Just be sure that each child is happy with his or her role, whatever it is.

Can adult children be involved? Of course! For older couples with adult children from previous marriages, including these children (and even grandchildren) in the celebrations only adds to the joy and community of the occasion.

A family addition to the service. After the couple is pronounced husband and wife, the children can be asked to come forward to join them. The officiant then addresses a special message to the children. A family prayer is often included in religious ceremonies. This brief part of the service usually emphasizes the creation of a new family, and the children are mentioned by name.

A candle-lighting ceremony. After the ceremony, the children and perhaps the parents of the bride and groom join the couple. Everyone lights candles as an expression of the union of the families.

Special remembrance gifts. The couple might present all the children with something unique to the occasion such as an engraved bracelet, watch, or necklace, picture frame with a picture of the new family, or a wedding photo album.

Wedding photos. Include the children in wedding photos. Be sure your photographer knows who they are and gets them in plenty of candids as well as formal photos. Seeing themselves in the picture afterward—literally—is a great way to emphasize their place of importance in the family.

A FEW FAMILY DOS AND DON'TS

As you and your fiancé(e) move forward with your plans to marry, the following guidelines can help you build family harmony:

Do consult each child individually to determine if he or she would like to be in the wedding. Avoid simply expecting them to participate. Respect the wishes of a child or teen who doesn't want to take part, but also leave the door open for a change of heart.

Do answer children's questions about your previous marriage. You can be honest without being explicit or overly negative.

Do speak respectfully about a former spouse. This is the time to create a positive, respectful atmosphere.

Do consult your former spouse to schedule events involving the children, especially if wedding activities may conflict with regular visits. Set the stage now for cooperation with ex-spouses.

Do invite your and your fiancé(e)'s respective children to your engagement party. Arranging a gathering for your adult children to meet is not absolutely necessary—and may not be possible—but it's a nice idea.

Don't question your future spouse's children about their other parent. Your interest may be benign, but questioning children may be seen as prying and can undermine their trust in you.

Don't expect your respective children to become friends right away. Don't push them together; give them some time to absorb the idea that you are remarrying and to get to know each other.

Flowers. Small tokens can mean a great deal. Whether they take part in the ceremony or not, be sure that each child has a boutonniere or flower. Wrist or pinned corsages are fine for girls, but a small nosegay or a miniature version of the bride's bouquet can be particularly meaningful.

Children and the Honeymoon

Sooner or later young children are likely to ask "What's a honeymoon?" followed by "Can we go?" Whether they raise the subject or you do, be very sensitive to their feelings. Sometimes an encore wedding followed immediately by a honeymoon trip can be difficult for children. The disappearance of their parent and new stepparent right after the wedding may be especially confusing for very young children. Older children may feel hurt or angry at your absence, especially if they worry that your remarriage will relegate them to second place in your affections.

Children tend to live in the present moment. They may not really grasp why you're going away after the wedding—no matter how well you explain. While it's fine to plan a honeymoon immediately after the wedding, if your children are genuinely troubled or upset, here are some alternatives that you might consider:

- Divide the honeymoon into two parts—for example, several days devoted to the children followed by time on your own as a couple.

- Delay the honeymoon. Give the children some time to settle into their new family life (and perhaps new home) and to adjust to the idea that you and your new spouse will be going away on a trip by yourselves.

This adjustment period could be several weeks, months, or longer, depending on the circumstances and the ages of the children.

- Plan simultaneous trips. Arrange for the children to spend special time with their other parent (your former spouse) or perhaps their grandparents. If you all return from your trips at the same time, the children are likely to see their time with relatives as something special, and you can all share your stories about your trips.

NEW MONOGRAM, OLD SILVER

Q: After my divorce, I kept my ex's last name and all the monogrammed wedding gifts including the sterling flatware. Now I'm remarrying, and I wonder what to do with these things.

A: Many encore couples dispose of monogrammed items like towels and table linens—either giving them away or passing them on to children from their earlier marriages. But something as valuable as sterling flatware can be another matter entirely. You might sell the sterling and replace it with a set you both choose. Or if your future spouse agrees, you could continue to use it. Today, people collect silverware that has been engraved with many different initials, so setting the table with your old monogrammed flatware may hardly be noticed. Alternatively, check with an engraver. If the silver isn't marked too deeply, it may be possible to buff down the old monogram and then remark it with your new monogram. Just be sure to discuss the options with your fiancé and make the decision together.

More Planning Particulars for Encore Weddings

For a number of reasons, including respect for your new spouse, avoid an exact duplication of your previous wedding. This is a time to consider all your options and to be open to doing things as the couple you are, not as the past bride or groom you were.

Attendants. While your wedding attendants also shouldn't be the same lineup as your first wedding, it's absolutely fine to include people who remain near and dear to you, whether they were attendants in your previous wedding or not. Sisters, brothers, best friends—all are eligible, but just make sure that whoever you ask is up for it a second time, both in terms of time and budget.

Attire. White is totally acceptable for bridal gowns, as it is a color of joy and celebration for both encore and first-time brides. Best advice? Choose a dress, suit, or gown that's appropriate to your age, figure, and the style of your wedding. The same advice applies to a veil, if you wear one. Choose one that suits your outfit, but forgo the blusher veil that's more appropriate for a very young or first-time bride.

Showers. Encore showers are acceptable, but tact and some good judgment come into play. A second shower is okay when it's carefully planned. Other than close friends and relatives, the guest list shouldn't include people who came to a shower for your first wedding. If hosts want to invite people who have already "showered" you, a luncheon or afternoon tea—sans gifts—would be a better way to go.

ENCORE GIFTS

Q: My husband's sister eloped a few weeks ago and is now having a reaffirmation ceremony and reception. Is a wedding gift for my sister-in-law and her husband appropriate? This is our family's first second marriage, so we are unsure how to handle the matter of a gift.

A: Many couples who elope or who have a small destination wedding host a celebratory reception for friends and family once back home. It sounds as if your sister-in-law is inviting you to such an event. Technically, a gift for either a reaffirmation ceremony *or* for a remarrying couple is optional, as traditional etiquette says that those who gave a gift for a first wedding don't need to give gifts again for subsequent marriages. Those who are close to a remarrying bride or groom usually want to give them a present nonetheless.

If you and your husband want to celebrate his sister's new marriage, by all means attend the ceremony and reception and, if you want, send her a gift.

Often theme showers work well because they allow the couple to be specific about what they need. For example, a monogram shower has lots of possibilities, from notepaper and luggage tags to towels and linens.

Gifts. *Technically*, gifts aren't obligatory for guests who attended your previous weddings, and many couples don't want them, as they may already own everything they need, especially after combining their two households. However, guests who weren't invited to a

NEW HUSBAND, OLD ENGAGEMENT RING

Q: Both my wife and I were married before. We are very happy together, except for one thing: She insists on wearing both the engagement and wedding rings given to her by her deceased first husband. Frankly, it bothers me to see her wearing the rings. Is it appropriate for her to do so?

A: A widow may certainly wear the rings from her marriage—up until she becomes engaged to remarry. Once she's newly engaged, she should stop wearing those rings, whether she receives a new engagement ring or not. She could keep her previous engagement ring for a son to use as an engagement ring for his future bride, or she might have the stone or stones reset into another piece of jewelry for herself or for a daughter.

Have a heart-to-heart with your wife. Hopefully, she will understand why you are upset. Encourage her to find a way to repurpose her rings or to set them aside. If you haven't already done so, perhaps the two of you together could choose a ring or other piece of jewelry that symbolizes your new marriage.

previous marriage—and some who were—often want to express their best wishes with gifts.

It's thoughtful to register for gifts. That's because new friends who've never given you a wedding gift before will probably want to give you something. If you decide to register, think about your interests: sporting goods, shop or garden tools, or books, for example. It's helpful to guests if you register at more than one place and, as with any registry, in a variety of price ranges. Another popular option for second-time couples is to set up a charitable-giving registry. (See also Chapter 13, page 161.)

How do you let people know if your preferred gift is "no gifts, please"? First of all, make no mention of gifts on your wedding invitation or enclosures, not even a "no gifts, please." Instead, rely on word of mouth, mentioning your wish to attendants, relatives, and good friends and encouraging them to pass the word. You could also mention "no gifts" on your wedding website, if you have one. Here's the one case where it makes sense *not* to register.

While adding "no gifts" to the invitation may seem thoughtful, the moment you mention gifts you put the emphasis on *gifts* instead of on the fact that the recipient is being asked to join you. If someone sends a gift anyway, receive it graciously and enthusiastically acknowledge it with a thank-you note.

Prenuptial agreement. The idea of a prenuptial agreement can be awkward to raise, but if you feel one is needed, discuss it as soon as possible after you decide to marry. A prenup can be very important for an encore couple who has children from former relationships, and who want to ensure that certain assets will be legally passed on to those children. (See also Chapter 3, page 43.)

PART SIX

MAKING IT YOURS

CHAPTER 19

WEDDING ATTIRE

Other than your rings, few wedding items are as iconic as the wedding dress. Many brides begin shopping for their gowns as soon as they become engaged. From elaborate and formal to streamlined and simple, your gown is one more way your wedding is a reflection of you. While expensive fabrics and designers can be tempting, budget and comfort often need to fit the bill, too. Fortunately, today's bride can have it all. In fact, some brides even have a separate dress for the reception, fulfilling their wedding dreams with a ceremony gown worthy of a royal wedding and then slipping into something more comfortable and contemporary to dance the night away with friends and family at the reception.

Before you dash off to the bridal salons, your first step is to determine how formal or informal your ceremony and reception will be, when and where they will take place, and how much money you're prepared to spend. Religious and cultural considerations can affect your selections, as will the choice of your bridal party. Bridesmaid's dresses should be chosen with the women who will wear them in mind.

Most brides purchase new wedding gowns, and it's smart to begin shopping as soon as the critical planning decisions—date, time, and location—are

made. Special dress orders can take months—sometimes as many as eight to ten months for couture gowns. If you're having your dress made, you need plenty of time to work with your designer or seamstress. Even off-the-rack dresses usually require alterations, so be sure to schedule fittings for yourself and your bridesmaids.

Men's clothing may be easier to select, but don't wait until the last minute. Many grooms and their attendants rent formal, and sometimes informal, wedding clothes. Because formal wear rental stores can run out of stock during the most popular wedding months, prom season, and holidays (June, September, May, and December), you should investigate rental sources and place orders well in advance.

The Wedding Gown

White is just one of a rainbow of colors that brides wear, and though it has been the fashionable choice since the 1800s—inspired by the white gown and orange blossoms worn by Queen Victoria at her 1840 wedding—it's not the only choice anymore. Until the late nineteenth century, most American brides wore their best dress, whatever the color, because the expense of a special gown was prohibitive except for well-to-do families. By the late twentieth century, white came to signify joy rather than virginity and is now considered appropriate for all brides.

Other colors—especially those drawn from non-European ethnic and cultural traditions—are equally lovely. Although white, in all its many shades and pastel tints, is still the conventional choice for formal bridal gowns, the ultimate decision about color belongs to the bride. In fact, more and more brides are opting for some color, whether it's choosing an accent such as a large sash or bow for the gown or a deep champagne- or rose pastel fabric from head to toe. While dresses in bright or bold colors are less common, they do exist. These days, the options are limitless. The key to wearing a colorful dress successfully is in knowing your audience. While the choice is yours as bride, if your choice would be upsetting to your family, it's worth considering a compromise.

Fabrics and Styles

As a general rule, the more formal the wedding, the more formal the fabric of the wedding dress. Fabrics are generally selected with the season in mind, but take the weather in your area into account. In a cold climate, for example, velvet or brocade might be worn earlier in the fall and later in the spring than in temperate and hot climates. Consider these possibilities:

Spring .... Lace and tissue taffeta

Summer .... Organdy, marquisette, cotton, piqué, linen

Fall/winter .... Satin, brocade, taffeta, velvet, moiré, crepe, peau de soie, wool (informal)

Year-round ... Silk, jersey, blends

Think about your comfort, and don't be guided by looks alone. Lace is beautiful but can be itchy over bare skin. Gowns of multilayered or bead-encrusted fabrics can literally weigh a bride down, especially after several

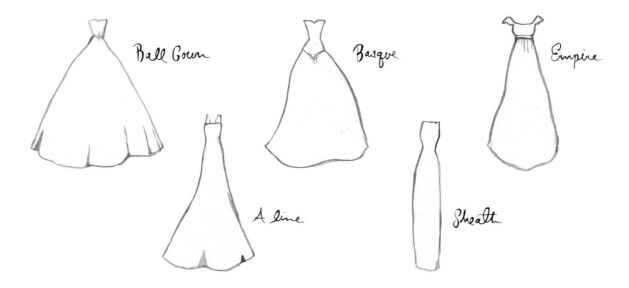

Ball Gown

Basque

Empire

A line

Sheath

hours of standing or dancing. Synthetic fabrics tend to be hotter than natural ones (they don't "breathe" as well as natural fibers), so a natural material or blend might be the better choice.

Since formal gowns may be boned and often require more structured undergarments than women today are used to, try on the dress with the correct undergarments to get a sense of its weight and ease of movement. Don't just check fit, either; move every way you might on your wedding day. Reach forward, bend down, turn, sit, and even do a little dance. Would you be comfortable throwing your arms up in the air to toss your bouquet?

Your cultural heritage might determine your style of wedding dress. Many of today's brides, grooms, and their wedding parties wear full cultural dress or adapt elements such as the Japanese marriage kimono, Indian sari, Turkish tunic, African *bubah* and symbolic patterned fabrics, and Chinese cheongsam.

Classic Wedding Gown Silhouettes

Your choice of silhouette and length is a matter of what is most flattering to you and most appropriate to the formality of the wedding. Floor-length gowns are usually worn for formal and semiformal weddings but are seen at less formal weddings, too. A long, summery, cotton or piqué dress might be just right for a casual garden or beach wedding. Here are some classic gown silhouettes:

Ball gown..... Floor-length "Cinderella"-style with big, full skirt

A-line .... Slimmer at the bodice and widening from the bodice down

Empire .... High-waisted with the bodice cropped just below the bust

Basque .... U- or V-shaped waistline dropped several inches below the natural waist

Sheath .... Narrow, following the body's contours; no defined waist

Neckline, sleeves, and back. Brides often ask how revealing their gowns may be. Your personal sense of comfort and taste is generally paramount, but it's also important to think about where and in what tradition your wedding will be held. For a religious ceremony, ask your officiant about any dress restrictions or expectations. Are bare shoulders and arms acceptable? Is a face veil required? Do dress rules differ for a religious service performed in a house of worship than at a secular location? For an interfaith or intersect service, there may be several traditions to observe, so talk to each officiant.

Issues of good taste and consideration for your guests apply equally for secular ceremonies. The focus of the day should be on your wedding ceremony—any dress choice that could detract from that focus is probably not the right one. If you will be married in a judge's chambers, for instance, respect your officiant, the civil office he or she holds, and the importance of the occasion by dressing up a bit.

Think about your guests. What is acceptable to friends your age—say a plunging back line—may make older guests uncomfortable. While it's tempting to say "My wedding, my way," a gracious bride never deliberately shocks or discomforts the people invited to share her wedding day.

Train. Trains add romance and visual interest to the back of a floor-length gown, but are by no means a bridal gown "must." The train can be sewn into the dress, and many sewn-in trains can be "bustled," or gathered up, at the back, so the bride need not carry her train after the ceremony. Detachable trains are easily removed for the reception. Either way, have a plan for the train to be off the floor for the reception so that you can navigate and dance with ease.

Popular styles include:

The sweep or
brush train .... Drapes from the waistline to 6 inches on the floor

The court train .... Extends 3 to 4 feet from the waistline

The chapel train........... Extends 5 feet from the waistline

The cathedral train....... Extends 2½ to 3 yards from the waistline; very formal and aptly named

The Watteau train........ Drapes from the back yoke of the dress

---

BUSTLING

Sure, you've done lots of hurrying and scurrying lately, but that's not the kind of bustling we're talking about. Wedding gowns without detachable trains need to be bustled. This involves gathering up the train and attaching its loop to a button on the lower back of the dress. This isn't something the bride can easily do herself, so at the fittings or at the rehearsal, the bridesmaids should practice bustling the train so that it falls smoothly and attractively.

The Bride's Accessories

You have many options, from regally elaborate to chic simplicity. Select accessories that complement your gown and the formality of the wedding and that you feel comfortable wearing.

Veil and headdress. Historically, the bridal veil relates to the face coverings worn by unmarried and married women in many cultures as a sign of modesty and

---

SOMETHING BORROWED, SOMETHING RENTED

The average cost of today's new wedding gown, plus headpiece and shoes, is between $1,000 and $1,800, with one-of-a-kind designer gowns running into the multiple thousands. Gowns can be purchased from department stores, wedding gown specialty shops, retail outlets such as J. Crew and Ann Taylor, and designer studios (for the more expensive creations).

Whether a new gown is simply too expensive or just seems wasteful regardless of your budget, there are plenty of other options, including renting, borrowing, or buying secondhand gowns from consignment or vintage stores and websites such as Nearly Newlywed. These alternatives are both acceptable and sensible ways to find a wedding gown, especially if you want to save money and feel no real need to preserve the dress. Nor do you have to purchase your gown and accessories from bridal industry sources. You may find just the thing for an informal or casual wedding at your favorite department or clothing store.

female subservience. Today's bridal veil is directly descended from a French and English practice beginning in the 1500s and is particularly related to the nineteenth-century fashion for veiled headgear, which was worn in a variety of social situations.

Veils and headdresses may be a matter of religious custom but otherwise are strictly personal choices. Many brides today prefer nothing more than a flattering hairstyle, perhaps enhanced with flowers or hair combs or elegant barrettes, often jeweled.

Veils can be worn over the face or trail from the top or back of the head and are usually attached to or draped under a headdress. They come in a variety of lengths and semitransparent materials, including lace and tulle. Among the most popular styles are:

The blusher veil .... Short veil worn over the face; may fall just below the shoulders, best suited to young brides

The mantilla .... Scarflike veil that drapes over the head and shoulders, usually lace

The fingertip veil .... Falls to the tips of the fingers

The sweep veil .... Touches the ground

The chapel veil .... Trails one to two feet behind the gown

The cathedral veil .... Trails one to three yards behind the gown

Blusher

Fingertip

Juliet Cap

Mantilla

Wreath of Flowers

Sweep   Court   Chapel   Cathedral

Some brides like to wear face veils for their wedding, and some religions even require them. The veil can be lifted by the bride's father or by the groom when she arrives at the altar or dais. If she chooses to wear a veil over her face during the ceremony, the part that covers her face should be short and about a yard square. When it's a separate piece attached to the headdress, the maid of honor either takes it off when she gives the bride back her bouquet at the end of the ceremony, or the bride or the groom may gently lift it back for the ceremonial kiss.

A face veil, worn for the processional and during the ceremony, is usually about a yard square and may be detachable.

Bows, headbands, tiaras, Juliet caps (small lattice caps, often decorated with pearls), and floral wreaths can be worn with or without a veil. Headbands and fashion hats such as pillboxes, worn with or without short veils, make for beautiful accessories with informal attire such as a wedding suit.

Undergarments. Your dress shop or dressmaker should be able to recommend bras, bustiers, and other undergarments. You should purchase them soon after you choose your dress. Wear these for your fittings and make sure they complement your gown. While women

WHEN MOM'S DRESS ISN'T RIGHT FOR YOU

Q: My mother has always hoped that I'd be married in her wedding gown. It's really beautiful and I'd love to wear it, but my mom is four inches shorter than I am. She's petite, while I'm more full-figured. She's offering to have her dress altered for me, but I'd rather get something new that really fits. How can I get out of this without hurting my mom's feelings?

A: Wearing an heirloom gown is a wonderful tradition when it's practical. On the basis of the differences you describe, however, your mother's dress would probably need to be completely remade. Talk with your mom, and be sure she knows that you would really like to wear her dress if you could. (You aren't criticizing her taste.) Be respectful, but also be clear that you won't feel comfortable in a dress that doesn't fit you. You might also talk with a seamstress or tailor who can explain to your mom how extensive the changes would be. Then involve your mom in your dress selection; seeing you in a beautiful new gown is likely to cure her disappointment. If it's feasible, incorporate something from her wedding dress, such as lace or trim (a piece of her jewelry, or her veil) in your outfit—a loving way to show how much you appreciate your mom. It may even create a new family tradition, one your daughter can adapt in her own way someday.

For a bride who might simply not care for her mother's dress, still pay her the respect of considering the possibility. You can discuss the option without committing. Respecting someone else's wishes isn't about giving in to them; it's about listening to them. Then be gentle but firm: "Mom, I know you had your heart set on this, but it just isn't me. I hope you understand."

today may be used to strapless bras, more elaborate support such as wired, boned, or waist-length and full-torso undergarments aren't normal everyday wear. Practice walking around, bending, moving your arms, dancing, and generally getting comfortable in all new undergarments. No one wants to be chafed, overly constricted, or otherwise uncomfortable.

Shoes. Color, glitter, rhinestones, and leather or patent leather have joined the ranks of traditional satin and dyeable peau de soie pumps. Flats, open-toe, and sandal styles have become popular, particularly for warm weather or more casual weddings (or for brides who are conscious about being taller than their grooms). Whatever the style, shop for comfort, avoiding stiletto-heeled shoes that can snag on a long gown, crinolines, and aisle runners and will sink into lawns. Low or flat shoes are mostly hidden under a long gown anyway, but if you

have your heart set on higher heels, you can always change into attractive flat or low-heeled shoes for the reception and dancing. Bring your shoes to your fittings so that your dress can be hemmed properly.

Gloves. Gloves can enhance the look of a wedding dress, but they are optional even at very formal weddings. Fabrics range from cotton and soft kid to satin and lace, in keeping with the wedding gown. A short, loose glove can easily be removed by the bride and handed to the maid of honor when rings are exchanged. Tight or long gloves are trickier. When it's difficult to remove a glove, you can snip open the seam on the underside of the ring finger ahead of time and then slip off that finger of the glove when you receive your ring. Fingerless gloves are another way to solve the ring-finger problem.

Jewelry. Traditional bridal jewelry is classic in design and neutral in color, such as a pearl or diamond-and-pearl necklace and earrings or simple gold ornaments. But colored stones are fine, too. Sometimes a bride wears heirloom family jewelry, either the gift of the groom and his family or something from her own family.

Bridesmaids' Attire

Because attendants generally pay for their own dresses and accessories, brides should be respectful when considering the cost of their outfits. It's also important to think about your bridesmaids' heights, figures, and coloring, and to look for styles that will be as flattering as possible for everyone. If your wedding ceremony is religious, be sure to check with your officiant about any attire requirements before selecting bridesmaids' dresses.

POSTURE PERFECT MAKES PICTURE PERFECT

Good posture is not quite as universal as it once was thanks to days spent hunched at computer screens. While it's a good habit for any day, your wedding day is one to stand up straight for. The beautiful dress you have spent so much and time and money on will show to advantage, and so will you—good posture slims and lengthens. Don't go overboard and thrust your chest out or hold yourself rigidly; imagine a string pulling up from the top of the back of your head, and then let the rest of your frame flow. Practice in the weeks leading up to your wedding day so your posture feels as natural as it will look.

Though traditionally the maid or matron of honor alone assists in the selection of bridesmaids' attire, consult with all your bridesmaids. When possible, let your bridesmaids do their own ordering. Unless someone requests that you order her gown, it's best to respect privacy and not ask for sizes and measurements. Alterations are usually handled by the store where the gowns are purchased, often for an additional fee. If a bridesmaid doesn't live nearby, have her dress sent to her so she can arrange to have it fitted by a local seamstress.

Variety

Countless tales have been told of unhappy bridesmaids who had to walk down the aisle in dresses they disliked or that were clearly unflattering to them. It is perfectly fine for your bridesmaids to each wear different dresses, but most brides choose a variation on a theme: all dresses in the same shade or fabric, with the style up to each bridesmaid, or a universal style with a choice of color. Some brides give even freer rein, asking that bridesmaids follow just one or two general guidelines so that the wedding party doesn't clash visually. You can have each bridesmaid wear the same color but in a cut that flatters her: A-line, tulip skirt, strapless, and so on.

Today, virtually all colors are acceptable, including black and shades of white. If choosing white, be careful that bridesmaids won't look like the bride. One bride asked her attendants to pick floor-length dresses in various shades of purple. The result was a glorious blend of lavender, violet, and magenta—a living, breathing wedding bouquet!

Harmony

In ancient Roman times the bride and her attendants dressed alike and traveled together from her home to the wedding ceremony site. The idea was to keep evil spirits from identifying the bride and causing trouble. Today, bridesmaids' dresses often complement (but don't exceed) the formality of the bride's gown. For example, if the bride wears satin, her attendants wear a similar material rather than something far less formal, such as linen. Gown lengths don't need to match, either; the bride can wear a long gown, with the bridesmaids' hems shorter. At very formal weddings, however, both the bride and her attendants traditionally wear floor-length gowns.

Whatever you decide, the goal is to create a look for the entire wedding party that is harmonious and suitable for the venue and level of formality.

<hr>

ARE FLIP-FLOPS A FLOP?

There's nothing wrong with flip-flops per se; the problem is their ability to be appropriate, even at casual weddings. Put simply, they are to shoes what jeans and T-shirts are to suits. Let's not even mention the audible flipping and flopping as bride and bridesmaids process down the aisle.

As the bride, if you suggest sandals to your bridesmaids, make a distinction about whether or not that includes flip-flops as an option. Keep in mind that one pair alone will stand out more than if every bridesmaid wears them. You may feel that more substantial colored leather flip-flops would be acceptable, while rubber or plastic ones wouldn't. Discuss, too, whether or not you are comfortable with your bridesmaids changing their shoes at the reception—if so, you may see flip-flops.

Accessories

Attendants' shoes are usually the same type—pump, flat, or sandal—and color but don't need to be exactly the same shoe. Many brides ask their bridesmaids to purchase a certain color, leaving style up to them. The trend today is toward whites, creams, black, or metallic colors, though fabric shoes dyed to match or complement the color of the dress are another classic way to go. (If possible, the bride might ask her bridesmaids to buy their shoes and deliver them to her or the maid of honor to be dyed together in the same dye lot. This ensures that the colors are a perfect match.) When bridesmaids are wearing knee-length dresses, you'll want to coordinate the color of panty hose, if worn, as well.

Although the bride selects her attendants' hair accessories, she should never dictate hairstyles. If you expect attendants to wear matching jewelry, you should provide it, perhaps as your bridesmaids' gifts. Otherwise, discuss jewelry with your attendants, but leave the final choice to them.

Clothes for Young Attendants

When children are included in the wedding, their parents are expected to pay for their outfits. The bride and groom or their families provide all the necessary accessories, including hats or hair accessories, flowers, baskets, and ring cushions.

Junior bridesmaids and junior ushers. These young bridal party members wear the same clothing as their adult counterparts. A young bridesmaid's dress, accessories, and flowers are the same color and style as the other bridesmaids', though the dress style can be adapted so that it's suitable for her age and size. A ten-year-old, for instance, could wear a strapped version of the bridesmaids' strapless dresses. A junior usher dresses like the other ushers and groomsmen. If it's a formal wedding, that usually means a tux or dark suit and tie.

Flower girls. A flower girl traditionally wears a white or pastel dress of midcalf length, white socks, and party shoes such as Mary Janes. The dress may be similar to the bridesmaids' gowns but should be appropriate for a young child. Headdresses might consist of wreaths of flowers, or ribbons or flowers braided in the child's hair. (If headwear makes a child uncomfortable, skip it.) Flower girls carry a small bouquet or a basket of flowers, but as a rule, they no longer scatter petals before the bride—they can make it slippery to walk. If it's okay with the venue, silk petals can be used instead.

Ring bearers, train bearers, and pages. Very young boys often wear white Eton-style jackets and short pants with white socks and shoes. Or they might wear boyish blazers and kid-appropriate good clothes. Older boys usually wear dark suits with matching socks, black shoes, and a boutonniere. It's best to forgo dressing young boys in tuxedos; wait until they're high-school age.

The Groom and His Groomsmen

Aside from updated cuts for trousers and lapels, formal and semiformal attire for grooms, groomsmen, and ushers hasn't changed significantly for a century. Today's groom does have more fashion choices, especially for informal and casual weddings. Even the traditional black tuxedo can be paired with a modern shirt or tie and cummerbund in colors other than black. The popular dark suit or blazer and trouser combination offers room for variation as well. Clothing from other cultural or religious traditions can be worn for any degree of formality.

The point is to select outfits for yourself and your groomsmen that are appropriate to the style of the

---

THE TUXEDO'S TALE

It's not uncommon today to see all formal male attire classed as "tuxedos," but in fact, a tux is a semiformal dinner jacket, worn with matching trousers to make a tuxedo suit. The man who started the fashion was tobacco tycoon Pierre Lorillard IV. Inspired by the traditional scarlet English hunt coat (and perhaps by the Prince of Wales, who reportedly had the tails cut from his coats while on a visit to India), Lorillard asked his tailor to make several tailless black jackets. Griswold Lorillard, Pierre's son, along with several young friends, debuted the jackets at a ball in Tuxedo Park, New York, in the fall of 1886—and a style was born.

The tux got its name from the town, but *tuxedo* goes back to the Algonquin word for "wolf." (Fun coincidence: Emily Post grew up at and later returned to live at Tuxedo Park, which her father had designed!)

wedding and solemnity of the marriage service. As you make your choices, think about the details, too, such as the style or type of shoes, tie, and collar; studs and cuff links (these make great groomsmen's gifts); vest/waistcoat versus cummerbund; and yes or no to the pocket square.

Formal evening. Black tie, meaning a **tuxedo**, is the typical choice for evening weddings. The outfit consists of:

- Black tuxedo jacket and matching trousers
- Formal (piqué or pleated front) white shirt
- Shirt studs and cuff links
- Black bow tie
- Black cummerbund to match tie, or a vest
- Black or dressy suspenders (braces) to ensure a good fit
- Black oxfords, dress pumps, or evening slippers and black dress socks

Variations can include a white dinner jacket instead in the summer or in tropical locations, as well as adding color with matching tie and cummerbund in the wedding colors.

The most formal evening wedding attire is **white tie**: This includes:

- Black tailcoat and matching trousers with a single stripe of satin or braid
- White suspenders (braces) to ensure a good fit
- White piqué wing-collared shirt with stiff front
- Shirt studs and cuff links
- White bow tie
- White waistcoat (vest)
- White or gray gloves
- Black patent oxfords, dress pumps, or evening slippers and black dress socks

Tuxedo   Tailcoat

Another option is the semiformal **stroller**. It is similar to the cutaway, but employs a single- or double-breasted jacket without tails.

Semiformal evening. Black tie (a tuxedo) is still an option for less formal evening wear, and in summer or warm climates a white dinner jacket can be substituted. Adding a bow tie and cummerbund in the wedding colors softens the formality of a tuxedo. Alternatively, the groom and groomsmen can wear dark suits. Suits must match, so groomsmen should rent or purchase the same suit.

Formal daytime. Before 6 PM, formal dress is the **morning suit** or **cutaway**:

Semiformal daytime. Suit-style dark gray or black sack (straight-backed) coat, matching trousers, dress shirt, and four-in-hand tie—groom's choice of color.

* Black or oxford gray cutaway coat (it has tails) and black or gray striped trousers

* Pearl gray waistcoat

* Stiff white shirt with stiff fold-down collar

* Black and gray striped four-in-hand tie or dress ascot

* Black oxfords and black dress socks

Informal day or evening. Lighter-weight suits or jackets and trousers, dress shirts, and four-in-hand ties. In warm weather, grooms and attendants might wear dark blue or gray jackets or blazers with white or gray flannel trousers, with socks to match trousers and closed shoes. In hot climates, white suits can be worn.

Morning Coat/
Cutaway

Stroller

Suit

Waistcoat

When the customary roles are reversed in the choice of attendants—a man as the bride's honor attendant or a woman serving as the groom's "best person"—there's always the question of what they should wear. The solution is surprisingly easy. A male honor attendant simply wears the same attire as the groom and groomsmen but perhaps chooses a tie coordinating with the bridesmaids' dresses or a boutonniere using the bridesmaids' colors or flowers.

A woman may wear a dress in the same color family as the bridesmaids, or she can choose a dress in black, gray, or whatever main color is worn by the groomsmen. Her attire is in keeping with the formality of the wedding, but she wouldn't wear a tuxedo or suit like the groomsmen. A woman can wear a wrist or shoulder corsage featuring the same flowers as in the groomsmen's boutonnieres.

Organizing Attire

There are basically two ways to organize wedding party attire. The groom might tell his groomsmen what he will wear and ask them to rent or purchase the same. Or it may be more convenient for the groom or best man to ask for sizes and measurements and then order all the outfits and accessories from a single rental source. (Formal-wear rental stores may offer discounts for multiple orders and normally provide alteration service.) Dress shoes can also be rented—this is a good way to ensure that everyone is wearing the same style shoe.

Except for boutonnieres (supplied by the groom), groomsmen are responsible for their rental and/or purchase costs as well as for any alterations that aren't included in the price. Sometimes the groom purchases the ties he'd like his guys to wear, perhaps sporting the wedding colors. It's normally the duty of the best man or head usher to see that everyone is dressed appropriately.

COMFORT AND FIT

Don't forget comfort and fit when selecting attire. To look your best, check these points and have alterations made if necessary:

- Coats should lie smoothly across the back but give you freedom of movement.

- Coat sleeves should reveal a half inch of shirt cuff when your arms are straight at your sides.

- Trousers are hemmed even with the tops of the backs of the shoes and have a slight break in front, so the hem rests on the shoes.

Mothers and Fathers of the Wedding Couple

This will be your children's day, but you have the right to shine, too. Parents and stepparents should choose clothing in keeping with the style of the wedding. Comfort matters as well, since you're likely to be busy for the entire event, so select outfits that feel good, fit well, and look great.

Mothers

Mother-of-the-bride or -groom outfits should correspond with the style of the wedding, and brides can be very helpful by encouraging "the moms" to work together in choosing their outfits. Tradition and courtesy say the bride's mother gets first choice, but that doesn't mean the groom's mother is limited to beige—unless that's her color. Matronly is out—fashionable and age-appropriate is in. Here are some other tips for the mothers of the bride and groom:

* Try not to wear colors that are the same as or very similar to the bride's and bridesmaids' dresses—you won't stand out.

* Wear different colors from each other. Variations on the wedding color scheme are fine as long as each mother's dress is distinct.

* The length of your gown or dress is your choice, even for formal weddings. Long dresses and skirts are fine for any wedding from noon on.

* Mothers of the bride and groom don't have to wear the same length, though many do, feeling that it creates a more harmonious look, especially in wedding photos.

* Gloves and hats or headpieces are normally worn for formal weddings but are optional otherwise, so be guided by the bride's preference and any religious requirements.

* If wearing gloves, keep them on for the receiving line. They can be removed afterward and are always taken off when eating.

Fathers

When they participate in the ceremony, fathers and/or stepfathers almost always wear the same outfits as the groomsmen. This is also the case for any man who escorts the bride down the aisle.

When the father of the groom doesn't have an active role, he can either match the formality of the groomsmen or "dress down" a bit—choosing, say, a dark suit instead of their tuxedos. But if the groom's father is to be in a receiving line, he might opt to dress like the bride's father and the groomsmen.

Attire for the Military Wedding

A military wedding can be anything from an informal service in a civilian setting to a full-blown, spit-and-polish affair complete with the American flag, unit standards, and the romantic Arch of Steel. The etiquette for military weddings varies somewhat from service to service, and members of the military should check their service manuals or consult with a protocol officer or base chaplain.

In general, brides and grooms in the service may wear either civilian clothes or their uniforms, as may their colleagues who serve in the wedding party. Depending on the formality of the occasion, everyday and dress uniforms are equally correct, since young and noncareer personnel often don't have dress uniforms. For commissioned officers, evening dress uniforms are the equivalent of civilian white tie, and dinner or mess dress is the same formality as a tuxedo. Noncommissioned officers can wear dress or everyday uniforms for formal and informal ceremonies. These correlations will help you guide your guests in what to wear.

Hats and caps are carried during an indoor ceremony. Even when it's permissible for an officer to wear

---

SAME-SEX WEDDING ATTIRE

Same-sex couples have all of the attire choices of heterosexual couples—formal or casual, traditional or adaptive. Incorporate gendered traditions only when they are meaningful to you. When Ellen DeGeneres and Portia de Rossi married, Ellen wore a simple white pantsuit (pantsuits being her normal style) and Portia donned a full-on wedding dress. They both looked fantastic, but they could just as easily have each worn pants or each worn bridal gowns. It all comes down to being true to yourselves and respectful of your guests and the occasion, whether you're gay or straight. Satisfy that, and the rest is just a trip to the tailor or seamstress.

---

a sword, swords aren't worn in a house of worship. Sword or saber bearers participating in the Arch of Steel always wear gloves. Flowers are never worn on uniforms—so no boutonnieres or corsages—but brides in uniform may carry a bridal bouquet. Service members not in uniform and nonmilitary members of the wedding party dress as they would for any ceremony, keeping in mind the level of formality of the service.

CHAPTER 20

FLOWERS

Fragrant, lovely, and romantic, flowers are central to decorating the wedding celebration. Flowers not only add visual pleasure and a note of festivity to the proceedings, but they also symbolize the blooming of new love and a new life—whether cascading from an altar, twined around an arch, spilling over a flower girl's basket, or tucked lovingly into a groom's lapel.

Many traditions retain a place in wedding events long after their origins have been forgotten, and wedding flowers have many traditions. For example, strewing flowers along the path the bride walks has its roots in ancient times, when a path of flowers and fragrant herbs was thought to keep evil spirits away. Centuries ago, wedding reception halls were decorated with sweet-smelling jasmine to entice angels to attend and bless the event. In a tradition that began in twelfth-century Spain, fresh orange blossoms were fashioned into wreaths to crown the heads of brides. Hundreds of years later, England's Queen Victoria wore fragrant orange blossoms in her hair at her marriage to Prince Albert, continuing and popularizing the tradition. Kate Middleton, now the Duchess of Cambridge, carried stems of myrtle cut from a tree planted by Queen Victoria in 1845 as well as a sprig cut from

a tree that grew from the myrtle used in Queen Elizabeth II's wedding bouquet of 1947, because myrtle is a symbol of love and marriage. Brides who could neither afford nor find fresh blossoms used wax ones; many a wax bridal wreath has become a treasured family heirloom, passed down from generation to generation of brides.

These days, flowers are used in nearly every aspect of the wedding celebration, from the decoration of church altars to topping the wedding cake. Flowers can be seen everywhere: in the hands of attendants, given to parents, stepparents, and grandparents; in centerpieces, on mantels, wrapped around candles; and even adorning serving platters.

Whether you select flowers for their symbolic meaning, for seasonability, for mix-and-match qualities, for color, size, or simply for fragrance, you'll find the process of choosing a delight. Make it a personal quest. The Victorians found nuance in the character of each flower and gave them unique meanings (see page 272). Whether you refer to the Victorian meanings or not, some flowers will resonate more with you than others, even if you don't know why. Make your wedding flowers an expression of your personality.

How to Choose Your Flowers

Peonies were the flower of choice for Anna's friend Nell's late-May wedding in New England. In fact, peonies are her favorite flowers and she planned the date of her wedding around their peak bloom time. While you may not have such a strong preference, here are some big-picture ideas to guide you:

The formality of your wedding. Generally, the more formal the wedding, the more formal the floral arrangements and bouquets. White is still the traditional color for very formal weddings.

The time of day. For an evening wedding, for example, white or brightly colored flowers stand out, especially if the ceremony is held in candlelight.

The season. Locally grown and seasonal flowers are usually fresher, last longer, and are less expensive than flowers shipped from distant suppliers.

Visual unity. Flowers can provide a unifying visual theme. You might work with a limited color palette (reds and pinks, for example) for both the ceremony and reception.

The theme of your wedding. Are you planning a country-style wedding with simple bouquets and baskets overflowing with wildflowers? Or do you favor a traditional, formal celebration with classic floral choices such as roses or calla lilies? If you're having a real theme wedding—romantic Victorian, for example, Hawaiian luau, or fifties-style—you'll want flowers and decorations that match.

The interior design of the wedding site and reception site. Choose flowers and greenery that comple-ment the architecture and decor of the wedding and reception site. For example, a high ceiling calls for taller arrangements or potted plants, and flowers can soften the space and add romance to a reception under a tent.

Whether the site is indoors or out. If you're marrying outdoors, you may need to supplement a blooming spring or summer garden site with only a few flower arrangements here and there along with bouquets, boutonnieres, and corsages. Think of the path both you and your guests will take. Strategically placed flower arrangements will help guide guests. For example, arrangements on the steps of the church, in an entrance-way, along a pathway to an outdoor ceremony site, or at the start of the aisle all say, "Wedding this way!"

Your budget. These days, flowers can account for an average of 10–16 percent of a couple's wedding budget. So, doing the math, for a $25,000 wedding, flowers could top out at $4,000. If you have a celebrity-style wedding in mind, a Preston Bailey–designed tall centerpiece could set you back more than $2,700—and that's just for one. Granted, that's for about 420 stems and five hours of labor and a $100 vase, but you can

---

PAINT THE PICTURE

One friend, Wendy, decided on her reception flowers well in advance of the wedding, and her step-mother, an artist, painted a beautiful watercolor of the planned centerpieces—colorful tomato tins artfully filled with Vermont wildflowers. The bride then used the watercolor on her wedding invitation, setting the exact tone of the wedding and reception to come for her guests.

see that at those prices you could easily spend a small fortune on flowers alone (and we haven't even discussed the bridal bouquet!). There are many ways to cut costs on flowers, including having friends help you do your own arrangements, using potted plants such as hydrangeas, using bridesmaids' bouquets as centerpieces, reusing your ceremony flowers at the reception, reusing reception arrangements at next-day brunches, and renting plants.

Wedding Flowers Checklists

As you begin planning your ceremony and reception, draw up lists of all your floral needs and bring copies to the florist at your first meeting. Determine what, if any, of the following items you need or would like to have: ribbons, greens, candles, vases, pots, or containers. The range of floral decorations can go far beyond bridal-party bouquets and altar decorations. You may want a plant for each entranceway, flowers to garnish serving platters, sprays for candles, corsages or boutonnieres for wedding helpers and grandparents—even a beribboned flower twined around the cake knife. To guide you are the following general (but not mandatory!) checklists of floral possibilities:

THE WEDDING PARTY

- [ ] Bride's bouquet
- [ ] Bride's headpiece
- [ ] Maid of honor's bouquet
- [ ] Bridesmaids' bouquets
- [ ] Bridesmaids' headpieces
- [ ] Flower girl: basket, nosegay, headpiece

- [ ] Tossing bouquet
- [ ] Groom's boutonniere
- [ ] Best man, groomsmen, ushers' boutonnieres
- [ ] Ring bearer's boutonniere
- [ ] Mothers' corsages
- [ ] Fathers' boutonnieres
- [ ] Corsages or boutonnieres for other special guests such as grandparents, godparents, readers

FOR THE CEREMONY

- [ ] Entranceway
- [ ] Altar/dais
- [ ] Chuppah
- [ ] Pew/chair decorations
- [ ] Candles
- [ ] Aisle decorations

FOR THE RECEPTION

- [ ] Table centerpieces
- [ ] Buffet tables
- [ ] Bar decorations
- [ ] Bridal table or chairs
- [ ] Cake topper
- [ ] Cake table, cake knife
- [ ] Mantel, stairway, entranceways
- [ ] Place-card table

- [ ] Garnish for serving platters, cocktail, or hors d'oeuvre trays
- [ ] Restroom arrangements
- [ ] Flower petals (real or silk) for tossing in the processional or by guests

ADDITIONAL ARRANGEMENTS AS GIFTS

- [ ] Party hosts
- [ ] Guests' hotel rooms
- [ ] Hosts who house members of the wedding party or family
- [ ] Thank-yous to friends and helpers

OTHER VENUES

- [ ] Out-of-town guest parties
- [ ] Rehearsal dinner
- [ ] Bridesmaids' luncheon
- [ ] After-party
- [ ] Next-day brunch

SEASONAL FLOWERS

Although the advances of modern growing techniques and transportation have resulted in the year-round availability of formerly hard-to-get flowers, you can save a lot by using seasonal flowers that are in bloom locally. They don't need to be shipped, can be cut close to the time they will be used, and tend to be hardier than blooms forced in a greenhouse out of season.

SPRINGTIME FLOWERS

Apple blossoms
Cherry blossoms
Daffodils
Dogwood
Forsythia
Iris
Jonquils
Larkspur
Lilacs
Lilies
Lilies of the valley
Peonies
Sweet peas
Tulips

SUMMERTIME FLOWERS

Asters
Bachelor's button
Dahlias
Daisies
Geranium
Larkspur

Queen Anne's lace
Roses
Zinnias

FALL FLOWERS

Asters
Celosia
Chrysanthemum
Dahlias
Hypericum
Marigolds
Shasta daisies

YEAR-ROUND FLOWERS

Flowers that aren't rare or difficult to grow in greenhouses are readily available year-round. These include:

Baby's breath
Calla lilies
Carnations
Daisies
Delphiniums
Freesia
Gardenias
Gerbera daisies
Hydrangea
Ivy
Lilies
Orchids
Roses
Snapdragon
Stephanotis

Floral Themes

There are many ways to use flowers to personalize your wedding. The following are some ideas to make your celebration special and unique.

The Language of Flowers

In the 1800s and early 1900s, romance was often communicated with flowers. A young man would present a red rose, which symbolized love, to a young woman. She would return a purple pansy, which silently relayed the message "You are in my thoughts." Traditionally, no words were spoken that would commit either party during this courtship, so knowing the language of flowers was of paramount importance if an accord was to be reached. Today, it is a charming idea to select flowers, and even herbs, that convey special floral messages between the bride and the groom.

Acacia—friendship

Anemone—expectation

Apple blossoms—hope

Aster—elegance

Azalea—temperance

Baby's breath—innocence

Bay laurel—glory

Calla lily—beauty

Camellia—loveliness

Carnation—devotion

Chrysanthemum—abundance

Daffodil—regard, esteem, respect

Daisy—gentleness

Freesia—innocence

Gardenia—purity

Heather—future fortune

Heliotrope—devotion

Ivy—fidelity

Larkspur—laughter

Laurel—peace

Lilac—humility

Lily—majesty

Lily of the valley—happiness

Myrtle—remembrance, love, marriage

Orange blossom—purity

Orchid—rare beauty

Parsley—beginnings

Peony—bashfulness

Queen Anne's lace—trust

Rose—love

Rosemary—remembrance

Sage—immortality

Stephanotis—marital happiness

Thyme—courage

Tulip—passion

Violet—modesty

Wheat—prosperity, fertility

Zinnia—affection

The Language of Color

Colors have meaning in many cultures. You may want to develop your floral color scheme around a particular color for its symbolic meaning.

Red or fuchsia The color of love in China and India.

Pink Represents romance, true love, purity and femininity in many cultures.

Green The ancient color of fertility. A color symbolizing luck to modern-day Italians and Irish.

Red and yellow The marriage colors of Egypt, India, Asia, and Russia.

Blue/turquoise Attached to wedding ceremonies in Western countries (" . . . something borrowed, something blue").

Purple Represented wealth in ancient Greece and royalty in Africa. The classical color of the soul.

Blue and gold Reinforces power, dignity, and rank.

Birth Month Flowers

Another special way to personalize and add meaning to floral choices is to combine the traditional birth month flowers of the bride and groom.

January—Carnation

February—Violet

March—Jonquil

April—Sweet pea

May—Lily of the valley

June—Rose

July—Larkspur

August—Gladiola

September—Aster

October—Calendula

November—Chrysanthemum

December—Narcissus

Fragrant Flowers and Herbs

A popular trend is including fragrance in your overall wedding theme, using flowers, herbs, and greenery not just for their visual appeal but also for their perfume. Often the white varieties have the most fragrance. Some choices to consider include:

Bay laurel

Carnations

Freesia

Gardenias

Scented geranium

Hyacinth

Jasmine

Lavender

Lilacs

Lily of the valley

Magnolia blossoms

Mint

Narcissus

Oriental lilies

Rosemary

Roses, especially old-fashioned or tea roses

Sage

Stephanotis

Stock

Tuberose

Violets (very tender)

Wisteria

Selecting the Florist for You

If you don't have a florist in mind, ask for recommendations from friends, local wedding vendors, caterers, local nurseries, or your ceremony or reception site. A florist who is closely affiliated with nurseries or wholesalers can often get good prices on flowers and plants in bulk. If you are holding your celebration in a hotel or reception site, get the names of florists who regularly work on wedding celebrations there. Some florists may be contracted to do arrangements for hotels and reception sites on a regular basis—in that case, you can view their work on site. Look for local florists who have firsthand experience working with a variety of area wedding venues—an invaluable plus.

When to Meet

It's never too early to book a popular florist, so if you know who you want to work with, you may want to book your date and make a deposit. Otherwise, wait until you have chosen your dress, the bridesmaids' dresses, and the color of any table linens before scheduling your initial consultation. Knowing the fabrics and colors chosen for the wedding will save the florist—and you—time.

When you are ready to interview possible choices, always make an appointment. It is unrealistic and discourteous to think you can walk in, unexpected, and snare a busy florist's undivided attention. If you are interviewing several florists, make it clear when you make your appointment that this is an initial consultation, and you aren't ready to sign a contract yet. Your goal at your first meeting is to find someone you trust, you feel comfortable with, and whose portfolio and ideas are compatible with your vision.

What to Bring

Be prepared for your appointment with the florist so that you can both use the time efficiently. The more information you provide and the better your research and planning, the more successful and satisfying your collaboration will be.

Bring visuals. Whether it's a Pinterest page, old-school pinboard, or a folder of photographs or magazine pages, a portfolio of floral arrangements, bouquets, and looks you like is very helpful. Give the florist swatches of your gown and your bridesmaids' gowns, if you have them, or a color wheel with the family of colors you've chosen to work with. Providing your wedding colors up front is an excellent way for the florist to match fabrics with complementary flowers. Photographs of bridal-party attire will also help the florist establish the style, as will pictures of the ceremony and reception sites.

Bring your floral list. It's a good idea to work up your flowers checklists before you visit the florist (see page 269)—or at least know what is essential to you and what is not. But don't worry—a good florist should also have an extensive checklist to prompt you.

What to Look For

Wedding experience. Look for a florist who is experienced in the business of wedding decorating, and preferably familiar with your sites. The florist should be capable of managing all the details, including the timing and the delivery of all your pieces. If yours will be a large wedding, make sure the florist has handled a wedding of that size before.

Portfolio. Ask to see the florist's album or portfolio containing photographs or illustrations of previous weddings. Is the style a match for your vision? Is there variety in the presentations, or do all the weddings look the same? When you see something you like, don't be afraid to ask how much it costs. Ask to see examples of weddings that were in the same season or venue as yours.

Creativity. Look for a florist who will work with you as a collaborator and who also offers creative input and advice on ways to do things more efficiently.

Compatibility. You'll want a florist you feel comfortable with, one who is willing to embrace your ideas, offer advice and suggestions, show you examples, and respect your budgetary parameters. Above all, your personalities should suit each other, and you should feel that this is someone with whom you will enjoy working.

Discussing the Nitty Gritty

Discuss your flowers checklists (see page 269) and the range of options for each item. Determine how many of your ideas, large and small, can be accommodated within your budget. The best florists are happy to suggest alternatives that allow you to achieve your vision and stay within your budget, and you will experience less stress if you remain flexible on floral choices.

If on the first pass your wish list results in a budget-busting estimated total, simply rethink your options. Ask your florist to recommend less expensive backup choices or suggestions for reprioritizing your list. To you, what is the most important floral expenditure? The bridal bouquet? The reception centerpieces? Can you splurge on these and rely on simpler choices for the less important arrangements? If you find mean-

---

SIMPLE DOES NOT ALWAYS EQUAL INEXPENSIVE

A clean, simple look can be stunningly elegant. But beware: Don't make the mistake of equating "simple" with "inexpensive." Take, for example, the current trend of single-flower-type bouquets. A "simple" bridesmaid's bouquet composed entirely of mini white calla lilies at $10 per stem could easily start at $100 apiece—and that's just for a ten-stem bouquet.

---

ing in your choices, it won't matter whether you used an expensive or exotic flower to express your joy.

Helping the Florist Help You

Florists are professionals, and those who handle weddings do them on a regular basis. They know what works—and what doesn't—at the various wedding venues in their area. They also know that even though they may have done the flowers for hundreds of weddings, yours is unique and it is their job to see that your wedding is like no other. Here are tips and advice on how you can work with the florist to achieve your goals:

Trust the florist. This is the most important piece of advice we can give you. Trust gives your florist the opportunity to be creative and do his or her best work. That won't be the case if you try to micromanage the process or make so many stipulations that the florist's creativity is hampered.

Have some flexibility in choosing your flowers. A florist is not unlike a chef: When going to the market to purchase the flowers for your floral arrangements, your florist will be most inspired if he or she can use the best flowers available—and the best may be what is in season at that time, not the exotics you've included on your must-have list.

Listen to the florist's advice. It's the florist's job not only to fulfill your needs and desires but also to advise you on the best ways to make it all happen—and that may entail offering solutions that run counter to your original vision. For example, you may be determined to use columbines in your bouquets and table arrangements, but because of their lack of sturdiness, they may not be the best choice. It is the florist's job to provide you with an informed opinion.

FLORISTS VERSUS FLORAL DESIGNERS

Q: What is the difference between a florist and a floral designer?

A: In the last few years, "floral designers" have become popular. Floral designers specialize in creating a unifying look for your entire wedding, integrating not only flowers into the decor but lighting and textiles as well. You'll have to decide whether you want to work with a full-service florist, who can provide soup-to-nuts floral needs in-house, or with a floral designer, who generally creates a design and then executes it by outsourcing jobs, adding another layer of cost. Although many floral designers don't have a shop, they often have a full staff to handle every aspect of the floral plans.

Be open to change. Remember that the floral plan is a work in progress right up until the week of the wedding.

Meeting Checklist for Your Florist

Be sure to discuss the following once you've committed to a florist:

- Confirm the date, time, and location(s) of the wedding and reception.

- Review your floral checklist.

- Review the overall ceremony decor. Bring information about your ceremony site with you, either visuals or a sketch. Don't forget to check with your officiant before your meeting with the florist about any floral restrictions or expectations. For example, are you expected to provide the altar flowers, can you affix pew ribbons, or are you allowed to decorate the chuppah with flowers?

- Review the overall reception decor, including linen colors. If the florist is unfamiliar with the reception location, provide a sketch of the layout and visuals showing key places for arrangements, greenery, tall plants, or other floral decoration. Schedule a walk-though, or ask the florist to schedule one with the site coordinator.

- Wedding cakes, buffet tables, cake tables, and passing trays can be decorated with real flowers and greenery. Find out if the florist needs to coordinate with the cake maker or caterer.

- Ask the florist about taking care of extras, such as:

  - Flowers for a unity candle

  - Tossing petals

  - Floral gifts for helpers—readers, soloists, or special guests—and those who host any of your wedding party or guests should be discussed up front. The florist might suggest simple flower arrangements to be delivered after the wedding day.

  - Thank-you flowers for bridal showers. If you know friends will be giving you a shower, flowers delivered before or after as a thank-you can be ordered at the same time you are ordering your wedding flowers.

- Discuss your budget. Your florist will prepare a proposal or estimate for you, but it's a good idea to let him or her know your limits. Ask that it be itemized so the job will be easier if you need to make cuts, changes, or additions.

- Discuss contract details. Ask if there is a deposit, when it's due, and when final payment is expected. Check whether the contract includes delivery costs, tax, and any gratuities. Add confirmation call reminders to your planner.

- Discuss when and where deliveries should be made. If you have contracted with the florist for deliveries and installation, provide a list of all the flower deliveries that need to be made, and discuss the best place and time to deliver each component of the decor. Review accurate dates, times, addresses, and instructions for access, as well as correct contact names and telephone numbers. Where, for example, do you want the bride's and her attendants' flow-

---

WELCOMING FLOWERS

It's by no means necessary, but small arrangements of flowers—a few stems and some greenery in a little vase—to welcome out-of-town guests staying in hotels or inns can be a nice touch. These can be included in the florist contract, making it one less detail to worry about. To truly personalize your welcoming gift, write individual cards beforehand and give them to the florist: "Dear Aunt Sara and Uncle Jay, We're delighted you are here for our wedding! Love, Heather and Tim."

---

ers delivered—the bride's home if everyone will be dressing there or directly to the ceremony site? Do flowers for the bride or bridesmaids' hair need to be delivered before the other flowers to be in time for the hairdresser? It's helpful to have the florist label the flowers not just with indications such as "bride's grandmother" but also with specifics: "Allison Jensen, bride's grandmother," especially if flowers have been chosen to coordinate with outfits.

- Set follow-up meetings, and discuss when to have a final meeting or call the week of the wedding.

Flowers for the Bride and Bridesmaids

The formality and style of your celebration and wedding attire will determine the flowers that complement it. The bride's bouquet is the most personal floral choice she will make and may set the tone for the rest of the wedding flowers.

Not all the bridesmaids' flowers have to be identical, but they should complement their gowns and echo the style of the bride's bouquet. For example, their bouquets can feature different flowers but in the same hue, with each bridesmaid carrying a nosegay of her favorite flower. Or the size of the bouquets can vary. Generally, the bouquet size is determined by the height and size of the attendant. A six-foot-tall bridesmaid holding a tiny nosegay looks as uncomfortable as a petite bridesmaid overwhelmed by a large cascade. Give their heights to the florist who can then choose a median size that will look proportional, especially in photographs. It's helpful to give your florist a photo of the bridesmaids lined up by height order or the order they'll be in the processional. You can also provide a personal touch by asking each bridesmaid what her favorite flowers are and surprising each with a specially designed bouquet.

Bouquets

Bouquets, by definition, are simply clusters of flowers, tied together or anchored in a bouquet holder. The shape of the bouquet generally determines the best flowers to use.

Formal bouquets are traditionally all white, generally of one type of flower or a combination of two or three different flowers, such as roses, gardenias, stephanotis, and lilies of the valley. The flowers can be fashioned into a cascade or a formal bouquet or nosegay and adorned with satin ribbons, chiffon, or organza. A formal bouquet can also be as simple as a single calla lily or white rose.

Unless it is a truly formal "black and white" wedding, the current fashion is to incorporate color, and a great way to do that is with flowers. All-white bouquets can be brightened up when wrapped with col-

---

CLASSIC BOUQUETS

Roses and peonies
Calla lilies
Tulips and freesia
Oriental lilies and roses
Gerbera daisies and hypericum
Local wildflowers

---

ored ribbon. Bouquets can be a combination of mixed colors or incorporate different flowers of the same hue or color scheme, such as pinks or corals.

BOUQUETS TO TOSS

If you would like to keep or preserve your wedding bouquet but still want to have the traditional bouquet toss, ask your florist to create a "breakaway" bouquet. Essentially, the bouquet separates into two parts, allowing you to keep one part and toss the other. Or you can order a completely separate "tossing" bouquet, often similar to but not as elaborate as the one you carry.

BOUQUETS AS DECORATIONS

Here's a lovely suggestion that's also a cost cutter: Use the bridesmaids' bouquets as floral arrangements on the bridal table, placing them side by side at the top of each place setting, with the flower sides turned out facing the rest of the reception, or in prepared vases. Alternatively, nosegays or bunched bouquets can easily be put in vases as table centerpieces. These are beautiful ways to display the bouquets, which might otherwise be relegated to a side table or tucked away out of sight in a safe place.

Neither the bride nor her bridesmaids are limited to carrying floral bouquets. Here are other possibilities:

- A single long-stemmed flower (or two or three)

- Bouquets of herbs or greens

- Pomanders (blossom-covered globes held by a loop of ribbon)

- Flower- and ribbon-decorated fans

- Flowers attached to a prayer book

Alternatively, they could choose to wear wrist corsages or flowers pinned to their dresses.

Bouquet Shapes

The formality and shape of a bouquet go hand in hand. There are four basic bouquet shapes.

Nosegays are circular, densely arranged arrays of flowers, approximately eighteen inches in diameter. A nosegay can be made up of or include posies, which are petite nosegays made of tiny buds. This is what most people think of when they picture a bridal bouquet. Single-flower nosegays are very popular today, but a traditional bouquet may use up to three flower types. A **tussie-mussie** is another type of small nosegay composed of tiny buds, flowers, greens, and herbs selected for their traditional Victorian meanings to convey a message. They can be carried in Victorian-period cone-shaped silver holders. Both of these smaller bouquets are suitable for mothers, grandmothers, flower girls, and bridesmaids. **Biedermeier nosegays** are arranged in rings of flowers, with each ring including only one flower variety. Nosegays can be carried with either long or short gowns.

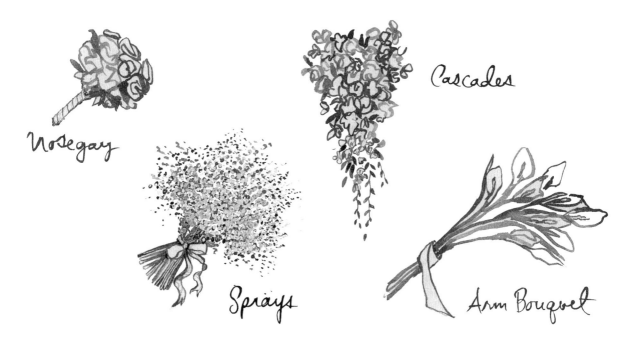

Nosegay

Cascades

Sprays

Arm Bouquet

ARM BOUQUETS

Arm bouquets are crescent-shaped arrangements, curved slightly to fit on the arm. Because they are larger than nosegays, they are usually best suited to long gowns.

CASCADES

A cascade is a bouquet that gracefully trails blossoms and/or greens. It can be any shape, from a nosegay to tear-shaped; it looks best with a long gown.

CAN THE BRIDE'S BOUQUET BE PRESERVED?

Technically, yes. It's possible to freeze-dry your bouquet, but the trouble and end result may be a disappointment. To truly do a proper job, you will need to provide a perfect bouquet. That means your actual bouquet ends up as compost and you'll pay for a new bouquet to go to the preserving service. Even then, the preserved bouquet ends up under a glass dome—destined to become perhaps more dust catcher than valued memento.

Your flowers provide their beauty and energy because they are alive and fresh. So maybe it's best to appreciate them for what they are. Take photos of your bouquet so you'll always remember its perfection. Then send big hints to your husband that it would be a sweet idea to send you the flowers featured in your bouquet on your anniversary.

You can also dry your bouquet. Hang it upside down in a dry place and use the dried buds and petals to create potpourri.

SPRAYS

Sprays are flowers gathered together in a triangular-shaped cluster. Sprays can be carried with either long or short gowns, since they can be of varying sizes.

Flowers for the Hair and Veil

Fresh orange blossoms were once the flowers that crowned the bride's veil, but today any number of flowers can be woven into bandeaux or circlets and Juliet caps with veils, or worn tucked into a chignon, French twist, French braid, or any other style of updo. Flowers can wreath the heads of the bride's attendants, too, or be as simple as a small spray attached to the back of upswept hair. You'll want to order "practice" flowers so the hairstylist can create the best look for your chosen blooms. On the big day, be sure to have these flowers delivered in time for hair prep for the bride and her attendants.

If you want to wear flowers on your veil, make sure the veil is delivered early enough in the planning process so that the florist can determine the prettiest look and the most secure way of attaching the flowers to it.

Flowers for Children

A flower girl may hold a tiny bouquet or carry a small basket of flower petals. Traditionally, fresh rose petals from the flower girl's basket were strewn during the processional. But fresh petals are notoriously slippery, so many brides choose dried or silk flower petals instead. Make sure that scattering petals is okay at your ceremony site.

Children also look enchanting carrying hoops decorated in satin and festooned with flowers in the spring and summer or swathed in evergreens in December.

It simply doesn't look right to have one attendant clutching her bouquet tightly at chest level while another has it dropped below her waist. It's rare that anyone would carry a bouquet outside of a wedding, and it's understandable to feel a bit awkward. But don't worry; follow these tips and you'll look the part. It's a good idea to practice carrying the bouquet at the wedding rehearsal. Use single flowers or tissue paper bunched into a bouquet shape and make sure all the attendants are carrying their flowers the same way.

Hold a nosegay with two hands, centered just below the waist. An arm bouquet rests along the lower half of one arm, with any falling sprays held in front. When walking in pairs, either with a groomsman or another bridesmaid, attendants walking on the right side hold their arm bouquets on their right arms with the stems pointing downward to the left, and those on the left hold their flowers on their left arms with stems toward the right. Whatever you do, try not to press the bouquet against your gown: It can get crushed or mark the gown with pollen.

An old English tradition, and popular in France, this custom is still practiced in the South today.

Children of either the bride or the groom from a previous marriage who aren't participants in the wedding ceremony might also receive flowers to wear or hold.

Flowers for the Groom and His Attendants

Boutonnieres, worn by the groom and his groomsmen on their left lapels, make for a festive and understated grace note to the men's attire. Subtle and small in scale are the key words: The groom and his groomsmen should never appear to be wearing corsages. A boutonniere can be any flower, but go for a hardy variety that won't wilt or crush easily. Usually, the groom wears a flower that is also used in his bride's bouquet, and groomsmen wear boutonnieres that complement those of the bridesmaids'. A small-scale white or ivory rose, lily of the valley, stephanotis, or freesia are equally elegant and may or may not be wired with greens. It's a good idea to order one extra boutonniere for the groom—in case his original is crushed or wilted by the time he arrives at the reception.

Wedding-party boutonnieres are usually delivered to the ceremony site where the groomsmen gather well before the wedding begins. But if all are dressing in the same location and traveling to the ceremony site together, their boutonnieres can be delivered there instead. Pins are provided by the florist for the grooms-

men to use to attach the boutonnieres on their left lapels, at the top of the buttonhole, stem down. (The stem does not go through the buttonhole.)

Flowers for the Ceremony

If your ceremony will be in a house of worship, ask the officiant or wedding coordinator to advise you on the types of decorations that work best there and what, if any, limitations there are on floral decorations or methods of attaching them. The range of options includes ceremony flowers or greenery for the altar or chancel, chuppah, and pulpit. The ceremony flowers may be as simple or as elaborate as the setting, your budget, and the formality of the ceremony.

In a Church or Synagogue

Traditionally, an arrangement or two of flowers that blends with the bridal-party flowers is all you need to provide. Placed on the altar in a church or on the read-

er's platform in a synagogue, they are lovely to look at when guests arrive and serve as a background for the ceremony. A unity candle can be wound with garlands of greens with a few flowers tucked in. When permitted in a synagogue, the chuppah, or canopy, can be decorated with garlands of flowers as well. If your budget permits, you can add more floral focal points:

- Drape entrance staircase railings with garlands.

- Adorn double doors at a church or temple entrance with floral wreaths.

- Decorate the ends of pews with satin ribbons or ribbons and flowers (there may be restrictions on how the ribbons and flowers can be attached).

- Add height in a very large church or cathedral with soaring ceilings with potted trees or arrangements on standards placed at the ends of every three or four pews.

If your house of worship requires that your ceremony flowers stay at the site as a donation, keep that in mind. Don't blow your budget on floral arrangements for the ceremony that can't serve double duty at the reception.

At Home, a Club, or a Wedding Facility

Ceremonies that take place outside a church or synagogue can be beautifully decorated as well. It is a good idea to take photographs of the areas that will be used, to have as a reference when planning your decorations. Use existing architectural elements to your advantage. For example, decorate a sweeping staircase with floral garlands and use it for the processional. Arrange chairs in rows, facing the altar or chuppah, and frame the aisle in well-secured standing arrangements, or tie ribbons at the sides of the chairs closest to the aisle. Frame the bride and groom with a backdrop or arch of greens and flowers. If there's a fireplace, it can be the center of the backdrop. Fill it with greens, and decorate the mantel with green roping or an arrangement of greens or flowers.

You can create an altar by covering an ordinary table with a white silk, lace, or damask cloth. Whether or not there are religious objects on the altar depends on the service, your faith, and the officiating clergy. Often there is simply a kneeling bench for the couple. Depending on the size of the room, you might consider an aisle runner. If the ceremony site is a club or a historic facility, check to see what elements are available.

It is likely your florist can provide a kneeling bench or stanchions for flowers.

Assuming that your reception will be held at the same place, you may want to carry over the same floral theme to the reception rooms.

Outdoors

A gorgeous outdoor setting will need little to embellish it in terms of decoration, but you will want to set the stage, so to speak, for your ceremony. Potted plants placed at strategic spots; an arched trellis woven with flowers, colorful ribbons, streamers, and garlands; as well as petals or fall leaves can define an aisle for the procession or the place where you will say your vows. At night, use lighting to provide a romantic ambience. Scents can be stronger in the evening; a sweet bay bush, phlox, or night-blooming jasmine can add fragrance to the setting as well.

Unless your wedding is being held under a tent, you'll need to come up with a floral design for the indoor backup site, too. Work with your florist to create a plan that will work well in both locations rather than designing (and paying for) two different schemes. If the site is located at a different address, make sure the florist has delivery instructions for both.

Flowers for the Reception

Most couples allocate a significant portion of their floral budget for the reception. It makes sense, because this is where you and your guests will spend most of your wedding time. The two most photographed locations at the reception are the table where the bridal couple is seated and the cake table. Another key focal point for guests is the table where the place cards are located. Consider this when you plan your reception decorations.

Arrangements can be placed on each dining table, on the place-card table, at serving stations or on buffet tables, and in restrooms. Flowers can encircle the wedding cake, coil around entranceways and archways, and frame the musicians' bandstand. Pots of beribboned topiary and standards may form a backdrop for the bridal-party table.

Centerpieces should be either low enough so that guests can easily see one another when seated or elevated in tall vases so that they are above the diners' heads. Bridesmaids' bouquets can form the floral focus at the bridal party's table, be used as table centerpieces, or be placed around the cake on a separate table. At an evening wedding, centerpieces can feature votives or candles in hurricane glasses surrounded with greens and simple flowers.

At an outdoor reception, you can embellish the setting with the same flowers and plants you used for the outdoor ceremony. Decorations don't have to stop with

---

THANKING YOUR FLORIST

While they may be ephemeral, flowers add so much to a wedding and take more care and work than meets the eye. In the days and weeks following your wedding, take some time to write your florist a note expressing your appreciation. Even better, enclose or email separately some photos of bouquets and arrangements as a thank-you.

---

flowers, however. Don't forget lighting for an evening wedding: Japanese lanterns, strings of lights dotted through the trees, or candle luminarias (pierced paper bags or metal containers) placed on the pathway to the site are all simple, but charming.

CHAPTER 21

LET THERE BE MUSIC!

Can you imagine a wedding without music? At different points, music adds joy, fun, gravitas, solemnity, and a sense of tradition to a wedding day. It serves as a ceremony cue, as pleasant background to conversation, as a call to dance the night away. The right music helps make a wonderful day even better. In fact, no other single element of your celebration has the power to engage the emotions the way music does.

There are a number of ways for the bride and groom to orchestrate and personalize their wedding music—and few professionals are more enthusiastic than musicians when it comes to talking about what they love.

Music at the Ceremony

Music sets the emotional tone for the ceremony. Striking the right note is about balancing the solemnity and joy of the event with your personalities and even the venue. The following are some guidelines to use when planning your ceremony music:

Finding music. Traditional favorites are often the best place to start—they are popular for a reason. Some

suggestions are listed starting on page 288, and you can also find compilations on CD or search online to find wedding ceremony favorites. If marrying in a house of worship, your officiant may refer you to an in-house music director, who can offer suggestions. But don't just take his or her word for it—you need to hear the music before you commit to it. Ask to hear samples of traditional and popular choices to help you decide what to use for the prelude, the processional, the recessional, and during the ceremony.

Restrictions. Many churches and synagogues have specific rules regarding music selections, and it's wise to check with your officiant about any restrictions. For example, some houses of worship only allow religious music, to the exclusion of even such well-known secular pieces as the "Bridal Chorus" (aka "Here Comes the Bride") from Wagner's *Lohengrin*, and Mendelssohn's "Wedding March."

Acoustics. Ask the officiant, music director, or site manager what type of music and instruments sound best in the space to make sure that your selections are a match for the acoustics of the site.

Consider your guests. If you plan on including songs to be sung by all, keep your guests in mind when making your selections. The less complicated and more familiar or beloved a hymn or tune, the more participation from your guests—and the more joyful your celebration will be.

Find out if you can use outside musicians. If your ceremony is at a house of worship, find out whether you are allowed to bring in an organist, soloist, or other musicians. The officiant or music director might be able to provide the names of musicians who have played in and are familiar with the site. You may have to pay a fee if you hire an outside organist or musicians.

Practice time. You'll need to coordinate access to the organ or the ceremony space in a house of worship or elsewhere so the outside musicians can practice.

The house organist. Who knows better than the house organist about the ins and outs of the organ, the acoustics, and the timing of religious ceremonies? Using the house organist might also save you on costs for ceremony music.

Discuss how and when payment will be made. If a house of worship provides a bill, the fee for the organist is often included and you can write one check. If not, he or she should be paid directly, either in cash or by check, before or right after the service. Traditionally, it is the best man's job to pass along payment, so it should be on his to-do list for the day of the wedding and on yours to have a check or cash prepared for him.

List the songs and the players. If you are providing a program for your ceremony, you will want to list the music that is performed during the prelude, processional, ceremony, and recessional. Get the correct names of each piece as well as the composer, information that may be of interest to your guests. It's also a good idea to list the names of the musicians. Check and double-check the spelling of everything you include.

The Order of Ceremony Music

Organize your choices into the four basic musical components of your ceremony.

The Prelude

Greet guests arriving at a wedding with the joyful sounds of music. The prelude music begins at least a half hour before the ceremony starts. It could be recorded music or it can be played by an organist, a single musician, or an ensemble, such as a string quartet. It could also include a choir or vocal soloist.

SAMPLING OF PRELUDE MUSIC

Bach: "Jesu, Joy of Man's Desiring"

Bach: Solo Cello Suites 1 & 3

Faure: "Pavane"

Handel: "Air" from *Water Music*

Handel: "Largo" from *Xerxes*

Vivaldi: Concerto No. 1 "Spring" from *The Four Seasons*

The Processional

The processional music begins as the mother of the bride is seated, the groom and his best man enter, and the bride and her father (or other escort) and her attendants are ready to begin their walk. The music can simply be that of an organ, piano, or guitarist. A trumpeter can accompany the organ, adding a celebratory and regal note. String quartets or solo cellists lend gravitas to the moment. Music played as the bride and her attendants walk up the aisle should be joyous and formal at the same time. The same piece can be played throughout the processional, but often the bride's entrance is accompanied by a different piece of music.

SAMPLING OF PROCESSIONAL MUSIC

Bach: "Air on the G String," Orchestral Suite No. 3

Clarke: "The Prince of Denmark's March" (aka "Trumpet Voluntary")

Guilmant: "Wedding March"

Handel: "The Arrival of the Queen of Sheba"

Pachelbel: "Canon in D Major"

Purcell: "Trumpet Tune and Air"

Wagner: "The Bridal Chorus" from *Lohengrin*

WALKING THE WALK

Thankfully, a slow, graceful walk has replaced the customary hesitation step, which often looks forced and stilted. Whatever processional music you choose, make sure it has an audible cadence to help everyone keep time when walking down the aisle.

The Ceremony

Having guests participate in the ceremony by singing hymns or a favorite song can add a communal spirit, especially when the ceremony is a brief one. In addition to one or two hymns, other musical interludes may be added at appropriate places during the ceremony. These can be vocal, performed by a soloist or a children's choir, or instrumental. Work with your officiant or the music director or organist to determine where music can be placed in the service. Make sure to schedule practice time for soloists with the organist or other instrumentalists.

SAMPLING OF CEREMONY MUSIC

Bach: "In Thee Is Joy"

Bach: "Jesu, Joy of Man's Desiring"

Beethoven: "Ode to Joy"

Bernstein and Sondheim: "One Hand, One Heart"

Hinsworth: "The King of Love My Shepherd"

Liszt: "Libestraum"

Schubert: "Ave Maria"

The Recessional

It is a jubilant time, and the music you choose for your recessional should be the most joyous of all. If at a church, ringing the bell note on the organ or bells in the bell tower can add to the festive ambience. Look for soaring, uplifting music, the kind that will have you and your attendants fairly floating down the aisle and out the door.

Beethoven: "Ode to Joy" from Ninth Symphony

Clarke: "The Prince of Denmark's March"
(aka Trumpet Voluntary)

Mendelssohn: "Wedding March" from *A Midsummer Night's Dream*

Purcell: "Trumpet Tune and Air"

The Postlude

Played as guests leave the ceremony, the postlude is either a continuation of the recessional music or a short piece or program that echoes the joyful mood of the recessional.

Music for the Reception

Music can make a party, and your reception should be just that: a full-tilt celebration of your marriage. Whether you hire a DJ, do it yourself with CDs or a playlist, or have the house jumping with a full-fledged band or orchestra, music sets the tone. While budget and personal taste are important considerations,

---

JUST WHAT IS "APPROPRIATE" MUSIC?

"Appropriate" boils down to music that is in keeping with the style and formality of the festivities, and is comfortable for your guests. This doesn't mean stuffy or bland. Think carefully about lyrics and avoid anything with strong sexual or violent content. Most people who react negatively to crude lyrics aren't prudes; they simply know what's appropriate for a wedding.

---

the kind of music and musicians you select depends largely on the time of day your reception is held.

Brunch, Lunch, or Tea Reception

At a brunch, lunch, or afternoon tea reception with no dancing, keep the music low-key so guests can talk. A single pianist, harpist, or violinist; a string quartet; or recorded music will add to the mood without being obtrusive. Classical or light jazz or pop selections set the mood for conversation and are meant to just be a background to the party.

Afternoon Cocktail Reception

Guests are mobile at cocktail receptions, moving from table to table, mingling and talking. Go for lively music, but not so loud that it drowns out conversation. This type of reception can be the perfect venue for instrumental combos, quartets, strolling musicians, or a single pianist. This isn't the place to have a vocalist—most guests would feel obliged to stop chatting and give the singer their attention.

Dinner-Dance Reception

The music for a dinner-dance reception can range from a band to a full orchestra to a disc jockey or your own preset playlist. The smaller the guest list, the smaller the group of musicians, and vice versa. Use this handy guide to help you decide what kind of group to hire: For an orchestra or band, you will need five or six pieces for 150 guests; six or seven pieces for 200 guests; and a full orchestra for 300 guests or more. This is just a general guide—some groups can produce a sound that is much bigger than they are. Select music or a recorded playlist that changes as the evening progresses from cocktail to dinner hours and then to dancing.

Selecting the Musicians for You

You'll want to start looking for musicians soon after you're engaged, as reception bands should be booked many months in advance of your wedding. Word of mouth is often the best place to start, so ask everyone you know for recommendations. But since not everyone has the same idea of what a great band is, be sure to listen for yourself. Try to see the musicians in concert or ask to attend a practice session. Request demos or a link to their website. Most bands will post video of themselves in action as well as an up-to-date playlist. When you start to interview musicians, look for the following qualities:

A varied repertoire. Quality and proficiency count, but so does diversity, especially if the couple has different tastes—say the bride loves country and the groom's into swing. Remember, too, that your guest list will likely be comprised of different generations. Make sure that the musicians you hire are capable of

moving from one kind of music to another, especially if your reception includes dancing. Have your musicians mix it up, combining upbeat tunes with tender ones. Don't subject your guests to three hours of slow songs or nonstop rock. For an ethnic wedding, you'll need to find musicians who can play your kind of traditional ethnic music.

The same band you hired. Often a variety of interchangeable instrumentalists and vocalists comprise a band, so make sure you get in writing that the group you heard on the demo is the one that will be playing at your wedding.

A well-rounded playlist and savvy pacing. Most musicians and DJs provide a song list of their selections. Having a playlist to review makes things easy—you and your partner simply check off the music you want to hear—or don't. A seasoned reception band will generally offer a large, wide-ranging repertoire and have a good sense of the audience. It is their job to pace the selections and know when to move from slow songs to old classics to popular hits.

Flexibility. You'll want to find experienced wedding musicians who are happy to work with you on special requests. You may want to select songs for special moments, such as music for the bride and groom's first dance, for the bride's dance with her father, and for the parents of the couple. Communicate special requests to the musicians in writing. (See page 294.)

Tasteful presentation. Sometimes a bandleader or DJ will also offer to serve as a master of ceremonies. You'll want to give some guidance as to how much announcing and commentary you want, as some really like to ham it up with jokes or risqué comments. If that's

---

THE VALUE OF A DJ

Cost containment is one compelling reason for working with a DJ; hiring a disc jockey to play music at your reception is typically half the cost of a live band. Plus, a DJ often has a larger playlist that can be expanded upon at your request—easily adding, for example, specific songs that may not be in the musicians' repertoire. Make sure to see the DJ in action before you make a decision to hire him or her. If he's never played at the reception site, have him schedule a trial run there to test the sound system and the acoustics of the space.

not your style, be clear about what you expect from the bandleader or DJ to avoid a misunderstanding. (See also page 294.)

Helping the Musicians or DJ Help You

The musicians and/or DJs are an important part of your wedding team. It's the musicians' job to tailor their skills to meet your needs and wishes. You can make that job easier by viewing the relationship as a collaboration. Here are suggestions and advice on ways to make working with musicians a positive experience for all involved:

- Coordinate the equipment needs of your musicians with the offerings of the reception site; for example, make sure that amplified musicians will have sufficient outlets and electrical power to play. Ask whether the reception site already has a sound system or piano on the premises.

- If you're on a budget, find musicians who can do double duty. When your ceremony and reception are small or held at the same location, it is entirely possible to have the same musician or musicians play for both, which may result in a better rate. Select musicians with the ability to play both classical and popular music.

- If your reception is large and lengthy, you don't necessarily need music the entire time. You can have recorded music or a cellist, guitarist, or pianist playing background music during cocktails and dinner, and bring in the band just before dancing begins. Ask the band representative if any of the band members

would be willing to perform solo (for a fee) during cocktails and dinner.

- If you have hired more than one group, make arrangements for the two to coordinate their performance time. For example, if your reception is 5 hours long and your band is willing to play for 1½ hours of dancing, during which they take two half-hour breaks, arrange for the jazz quartet you hired for dinner to be on call during those breaks.

- Make arrangements for meals for the musicians. You are expected to feed any members of the band or the DJ at some point during the reception. A club or caterer can give service providers a different meal than your guests' or may offer the same meal at a reduced price.

- Give the musicians a rough idea of the timing of everything—when dancing will start, when the cake will be cut, when toasts will be held. (See page 294.)

- Just as you should be specific about the music you want played, it's equally important that you be specific about songs you don't want played. If you absolutely cannot bear to have "The Chicken Dance" played at your reception, by all means let the musicians know ahead of time.

Questions for the Reception Musicians

When interviewing musicians or DJs, make a list of questions to ask and provide any important information. Make sure that the songs you definitely want played will be played. Questions you might ask include:

- How many weddings has this band/DJ played? In the last year?

- How many hours of play time are included?

- How many musicians or soloists can be provided?

- What is the scope of the repertoire? (Most bands know 200–500 songs, from swing to Top 40 to oldies to ethnic.)

- Is the band willing to learn a new song for the wedding if requested?

- How many breaks will be taken, how often, and for how long? (The standard is one per hour, for five to ten minutes.)

- What music, if any, will be provided during breaks?

- What will the band members or DJ wear? For example, is there an extra charge if they wear tuxes, or do they own them?

- Are there any other costs not included in the quoted fee, such as travel time and music between breaks?

- Is the band (or DJ) willing to play overtime, and if so, what's the charge?

- What is the cancellation policy?

- Will the musicians you are contracting be the ones at your reception?

- Will the band (or DJ) take requests from guests at no extra charge?

- Do the vocalists sing in any other languages? (This is important for ethnic weddings.)

Get It in Writing

Ask for everything in writing. Understand precisely what you will be getting in return for the price you are paying. Make sure the contract lists the following:

- The date, time, location and address of the event; start and ending time of the music

- Amounts and payment dates for the deposit and the balance

- Whether a refund is available if you cancel and any taxes or other charges

- How many hours of playing time is contracted

- How overtime hours will be billed

- How many breaks the band will take and for how long

- The number of musicians and vocalists (ask for their names)

- Specific attire

- Statement of liability insurance

The Details

When you've chosen your band or DJ, or if you are creating your own playlist, you'll want to specify songs/music/type of music for:

- Cocktail hour

- Dinner hour

- Couple's first dance

- Bride and her father's dance

- Groom and his mother's dance

- Guests' first dance

- Dancing

- Cake cutting

- Last dance

- The "do not play" list

DIY Music

There's no question that the digital music revolution has made it possible to have great music at your wedding at a fraction of the cost of a DJ or band. The playlist can be completely tailored to the event: the rehearsal dinner, ceremony, reception, after party—even brunch the next day.

Building a Playlist

What you won't spend in dollars you will spend in time to create your playlists. Check online for sites that offer suggested wedding playlists that can be downloaded—just be sure to edit out songs you don't like or want.

THE MC

The DJ, bandleader, a groomsman, or even the father of the bride can act as master of ceremonies, if you choose. Or the duties may be split among those who need to call on guests' attention at various points during the reception, such as the best man when he gives his toast—a more low-key approach. Make a schedule of any announcements you'd like made (say, for the cake cutting, or your first dance as a couple) and any planned toasts. Note who will make the announcement and when. In addition, it's a good idea to give the MC a list of the names of any persons who will be introduced—parents, grandparents, siblings, maid of honor, best man—and the phonetic spellings so their names can be pronounced correctly. If you're going to be introduced as a couple, let the MC know how you'd like it done: "Mr. and Mrs. Scott Jones" or "Scott and Maureen" or, in the event the bride is keeping her maiden name, "Scott Jones and Maureen Sepulveda." The MC is not listed on the ceremony program as he or she has no ceremony duties.

Using iTunes or Spotify is easy and fast and allows you to add professional touches such as cross-fading songs so there are no long, empty pauses or abrupt song changes. You can also create a wedding playlist folder with subfolders for each different component: prelude, processional, ceremony, recessional, cocktail hour, dinner, and dancing.

When it comes to creating your dance list, keep your guest list in mind. If it's multigenerational, as it is for many weddings, try to include memorable dance hits that will resonate with your oldest and youngest guests. Pace the music, too. Most guests—unless they're aerobics instructors—need a break, so sprinkle in one or two slow songs after three to four fast numbers.

Don't run out of music! Make your playlists longer than you think they need to be by thirty to forty-five minutes to be safe. Better to have too much music than to have to repeat.

Testing, Testing . . .

You'll have to be sure that your venue has amplifying equipment you can use or a place to hook up your computer, smartphone, or rental gear. Ask if you need to bring connecting cables. Test everything out to be sure the speakers can do the job in the space, and check volume levels. Better to begin the music too low and turn it up than to jolt guests with it up too high at the start.

Consider running your playlist from a laptop; it can make manipulating the playlist faster and much eas-ier. Don't forget to bring any chargers and plug in your speakers, laptop, or music player.

Then ask a friend to be in charge of the Play button—you'll have other things to do during the ceremony and reception. Run through the music with him before the wedding so he can cue the right music for the right event.

Other Considerations

Here's a rundown of what to consider if you're thinking about DIY music for your wedding:

- ❖ Will you need to hire additional equipment such as speakers or cables?

- ❖ What are the comparative costs? Will renting appropriate equipment make DIY music more expensive than a DJ?

- ❖ Is the time involved with creating the playlists worth the savings?

- ❖ What are your priorities for the wedding, and is music important enough to spend the money on?

- ❖ Is the venue and style of your wedding appropriate for this informal approach to music? More casual events are well suited to DIY music; more traditional weddings (with announcements and such) may need personal attention to music cues.

Bottom line: Music can be one of the most memorable aspects of a wedding, so if DIY music can't be executed well, or if the bride and groom don't know someone who can handle it effectively, it's worth it to go with professionals.

And the Band Played On

Dancing can take place before, during, and after the reception meal depending on the time of day and preference of the bride and groom. At most late-afternoon and evening weddings, the bulk of the dancing occurs after dinner and can go on late into the night. When the bride and groom cut the wedding cake, that's the signal that guests who want to call it a night may politely depart. For those that want to stay on, the music shifts into high gear and dancers rarely leave the floor.

These days, the bride and groom don't necessarily leave for their honeymoon right after the reception; instead, they stay and make a night of it dancing and partying with their friends. Typically, the band is asked to play for an extra hour or two or at least until the venue closes. If that may be the case, be prepared to pay the overtime fee at the end of the evening. Or plug in an iPod loaded with dance tunes once the band has called it quits.

SO YOU THINK YOU CAN'T DANCE

You've picked the band or the DJ, vetted the playlist, and chosen your special song for your first dance. Only one problem: You—or your fiancé(e)—can't dance, and all eyes will be on you when you take to the dance floor. The solution? Dance lessons!

Call your local dance studio and ask about private, semiprivate, or group lessons. Most studios charge between $65 and $140 for a one-hour private lesson, but group lessons can be a bargain at $15–$25 per hour. Recognizing the need for an engaged couple to get up to speed quickly, many studios offer special wedding packages—a series of ten or more lessons, for example, or a crash course of one or two sessions for those couples tight on time or money. Here are some tips to get the most out of your tango:

- Check out local dance studios for special deals and to get the best price.

- Schedule lessons early, four to six months before the wedding to allow for practice time.

- Get the wedding party or your parents (don't forget the father–daughter and mother–son dances) to join you and take advantage of less expensive, semiprivate lessons. The price per person drops as more couples are added to the lesson.

- If you're going to be dancing to a specific song, bring it along so you can practice to it. The instructor can also help you choreograph any special moves.

- Think about your wedding dress and how its weight or style might affect your dancing.

- Practice in the shoes you'll be wearing.

CHAPTER 22

PHOTOGRAPHY AND VIDEOGRAPHY

While your wedding is "the big day," in the end, it does draw to a close. But your memories live on for the rest of your lives, strengthened through your wedding photos. Years after minor details are forgotten, your photos will be there to remind you, vividly bringing back the joy and importance of your wedding, and ready and waiting for you to show to your children and grandchildren. That's why choosing the right person for the job is so important. No one else has such VIP access to the couple throughout the wedding day, and the right photographer isn't just one who knows his or her craft; you`ll also need someone with whom you have good chemistry and who you can trust to do a good job. There are also many styles of wedding photography, so when you look for the right photographer for your wedding, consider carefully the aesthetic approach that best articulates your vision.

Before hiring a photographer and/or videographer, couples need to consider several questions. Budget and compatibility are primary, but almost as important is the variety of photos you prefer. Do you want the traditional album of posed wedding photos, mostly candid shots, or a mix of both? Do you want rehearsal dinner and day-of preparation shots or just a record of the ceremony and reception? Do you want a video recording as well, or are photos alone how you think you'll want to relive the day?

Be honest as you discuss your wishes with each other. Your goal is to take great pleasure in looking at your wedding album and video for years to come. Don't overlook practical matters such as budget, but don't get talked into anyone else's idea of what your wedding photos should look like. Ultimately you should choose what you think suits you best.

Photography: What's Your Style?

Each photographer has his or her own distinct aesthetic, which is reflected in the photographer's portfolio of work. While the current trend in wedding photography is photojournalistic, many brides and grooms want a mix of styles. Look for a photographer whose work shows range and discuss, using examples from their portfolio when possible, the variety you would like to see.

Traditional. A traditional photographer generally treats every image as a posed portrait, even shots you may think of as candid. That doesn't mean that the photographs will appear forced or posed, but there likely won't be many spontaneous "action shots" included in the mix. Think "Everyone look at me and smile!" The emphasis with this style is on the classic, big moments, such as the first dance, not on the smaller, in-between moments. Traditional wedding photographers look to capture perfect moments with artistry and generally produce excellent, albeit formulaic, shots of the wedding party, families, and planned events.

Photojournalistic or reportage. A wedding photographer who takes a photojournalistic approach considers it the photographer's job to record events, not stage them. Think of it as more of a documentary style. This photographer will still capture the big events and take the group shots you want but will also include candid and spontaneous images. They look to tell the unique story of your day, often found in the unscripted moments. There are few formal "say cheese" roundups of guests smiling for the camera; this photographer prefers to blend into the background and capture close-ups, spontaneous reactions, and the emotions

surrounding them, not orchestrated or posed tableaux (outside of the formal wedding portraits).

Commercial. These photographers will perfectly capture staged shots of the centerpieces, cake, flowers, and decor and could be hired just for this purpose, supplementing another photographer hired to handle "people pictures." A commercial photographer's sense of style may be more formulaic and less spontaneous than that of a journalistic photographer. Just the same, this type of photographer is a professional and capable of taking magazine-quality images.

Selecting the Photographer for You

Once you have agreed on the style of photography that will make you the happiest, you can begin seeking a wedding photographer in earnest. When you have some names and are ready to interview people, consider the following criteria in your search for a photographer:

Portfolio. When you visit a photographer or videographer, always ask to see his or her portfolio (selected samples of his or her work). This is the most telling element of a photographer's background. A so-so photographer can't hide behind impressive references; the picture tells it all. When reviewing a photographer's portfolio, look for images that speak to you and convey emotion and feeling. Don't be dazzled by special effects or complicated setups; the basic composition and emotion need to work or no amount of postproduction tweaking will help. Keep in mind, too, that you are being shown the photographer's showcase work. The photos won't get any better than that, so be sure you like what you see.

Q: My fiancé and I found a photographer we really like, but he isn't on our venue's recommended vendors list and he has never shot at our venue before. Should we keep looking?

A: While it's great to work with a photographer who is familiar with your venue, it shouldn't be a deal breaker. Recommended vendor lists are a great place to start, but in most cases it's not required that you choose from among them. A good photographer can go into any situation, especially after scouting it, and take beautiful photographs. Remember, too, every vendor on the recommended list was also once new to the venue.

Depth of work. It's easy for a photographer to put one or two dozen of their best photographs on their website, but is that it? Ask to see multiple highlight slideshows or client albums to get a sense of how consistent they are and how his or her work translates in different settings. This will also help you judge their versatility: Can they shoot equally well in different venues, lighting situations, seasons, and kinds of weather?

Compatibility. Compatibility can't be stressed enough. If you like the photographer's work but don't like the photographer, keep looking; your annoyance and hesitation will show up in your photos. This person will be by your side most of the wedding day, so look for someone who is both respectful and easy to be around. If you meet with several photographers at a large professional studio but prefer one in particular, ask specifically for that person to be assigned to your wedding.

Price and service comparisons. While your first consideration is your ability to relate to the work the photographer has done in the past, you will need to incorporate price and service comparisons into your decision-making process. Ask about package options and the cost of any add-on services.

Wedding philosophy. The one factor that makes the difference between two equally competent professionals is their wedding philosophy. Ask the people you interview how they feel about weddings to try to ascertain if they are truly enthusiastic and dedicated—or if this is just another job.

Meeting Checklist for the Photographer

Be prepared: Take a list of questions with you when interviewing photographers. Following are some sample questions:

- Is a wedding package offered? If so, what does it consist of? For example, does the photographer provide an album for the bride and groom and smaller albums for their parents and perhaps grandparents? Is the package mandatory, or are there options, such as additional prints or albums?

- What is the number of photographs in the standard couple's album?

- What are the sizes and costs of extra albums, such as parent or attendant albums?

- What does it cost for additions to a package?

- What is the average number of pictures taken during the wedding and reception?

- If you are planning formal portraits ahead of time, for example for the newspaper, does the photographer have a dressing room in the studio? Is there a "prop" bouquet for you to hold? (See more on page 302.)

- If the option is available, discuss whether or not you should have a second photographer. The more guests, the more challenging it is for one photographer to cover the event adequately on his or her own. Photographers' comfort levels will vary, but consider bringing this up if your guest list is over 150.

- May the rights be purchased? How long does the photographer wait, if at all, to license the photos to you after the wedding?

- How long will the photographer stay at the reception? What is the per-hour fee for overtime?

- Is the photographer familiar with the ceremony and reception sites? Are there extra charges for site scouting and/or travel time?

The Photography Contract

When you find the photographer you want and agree to the date and terms, have him or her write up an itemized cost breakdown, including in the contract the wedding date, the agreed-upon arrival time, how many hours of photos or footage will be taken, breakdown of package cost and inclusions, overtime fees, fees for any additional photographers, extra charges, schedule for reviewing proofs, and estimated delivery dates of the final photos, finished album, slideshow DVD, and/or edited video.

Make sure that price guarantees for additional prints, enlargements, and extra album pages/prints and upgrades are included in your agreement. Ask whether the photographer offers a package discount when you buy extra albums for parents and other relatives. All packages are negotiable to a point. If you'd prefer not to have a finished album from the photographer, choosing to purchase customized prints or a disc of hi-res images instead, discuss your options.

You should also have a record of the number of hours, the number of staff (assistants or a second photographer may be needed for a very large wedding), delivery and payment schedules, and what the final products to be delivered are, such as a DVD of photos or video, albums, or the number of prints.

In return, provide your photographer with a copy of the venues' photography regulations and restrictions regarding proximity or site access and the use of cameras, flash photography, or lights. You will also need to give him or her the name and phone number of the officiant and the reception site's venue coordinator so that the photographer can ask any questions directly or scout out the wedding location if necessary. Otherwise, you can show him or her the sites yourself. Closer to the date, supply your photographer with a timeline of the wedding day (right down to details such as toasts so they don't miss any important moments), lists of formal portrait groupings for family and wedding party shots, and any other shot lists, such as informal group portraits of high school and college buddies.

Helping the Photographer Help You

Most people have never worked closely with a photographer and are not that familiar with wedding photography. How well your photographs and videography turn out is in large part dependent on your success in conveying your vision and desires to your photographer and/or videographer. Here are a few tips on how to make your collaboration with your photographer a success:

- The most important thing is to trust the photographer—and on the wedding day let the photographer do what he or she does best. You chose this person because you love his or her work; now trust the photographer to make work that you will love.

- If you have examples of photographic styles you like and want to emulate, bring them along when you meet with the photographer. Articulate what it is you like about your examples to help the photographer translate them to your day. Just remember that you might not end up with those exact photos—they are for inspiration and direction, not necessarily exact duplication. Samples can also give the photographer a sense of who you are and how to direct you during your wedding day portraits.

- Have an engagement photo session. This is a chance for the photographer to get to know what works for you as a couple. For you, it's a chance to get comfortable with someone who will be by your side throughout the wedding day. (See also page 302.)

- It's very helpful to have a small list of special people (or moments) you want photographed ready before the wedding day.

- It's also very helpful to assign a guest or a member of the wedding party who knows the family to organize group or single portraits. Instead of fishing guests the photographer doesn't know out of the crowd, he or she is free to concentrate on taking the pictures.

- Don't feel pressured to do something you're not comfortable with or that doesn't feel natural, especially during your couple portraits. This is your record of your wedding, so give feedback if it's just not feeling right.

- On the other hand, be open and willing to take a few risks, especially if having your picture taken isn't your favorite thing. Keep in mind that many photographers appreciate the opportunity to be a little creative—and sometimes the results can be the most endearing shots of the wedding.

Getting the Photographs You Want

Wedding photographers can capture a number of different special moments and events, including: engagement photographs, formal wedding portraits (taken in advance of the wedding and often for use in the newspaper), preparation photos of the bride and groom getting ready on the big day, the "first look," formal day-of portraits, and photographs of the ceremony and reception.

Engagement Photographs

In the past, engagement photographs were typically black-and-white head-and-shoulder shots of the bride alone, taken for publication alongside the engagement announcement. Today, the bride and groom usually appear in engagement portraits together. The trend now is for photos that are more casual than in the past, tell more of the couple's story, and are unique to who you are. Whatever you decide on—a photo of you alone or both of you—is fine.

Engagement photos are often used for save-the-date cards, so plan your timing accordingly if you wish to do this. If you plan on using a photo for a newspaper engagement announcement, let your photographer know the format the paper needs.

You may have the engagement portrait taken before you have begun the search for a photographer. Try to use someone you might consider booking for the wedding, too. In fact, some photographers include engagement shoots in their overall package (they want the trial run, too!), whereas for others it's an add-on or separate service. Either way, it's a good introduction to the way the photographer works—and an introduction to the quality of the work as well. If you find he or she fits the bill, you'll have a head start on your working relationship.

Advance Formal Wedding Portraits

The portrait photograph of the bride is traditionally the one you send in with your newspaper wedding announcement—and it is usually the shot that ends up on the living room wall or perched lovingly atop your parents' piano. Photographers usually shoot a formal portrait in the studio, against seamless paper, in a controlled lighting situation. You may, however, prefer having your picture taken at home or even at the bridal salon on the day of your final fitting.

If you're submitting your photo for publication in a newspaper, find out the format and deadline for submission. Then ask your photographer how far in advance of that date to schedule the shoot. This is

---

BANG FOR YOUR BUCK

You can get quite a lot of mileage out of your engagement photographs. Consider using them for:

- Newspaper announcements
- Save-the-dates
- Your wedding website
- A rehearsal dinner slideshow
- Your guest book
- Table cards (each table number could be displayed with a different photo)
- Photo table at the wedding along with pictures of your parents' weddings
- Thank-you cards

Whether it's for engagement pictures, wedding portraits, or any other photos, be in the moment. You can't do that if you're micromanaging the photographer or taking just as many photos yourself. You've carefully selected your photographer, and now it's time to let that person do his or her work. It's the photographer's job to capture the day; it's yours to live it to the fullest.

the date when your gown and accessories also need to be ready.

Because you will want the formal portrait to look as though it were taken on the day of the wedding, have your hair and makeup done in the style you will wear on your wedding day (a good way to put a test run to good use). For a picture-perfect portrait, make sure that your gown is wrinkle-free and that you are wearing the jewelry you plan to wear on your wedding day, too.

Today, the newspaper photo often includes the groom. If you'd like a portrait of the two of you, book the appointment at a time that is convenient for you both, and make sure the groom's attire has been fitted, if necessary.

The formal bridal portrait can also be a lovely gift for parents and grandparents. Ask the photographer for prices on extra prints.

Preparation Photographs

Preparation photographs—photos of the bride and groom getting ready—are becoming more and more popular. These shots are often very emotional and introspective, as the couples' closest friends and fam-

ily help them get ready for their vows. Discuss with your photographer how these shots will affect the start time of your day. Agree on the photographer's arrival time, the kinds of shots you want, and how much time to plan for them. For example, it might technically take just a minute or two to button your dress, but more time may be needed to photograph this. Possible shots to consider include:

- ☐ Buttoning up the dress
- ☐ Putting on shoes
- ☐ The bride putting on the finishing touches, such as a necklace or headpiece
- ☐ The bride's mother helping her with her veil
- ☐ The bride kissing her mother good-bye as she prepares to leave for the ceremony
- ☐ Signs leading to the ceremony site
- ☐ Ceremony entrance decorations
- ☐ Guests arriving at the ceremony site
- ☐ The bride and her father arriving at the ceremony site

This is also a great time to take detail shots of the couple's attire, including:

- ☐ The bride's dress (while it is still hanging), shoes, and veil
- ☐ Jewelry and other accessories (such as her clutch, shawl, handkerchief, pin, and other heirlooms or keepsakes)
- ☐ The bouquet or other flowers
- ☐ The groom's suit, tie, shoes, cuff links, and boutonniere

Ceremony Photographs

With the advent of digital cameras, the flash is usually no longer necessary to take quality ceremony photographs. But that doesn't mean that cameras are welcome in every church, chapel, or synagogue. Some officiants won't permit the clicking of cameras during the ceremony, an occasion they consider sacred. Photographers may also be restricted from places like the altar or behind the chuppah. So before you contract with a photographer for ceremony shots, be sure to ask the officiant precisely when photographs are permitted and when they aren't, and what kind of access photographers will have within the ceremony space.

It's also very courteous for the photographer to speak to the officiant ahead of time (especially when it is a religious venue) to discuss any restrictions or preferences he or she may have, such as remaining outside the altar area. A little respect ahead of time might gain the photographer more latitude during the ceremony.

Lastly, don't forget about any detail shots you may want of the space or the decorations. These could include the altar, chuppah, other religious fixtures or objects, the flowers, and any row or pew decorations.

When photography isn't permitted during the ceremony at all, you can have the photographer take simulated ceremony shots before the wedding or re-create them afterward. If staging the photos before, take them well before the start time of the ceremony, not as guests begin to arrive or are being seated.

If you are having photographs taken between the wedding and the reception, don't think you have to

rerun the entire wedding ceremony to get the right shots. Keep it brief! Preselect specific images you want to re-create. Otherwise the process could drag on, and guests will be left with too much downtime between the wedding and the reception.

Possible re-created photos might include:

- ☐ The bride and her father walking up the aisle
- ☐ The bridesmaids, maid of honor, flower girl, and ring bearer walking up the aisle
- ☐ The groom and best man turned as they would be to watch the bride walk up the aisle
- ☐ The bride and groom standing or kneeling at the altar and/or exchanging vows
- ☐ The bride and groom with their children, if they have any
- ☐ The entire wedding party as they stand for the ceremony
- ☐ The bride and groom kissing
- ☐ The bride and groom walking down the aisle after the ceremony

If there are other special moments or people you want photographed at this time, be sure to delegate a friend to ask these people to stay after the ceremony. Included could be shots of your grandmothers being ushered to their seats or of the organist or soloist at work.

Formal Day-of Wedding Portraits

Your formal wedding portraits are the group photos of you with your respective families, with your wedding party, and of just the two of you. The timing of these photos is important to how you schedule your day. Portrait shots might be taken before the ceremony,

between the ceremony and the reception, or while the reception is beginning if there is no lag time.

BEFORE THE CEREMONY: THE FIRST LOOK

Taking your formal wedding portraits before the ceremony does mean that the groom will see the bride before the vows, something that used to be taboo. Now, however, couples are turning this to their advantage by creating what is called the first look. This is that special moment that only happens once, when the groom first sees the bride on the wedding day in all of her bridal glory. Capturing this first look is becoming more and more popular, and the emotion of it can go a long way toward smoothing any parental feathers that might be ruffled by the idea of breaking with older traditions.

Beyond the beauty of first-look photos, taking your formal portraits before the ceremony helps your day run smoothly. Your time for photos is only constrained by when you can start shooting—critical if you are using

---

MAKING THE MOST OF A PHOTO DO-OVER

The re-created photo list above will do a great job of capturing ceremony highlights, but will fall short in one essential: There won't be any guests in your photos. This could make processional and recessional shots look awkward. Concentrate instead on the "altar shots," such as the father of the bride handing his daughter to the groom. If you do go for processional shots, say of the bride and her father, ask the photographer to keep them tight, so the lack of guests in the pews won't be noticeable.

multiple locations or wish to travel to have your picture taken in front of any local sites or monuments. More important, though, you won't have to worry about keeping your guests waiting for you at the reception, and you won't miss a second of it. Just be sure that your wedding party and relevant family members know where and when to gather before the ceremony for photos.

AFTER THE CEREMONY

If taking photos after the ceremony, plan on 1–1½ hours to take all the portraits. Be prepared that you will miss part or all of the cocktail hour, especially if the reception starts immediately after the ceremony. If there is some lag or travel time between events, use this time efficiently so that you don't keep guests waiting for you longer than necessary. Whenever possible, it's best to start the reception not more than forty-five minutes to an hour after the ceremony, even if this means you miss part of the cocktail hour while you finish photos.

FAMILY PHOTOS

Plan to have your family photos taken first. They often require the most people to round up, and it's easier to start with family members assembled and ready to go than to hunt them out of the reception crowd. It also allows them to rejoin the reception ranks first. This is especially important in the case of parents, who are often the hosts or can act as hosts, helping to bridge the gap with guests while the couple are still smiling for the camera with their wedding party.

Provide in advance your list of "must have" shots to the photographer. Your list will be as unique as your family dynamics. Think about the combinations that will best suit you and your family—and your allotted time. Plan three to five minutes per group shot, allowing more time for very large groups. Aim for about eight family combinations or twenty to thirty minutes of family portraits. This may sound short, but when you add the wedding party and couple portraits, the time can add up quickly.

It's also a good idea to take pictures with grandparents and children at the beginning so they aren't kept waiting. Share your list with your parents ahead of time so that they won't suddenly request additional combinations once you've begun taking the portraits. Possible formal family portrait groupings might include:

- ☐ The bride with her parents (or each parent, plus stepparent, as applicable)
- ☐ The groom with his parents (or each parent, plus stepparent, as applicable)
- ☐ The bride with her mother
- ☐ The bride with her father
- ☐ The groom with his mother
- ☐ The groom with his father
- ☐ The bride and groom with the bride's family (parents, siblings, aunts, uncles, cousins)
- ☐ The bride and groom with the groom's family (parents, siblings, aunts, uncles, cousins)
- ☐ The bride and groom with their siblings if they are not all in the wedding party
- ☐ The bride with her parents and grandparents
- ☐ The groom with his parents and grandparents

WHO'S IN THE PICTURE?

Posing for pictures with your respective families can get a little complicated these days. If your parents are divorced, it is simply not appropriate to ask them to flank you in a photograph in a semblance of a united family. Instead, a portrait of you with each of them individually is fine—and if they have remarried, have a portrait taken of you with each of them with their spouse. Placing this photo on your list of portraits can make your parent and step-parent very happy. If enmity toward the new spouse is great, you don't have to do it—just don't try to re-create the family you once were.

SAMPLE WEDDING PARTY AND FAMILY PHOTO SCHEDULE

Plan on: 5 minutes per group

Hamlin-Flynn Wedding
Family Photo Schedule

Scott and Lila
May 14, 2016
Middlesex Farms
Middlesex, VT 05602

5:45 PM immediately after the ceremony

All members in the family pictures please gather by the gazebo (good weather) or the Farmstead Room to the left of the entry (poor weather).

Maureen Hamlin and **Carolyn** Flynn will be the point people for the family pictures and will make sure everyone gets to photo location and help identify people in the photos.

Our goal is to be finished in 45 minutes or **less.**

1. **Scott and Lila with:** Full wedding party, both sets of parents
2. **Scott and Lila with:** Hamlin Family (Peter, Sara, Anna, Liz, Josh) and Flynn Family (George, Suzanne, Michael, Carolyn)
3. **Scott and Lila with:** Hamlin Family (Peter, Sara, Anna, Liz, Josh) plus grandparents (John, Patsy, Betty)
4. **Scott and Lila with:** Flynn Family (George, Suzanne, Michael, Carolyn) plus grandparents (Frank and Barbara)
5. **Scott and Lila with:** Hamlin siblings (list names here)
6. **Scott and Lila with:** Flynn siblings (list names here)
7. **Scott and Lila with:** Hamlin cousins (list names here)
8. **Scott and Lila with:** Flynn cousins (list names here)

Schedule your wedding-party portraits second. If you are taking photos after the ceremony, this allows your wedding party to rejoin the reception when they're finished instead of waiting while you have your couple photos taken. While these photos can be the classic line-ups, couples today often want a more unique approach. From taking advantage of an interesting backdrop to asking everyone to jump in the air at the same time or run toward the camera, it's often all about creativity. The time you spend on your wedding party portraits will depend greatly on the style of photography you and your photographer decide on. If you do traditional, lined-up photos, plan on ten to fifteen minutes. For more creative shots, plan twenty to thirty minutes of time. Remember, the more creative you go or the greater variety of shots you want, the more time the shoot will take. Some combinations of people to consider:

- ☐ The bride with her maid or matron of honor
- ☐ The groom with his best man
- ☐ The bride with her bridesmaids
- ☐ The groom with his groomsmen
- ☐ The bride and groom with the full wedding party

THE COUPLE

Many couples still want traditionally posed portraits, but the emerging style in wedding portraiture is more about a creative expression of who the couple is. From fields with horses to towering skylines and neon city lights, it's about pictures that are tailored to you. The idea isn't to be gimmicky; it's to find or create the setting (or even just mind-set) and then capture that moment.

For bride and groom portraits taken before the ceremony, schedule about one hour. For those taken after the ceremony, plan no more than thirty minutes at the most. (You can also use less time either way if you wish.) Compositions include:

- ☐ The bride alone
- ☐ The groom alone
- ☐ The bride and groom together

Reception Photos

For planned events at the reception—both the traditional ones, such as the cake cutting, and those that personalize your wedding—provide the photographer with a timeline of events and where they will occur, for example, "After the salad, two speeches. Dinner. After dinner, two toasts." Events can include:

- ☐ The bride and groom's introduction at the reception (and also possibly parents and/or wedding party)
- ☐ Guests going through the receiving line
- ☐ Any toasts or speeches
- ☐ The cake cutting
- ☐ The bride and groom's first dance
- ☐ The bride dancing with her father
- ☐ The groom dancing with his mother
- ☐ The bride tossing her bouquet
- ☐ The groom tossing the bride's garter
- ☐ The bride and groom leaving the reception

PHOTO BOOTHS

Photo booths at receptions are a hot trend right now. Couples either rent an arcade-style booth that spits out the classic four-shot strip or hire an additional photographer to set up a mini studio complete with props. No smartphone can replicate this kind of fun!

Let your photographer know up front the kinds of candid photographs that mean the most to you. If you want shots of every table of guests, make that clear so no one is left out. If you prefer shots of people mingling and dancing, say so. Guest candids at the reception are often some of the most spontaneous and fun pictures. The unplanned photo of the groom dipping the bride on the dance floor might become your favorite shot!

Also, be sure to tell the photographer about any informal group photos you would like to take, such as your high school or college friends. Take these pictures after the main events, such as cake cutting and first dances, are done. Put one person from each group in charge of gathering the group, or ask the DJ or band-leader to make announcements when you're ready to take each group's photo.

To the best that you can, let the photographer know about any surprise events in advance (both when and where they will occur) so he or she can be ready to capture the moment. This could be a surprise guest arrival, a gift to the couple or from the couple to their parents, a special toast, or even another proposal or big announcement.

Lastly, review with the photographer any detail shots you would like of the cake table, centerpieces, and other special decorations.

Videography: What's Your Style?

A wedding video can be a wonderful addition to your collection of memories. It will be there on your first anniversary and, technology to view it permitting, it will be there on your twentieth. It provides a wonderful record for your children, capturing like no other medium the mood and moments of your wedding day.

When reviewing a videographer's work, ask to see footage of previous weddings. You'll be looking not just for artistic quality but also for a personal sensibility that matches your own. Do you want a wedding video that is a lush visual record of a beautiful day in a beautiful setting? Or do you want a video that focuses on telling a story, one that has a point of view? Do you want a videographer who presents a cinematic sensibility? One who is proficient at editing and cutting the footage? Is a sense of humor important to you? Are you interested in capturing special little moments and not just the standard orchestrated ones (like cutting the cake and throwing the bouquet)? Do you want a videographer who blends into the background, or one who orchestrates events? Consider these criteria when choosing the style of your video.

Video Options

While the costs of filming a wedding have gone up in the past few years, so have the credentials and professionalism of dedicated, full-time videographers as well as the quality of the equipment they use. Standard video packages include your entire wedding story, from the time you arrive at the ceremony (or even before, if you wish) until you depart from the reception. Finished recordings are usually thirty minutes to two hours long, edited down from three to five hours of raw footage.

A wedding video usually includes the entire service and all or part of the reception. The final product you receive is generally an edited DVD. The editing is done in a studio, and the edited recording can contain not only scenes from your ceremony and reception but interviews with guests, reflections by your parents, and messages for each other as well as still images, such as old family photographs and your invitation. Naturally, the more special effects, music, extra photography, and other elements that are added, the more your wedding video will cost.

Another, less expensive option is a wedding-highlights video. Usually lasting only about fifteen minutes, a highlights video is a fast-paced montage of special moments of the day. It makes an ideal gift to send to those who were not present. Sometimes a videographer will provide a highlights video as an extra to couples who contract for a full video.

Selecting the Videographer for You

Consider the following criteria in your search for a videographer:

Equipment. Look for a videographer who uses high quality, professional-grade, full-featured cameras that can shoot in both high definition and standard definition. This type of equipment doesn't need additional lighting to capture indoor, evening, or other low-level lighting scenes. Wireless microphones are now standard. Ask if the videographer has backup equipment as well.

Style and content. You'll want a videographer who shares your style and content sensibility.

Credentials. Talk to more than one professional, and view any previously made wedding videos. It's a big commitment of your time to preview other videos, but it is worth it to make sure the investment of money you make will be a good one. Seeing the videographer's work will give you the opportunity to see his or her training, experience, talent, and style.

Details indicating quality. Specifically, keep an eye out for:

- Steady (not shaky) images
- Clean, crisp focus
- Continuity of sound
- A mix of distant and close-up images
- Seamless editing from one scene to the next

References. Do check references. The videographer should be able to facilitate a call with previous clients. Ask other couples not just if they were satisfied with their video but if they were also happy with the way the videographer conducted him or herself at the wedding.

Questions for the Videographer

Be prepared: Take a list of questions with you when interviewing videographers. Following are some sample questions:

- Will background music be dubbed on the video? If so, who selects the music?
- Can credits be added so that the names of the wedding party and others can be listed on the video?

- How much editing is done? Is the videographer the only person involved in editing the final cut?

- What special effects are usually used, and when can you decide whether you want them?

- What do additional copies cost?

- Who keeps the original video footage?

- What happens to the footage if it is the property of the videographer?

- How long is the original kept on file in case you want to order extra copies?

- Can you buy the original footage, and if so, for how much?

- When will you see the video? Will you receive a disc, or will it be posted online?

Getting the Footage You Want

Both your preferences and your budget can determine what you arrange to have taped. Do you want the videographer recording the wedding party getting ready for the ceremony? You and your father arriving at the ceremony? The mothers being seated? Guests arriving? Do you want the ceremony recorded (if your officiant permits it), or just the reception? Do you want your guests "interviewed" by the videographer, or do you think this might make them uncomfortable? Looking at the wedding videos of friends or those provided by the videographer may help you decide what elements of your day you want recorded.

Ceremony Video

The videotaping of your ceremony must be cleared with your minister, priest, rabbi, or other officiant before you sign any contracts with videographers. Any specific guidelines should be discussed with the videographer, such as the placement of equipment, lighting restrictions, and whether events can be restaged later.

Most churches and synagogues allow videographers to film from a specific location, either from the side of the altar or the rear of the balcony, to prevent disruption. Lights generally aren't allowed, so newer equipment that requires little or no extra lighting is essential. A wireless microphone attached to the groom's lapel will record vows clearly.

If your ceremony will be recorded, meet with your videographer in advance to describe the ceremony plans. You will need to answer such questions as these: Will you face each other? Is there a soloist? How many members of your bridal party will there be? Will you have a receiving line at the ceremony site? Will guests shower you with anything as you leave the ceremony?

Reception Video

First decide what video memories and planned events you want recorded at your reception and then give the videographer a specific list. He or she will need to know whether there will be a receiving line, whether guests will be seated at assigned tables or mingling through the room, whether there will be dancing, and the timing of the toasts, cake cutting, and other festivities.

Many videographers offer to interview guests. If you would like this component for your wedding video, prepare a list of candidates ahead of time, such as your parents, grandparents, siblings, members of the wedding party, and special guests. Let the videographer know not to push it, that it's okay to move on if a person declines to be interviewed.

A LITTLE DISCRETION, PLEASE!

Let your videographer know that as far as you are concerned, discretion is the better part of valor. You're not looking to have intimate conversations recorded by hidden mics or someone's intoxicated behavior captured on film.

CHAPTER 23

THE MANY LAYERS OF WEDDING CAKE

Eating and sharing cake is among the oldest wedding traditions—almost certainly because wheat and other grains, seeds, and nuts are universal symbols of fertility. The ancient Greeks served sesame seed pies. Small wheat cakes were shared at Roman weddings. Wheat biscuits were broken over the bride's head at early Anglo-Saxon weddings. In Hindu and Hebrew cultures, the bride and groom's first shared food after their marriage is something sweet—a symbol of the sweetness of their union and the life they will share.

In the 1800s in Europe and the United States, the height of wedding cakes began to soar. The cake for the 1871 marriage of Queen Victoria's daughter Princess Louise stood five feet high and weighed almost 225 pounds. The 1947 wedding of Princess Elizabeth and the Duke of Edinburgh featured a four-tiered cake—nine feet high, 500 pounds, and decorated with, among other things, sugar replicas of Buckingham Palace and Windsor and Balmoral Castles. Imagine being in charge of moving it!

While most brides don't dream of such lofty creations, highly designed and decorated wedding cakes are still the visual focal point of many receptions. In the last decade, wedding cakes have become as central an element as the wedding dress, thanks to the special bridal issues of lifestyle magazines and popular television shows such as *Amazing Wedding Cakes* and *Cake Boss*. While the traditional cake is round or square, multitiered, and frosted in white or pale pastels, there's no real limit on the size, shape, color, and style of your wedding cake. Generally, the more formal the wedding, the more formal the cake, but that's not a rule set in fondant!

New Trends in Wedding Cakes
One Cake, Two Cakes . . .

Some couples skip the cake cutting and serve individual cakes to guests. Or, instead of one huge cake, they opt for several smaller cakes in different flavors, shapes, and/or sizes. Cupcakes continue to be popular, and one recent bride served them in three sizes: small, medium, and large—perfect for guests who want "just a sliver." At a small wedding, multiple cakes can serve double duty as centerpieces. Another idea is to display a variety of cakes on a dessert table. The bride and groom cut one, and then guests choose their favorite flavor. By setting up several dessert stations, guests can travel around the room and sample different cakes. What a great way to mingle and meet other guests!

Red Cake, Blue Cake . . .

Color is everywhere in weddings today, and the wedding cake is no exception. Cascading pink roses, white lilies of the valley on a Wedgwood blue fondant, real flowers matching the bridesmaids' bouquets adorning basket-weave buttercream tiers, polka dots, chevrons, ombré, metallic icing, or fondant—when it comes to the cake, you're only limited by your budget and imagination.

Carrot Cake, Cheesecake . . .

More and more, couples are indulging taste buds by selecting cheesecakes, meringues, baked Alaska, chocolate cake, fruit cakes, pound cakes, mousse cakes, angel food cake, carrot cakes, or your mom's famous lemon cake. No longer is the wedding cake for

---

THE FIRST SCOOP

A wedding without cake and its traditional cutting sounds lacking—until you replace it with ice cream! That's what Daniel and Jessica did: Instead of a cake, they had an ice-cream sundae buffet, and rather than cutting the first slice of cake together, they had photos taken of them making the first scoop. It was far less expensive than cake, suited their personalities, and was a hit with kids and grown-ups alike. Perfect for a country wedding in July!

---

looks only. It's just as important that the cake, even traditional white cake, is delicious. Always sample!

Fake Cake . . .

It's perfectly fine to display a frosted cardboard or foam-core "faux" cake on top of one tier of real cake for cutting, and serve slices of real cake from the kitchen. You can go crazy with an elaborate design and no one has to worry about how to cut—or pay—for a monstrous cake.

No Cake?

How about a dessert table in lieu of or in addition to cake? Dessert tables can include a variety of pastries, cookies, brownies, cupcakes, fruits, cheeses, mini desserts, ice cream, and more. Including a couple's favorite treat or a family ethnic specialty is a nice way to add a personal touch. One recent bride wanted to serve shortbread cookies with coffee after dessert and had a stamp made with her wedding motif to mark each of the silver-dollar-sized cookies. (See also page 318.) Not into cake at all? A table of pies—apple, peach, blueberry, lemon meringue, key lime, Boston cream—could be the perfect solution.

Cake Vocabulary

Don't know the difference between a marzipan paste and a fondant finish? The world of wedding cakes is an extraordinarily varied one. You can choose a cake with a traditional look and an adventurous taste. Inside a classic tiered facade, for example, may be a rich but homey carrot cake. You can mix textures—combining a tender cake with a smooth filling, for example, or using a hard-finish royal icing decorations over a smooth-finish fondant. You can mix and match flavors: devil's food with hazelnut; German chocolate with French crème; Amaretto with chocolate mousse; fudge truffle with strawberry crème. A good baker will help you choose a texture, filling, and icing that marry nicely.

Here's a primer on some of the terms your baker may use:

Buttercream

Cakes iced in buttercream are the best value in terms of price per slice. Buttercream is smooth and creamy but not too sweet. It takes flavors well; remains soft, making it easy to cut; and is perfect for finishes like basket weaves, swags and swirls, fleurs-de-lis, and rosettes. Genuine buttercream is made with real butter. Heat and humidity make it bead, run, and drip, so cakes iced with buttercream need to be refrigerated and then brought to room temperature just before serving. Alternatively, bakers can counter this effect by adding shortening to the icing to give it a measure of stability, but some people don't like the taste. If your cake will be kept cool in an air-conditioned reception room, the added shortening is unnecessary.

Ganache

Ganache is the ultimate choice for chocolate lovers. It's a mixture of chocolate and heavy cream, but additional flavors can be added, such as orange, raspberry, hazelnut, or coffee. Like buttercream, it doesn't hold up well in heat or humidity. It can be used as an icing, glaze, or a filing between cake layers.

Whipped Cream

Whipped cream can be used as a light, soft icing, and like buttercream, is temperamental in heat and humid-

ity. A whipped cream cake must be kept refrigerated until just before it is served. Bakers may also use stabilizers when working with whipped cream. If you don't want stabilizers used, discuss with your baker whether this will affect the appearance of the cake. Whipped cream can also be used to lighten buttercream or chocolate ganache, in which case it's called mousseline. Alternatively, whipped cream or mousseline can be used as a filling.

Fondant

Rolled fondant icing is a combination of sugar, corn syrup, gelatin, and usually glycerin. It doesn't get high marks for flavor, but it's perfect for elaborate decorations. It can be rolled out in sheets and wrapped around each tier of the cake, presenting a smooth surface with a matte, porcelainlike sheen. It serves as an excellent base for flowers and decorations piped in royal icing (see "Royal Icing" on the following page) because of its smoothness. Fondant can't be refrigerated; the condensation that forms as it comes to room temperature looks unattractive and can hurt the finish. While lack of refrigeration isn't a problem for the cake (it actually can help preserve it), it may be for a filling that requires refrigeration. (Note: Because of the gelatin, fondant isn't an option for vegetarians or vegans.)

Royal Icing

Soft when piped onto a cake, royal icing dries to a hard finish, which makes it perfect for decorative touches but not for icing an entire cake. Made with egg whites and confectioners' sugar, it takes color and flavor well and is what bakers use for creating latticework, flowers, and beading around the edges of the cake.

Spun Sugar, Pastillage, and Marzipan

Finishing touches can be made from any of these decorative icings, all of which are edible. Spun sugar is caramelized sugar that is pulled into strands and quickly formed into bows and other shapes. It melts into a gooey mess in heat and humidity, so it isn't a good choice for a non-air-conditioned room. Pastillage is a paste of sugar, cornstarch, and gelatin that hardens as it dries to a porcelainlike finish (gelatin alert again!). It's used to create realistic-looking flowers and decorations. Marzipan is also a paste, made of ground almonds, sugar, and egg whites. It is sometimes rolled in sheets, like fondant, but it is usually molded into flowers and other decorative shapes and painted with food coloring.

Genoise

A rich, dense, European sponge cake, a genoise is usually soaked in a liqueur-flavored syrup and layered with fruit, mousseline, ganache, or buttercream fillings.

Tiers and Layers

Tiers describe a cake that is stacked and then decorated. A five-tiered cake may have five graduated sections, one stacked on the other with the smallest at the top. If you want variety, this allows nicely for each tier to have a different flavored cake.

A cake that is layered is sandwiched together with filling—fruit, chocolate, whipped cream, ganache, buttercream—and then iced and decorated. Each section of cake is a layer, either baked as one piece or split horizontally into two or more layers. A three-layer cake has three layers of cake, sandwiched together with two layers of filling and then iced. These terms can be confusing, so be sure to discuss the difference with the baker.

Cost

The cost of the cake depends on the cake size, the relative simplicity or elaborateness of the decoration, the ingredients, and who does the baking. A custom-designed, professionally baked cake can cost thousands of dollars. As weddings have become more elaborate, the expenses have increased. Today, the wedding cake can take a big slice out of your wedding budget, costing $535 on average. Price can be determined as a flat fee or on a per-slice basis, ranging anywhere from $1.50 to $10.00 or more per serving.

There are also some hidden costs to consider. Some reception sites require you to purchase an in-house cake or pay an additional fee to bring one from outside, or they charge a slicing fee to prepare the cake for serving to guests. A delivery fee is also standard.

FLOWERS ON YOUR CAKE

Check with your florist to be sure that flowers and greens used for your cake decorations are either edible or at least nontoxic and removed before serving. This is a good time to choose organically grown flowers.

It is possible to have your cake and eat it, too, without breaking the bank:

- Serve cupcakes or individual pastries and avoid slicing charges.

- Have a small decorated cake for the bride and groom to slice, and then serve the same type of cake as undecorated sheet cake for dessert. (Added bonus: It doesn't take very long for the kitchen to cut and plate a sheet cake.)

- Use real or candied flowers instead of expensive handmade marzipan or pastillage ones.

- If cake is not your only dessert, a simpler, less expensive cake may fit the bill.

Cake Bakers

Your caterer or your reception site may be your best source for information on cakes and bakers, if they don't provide the service themselves. You can use a bakery or grocery bakery department, but be sure to sample so that you are pleased with the quality and presentation. You may have a favorite restaurant that has a bakery or a master baker who also does wedding cakes. You were born under a lucky star if you have a relative or friend who is a skilled baker and offers to make the cake!

Working with the Baker

Make an appointment to meet with the baker, whether he or she is the baker at the site, the one used by the caterer, or one you find and interview yourself. Even if you've seen his or her work online, ask to review the baker's portfolio. You'll want your cake to look good, but looks aren't everything—you'll want it to taste as good as it looks. Ask to see a list of ingredients. To get the best-tasting cake, you'll want high-quality ingredients such as real butter, eggs, fruit, and cocoa.

Now for the best part! Most reputable bakers offer tastings of cakes, fillings, and icings for a fee, so indulge and sample a baker's work before signing a contract.

Once you've settled on a baker, provide him or her with the following information:

- The date and time of the wedding reception

- The address and phone number of the reception venue

- The names and phone numbers of the caterer, florist, and wedding planner, as well as the site location manager to coordinate delivery

- Very clear directions to the reception site

- The room decor

- The general room temperature

- Refrigeration options

- The table linen colors

- The wedding-party colors

- The floral scheme (flower types and colors)

- The formality of your wedding

- The number of guests

- Your intention to freeze the top layer for your first-month anniversary (which could affect the choice of icing or ingredients as some freeze better than others)

Be sure that any contract you sign—whether with an outside baker or with a caterer—spells out all the details of your arrangements, including flavors, ingredients, decorations, and the date and time of delivery. Inquire about extra charges for cake stands, pillars, assembly, and delivery. Some reception sites charge an extra cake-cutting fee if your cake is not ordered through them, so be sure any fees are clearly listed.

Bringing in an Off-Site Cake

If your cake is baked at another site and transported, let the site caterer or manager know when the cake will be delivered. A cake consisting of more than three tiers is generally transported unassembled and is put together and decorated on-site. It's a really good idea to let the baker be responsible for delivery and assembly. Find out from the location manager if there is space for the baker to work and the best time to do so.

When to Order

Cake orders are usually placed at least three to six months in advance of the reception—earlier if you

---

want a popular baker during the busiest wedding months. If you're marrying on very short notice, you can get a good-quality cake from a professional bakery or grocery store bakery.

How Much Cake?

Most experts say to order 10–15 percent less than the number of guests because usually not all the guests want to eat cake and a fair bit can go to waste otherwise. Discuss this with your baker and don't forget to let him or her know if you are planning on saving the top layer. (See also page 320.)

The Wedding Cake on Display

The cake display is one of the most photographed spots of the reception, so you'll want to make sure it looks just right. If temperature allows, the wedding cake can be in place and on display when guests enter the reception location. How to display the wedding cake is up to you. It can be placed on the bridal-party table, in the center of a buffet table, or on a small table or cart of its own.

You can decorate the cake table in a variety of ways: with a favorite family tablecloth, your mother's wedding

---

CAKE AND DESSERT?

Some couples opt to serve both cake and some other dessert. It could be another rich dessert or something light and refreshing like fruit or sorbet to accompany the cake. A separate dessert or sweets table comprised of traditional ethnic goodies or an assortment of desserts is popular in some parts of the country. If you know that a number of your guests would prefer a choice, and the extra cost is not prohibitive, it's a nice way to personalize your reception.

veil over an undercloth, or even with the bridesmaids' bouquets circling the base of the cake. Another option: Use an overcloth gathered in swags caught up by fresh flowers, and repeat the design on the cake with real or similar-looking flowers made of edible icing.

You can wrap the handle of the cake knife with a ribbon or flowers and place it on the table next to the cake. Perhaps you have a special cake knife, such as a family heirloom, to use.

Sometimes the presentation of the cake is an event in itself. The cake is kept hidden in the kitchen until it is time for you to cut it. The lights are lowered, the music stops, and the room becomes hushed. The cake is wheeled into the middle of the room and spotlighted. Then everyone gathers around to witness the cutting of the cake.

The Art of Cutting the Cake

Cutting the wedding cake is a traditional part of the reception. At a seated dinner, the cake is cut just before dessert is served. At a buffet, luncheon, tea, or cocktail reception, the cake cutting takes place closer to the end of the reception. Be sure to give your caterer or club manager the approximate time you plan to cut your cake so that the kitchen staff can be alerted to remove the cake for serving after the cutting. Tell your photographer in advance, too, in order to set up the shot. Remember that it takes a while to cut, plate, and serve the cake, so don't leave it to the very end of the reception. Here is the traditional sequence of events in cutting the cake:

The announcement. Typically, the host, best man, DJ, or bandleader announces the cake cutting, at which point the bride and groom proceed to the cake table and their attendants gather round.

Cutting the cake. To start, the bride puts her hand on the handle of the cake knife and the groom puts his hand over hers. It is easiest if they pierce the bottom tier of the cake with the point of the knife and then carefully make three cuts (i.e., two slices worth), then remove a small slice onto a plate set with two forks and napkins. (The three cuts make it easier to remove the first slice.)

The first bites. The groom gently feeds the bride the first bite, and she feeds him the second. This tradition, symbolizing their commitment to share with and support each other, begins their sweet life together. No smushing! It's tacky, messy, and requires makeup repair. (And no bride wants the nightmare of chocolate cake on a white wedding gown.)

The wedding cake kiss. At this point, the couple may share a kiss, and then the caterer whisks away the cake so it can be cut and served to guests.

Slices for the parents. Before the cake is taken away it's a lovely gesture for the bride and groom to cut cake slices for their parents. Tradition has it that the bride serves the groom's parents, and he serves hers.

Saving the top layer. Many couples want to save and freeze the top layer of the cake for their first anniversary. If that's what you'd like to do, be sure to tell the caterer or manager in advance so that it isn't cut and served to guests. Some couples don't like the idea of eating a year-old, possibly freezer-burned cake, preferring to take it out of the freezer and share it on their one-month anniversary. Alternatively, you can choose to freeze only one piece of cake and eat the pretty top layer at the reception.

Cake Cutting 101 for the Home Wedding

If the wedding is small or at home, you'll want someone in charge of cake cutting once you and your new spouse have made the traditional first cuts. In this case, it's a good idea to review the art of cake cutting in advance.

For a three-tiered cake: About two inches in from the outside, cut all the way around the bottom tier (the cut runs parallel to the outside of the layer, in a circle). Individual slices are cut from this section, and each is lifted onto a cake plate to be served.

Next, repeat the process with the middle tier: Cut a circle about two inches in from the outer edge, but only cut through the middle tier, not the bottom tier. There should be a cardboard round separating the layers so you don't cut into the layer below. When this outer ring has been sliced and served, remove the top layer and set it aside, especially if the bride and groom want to save it.

Finish cutting the middle layer, into slices if it's been reduced to the size of a regular cake, or continue to use the circle/slice method if it is still large.

When the middle layer has been completely sliced, remove the cardboard round if used and slice the bottom layer, using the circle/slice method until the remaining circle is small enough to slice like a regular cake.

The Groom's Cake

Traditional groom's cake is a dark, rich fruitcake that was served alongside the brides' cake. Alternatively, it wasn't displayed at all but sliced, wrapped, and presented in little white ribbon-tied boxes for guests to take home. It was believed that if the cake was placed under a pillow, singles would dream of the person they were to marry. (That's why the cake was boxed—who wants to wake up with cake smeared on their pillowcases?) These little boxes are still available from cake supply companies and can even be marked with the couple's initials. If the custom intrigues you,

---

CAKE TOPPERS

The little plastic bride and groom figurines of old may be what come to mind, but times and trends change. The current fashion is a delicate cascade from the highest tier down of fresh, silk, buttercream, or pastillage flowers and ivy or ribbons—or some combination thereof. Or, if bling is your thing, top the cake with your initials created from crystals.

Before you invest in a personalized cake topper, consider the entire cake design. A tiny model of the car you drove on your first date, for example, may detract from an elegant-looking cake, but a miniature Eiffel Tower recalling the proposal in Paris could be just right. Inform your baker of your preferences in advance.

or is part of wedding tradition in your area, ask your baker if he can provide the boxed fruitcake. Baking the cake and packaging it yourself could also be a fun DIY project.

Like many wedding traditions, the groom's cake has gotten an update. Today, the cake is more likely to be the groom's favorite—chocolate, carrot, poppy seed—

or decorated to reflect his interests—say, football, golf, or music. (Red velvet armadillo, anyone?) Often, the bride organizes the cake as a surprise for the groom. The cake can be presented and served separately at the reception, but that may be cake overload. Instead, it could be the featured dessert at the bachelor dinner, the rehearsal dinner, or a next-day brunch.

THE ULTIMATE BRIDE'S CAKE

Lizzie has some good friends who were doing their own home wedding on a shoestring. Many family and friends offered to help out, in the Vermont community barn-raising tradition. Lizzie volunteered to make the cake, a giant bride's cake to be exact.

For those of you who don't know, bride's cake is also known as icebox cake or Famous Chocolate Wafer Refrigerator Roll. It's made exclusively with Nabisco's Famous Chocolate wafers—thin, not-too-sweet cookies—and whipped cream with a touch of vanilla. It was a staple dessert when our mom was growing up and was so easy to make that, as the saying went, "even a new bride could do it!" And it is: Layer the cookies with the vanilla-flavored whipped cream into small stacked sandwiches about six cookies high. Then, on a platter, lay the stacks on their side and connect them end-to-end making longer rows, ultimately forming any shape you like and ice all over with the remaining whipped cream. Refrigerate for at least four hours, slice, and serve. Somehow the cookies absorb the cream, turning into "cake," and the whole thing is sinfully delicious.

The wedding cake Lizzie made used multiple stacks to make a four-tiered square cake. It was a huge

hit—as impressive as any wedding cake—and there wasn't a speck left at the end of the evening.

FAMOUS CHOCOLATE REFRIGERATOR ROLL

Serves 4–6. Can be multiplied as many times as needed.

1 teaspoon vanilla

2 cups whipping cream (do not substitute artificial whipped cream from a tub or spray can)

1 9-ounce package Nabisco Famous Chocolate Wafers

Add the vanilla to the cream in a medium bowl.

Beat together the cream and vanilla with a mixer on high speed until stiff peaks form.

Spread 1½ teaspoons whipped cream onto each wafer. Stack and then stand on edge and arrange together in any form you like on a platter. Frost with remaining whipped cream.

Refrigerate for 4 hours. Keep refrigerated until served or until cake cutting. To serve, cut into diagonal slices.

PART SEVEN

YOUR WEDDING DAY

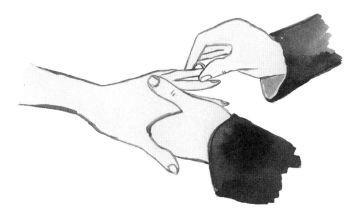

CHAPTER 24

THE WEDDING REHEARSAL

Most likely, you scheduled the rehearsal when you first met with your officiant or booked the venue where the ceremony will be held. Generally, the rehearsal takes place the day or evening before the wedding and takes 1–1½ hours, depending on the number of elements and complexity of your ceremony. This chapter will walk you through a few key things to know about the rehearsal, and Chapter 25, page 329, gives an overview of the general order of the ceremony, from guest arrival and seating, right through the recessional and optional postceremony receiving line. It's a good idea to read it through a few times, both when you are planning your ceremony and just before the rehearsal as a refresher. It's a lot to remember, not just for the couple but for their wedding party and parents as well. Fear not, those performing your ceremony are usually old hands and will help guide you through.

What to Expect from Your Rehearsal

WHO ATTENDS?

- The bride and groom and their officiant, the wedding party, and the bride's parents. While the groom's parents don't usually have a role that needs practicing, they may like to attend as well.

- Any children in the ceremony, accompanied by their parents

- Readers or others with an honor role that needs instruction or practice

- The organist or musicians

- The wedding consultant, if one has been hired. The consultant can help instruct the groomsmen and ushers regarding seating and other duties, line up the wedding party for the processional, and guide their spacing and pace.

WHAT SHOULD YOU WEAR?

- In a house of worship, rehearsal participants should dress in a manner that respects the venue. That means no shorts or jeans or low-cut blouses. In some cases it also means no bare arms or that head coverings are required.

- At a secular location, clothing might be more casual. If the rehearsal dinner follows immediately after, participants wear their dinner clothes to the rehearsal.

❖ This is the time to instruct ushers or groomsmen on the seating order (best to give them a written list); what to do with pew cards, if used; and for them to practice escorting guests to their seats. Since they are the first people your guests see, they should be confident when doing so. Have them practice giving an arm to a female guest or elderly gentleman and show them how to remove and reattach pew ribbons. (See also Chapter 25, page 332.)

❖ In the rare case that an aisle runner is being used, the groomsmen or ushers will practice rolling it out. This occurs after the bride's mother is seated.

❖ The order of the procession is established and pace and spacing is practiced in time to the music. This may take two or three tries until everyone is comfortable. Bridesmaids mime holding their bouquets (tissue paper bouquets can be good props), and the flower girl mimes scattering petals, if that's her job.

❖ Everyone lines up at the altar, chancel, chuppah, or dais, and adjustments are made so that the group looks comfortably spaced and symmetrical.

❖ The officiant reviews the order of service. This includes:

• Instructing the maid of honor when to take the bride's bouquet and discretely adjust her train.

• Instructing the best man (and maid of honor) when to give the wedding rings to the officiant. If the rings are pinned to a pillow, it's a good idea to practice unpinning them.

DON'T FORGET THE "THANK YOU"

Before everyone departs for the rehearsal dinner, take a moment to thank your team sincerely for their hard work, good humor, and support.

• Explaining when the bride's veil is turned back and who will do so.

• The couple doesn't say their responses or vows at the rehearsal. (They should practice them, out loud, on their own.) It's a good idea for them to recite or read something else aloud to adjust tone and volume. If there isn't a microphone, they may need to practice projecting so the audience can hear them.

❖ The cue for the recessional is reviewed, as is the pairing up of the bridesmaids and ushers. The bride and groom set the pace, and the others follow at a natural walk.

❖ Ushers or groomsmen then return to remove pew ribbons and lead guests out of their rows.

Last-Minute Instructions

The wedding rehearsal is often the last time you'll have your team assembled in one place before the wedding. Take advantage of this time and their focus to review schedules and duties for the big day. While you may have made these lists and emailed or texted them to the appropriate parties ahead of time, bring printed copies just in case. Here are some things to review:

- Give a general reminder to turn off electronic devices when arriving at the ceremony site.

- Review the wedding day schedule, including what time to be ready for photos or the ceremony and a general rundown of the day.

- Review the floral delivery schedule. The wedding party will need to know where and when their bouquets and boutonnieres will be delivered.

- Review special assignments:

  - Make sure a groomsman or usher is assigned to deliver any corsages or boutonnieres for special guests such as grandparents and readers and that he has a list.

- Assign the person who will make any announcements about phones, photos, and posts before the start of the ceremony.

- Hand out reserved seating charts and lists of assigned escort duties to ushers/groomsmen.

- Review who any point people are, such as who will be the liaison(s) with the site manager, caterer, bandleader or DJ, and photographer.

- Hand out the photo schedule for the wedding day. Deliver schedules to grandparents and other relatives at the rehearsal dinner so they know when to be available.

- If you're having a receiving line, identify the participants and let them know where and when it will start.

SAMPLE WEDDING DAY TIMELINE

(Hours Before / After the Ceremony)

	-7:00	Hair and makeup for bride and bridesmaids
Bouquet, etc. deliveries for bridal party	-4:00	Bridal party dresses
Photographer arrives		
	-3:00	Photos of bride/groom getting ready
	-2:00	Bridal party leaves for ceremony site
Bouquet, etc. delivery to ceremony		
	-1:30	Bridal party arrives for pictures at ceremony site
Ceremony musicians set up	-1:00	
	-:30	Guests arrive
Reception musicians set up	0	Ceremony starts
	+:45	Ceremony ends
		(Photos/receiving line/travel)
	+1:15	Reception begins
		(Cocktail hour/photos/receiving line)
	+2:15	Opening activities
		(Announce bride and groom/first dances/cake cutting)
	+2:30	Meal service
		(Blessing/Toasts/Table visiting)
	+3:30	Dancing
		(First dances/table visiting/cake cutting)
	+4:45	Closing activities
		(Bouquet toss, garter toss)
	+5:00	Reception ends
		Bride and groom depart

Plan on:

30–45 minutes per bridesmaid for hair

30–45 minutes per bridesmaid for makeup

1–1½ hrs for bride's hair

1 hour for bride's makeup

30 minutes to 1 hour for photographer set up

30 minutes to 1 hour for musician set up at venue

1 hour for getting ready photos

1 hour "first look" photos

1–1½ hours for family, wedding party, and couple photos

30–45 minutes for receiving line

5 minutes per table for table visits

10–15 minutes for toasts

10 minutes for first dances

10 minutes for cake cutting

10 minutes for bouquet/garter toss

CHAPTER 25

AT THE WEDDING CEREMONY

After so many weeks and months of planning and preparation, your day has finally arrived! What couple doesn't look forward to a happy celebration with family and friends? This is what all of your hard work and preparation was for, and now you get to live it.

Are glitches still possible? Of course, though at this point it's all about how you handle them. Your mood will set the tone for the day, and reacting to anything unexpected with grace and acceptance will help others to do the same—turning a table arrangement into a bridesmaid's bouquet when the florist's delivery was one short; drafting a friend to stand in when the best man fell ill at the last moment; arriving at the reception in an usher's old VW Beetle because the rented limo broke down on the expressway.

As the hour approaches, take a deep breath and relax. So many couples say this day goes by in blur, so throughout your day take a moment or two to say to yourself, "This is really happening!" The day is yours to savor . . .

Getting Ready

The Bride and Her Attendants

Dressing. This is the magical transformation from single woman to bride, when everything about her suddenly becomes perfect and radiant. The bride generally dresses at home, and if space permits, her attendants dress there as well. Alternatively, many ceremony sites offer "getting ready" rooms where the bridal party can dress for the wedding, or if the wedding party is staying at a nearby hotel, the bride may join them there to dress for her wedding.

You'll want this to be a relaxed, happy, stress-free start to your wedding day. Schedule enough time for a shower or bath, hair and makeup, and to dress so that everyone is ready and can get together at least an hour before it's time to leave for the ceremony. If you are planning on having a professional hairdresser and makeup artist on hand to help prepare the bridal party for the wedding, be sure to schedule enough time for them so no one feels rushed. Stress might take a toll on that bridal glow.

Once you're dressed, your mom and maid or matron of honor can help with the finishing touches. Your maid of honor and bridesmaids check that you are wearing something old, something new, something borrowed, something blue (and, to finish the rhyme, "a silver sixpence in her shoe").

Bouquets. Bouquets will be delivered to dressing sites or the ceremony site, according to the arrangements made with the florist. Treat them carefully so they're in prime condition for the ceremony and for photos.

Photographs. Pictures of the waiting wedding dress, the bride and her attendants getting ready, and the bride's mother helping her with finishing touches are all lovely wedding day preparation photographs. You could have similar photos of the groom, too. Work out the schedule so the photographer has time to take these pictures and still get to the ceremony site in advance of guests to catch them arriving and set up for ceremony shots.

Transportation. The bride usually rides with her father. The bridesmaids travel together; the bride's mother accompanies them or any children who are in the wedding party and/or the bride's children from a previous marriage. If the groom has children from a previous mar-

---

MAID OF HONOR'S WEDDING DAY EMERGENCY KIT

Help your bride with this handy survival kit for the wedding day:

- Needle, prethreaded with color matching the bride's dress
- Small scissors
- Pins
- Double-sided tape
- Hairbrush or comb
- Hairpins or tiny clips
- Hairspray
- Makeup for touch-ups: concealer, bronzer, blush, lipstick/gloss, mascara, eyeliner
- Oil-blot sheets
- Tide To Go stick (or similar stain remover)

- Nail file
- Nail polish for touch-up
- Compact mirror
- Tweezers
- Deodorant
- Baby powder
- Hand lotion
- Band-Aids for blisters
- Tissues
- Aspirin/acetaminophen/ibuprofen
- Mints
- Bottle of water
- Any special requests from the bride, such as her favorite perfume

riage, they are taken care of by the groom's parents or other family members. The flower girl and ring bearer ride to the ceremony with the bride's mother if their parents don't take them directly to the ceremony site.

The Groom and Best Man

Dressing. Like the bride, the groom should be dressed and ready to go at least an hour before the ceremony. He usually spends this last hour with his best man. They should arrive at the ceremony site *at least* half an hour before the ceremony is scheduled to start. Once there, the best man drops the groom off in a private room, such as the vestry or officiant's study and retrieves his and the groom's boutonnieres. Returning to the groom, they help each other pin on their boutonnieres. The best man waits with the groom until the signal comes that the ceremony is about to begin.

The Groomsmen and Ushers Arrive

Arrival. The ushers should arrive at the ceremony site about an hour before the ceremony is scheduled to begin. Generally, they're responsible for their own

PINNING ON THE BOUTONNIERE

Contrary to what its name implies, the boutonniere (French for "buttonhole") doesn't go through the buttonhole of the lapel. Instead, pin it just above the buttonhole, with the stem down.

1. Push the pin through the left lapel from the back.

2. Weave it through the wide base of the boutonniere, where the flowers are gathered and wrapped.

3. Push the pin back through the lapel.

The pin, even one with a pearl head, shouldn't show at all, and the point is tucked safely behind the lapel.

transportation, but a head usher or groomsman might organize group transportation to the ceremony and then to the reception.

Flowers. The groomsmen's boutonnieres are usually delivered to the ceremony site. Ushers or groomsmen are also responsible for presenting corsages to mothers, grandmothers, and any special friends helping out. The florist should provide a list indicating who receives which flowers but it's a good idea for the bride to give a duplicate list to the head usher, just in case.

General Duties. The ushers and/or groomsmen are responsible for all the front of the house duties: seeing that the ceremony site is ready; greeting and escorting guests to their seats; handling late arrivals; and doing everything to ensure guests are comfortable and the ceremony runs smoothly. At the end of the ceremony, they tidy up the site and are generally helpful in assisting guests to get to the reception. In particular, their duties cover:

- **The seating plan.** The ushers make sure that everyone gets a seat and that special guests get to their assigned seats. The bride and groom should give a copy of their seating plan to the groomsmen or head usher a few days in advance so they can familiarize themselves with it. Ushers will have practiced seating the grandparents and parents of the bride and groom at the wedding rehearsal the day before.

- **Programs.** Ushers hand them to guests as they seat them; however, this job can also be given to children related to the bride and groom who don't have another role in the ceremony or anyone else on hand to help.

- **Last-minute details.** Ushers make a final check before the processional begins. If the room is stuffy or hot, they can open windows or adjust the heat or air-conditioning. They should familiarize themselves with the location of restrooms, should a guest ask.

- **After the ceremony.** Ushers are responsible for a general tidy-up of the site—picking up extra programs, closing windows, removing pew ribbons. They're also available to give assistance to elderly guests or those with a disability and to provide directions to the reception site.

DOUBLE DUTY

Groomsmen may perform the duties of ushers, but ushers aren't necessarily groomsmen. The title is sometimes used interchangeably, and that can be confusing. At most small- to medium-sized weddings, the groomsmen perform ushering duties, escorting guests to their seats and laying the aisle runner if one is used. Then they switch gears and take on the wedding attendant role of groomsmen, walking in the procession and standing with the couple during the ceremony.

At larger weddings, male friends or relatives of the couple who aren't members of the wedding party may be asked to usher. They don't necessarily wear the same attire as the groomsmen, but they do wear a boutonniere to designate their status. They do most of the escorting and are responsible for rolling out (and rolling up) the aisle runner, if used, but they don't walk in the processional or stand with the couple at the ceremony. Instead, they sit with the other guests. During the ceremony, they seat latecomers or assist guests as needed. If your groomsmen are doubling as ushers, consider appointing a male friend to take over ushering duties once the groomsmen start the processional. (See also Chapter 6, page 79.)

The Guests Arrive

Greeting Guests. On a nice day, if the couple's parents arrive early and are so inclined, they may want to greet guests for a while outside the ceremony site as they arrive. Their presence is welcoming and lends a personal note to the start of the wedding festivities.

They should keep conversations warm but brief and encourage guests to enter and be seated.

Escorting Guests. The ushers or groomsmen show all guests to their places. Older guests may request to sit on the bride's side (the left) or the groom's side (the right). At a Jewish wedding, the bride's side is the right, because she stands to the right under the chuppah. It was customary for the family and guests of each family to support "their person." If a guest doesn't have a preference, the ushers should try to keep the seating divided evenly between the two sides. Same-sex couples don't have a "groom's side" and "bride's side" so at the rehearsal choose who will stand on which side and offer guests who have a preference "Will's side" or "Dave's side."

In taking guests to their seats, an usher offers his crooked *right* arm for the women guests to hold on to while their escorts walk behind them. Or the usher may lead a couple to their seats. When a single male guest is escorted alone, the usher walks on his left.

Ushers don't need to be somber. This is a happy occasion so they should smile warmly and exchange a few quiet remarks as they escort the guests.

PEW CARDS

Pew cards alert the ushers that the recipients are seated in designated front pews. They're usually sent to close relatives, such as grandparents, or others close to the couple or their families, such as godparents or longtime friends. Recipients present them to the ushers upon arrival. Determine ahead of time if certain ushers will escort particular guests with pew cards. For example, if the groom's brother is ushering, he would escort his grandmother and mother, just as the bride's brother would escort his own grandmother and mother.

Seating Family

Seating parents. The parents of the bride always sit in the first pew or row on the left, facing where the ceremony will take place; the groom's parents sit in the first row on the right. If there are two aisles, the audience sits in the center section. The bride's parents sit on the left side of the center section and the groom's parents on the right. At a Jewish wedding, the couple's parents stand with them under the chuppah.

Seating widowed parents. The widowed parent of either the bride or the groom may prefer to have someone by their side during the ceremony. This is perfectly correct, and the companion is treated as an honored guest.

Seating immediate family. Behind the front pews, several pews on either side of the center aisle are reserved for the immediate families of the couple. These people may have been sent pew cards to show their usher, or the usher may keep a list of guests to be seated in the first few pews. Reserved pews are usually marked in some way.

SEATING FAMILY

DIVORCED PARENTS	BRIDE'S FAMILY	AISLE	GROOM'S FAMILY	DIVORCED PARENTS
Bride's mother (stepfather)	Bride's parents		Groom's parents	Groom's mother (stepfather)
Bride's siblings / bride's mother's parents	Siblings / grandparents		Siblings / grandparents	Groom's siblings / groom's mother's parents
Aunts, uncles, their spouses on bride's mother's side	Aunts, uncles, their spouses		Aunts, uncles, their spouses	Aunts, uncles, their spouses on groom's mother's side
Bride's father (stepmother)	More family / special guests of bride		More family / special guests of groom	Groom's father (stepmother)
Bride's father's parents				Groom's father's parents
Aunts, uncles, their spouses on bride's father's side				Aunts, uncles, their spouses on groom's father's side
More family / special guests of bride				More family / special guests of groom

Seating parents who are divorced. When either the bride's or groom's parents are divorced, the seating needs to be planned carefully and the ushers need clear instructions. Divorced parents may or may not get along, or the bride may be close to one parent and not the other. Tact and diplomacy will be critical to keep the peace.

In the lucky event that all the parties get along, there's no reason why divorced parents can't share the front row. But when there is strain or outright bit-terness, it's necessary to use a careful, well-thought-out alternative plan that keeps the parties separated.

When divorced parents sit separately (using the bride's parents as an example), follow this order:

- The bride's mother (and stepfather if she has remarried) sits in the front row.

- Members of her mother's immediate family—the bride's grandparents, any siblings who aren't atten-dants, and aunts, uncles, and their spouses—sit immediately behind in the next one or two rows.

- The bride's father, after escorting his daughter down the aisle and presenting her to her groom, sits in the next row behind the bride's mother's family—usually the third or fourth—with his wife, if remarried, and their family members. This protocol is followed even if the bride's father is hosting the wedding.

When the groom's parents are divorced, they're seated in the same manner: The groom's mother, accompanied by close members of her family, sits in the first row (or rows) on the right side of the aisle. The groom's father and family sit in the next rows behind

the groom's mother's family. (For more complicated family dynamics, such as when the bride is estranged from her mother or there is rancor between former and current spouses, see Chapter 1, page 10)

The Ceremony

While this section describes the traditional Christian order of seating, processional, ceremony, and recessional, many secular weddings use the same format. (For Jewish ceremonies, see page 340.)

Places, Everyone

The guests have arrived and been shown to their seats and it's about two minutes before the starting time on the invitation. Before the procession begins, the ushers seat the immediate family of the bride and groom, a signal that the wedding is about to begin.

The grandparents are seated. Grandparents may be seated when they arrive (a good idea if they would get tired waiting for the ceremony to begin) or escorted to their seats just before the groom's parents. If this is the case, escort the groom's grandparents to their seats, followed by the bride's grandparents.

The groom's parents enter. The groom's mother and father are the next to the last people to be seated. The groom's mother may be ushered by one of her sons or the head usher, and the groom's father follows them. Once they're seated, the bride's mother is escorted to her seat.

The bride's mother enters. This is the signal that the wedding processional is about to begin. The mother of the bride is escorted by a son, brother, or the head

---

WHICH DAD?

Q: I have a problem deciding who should walk me down the aisle. Naturally, my father would be the logical choice, but my stepfather helped raise me and is an important part of my life. What do I do?

A: Choosing between parents and stepparents may be one of the hardest decisions a bride has to make. If they're cordial to each other, you could ask both to escort you down the aisle, one on either side. Or your biological father could walk you halfway and meet your stepfather, who then escorts you to the altar. If neither of these solves your dilemma, you could ask your mother to escort you, or choose to walk alone.

Whatever you decide, you'll need to discuss this with those involved well in advance of the ceremony. It wouldn't be fair and most likely would be hurtful to spring this news in public at the wedding rehearsal. Better to let everyone have time to adjust to and accept your choice.

usher. After she is taken to her place, no guest may be seated from the center aisle. If guests arrive after the bride's mother is seated, they must stand in the back, go to the balcony, or slip into a row from the side aisles. The ushers may assist them.

The aisle runner is unrolled. Aisle runners aren't used that often anymore, but if one is, here's how: Once the bride's mother is seated, two ushers pick up the runner, place it at the head of the aisle (near the altar or dais), and carefully unroll it back to the rear.

The countdown begins. Minutes before the wedding is to start, the bride and her father (or other escort) arrive or step out from the waiting area, and the procession forms in the vestibule or entrance at the back. As soon as the attendants have taken their places, a signal is given—usually the opening bars of the processional music—and the officiant enters.

The groom and the best man take their places at the right side of the head of the aisle or, in some churches, at the top of the steps to the chancel. The best man stands to the groom's left and slightly behind him, and they both face the guests. As soon as they take their places, the procession begins.

The Traditional Processional

1. The groomsmen lead the procession, walking two by two, the shortest men first. Junior groomsmen follow the adults.

2. Junior bridesmaids come next.

3. The bridesmaids follow, walking in pairs or singly. The space between each couple or individ-

ual should be even and approximately four paces long. A slow, natural walk is more graceful than the old-fashioned hesitation step.

4. The maid or matron of honor follows the bridesmaids.

5. The ring bearer comes next, followed by the flower girl. She finishes walking down the aisle before the bride and her father begin.

6. The music might change, say to the "Wedding March," the guests stand, and the bride enters on her father or other special person's right, her left arm looped through his (or her) right arm, and they proceed down the aisle.

MARCHING TO A DIFFERENT DRUMMER

There are many variations to the traditional processional, some made by practical necessity and some by creative whimsy. Groomsmen could escort the bridesmaids or enter with the groom and best man from a side door. The entire wedding party could be preceded by the family dogs in beribboned collars. And there's a world of music beyond the wedding march.

However you choose to make your entrance, it should fit with the venue and let the bride—and possibly the groom—star. Two-year-olds dressed to the nines and pulling a wagon may be adorable, but the "awww" factor—and possible mishaps—could distract from the bride's entrance. And what if Rover starts acting more like the dog he is than as an escort? Think through the real-life possibilities that could result from trying to re-create an adorable wedding photograph from your favorite magazine or website.

At the Altar or Dais

The arrangement of the attendants at the altar or dais varies. The groomsmen may divide and stand on either side, as may the bridesmaids, or the groomsmen may line up on one side and the bridesmaids on the other. You and your officiant will help determine what looks best during the rehearsal.

- The maid of honor stands to the bride's left and below or behind her.

- The best man remains in the same position, but because he turned to face the altar as the bride and her father arrived, he should now be on the groom's right.

- Usually, the flower girl stands next to the maid of honor, while the ring bearer stands next to the best man. (Children too young to stand for the entire ceremony sit with their parents who should be seated close by so the children can join them.)

The Ceremony

1. When the bride reaches the groom's side, she lets go of her father's arm, transfers her flowers to her left arm, and gives her right hand to her groom. He puts it through his left arm, and her hand rests near his elbow. They may also stand hand in hand or merely side by side. The officiant faces them.

2. Just before "giving" her to her groom, her father lifts her veil (if she's wearing one that covers her face), gives her a kiss, and either replaces the veil or not, depending on the couple's preference.

3. The bride's father remains by her side or a step or two behind until the officiant says, "Who will support and bless this marriage?" or "Who represents the families in blessing this marriage?" The bride's father says, "Her mother and I do," or her parents together say, "We do." He then turns and takes his seat.

4. If there are children from the bride or groom's previous marriage, the officiant could ask, "Who will support this new family with their love and prayers?" In this instance, the bride, groom, children, and often the guests answer together, "We do."

5. Just before the bride receives her wedding ring, she hands her flowers to her maid of honor. The bride's bouquet is returned to her just before the recessional.

6. At the conclusion of the ceremony, the officiant may say, "I now pronounce you husband and wife" or, for gay and lesbian couples, "I now pronounce you married" or "I pronounce you partners for life."

SHARING THE PEACE

When communion is offered at a Christian wedding, the minister or priest will often ask everyone to reach out and share a message of peace with one another, by turning to the congregation and saying, "Peace be with you." At this time, and especially if the guests are few in number, the wedding party may move out into the congregation, offering handshakes, hugs, and kisses to guests. It is only a small break in the ceremony, but it gives the bride and groom the opportunity to connect with their guests.

---

7. If the bride has remained veiled throughout the ceremony, the groom now lifts her veil.

8. The bride and groom kiss. In some ceremonies, the officiant announces the newly married couple by name.

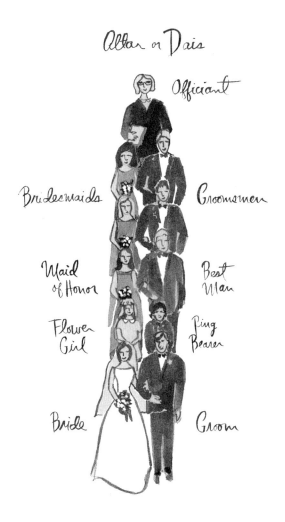

Altar or Dais

Officiant

Bridesmaids

Groomsmen

Maid of Honor

Best Man

Flower Girl

Ring Bearer

Bride

Groom

"YOU MAY KISS THE BRIDE"

Why does a wedding ceremony end with a kiss? A kiss was long believed to be the medium for the exchange of spirits, where a part of the bride's soul joined the groom's soul, and vice versa, truly uniting the couple as one. In some cultures, a kiss literally seals the wedding contract, whereas in others a kiss is not required. Most people just think of it as an expression of love.

The Recessional

1. The maid or matron of honor hands back the bouquet to the bride and straightens her gown and train. The bride and groom turn, she loops her left arm through his right, and they head up the aisle.

2. The flower girl and ring bearer walk together behind the bride and groom, followed by the maid of honor and the best man.

3. The other attendants step forward and follow behind the couple either singly or side by side, depending on their number. They may walk together as they entered: groomsmen with one another and bridesmaids together, or bridesmaids may pair up with groomsmen (in the event of an uneven number, one bridesmaid or groomsman either walks alone or three walk together). Each member of the wedding party should know how to fall in line, since the recessional will have been practiced during the rehearsal.

4. Family and guests follow the processional row by row, starting with those in the front rows.

SIGNING THE PAPERS

At some point during the proceedings, the bride and groom must sign their wedding papers, witnessed by the maid of honor and best man. If this hasn't been done before the ceremony, then it should be done before they leave for the reception.

The Jewish Wedding Ceremony

This section details the order for a traditional Jewish ceremony.

Before the Procession

The wedding ceremony begins in private, with the signing of the *ketubah*, or marriage contract, and may be followed by a *bedeken*, or veiling ceremony.

The Conservative or Traditional Jewish Processional

The public ceremony begins with the procession to the chuppah. Both parents accompany their children. The bride's parents don't "give her away"; rather, the two families join when their children marry.

1. The rabbi and the cantor lead the traditional Jewish processional.

2. The groom's attendants—groomsmen, then best man—follow.

3. Then the groom is escorted by his parents—his father on his left and his mother on his right.

4. The bridesmaids process, followed by the maid of honor.

5. The bride is escorted by her parents—her father on her left and her mother on her right.

6. The bride and groom's grandparents may also be included. They follow the rabbi and cantor and are seated in the front rows as the rest of the party approaches the ceremony area.

Under the Chuppah

The bride, groom, their parents, maid of honor and best man, and perhaps the rest of the wedding party gather under the chuppah. At the rehearsal, the rabbi will determine how many of the wedding party can be accommodated under the chuppah. The bride stands to her groom's right. The first of two parts of the wedding ceremony begins with the betrothal, or *erusin*.

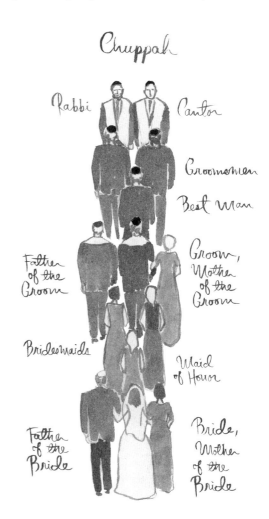

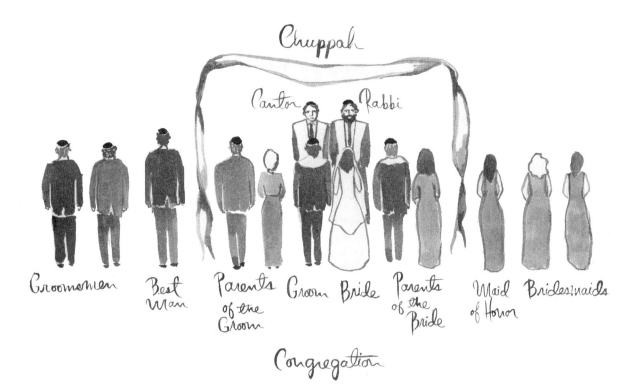

1. The rabbi recites a blessing.

2. The bride and groom drink from the same cup of wine.

3. The groom places the wedding ring on the bride's right forefinger.

4. The *ketubah* is read and presented to the couple, concluding the betrothal ceremony.

The second part is the actual wedding ceremony, or *nisuin*.

1. It begins with the chanting of *Sheva Brachot*, or Seven Blessings.

2. At the end of the blessings, the couple drinks from a second cup of wine. At this point, the bride may give the groom a ring.

3. The ceremony concludes when the groom breaks a glass with his foot and the entire congregation shouts "Mazel tov!"—"congratulations" or "good luck"—and the celebrating begins.

The Recessional

The recessional is led by the newlyweds, followed by the bride's parents, groom's parents, wedding party (men and women in pairs), the rabbi, and finally the cantor. Women are on the men's right.

After the Recessional

1. Immediately after the ceremony, the bride and groom retire alone for the traditional *yichud*, or seclusion, to enjoy the first moments of their new life together and to share the first bites of food as a married couple.

2. Then the *simcha*, or celebration and reception begins. (For more on these traditions, see Chapter 15, page 198.)

The Celebration Continues
Photographs and Videos

If you didn't have your wedding photos taken prior to the ceremony, now is the time to take pictures. If certain aspects of the ceremony need to be re-created for the photographer, the wedding party reenters the building so pictures can be taken *as quickly as possible*. The guests either wait, taking their cue from the parents, or depart for the reception if it's suggested they do so. (For more on scheduling photographs, see Chapter 22, page 305.)

Ceremony Receiving Line

When a receiving line isn't planned for the reception, the bride and groom, their parents, and the maid of honor (and sometimes the bridesmaids) may form one and greet guests as they exit the ceremony site.

If either the bride or the groom has children, they may want to have them stand in the receiving line, too, as a part of the new family. The idea is for all guests to have a chance to greet the families and congratulate the couple. Having a receiving line at the ceremony site encourages guests to keep greetings and comments short, so they don't hold up the rest of the guests still waiting to exit.

Transportation to the Reception Site

Cars taking the wedding party to the reception should be waiting near the entrance of the ceremony site. The bride and groom are helped into the first car by the best man and are the first to leave for the reception. The bride's parents ride together, and the maid or matron of honor and bridesmaids depart in the same cars in which they arrived. Groomsmen and ushers are responsible for their own transportation unless group transport has been arranged. The flower girl and ring bearer may travel with their parents or they may ride with either the bride's parents or the bridal party.

CHAPTER 26

AT THE RECEPTION

No matter how large or how small, your reception is a celebration, and you and your family are the hosts. This is the time for all the planning details to melt into the background and for you to turn your focus to enjoying the company of your guests. You will bask in congratulations and toasts and in turn will set a welcoming tone and thank each person for coming. Make sure that you greet all your guests, either with a receiving line or by visiting each table to let each guest know how happy and pleased you are that they are there to celebrate with you.

In order for you to enjoy the moment, there's lots to schedule in advance: greeting guests, a reasonable amount of time for food and drink, toasts, dancing, cake cutting, and the bouquet and garter toss. You'll want to keep the reception flowing and leave people feeling that they weren't rushed but weren't stuck at a long, drawn-out affair, either. Map out a timetable of your reception, and then designate a person to be in charge of keeping things moving along on the big day. This could be your wedding coordinator; the bandleader, DJ, or MC; or even the bride's dad or the best man.

From Here to There

One of the trickiest timing elements of the wedding day is the lag time between the ceremony and the reception. The reception hosts and the bridal couple should get to the reception as soon as possible. Since wedding photographs are the typical delay culprit, time the photo session so that the shots including parents, other family members, and attendants are taken first. While the bride and groom are having their photos taken, family and attendants can proceed to the reception to greet and entertain guests.

If there's a long interval between the arrival of guests and the wedding party, arrange to have special helpers at the reception site ready to greet guests, make introductions, and see that guests are offered drinks and hors d'oeuvres. It's nice to have music (live or recorded) to set the mood. Guests do expect some delay between the ceremony and the start of the reception. Begin the cocktail hour or start serving refreshments within thirty to forty-five minutes after the end of the ceremony at the latest. Any longer is excessive unless your invitation indicated a later starting time for the reception.

Greeting Your Guests

When mapping out the schedule for your wedding day, be sure to plan time to be available for all your guests, to greet them and thank them for attending. Generally, there are two options to accomplish this gracefully. You can visit each table and chat with your guests during mealtime, or you can have a traditional receiving line, either at the conclusion of the ceremony, as noted in the previous chapter, or at the reception. Your decision will be structured to some degree by the style of your reception and the amount of time you have available to you. Both a receiving line and table visits are equally correct, and you are free to choose what is most practical and comfortable for you.

We'll never forget this letter we received from a bride's aunt, who had traveled 600 miles to attend her niece's wedding:

I recently attended my niece's wedding and never got a chance to meet her new husband or wish them well. They spent ninety minutes taking pictures following the ceremony and then went directly to their seats at the bridal table. After dinner, there were many toasts, and then the couple took to the dance floor without any welcome to their guests. After four hours, I left with my ninety-three-year-old mother, the bride's grandmother, without even a "hello" to either of us from my niece.

This sad story illustrates why it is so important to take the time to greet your guests. In the long run, most guests won't remember the color of the table-cloths or even the menu. What they will remember is their reason for being there in the first place: the affection they have for the marrying couple.

Table Visits

Today, many couples forgo the formal receiving line and opt to visit each table instead. It's certainly a more relaxed and personal way to spend time with guests, allowing for conversation that goes beyond the for-mulaic greetings exchanged in a receiving line. This approach works best when a sit-down meal is planned because it guarantees that all your guests will be available and in the same spot. It is also a smart move when there wouldn't be enough time to schedule both wedding photos and a receiving line.

It will take about five minutes per table to visit and chat. So, for a wedding with one hundred guests (which translates to twelve tables of approximately eight guests each) plan on a full hour. Sprinkle the visits during the different courses—first course, entrée, and dessert. (You'll want to be sure that you have time to enjoy the meal, too!)

As the guests of honor, and possibly the hosts as well, take a moment to publicly welcome and acknowledge your guests and to thank them for being with you on your wedding day either after you make your entrance to the reception or during the toasts. It's a small gesture, but it does so much to show your appreciation for the kindness and affection of friends and family.

The Etiquette of the Receiving Line

A receiving line is a traditional and *efficient* way for the wedding party to greet guests, either after the ceremony or upon their arrival at the reception. It gets the job done and guarantees that you say hello to all, or almost all, your guests. Even though it's more formal, it doesn't mean that it has to be somber. There is plenty of joy and laughter in the greetings, even if they are kept short.

When is a receiving line recommended? It's helpful to have a receiving line for a larger wedding, say seventy-five or more guests, or when you are not serving a seated meal during your reception. It's an effective way to greet and thank your guests since you may not have the chance to speak personally with everyone during the course of a stand-up cocktail reception, for example.

When is it best not to have one? If the combination of picture taking and receiving line means guests could be left hanging for an hour or more with little to do, it's better to skip it. Just be sure that you speak to each guest at some point during the reception. Also, have the DJ or bandleader introduce the bridal party and the bride's and groom's parents so that guests will know who's who.

WHERE TO PUT THE COCKTAIL?

See that a small table for used glasses, plates, and napkins is placed near the start of the receiving line itself. Guests shouldn't carry food or beverages while greeting the hosts and the wedding party—think how awkward that would make it to shake hands.

Where should it be? When the receiving line is at the reception site, the ideal location is one that flows into the reception area or lets guests have refreshments while they are waiting their turn. If you choose the refreshment option, position a waiter with a tray of beverages where the guests join the line to offer to guests. Waiters could also pass hors d'oeuvres to those waiting to go through the line.

Who stands in the receiving line? Usually the couple, their parent(s), the maid of honor, and possibly the bridesmaids form the line. The basic order is:

- The wedding hosts—traditionally the bride's parents (her mother first, then her father); when the couple host, they can be first, or give that honor to their parents

- The groom's mother and father

- The bride and groom

- The maid or matron of honor

- The bridesmaids

Fathers aren't required to stand in line—they can circulate among the guests—but if one father participates, the other should as well. When there is a large number of bridesmaids, they might take turns in the line a few at a time, or be excused altogether (the maid or matron of honor would remain).

If the receiving line is short, the best man and groomsmen can be included. Sometimes the children of the couple participate, if they're willing and mature enough to greet people. Ushers, flower girls, and ring bearers aren't included, nor are siblings who are not members of the wedding party.

Where do divorced parents stand? Individual situations vary so much that the arrangement should be one that's the most sensible and comfortable for your family. If there's serious discord between parents and stepparents, it may be best to forgo the formal receiving line altogether.

When relations between divorced parents and their current spouses are amicable, they may all be in line—but separated by the other sets(s) of parents to prevent confusion or embarrassment for guests. When all the parents are divorced and remarried, the order can be:

- ❖ Bride's mother and stepfather
- ❖ Groom's mother and stepfather
- ❖ Bride's father and stepmother
- ❖ Grooms father and stepmother

And if this is the case, excuse the bridesmaids—the line is long enough!

How do you greet guests? The trick is to be gracious and brief at the same time! Usually, a guest says his or her name to the first person in line, who, after a very brief exchange, might introduce the guest to the next

Bride Groom

Mother & Father of the Bride   Mother & Father of the Groom   Maid of Honor   Bridesmaids

Pouring the Champagne. At a sit-down reception, Champagne is poured as soon as everyone is seated. At a cocktail reception where guests are either seated at small tables or standing, it's poured and passed after everyone has gone through the receiving line or after the couple has entered the reception and been introduced. If Champagne isn't being served (or some guests don't want any), toasts are then made with whatever beverage guests have in front of them.

person in line if this doesn't keep the next guest in line waiting—and if they are good at remembering names!

Guest 1 extends her hand for shaking and says, "Hi, I'm Tonya Wilkes. It was such a beautiful wedding. Clara looked radiant! Thank you for including me!"

Mother of the bride, shaking hands, responds, "It's lovely to meet you, Tonya, and we're delighted you could be with us today. John (father of the bride), this is Tonya Wilkes, Clara's friend from college."

Obviously, if guest and host know each other, the guest doesn't introduce him or herself. However, if the next person in line doesn't know the guest, it's nice for the person handing off the guest to make a quick introduction when possible.

Toasts

Toasting the happy couple at the wedding reception is one of the event's most cherished traditions. The customary toasting drink is Champagne. It's fine to toast with plain water, but consider offering something more festive for your guests who don't drink alcohol: ginger ale, sparkling water or cider, or fruit spritzers are all great options.

Who gives a toast? Traditionally, the best man gives the first wedding toast to the bridal couple. He attracts the attention of the guests, either from his table or from the microphone, and proposes a toast to the bride and groom. It's completely acceptable for his to be the only one offered. The maid or matron of honor may then take her turn if giving a toast, or she might wait until after others toast. The fathers of the bride and groom may each follow with a toast or speech of their own, welcoming guests and congratulating the newly married couple. It's perfectly fine for mothers to toast as well.

Then, if he wishes, it's the groom's turn to toast his bride, and the bride may reciprocate with a toast to the groom. Both the bride and groom may toast and thank their parents and new parents-in-law. After that, anyone may propose a toast. Typically, more—and longer—toasts are offered the evening before at the rehearsal dinner. Friends should keep their toasts to about a minute at most, which will give family members and other attendants more time to propose their own.

Who stands, who sits? Everyone should rise for the toasts to the newlyweds except the bride and groom, who remain seated. If a toast is directed to the bride only, the groom rises; if it is directed to their parents, both the bride and groom rise. If there is no seating

and everyone is standing, those toasted just smile and say, "Thank you."

When the bride and groom toast together. When making a toast together, the bride and groom don't speak in unison, but rather stand together while one speaks or take turns speaking.

How should the bride and groom respond to a toast? When toasted, the bride and groom don't stand or drink. They smile appreciatively and, when the toast is finished, acknowledge it with a thank-you.

Sample Wedding Reception Toasts

There are entire books devoted to the subject of wedding toasts, so pick one up if you're really struggling with what to say. Don't be intimidated. It's more important for wedding sentiments to be heartfelt than long or eloquent.

BEST MAN OR MAID OR MATRON OF HONOR TO COUPLE

- After a brief speech, a toast is offered, something along the lines of, "To Keisha and Michael—may they enjoy every happiness in their life together."

GROOM TO BRIDE, BRIDE TO GROOM

- "All my life, I've wondered what the woman I'd marry would be like. In my wildest dreams, I never could have imagined she would be as wonderful as Keisha. Please join me in drinking this first toast to my beautiful bride."

- "I'd like you all to join me in a toast to the man who's just made me the happiest woman in the world. To Michael!"

PARENT(S) TO COUPLE

- "We're thrilled you're now a part of our family, and we know that Michael's [Keisha's] life will be blessed and enriched by having you as his [her] wife [husband]. Michael and Keisha, we wish you health, wealth, and lifelong happiness as you set off on your greatest adventure together."

- "As long as I've known Keisha, she's kept the perfect man in her mind's eye. And the first time I met Michael, I knew immediately that she had found him. Kids, you were no doubt meant for each other, and I want to wish you a long and happy life together."

Blessing the Meal

If your reception includes a meal, saying a blessing beforehand is certainly appropriate. Here's a wonderful opportunity to honor a relative or friend by asking him or her to participate. No matter who gives the blessing, you should be sure to ask him or her ahead of time, so that they can prepare. If you are concerned about your guests who aren't religious or are of other faiths, don't be. They can simply lower their heads and remain respectfully silent during the blessing.

Just before the meal service is to begin, the best man, DJ, bandleader, or MC can request everyone's attention. Usually the best man makes a brief introduction; the person you've asked offers the blessing; and then the best man thanks the person, signaling to waiters that they may begin serving and guests may begin eating. At a buffet, when guests may be milling around and waiting in line, start the blessing once everyone is seated with their meal, even though many guests may have already begun eating.

Dancing

Dancing is often an essential element of the reception. Almost every culture has a tradition of joyous dancing at the wedding celebration: the Greek *kalamatiano*, the Jewish hora, and the Italian tarantella. While there are many types of dances and a wide variety of customs, here are a few general guidelines for dancing at the wedding reception:

When does the dancing start? Dancing follows dessert at a seated dinner, but at a buffet reception, it might start after the receiving line or photo session. At an afternoon reception when a meal is served later, the bride and groom might begin the dancing before they go to their table.

Who dances first? The bride and groom dance the first dance together while guests watch and applaud.

What is the second dance? For the traditional "second dance," the bride dances with her father, and the groom dances with his mother. Then the groom's father might dance with the bride, and the groom with his new mother-in-law, or the groom might dance with the maid or matron of honor, and the bride with the best man. At this point, other guests usually join them on the dance floor. The "second dance" is completely optional. Some couples prefer not to have it.

When do the bride and her father and the groom and his mother dance? If there is no prearranged "second dance," at some point during the dancing, the bride and her father usually have a special dance of their own. The groom and his mother may do the same. The bride and groom may want to select special songs in advance for their respective parents. The bride and her father may either dance the entire song alone, or be joined by the bride's mother who dances with the groom and the groom's father who cuts in on the bride's father to dance with the bride. They may change partners halfway through the song and join their respective spouses, and the other guests may join them on the dance floor.

Stepparents and blended families. When family relationships are more complicated, everyone can join the couple after their first dance. The newlyweds should then make a point to dance with all parents and stepparents at some time during the reception.

Traditional Closing Activities

In bygone eras, guests waited for the bride and groom to make their grand departure before leaving. Today, cutting the cake is the signal that guests may take their leave. However, it's much more likely that the bridal couple will see their older guests off and then continue the celebration. As a courtesy to elderly guests and those with young children, consider cutting the cake earlier in the reception so that guests are free to leave when they're ready.

Cutting the Cake

At a seated dinner, the cake is cut just before dessert is served. At buffets or passed-tray receptions, the cake cutting usually takes place nearer the end of the reception. Be sure to give your caterer or site manager and your photographer an approximate time for the cutting. Remember, too, that it takes a while to cut, plate, and serve the cake, so don't leave it till the very end.

Typically, the person acting as MC announces the cake cutting, at which point the bride and groom proceed to the cake table and their attendants gather round. (See also Chapter 23, page 319.)

CUT THE CAKE FIRST!

When the bride and groom cut the cake, it's the time-honored signal that it's okay for guests to say their farewells and depart without appearing rude. While this mainly applies to elderly guests for whom a five- to six-hour stint at a big social event could be tiring, other guests, too, may need to make an early exit.

We know one couple who scheduled the cake cutting after they arrived at the reception and just before their first dance. Their elderly guests—of which there were a number—were then free to enjoy as much of the reception as they wished, and then say their thanks and good-byes when they were ready to leave.

Tossing the Bouquet

Just before the couple leaves the reception, the bride or her maid or matron of honor gathers the bridesmaids and all single women guests together at the foot of a staircase, in the center of the dance floor, or by the door. The bride then turns her back and throws her bouquet over her shoulder. (If she wants to keep and preserve her original bouquet she can throw a "tossing bouquet"; see Chapter 20, page 278.) Tradition has it that whoever catches the bouquet will be the next one married. (By the way, the lucky lady who catches the bouquet gets to take it home.)

Throwing the Garter

In some places, the garter toss is traditional. The bride wears an ornamental garter just below her knee, so the groom can remove it easily. The best man and the groomsmen gather, and the groom throws the garter over his shoulder. According to tradition, the man who catches the garter will be the next to marry. Throwing the garter should never be done in a tasteless or crass way. It would be embarrassing, for both the bride and for the guests.

Both throwing the garter and tossing the bouquet are completely optional activities, and you can do one without doing the other. Or the bride could give her bouquet to the couple married the longest, to her maid of honor or her sister, or to any other special guest. Plan in advance whether or not you'd like to include these traditions, so that your DJ or bandleader will be prepared (or know to skip them).

And You're Off!

The bride and groom may leave still dressed in their wedding clothes, or they may change into casual or travel clothes. If they decide to change at the site, the maid of honor and the best man generally attend to the bride and groom in their separate changing rooms and collect the wedding clothing. At some point, parents and relatives join them for a good-bye.

Sometimes the groomsmen decorate the departure vehicle with "Just Married" written in shaving cream or something similar that is (hopefully) easy to clean and won't damage the paint. When the newlyweds are ready to go, the attendants and guests form a corridor and the happy couple dashes through to a waiting car, limo, boat, plane, or horse-drawn carriage while being showered with bird seed, rose petals, bubbles, or other such biodegradables or, better yet, colorful flags, streamers, or even sparklers (when safe to do so). (See Chapter 25, page 342.) Make sure to have someone take photos or video when you make your grand leap into your new life.

Dancing the Night Away . . .

Many couples don't want their party to end, and the after-party has become part of the reception repertoire, particularly for couples who aren't leaving for their honeymoon right after the reception. All of your guests are invited, but chances are your elderly guests or those with little ones awaiting them at home will say good-bye soon after the customary closing activities, such as the cake cutting, bouquet toss, or send off. Many couples make the traditional departure and then return for more dancing, or head to an alternate venue. If there is no obvious break between reception and after-party, be gracious and unhurried in saying your good-byes to those leaving now. (For more on after-parties, see Chapter 12, page 158.)

CHAPTER 27

AFTER THE WEDDING

Congratulations! You're married! Time to relax and share just how much you enjoyed your wedding. If you're like many couples, you'll be off on your honeymoon, your first of many adventures in your future as a couple. Or you'll be back to normal life and perhaps looking forward to a honeymoon at a later date.

While the majority of wedding-related checklists are behind you, there are still a few details that need your attention in the week following your wedding. It's up to you to make sure postwedding loose ends are taken care of, so that they don't become a burden to anyone else while you are away on your honeymoon. These could include making arrangements for gift deliveries and delegating rental returns, mailing wedding announcements or posting your news on social media, and cleaning and storing wedding clothes. If you are heading out on your honeymoon immediately, many of these duties can be delegated to members of your wedding party and relatives.

It's not all chores after the big day, though. You'll also have your wedding photos or video to look forward to seeing and lots of stories from the wedding to hear and share.

Your Wedding Attire

After all the fuss of being measured and fit for wedding attire, you'll want to see it cared for after the big day. Whether it's a gown destined to be an heirloom or a rental in need of returning, their journeys aren't done yet.

Bridal Attire

Take as much care with your wedding clothing after the event as you did before. Here are some practical ways to store your wedding attire so that it will be preserved for years to come.

Wedding gown. Have an attendant or relative hang your gown up as soon as you take it off. Get it to a professional cleaner who specializes in wedding gowns, particularly in the event of spots or spills. They will clean the gown and put it in a sealed box or container for storage. Store the box or container in a dry place, such as on a high shelf in a closet or in the attic.

Train and veil. Have each cleaned professionally with the wedding gown and stored in the same manner.

Headdress. Any headdress not attached to a veil should be cleaned professionally and placed in a hatbox.

Gloves. Launder cotton gloves. Wrap in acid-free tissue and keep in a box. Have kid or other leather cleaned professionally and returned ready for storage.

Shoes. For cloth shoes, sponge with a mild detergent; when dry, put them away in acid-free tissue in a box. For leather shoes, polish and store. For tough grass stains, have shoes cleaned professionally, no matter what the fabric.

Bouquet. If you plan on saving your bouquet, arrange for your maid or matron of honor or a family member to deliver it to your florist for preserving.

Returning Rental Attire

The best man or the groomsmen individually are responsible for returning their tuxes and any other rentals that have been used. Still, a heads-up reminder to them isn't a bad idea, either at the rehearsal or the next day in a text. Return a rented wedding gown or bridesmaid's dress according to the instructions in the contract. If you're off on your honeymoon, ask your maid of honor or another bridesmaid (or your mom, if it's more practical) to oversee or take care of the returns.

Seven Honeymoon Tips

The honeymoon is the romantic interlude bridging your past and future lives. It's the time to revel in your happiness and recuperate from the hectic planning and activities of the weeks and months before the wedding—and from the big day itself. Here are some tips to help make the honeymoon live up to your romantic expectations—and to create an unforgettable experience.

1. Honey + Moon. In the Middle Ages, the bride and groom drank mead, a fermented drink made with honey (the symbol of fertility, health, and life), for one full cycle of the moon. During this period, the couple stayed hidden from their parents and friends—the mead no doubt loosening their inhibitions and getting the marriage off to an auspicious start. Even if you've been together for quite some time or don't drink alcohol, you can get into the spirit of the honeymoon as a period of treasured bonding between the two of you—a time like no other. If you want to take the tradition literally, make a pact to shut off your smartphones, log off of Facebook, and enjoy a real retreat from the world. If that seems impossible, agree to at least limit your screen time.

2. Plan together. Both of you should be involved in planning the honeymoon. That includes doing the research, meeting with a travel agent, and making reservations. Discuss what type of honeymoon experience you want. A lazy beach retreat? A tour of a foreign country? A week of sky or scuba diving? Make sure you are in agreement. If you dream of biking in Italy, but your new spouse or partner is visualizing cocktails by the pool, aim for something in the middle.

3. Plan ahead. The honeymoon, for many couples, is a top-priority decision—with good reason! Some couples make all of their other wedding decisions around their honeymoon plans. Make the preliminary decisions as early as possible, such as the honeymoon date, location, transportation, accommodations, and length of stay. If you plan to travel outside of the United States, apply for passports as soon as possible if you don't have them— and if you do have them, make sure they are up-to-date (and will be so at the time of the honeymoon).

4. Set a honeymoon budget. Honeymoons need to be planned in advance for budgetary reasons as well. It is all too easy to get caught up in the frenzy of planning the wedding and reception, only to find you don't have the funds you need for the honeymoon you've dreamed of or that plane tickets and hotel reservations are now exhorbitant—or sold out—so close to the date. So don't forget to add up all of the expected (and unexpected) costs of the honeymoon, such as:

- Transportation, transfers, lodging, and meals
- Sightseeing and sports-related costs
- Little luxuries, like a massage or poolside charges for lounge chairs and towels
- Tips and taxes
- Souvenirs

5. Plan for children and your honeymoon. Some couples with children from previous relationships decide to take their kids on the honeymoon with them, making the trip a family vacation. This is fine—as long as you and your spouse or partner are enthusiastic and in complete agreement about this. Others find ways to divide their honeymoon, with the first part a time for the two of them alone and the second part a trip as a new family. This gives your children something to look forward to during the few days you are away from them.

If you do decide to take a honeymoon away from your kids, think of ways to remember them while you are gone. Call often and send plenty of postcards or emails. You can even video chat or Skype with your kids, describing your vacation spot and sending your love. (See also Chapter 18, page 246.)

6. Take care of the caretakers. As a matter of security as well as courtesy and common sense, leave a written schedule of your trip (including contact numbers where you can be reached) with the people who maintain your home, take care of pets, water plants, or pick up mail, and provide written instructions for anything they might need to know about, such as pet medications.

The same applies if you have children and you're leaving them with a relative or other caregiver. Be sure to give your parents or other close relatives copies of your schedule as well. Take the phone numbers of any caretakers with you, or add them to your smartphone. Be sure to stock up on food and other daily items so that caretakers—for kids or pets—aren't stuck spending money on supplies. When you return, write thank-you notes and perhaps even give small gifts to those people who took care of things while you were away.

7. Pamper, indulge, relax. This is a once-in-a-lifetime event for the two of you, so don't be afraid to splurge on a few extras. It could be couples' massages at the hotel spa—or goodies for giving each other spa treatments in the privacy of your own room. Other possibilities: a sunset sail, an extravagant meal, or tickets to a concert. Whatever the indulgence—enjoy! This is a special time for you and your new spouse.

Thank-Yous

Ideally, you've kept up with your thank-you notes throughout the prewedding period. Most likely you'll be inundated with more gifts in the weeks following your wedding or upon your return from your honeymoon—and thus will have a whole new batch of thank-you notes to write. Remember: Both partners write thank-you notes these days, so writing them can be one of the first shared tasks you tackle as a married couple. (See also Chapter 13, page 161, and Chapter 14, page 177.)

It's a nice touch to send your parents a thank-you note and a gift, perhaps a souvenir picked out on your honeymoon travels. Don't forget to thank your attendants for being in your wedding when you thank them for their gifts. Other important thank-yous? Your wedding planner, site manager, officiant and any vendors, such as your florist, photographer, or baker. In addition to a note, some couples choose to give a small gift, such as a certificate to a restaurant, to any vendors with whom they've worked closely. It means a lot to these professionals to know that you were pleased with their efforts to make your wedding a success. Better yet, if you were really pleased with their services, offer to be a reference or provide a testimonial for their website.

Selecting Wedding Pictures

Before your wedding, you probably discussed with your photographer and/or videographer a date when you can expect to see photos and videos. Most likely, he or she will post the photos or videos to a website, but it's fine to arrange a time to meet at the studio for a viewing. Also, don't forget to retrieve photos that guests posted to a shared site to create a separate album on your own.

Make choosing your photos a priority; otherwise, you may end up letting the proofs or DVD languish in a drawer. You won't regret putting in the time now to create a lasting memory of your wedding day. Once you've made your selections, decide the size and quantity of each photograph to be printed, their order in the photo albums, and how many albums you want to purchase. Make sure the wedding negatives or the digital equivalents are stored in a safe place.

The following is list of suggested people for whom you may wish to order photos or an album:

THE POSTWEDDING BELL BLUES

The two of you have been planning and looking forward to your wedding for a year or longer. You've been feted and fussed over, showered with gifts, and been the center of attention for friends and family alike. Now the big day has come and gone in a blur of excitement and happiness.

Don't be surprised if at some time in the days following your wedding you feel a little low or let down. It's natural and normal, especially if you're returning to daily life right after your wedding. Take extra care of yourselves. Spend some time reliving your wedding day by talking about it and looking at photos. Keep a good attitude about writing thank-yous and taking care of other postwedding to-dos, seeing them as an opportunity to hold on to the excitement rather than as chores. And plan something to look forward to, something fun that you both enjoy.

- Bride and groom
- Bride's parents
- Groom's parents
- Bride's grandparents
- Groom's grandparents
- Other relatives
- Special friends
- Bridal party: best man, maid/matron of honor, bridesmaids, groomsmen, flower girl, ring bearer

The Two of You: Life After the Honeymoon

Some newlyweds returning from their honeymoon will be living together for the first time. As part of making the transition from "me" to "we," here are some things to decide on together:

Household management. Start with the practical details. It's a good idea to have made any financial and name-change arrangements before your wedding day particularly if you'll be sharing a bank account. (See also Chapter 3, page 41.) Discuss the division of household duties: Who will be responsible for keeping a household budget, for example, or buying groceries or taking out the trash? Even though you may plan to share household duties, you may quickly discover that one of you naturally falls into the role of cook or bookkeeper or that each of you has a distinct preference in household chores. Whatever you do, try to keep the balance of duties equal. There are also adjustments to be made for differing styles: Your spouse wants all the counters clear, for example, and you don't mind a lived-in look. The key words here are *flexibility* and *communication*.

Personal space. Other little sticking points you and your spouse should work out include:

- Which side of the bed to sleep on
- Closet and drawer space
- Making sure each of you has your own private place, even if that's just a desk or reading chair
- Digital rules, especially established times when screens and devices are off
- Privacy boundaries, such as always knocking before entering an occupied bathroom
- Your policies on drop-ins, such as in-laws or sports buddies popping by without calling first

Communication. Finally, continue to affirm your mutual commitment to open communication. If something is making either of you increasingly unhappy or irritated, you'll want to feel free to express that unhappiness in an open forum—and the sooner you deal with a problem, the less time it has to fester into resentment. Do so sensitively without playing the "blame game."

At the same time, promise to listen open-mindedly to any complaints the other may have. When conflicts arise, as they inevitably will, it is a great help to have practiced your communication skills in many small ways and to have built mutual trust in your willingness to listen, be flexible, and compromise.

Anniversaries

Anniversaries are milestones honoring your commitment to each other, past and future. Tradition says that different kinds of gifts are given to couples on each subsequent anniversary of their wedding vows. Iron and wool may not seem as obvious a choice for a gift as gold or diamonds, but get creative. A cast-iron skillet given along with cooking lessons for two or a cozy alpaca wool throw blanket for cuddling up in paint much more romantic pictures than their names alone imply. Here is a list of traditional gifts and their modern options:

YEAR	TRADITIONAL	MODERN
1	Paper or plastics	Clock, watch
2	Calico or cotton	China
3	Leather or simulated leather	Crystal, glass
4	Silk or synthetic material	Linen, appliances
5	Wood	Silverware
6	Iron	Wood
7	Copper or wool	Table sets
8	Electric appliances	Linen, lace
9	Pottery	Leather
10	Tin or aluminum	Diamonds
11	Steel	Fashion jewelry
12	Linen (table, bed)	Pearls, gems
13	Lace	Fur (faux), fabrics
14	Ivory (skip as now endangered)	Gold jewelry
15	Crystal or glass	Watches
20	China	Platinum
25	Silver	Silver jewelry
30	Pearls	Diamond
35	Coral (endangered) and jade	Jade
40	Ruby	Ruby
45	Sapphire	Sapphire
50	Gold	Gold
55	Emerald	Turquoise
60	Diamond	Gold
70	Diamond	Diamond
75	Diamond	Diamond

THE AFTER-AFTER-PARTY

By no means a must, a postwedding party hosted by the newlyweds can be a great excuse for reuniting with loved ones and close friends. Whether held a month or six months after the wedding, the gathering of the wedding party, family, and close friends can also be an occasion to view wedding videos and photo albums—but keep it short and optional in case your guests are suffering from wedding fatigue. It can be as casual as you like but can also be a chance to show loved ones your new home and entertaining skills as a couple.

Farewell, Dear Couple . . .

Thank you for using this book on your journey. We hope that it helped form your thinking about weddings from a perspective of caring and consideration for yourselves, your guests, and all who worked with and for you to make your wedding day one of the best of your lives.

As a couple, we are sure you've learned a lot throughout the planning and preparation for your marriage—not just how to organize an important social event but about how to problem solve and compromise. All of these skills will serve you well in your life together.

Our best wishes to you both!

WEDDING PLANNING CHECKLIST

First things first:

- [ ] Tell family and friends and about your engagement.

- [ ] Brainstorm about your vision of your wedding to get ideas for the real thing. Create a Pinterest page, snap photos with your smartphone, or start a wedding folder.

- [ ] Set up an organization system—buy a wedding notebook, create an electronic file, or choose planning apps that work with your computer, smartphone, or tablet. Include sections for reception, music, flowers, wedding attire, photography, stationery, etc.

9+ months before:

- [ ] Set a budget: consider who might contribute, and add a cushion for cost overruns

- [ ] Set the date: be sure it works for important guests, the location, and the officiant

- [ ] Choose your ceremony and reception sites: book wedding date immediately and schedule rehearsal time

- [ ] Obtain permits if the ceremony will be held in park or recreational area

- [ ] Choose an officiant and discuss ceremony structure and marriage requirements

- [ ] Research vendors (florist, photographer, caterer, baker) and/or hire a wedding consultant or event designer

- [ ] Draft a guest list: Ask for input from your families

- [ ] Choose your attendants and invite them to participate

- [ ] Build a wedding website

- [ ] Start shopping for your gown

- [ ] Begin a prewedding fitness and beauty regimen

- [ ] Announce your engagement in local papers

- [ ] Begin planning your honeymoon

6 to 9 months before:

- [ ] Register for wedding gifts (especially if a shower is planned)

- [ ] Send out save-the-date notices, especially for a holiday weekend or if guests will have to make travel arrangements

- [ ] Arrange group rates and accommodations for out-of-town family and guests to book
- [ ] Place stationery order for invitations, envelopes, announcements, and thank-you notes
- [ ] Reserve a caterer: sign a contract and make a deposit; develop menu and alcohol list
- [ ] Choose your photographer (and videographer) and schedule any engagement portraits
- [ ] Select your florist and discuss bouquets, boutonnieres, and arrangements
- [ ] Select musicians for ceremony and reception; take dance lessons
- [ ] Order your gown and schedule fittings
- [ ] Determine your accessories (shoes, headpiece, jewelry, lingerie) for the wedding day
- [ ] Choose bridesmaids' dresses and schedule fittings
- [ ] Schedule time off from work for wedding preparation, wedding weekend, and honeymoon
- [ ] Reserve flights, hotel rooms, and transportation for the honeymoon, and if needed secure passports, visas, and vaccinations
- [ ] Reserve your accommodations for the wedding night

4 to 6 months before:

- [ ] Meet with officiant to discuss the ceremony, arrange rehearsal times, and select readings
- [ ] Plan the rehearsal dinner
- [ ] Finalize the guest list
- [ ] Discuss any shower and other party plans with those who have offered to host
- [ ] Arrange wedding transportation for yourself, attendants, and guests (if needed)

- [ ] Re-confirm group hotel rates for out-of-town guests
- [ ] Make hair and makeup appointments for wedding day, including practice dates 1–2 months prior to the wedding
- [ ] Book calligrapher, if using one (allow at least two weeks for calligraphy)
- [ ] Pick out or design a *ketubah* and arrange for a chuppah
- [ ] Order the wedding cake
- [ ] Meet with cake bakers and schedule tastings
- [ ] Meet with florist, photographer, and musicians

2 to 4 months before:

- [ ] Contact the local clerk's office to inquire about marriage license requirements
- [ ] Change insurance policies and create prenuptial agreement, if necessary
- [ ] Follow up or have progress meetings with florist, photographer, musicians, caterer/site manager
- [ ] Arrange ceremony and reception decoration needs
- [ ] Select and order attire for groom and groomsmen
- [ ] Shop for and order wedding rings; have them sized and engraved
- [ ] Reserve rental equipment such as tables, chairs, linens, and tents, if necessary
- [ ] Prepare maps and directions for ceremony and reception; add to website
- [ ] Order (or make) wedding favors and welcome bags
- [ ] Shop for attendants' gifts
- [ ] Purchase a gift for your fiancé(e)
- [ ] Address wedding invitations

1 to 2 months before:

- ☐ Mail wedding invitations eight to ten weeks prior to the date
- ☐ Mail rehearsal dinner invitations four to six weeks prior to the date
- ☐ Send thank-you notes for shower or wedding gifts as they arrive
- ☐ Decide on any extra liability or event insurance
- ☐ Prepare any documents for name and/or benefit changes at your workplace
- ☐ Gather information from the town/city clerk's office to change your name if desired
- ☐ Send change-of-address notices to post office
- ☐ Meet with caterer to finalize menu
- ☐ Finalize wedding-weekend activities or day-after brunch
- ☐ Choose ceremony and reception music and create a "must play" and "don't play" song list for the reception
- ☐ Finalize ceremony readings; invite readers
- ☐ Send programs, menus, and table cards to stationer to be printed
- ☐ Buy guest book or prepare cards or other vehicle for guest notes or sign-in
- ☐ Do hair and makeup run-through
- ☐ Check that bridesmaids have their dresses, shoes, and accessories; check that groomsmen have made arrangements for or acquired their attire
- ☐ Arrange a wedding-day dressing room for the wedding party
- ☐ Send wedding announcement to local newspapers
- ☐ Check your registry to update or add items

2 weeks to 1 month before:

- ☐ Contact your vendors to re-confirm all details and timeline for the wedding day
- ☐ Write welcome letter and guest schedule
- ☐ Create and assemble guest welcome bags
- ☐ Pick up wedding rings
- ☐ 3 weeks out, start calling guests who haven't responded for the wedding and rehearsal dinner to get final head count
- ☐ Develop wedding day timing and details
- ☐ Get marriage license and any other legal documents, pick witnesses, and make appointments for blood tests
- ☐ Create a seating chart for the reception
- ☐ Once you have the final count, prepare table or place cards or send to calligrapher
- ☐ Choose or write your vows
- ☐ Write a toast to give at the rehearsal dinner or during the reception
- ☐ Write ceremony program
- ☐ Have your final dress fittings (include all accessories)
- ☐ Visit the salon for one last haircut and color
- ☐ Re-confirm wedding-night and honeymoon reservations; give your itinerary to a friend or family member in case of emergency
- ☐ Designate someone to look after your home or pets while you are on your honeymoon
- ☐ Create a list of important people and events for photographer and/or videographer
- ☐ Find out where guests will be staying if you plan to deliver welcome notes or bags
- ☐ Break in your wedding shoes

1 week before:

- [ ] Pick up dress or have it delivered
- [ ] Deliver a final headcount to the caterer
- [ ] Re-confirm date, location, time, final payments, etc. with officiant, musicians, caterer, baker, florist, and any other vendors
- [ ] Re-confirm all travel plans (including transportation to airport, etc.)
- [ ] Make sure wedding announcements are ready for mailing
- [ ] Organize wedding-day payments, tips, and fees in envelopes and give to someone (often the best man) to distribute
- [ ] Delegate ceremony and reception responsibilities to your wedding party
- [ ] Distribute directions, schedule, and contact list to wedding party and families
- [ ] Deliver welcome notes or bags to guests' lodgings
- [ ] Take care of last-minute beauty treatments: waxing, facial, manicure and pedicure, and confirm hair and makeup appointments for wedding day
- [ ] Pack for the honeymoon

Day before:

- [ ] Assemble dress, shoes, accessories, and a last-minute emergency kit
- [ ] Greet out-of-town guests, if possible
- [ ] Rehearse the ceremony
- [ ] Hold rehearsal dinner
- [ ] Give gifts to wedding party and/or parents

Day of:

- [ ] Eat breakfast; arrange for other meals or snacks during the day
- [ ] Have overnight bags and honeymoon luggage delivered to hotel, if leaving from there
- [ ] Have your hair and makeup done
- [ ] Allow plenty of time to get dressed
- [ ] Make sure the best man has the rings and the marriage license
- [ ] Switch your engagement ring to your right hand for the ceremony

After the wedding:

- [ ] Have gown and veil cleaned and preserved by professional dry cleaner
- [ ] Have the wedding party return any rental attire
- [ ] Have someone mail prepared wedding announcements
- [ ] Turn in name-change forms for all legal documents, bank accounts, medical forms, etc.
- [ ] Continue to send thank-you notes for wedding gifts
- [ ] Send thank-yous to vendors
- [ ] Take care of any gift returns
- [ ] Collect photos from your photo-sharing site
- [ ] Create photo album(s) and order individual photos

INDEX

A

abbreviations, wedding
    invitation, 108, 118
    outer envelopes, 122, 123
accessibility, of reception site,
    210, 213
accessories
    bride, 254–57
    bridesmaids, 259
acolytes, 187
address change, 43, 363
addresses, wedding invitation
    abbreviations, 122, 123
    outer envelopes, 109, 111,
        122–24
    return address, 109,
        122
    titles, 123, 124
admission cards, 127
affirmation ceremony, 113
African American traditions,
    231, 232, 253
after-after-parties, 360
after-parties, 158, 353
aisle runner
    groomsmen/usher duties,
        79, 326, 332, 336
    order of service, 336
    provision of, 187, 283
    wedding ceremony, 336
    wedding rehearsal, 326,
        332
albums, photo, 34, 245, 297,
    299, 300, 358, 364
alcoholic drinks, 221–23
    bachelor/bachelorette party,
        151
    cash bar, 221
    caterers and, 215, 217,
        222–23

champagne. See champagne
cocktail hour. See cocktail
    hour
cost, 215, 221
designated drivers, 151, 225
inebriated guests, 212
local laws/licenses, 212,
    213, 222
open bar, 215, 217, 222
toasts. See toasts and
    toasting
wedding invitation notice,
    115
wedding reception, 212,
    221–23, 349–51
See also beverages; drinks
allergies
    flowers, 270
    food, 220–21
altar
    flowers/decorations, 269,
        270, 276, 282, 283
    honoring the deceased,
        192–93
    order of service, 337
    photographs of service at,
        304, 305
altar assistants, 82, 187
anniversaries, 360
    traditional gifts, 360
    vow reaffirmation, 204–5
    wedding cake, 317–18, 320
announcements
    engagement, 3–6, 302
    newspaper, 8–11
    wedding, 135–37
    wedding cancellation, 104–5
annuities, beneficiary
    changes, 45
annulment, 3, 39, 197

Arch of Steel, 203, 264
assigned seating, 224, 225
assigned tables, 225
at-home cards, 43, 127
at-home weddings, 211–213,
    227
attendants. See bridesmaids;
    ushers; wedding
    attendants
attire. See wedding attire

B

babysitters, 80, 212, 357
bachelorette party, 150–52
bachelor party, 65, 78–79,
    150–52
bakers, wedding cake, 217,
    317–319
bandleaders, 291, 292, 294,
    319, 351
bands. See musicians
bartenders, 214, 222–23
    gratuities, 36
    insurance, 217, 222
bedeken, 198, 340
belated wedding receptions,
    158–59, 169
bells, ringing of, 233, 236, 289
beneficiary changes, 45, 359
best man/person
    bachelor party, 78, 151, 152
    boutonniere, 269, 281–82,
        331
    bridal table seating, 223
    ceremony fees, 33, 38, 187,
        288
    dressing for ceremony,
        331
    duties, 78–79, 326, 331
    expenses, 31, 76, 77

gifts to/from, 31, 78–79,
    153, 156, 165, 171
multiple attendants, 71–72
opposite sex, 72, 262
photos, 303, 305, 306, 308
processional, 336, 337, 340
program listing, 134
receiving line, 348
toasts, 156, 350, 351
transportation, 225, 226,
    343
wedding attire, 21, 251,
    260–63
wedding attire return, 356
wedding cake
    announcement, 319
wedding ceremony, 331–32,
    336, 337, 339, 340
wedding day tasks, 78–79,
    331, 336, 337, 339, 340
wedding rehearsal, 325,
    326, 327
wedding ring, 79, 331, 338
beverages, 221–23
    cost, 215, 221
    local laws/licenses, 212,
        213, 222
    wedding invitation notice,
        115
    See also alcoholic drinks;
        champagne; drinks
black tie, 53, 115, 261
blended family. See stepfamily
bouquets, 278–80
    alternatives, 270, 279
    bridal, 269, 277–80, 338,
        339, 353, 356
    bridesmaids, 269, 277–78
    delivery, 327, 330
    preserving, 280, 356

email (*cont.*)
   wedding shower invitations, 49–50, 98, 143
   wedding updates, 50
embassies, 27, 40, 41
embossing, 103
emergency kit, wedding day, 330
enclosures, wedding invitation, 103, 125–28
encore weddings. *See* remarriage
engagement, 3–16
   addressing future in-laws, 8
   announcement, 3–6
   breakup, 15–16
   during difficult times, 6
   divorced people, 3, 8, 9–10
   family disapproval of, 6–7
   fiancé/fiancée death, 16
   gifts, 14, 15–16, 166
   length of, 3
   parent introduction, 7
   party, 13–15
   photographs, 301, 302
   ring. *See* engagement ring
   sharing good news, 3–6
engagement ring, 11–13
   family heirlooms, 11, 12, 16
   remarriage and, 243, 248
   return after breakup, 16
   wearing with wedding rings, 23–24
English traditions, 232–33, 281
engraving
   wedding invitations, 96, 101–2, 127
   wedding rings, 24
   See also monograms
envelopes, wedding invitation, 95, 121–25
   addressing, 121–24
   design elements, 101
   handwritten, 122
   inner, 121, 124–25
   ordering, 24, 96
   outer, 121–24
   plus-ones, 123–24, 125
   printing, 102
   stick-on labels, 115, 122
   stuffing, 96, 128–29
environmental concerns, xi
   wedding cake, 318
   wedding flowers, 282, 284
   wedding gifts, 163
   wedding invitations, 48

Episcopal weddings, 196
ethnic customs
   reception musicians, 291, 293
   wedding attire, 252
   wedding ceremony, 230, 252
   See also cultural customs
Eucharist, 196
ex-spouses
   engagement announcement, 4, 242
   remarriage of, 241–45
   seating arrangements, 334–35
   as wedding guests, 243
   See also divorce
extended family, xiii, xvi
   engagement announcement, 5
   wedding ceremony seating, 334
   as wedding host, 116
   wedding rehearsal dinner, 156
   See also grandparents; siblings

F

Facebook, 47–50
fake wedding cake, 314
family, xvi
   broken engagement and, 15–16
   engagement announcement, 4–5, 241, 242
   engagement party, 7–8, 13
   fiancé/fiancée disapproval, 6–7
   first get-together of, 7–8
   getting to know "new," 60, 63, 66–67, 69–70
   guest list, 84–85, 87–88, 90
   honoring of deceased, 192–93
   marriage legalities, 38
   party welcoming bride, 159
   remarriage and, 241, 242, 244
   unity candle lighting, 230, 282–83
   wedding ceremony seating, xvi, 333–35
   wedding gift to, 171

wedding invitation wording, 114–15, 116, 117, 124
   in wedding party, 59–60, 71–72, 82
   wedding photos of, 306, 307
   wedding rehearsal dinner, 156
   wedding showers, 142
   See also children; extended family; grandparents; parents; siblings; stepfamily
family crest, wedding invitation, 101
family heirlooms
   bridal jewelry, 257, 303
   cake knife, 319
   engagement rings, 11, 12, 16
   wedding gown, 256
father of the bride, xx, 14, 51–2, 68, 69, 157, 269, 271, 281–82, 303, 305, 306, 308, 330, 334–35, 337, 340, 347–49, 350, 351
father of the groom, 70, 156–57, 264, 269, 281–82, 306, 334–35, 348–52
farfallette dolci (wedding knots), 237
favors
   almonds, 234, 236, 237
   cost, 35
   personalized, 135
fee envelopes, 36, 38
finances, xvii, xix, 29–37
   bank accounts, 45, 359
   beneficiary changes, 45, 359
   disclosure of, 44
   premarital/prenuptial agreements, 43–45
   wills, 45
   See also money; wedding budget
financial registries, wedding gifts, 164
flag, U.S. military weddings, 203, 264
flat printing (lithography), 102
florists, xiv, 25, 274–77, 285
   allergy concerns, 270
   cake decorations, 316
   ceremony site considerations, 187
   contracts, 37, 277
   floral designers vs., 276

floral needs checklist, 269–70, 274, 275, 276–77
   wedding planning, 25, 155
   See also wedding flowers
flower girl, 80–81, 134
   attire, 260
   expenses, 81, 260
   parents of, 81, 85, 156
   photos for, 359
   processional/recessional, 80–81, 337, 339
   transportation, 331, 343
   wedding flowers, 80, 188, 269, 280–81
   wedding receiving line, 348
   wedding rehearsal, 81, 326
   wedding rehearsal dinner, 81, 156
flowers. *See* florists; wedding flowers
food allergies, 220–21
formal invitations, 21, 100–102
   envelopes, 121–25
   wording, 107–11
formal portraits, 302–3, 305–6, 346
formal weddings, 21
   attendants, 21, 71, 73, 75, 81, 261, 262–63
   attire, 21, 251, 252, 253, 254, 257, 259, 261, 262–63
   ceremony, 29, 261, 262–63, 268, 278
   costs, 32
   flowers, 268, 277, 278, 282
   invitations, 100–102, 121–25
   reception, 29, 32, 210
   train bearers/pages, 81
fraud, 39, 42, 44, 45
French service, wedding reception, 219
French traditions, 232, 234
friends
   broken engagement and, 15
   engagement announcement, 5–6, 8, 242
   engagement party, 13
   guest list considerations, 83, 84, 85–86, 88, 89, 90
   as hosts of guests, 179
   remarriage and, 242, 243, 247
   thank yous to, 168, 179, 247, 270, 349
   wedding attendants, 72, 82